Wolfgang Schlüter
Urs Engeler Editor

My Second Self
When I Am Gone

Englische Gedichte
übersetzt von
Wolfgang Schlüter

in memoriam Muzio Clementi

Inhaltsverzeichnis

Now goth sonne 1
Sing! cuccu 2
Mirie it is 3
Richard, thah thou be ever trichard 4
Wanne mine eyhnen misten 5
Foweles in the frith 6
Now springes the spray 7
   ANONYM
   (13. Jahrhundert)

Mon in the mone 8
Ich am of Irlaunde 9
Lollay, lollay, little child 10
Why have ye not reuthe 11
I am Jesu 12
Ye that pasen by the weiye 13
Of thes Frer Minours 14
   ANONYM
   (14. Jahrhundert)

Hide, Absalon 15
Now welcome, Somor 16
A Song to his Purse for the King 17
   GEOFFREY CHAUCER
   (1340 (?) -1400)

Of my lady 18
   THOMAS HOCCLEVE
   (1368 -1450 (?))

Bewar, sqier, yeman 19
I have a yong suster 20
I sing of a maiden 21
A celuy que pluys 22
The Agincourt Carol 23
I have a gentle cock 24
Kyrie, so kyrie 25
Tutivillus 26
Go! hert 27
Epitaph 28
O! Mankinde 29
It semes white 30
Alanus calvus 31
At a springe wel 32
Inordinat love 33
Swarte-smeked smethes 34
Whan netilles in winter 35
To my trew love 36
Continuaunce 37
For a man that is almost blind 38
   ANONYM
   (15. Jahrhundert)

My ghostly fader 39
For dedy liif 40
   CHARLES OF ORLEANS
   (Mitte 15. Jahrhundert)

Done is a battell
  on the dragon blak! 41
    WILLIAM DUNBAR
    (Ende 15. Jahrhundert)

Most soveren lady
  (MARGERET) 42
My lefe is faren in a lond 43
I must go walke the woed 44
Westron winde 45
Burgeis, thou haste so blowen 46
    ANONYM
    (um 1500)

With «Lullay! lullay!»
  like a childe 47
    JOHN SKELTON
    (um 1500)

The lover compareth his state
  with a ship in perilous storm
  tossed on the sea 48
Vixi Puellis Nuper Idoneus . . . 49
What menethe this? 50
    SIR THOMAS WYATT
    (1503 (?) -1542)

Description of a spring,
  wherein each thing renews,
  save only the Lover 51
    HENRY HOWARD,
    EARL OF SURREY
    (1517 (?) -1547)

One day I wrote her name 52
Epithalamion 52B
    EDMUND SPENSER
    (1552 (?) -1599)

A secret murder 53
What is our life? 54
My body in the walls captived 55
Like to a hermit poor 56
To his son 57
Last Verse 58
Epitaph (anon) 59
    SIR WALTER RALEGH
    (1552 (?) -1618)

In night when colours all
  to black are cast 60
    FULKE GREVILLE,
    LORD BROOKE
    (1551 -1628)

With how sad steps 61
Thou blind man's mark 62
Come Sleep; O Sleep! 63
    SIR PHILIP SIDNEY
    (1554 -1586)

A Summer Song 64
    GEORGE PEELE
    (1558 (?) -1597)

What meant the poets   65
  ROBERT GREENE
  (1560-1592)

Of his mistress, upon occasion
  of her walking in a garden   66
On the Death
  of Sir Philip Sidney   67
  HENRY CONSTABLE
  (1562-1613)

Care-charmer sleepe   68
  SAMUEL DANIEL
  (1563-1619)

How many paltry, foolish,
  painted things   69
  MICHAEL DRAYTON
  (1563-1619)

To the moon   70
  CHARLES BEST
  (? - ?)

Tired with all these   71
from «Love's Labour's Lost»   72
  WILLIAM SHAKESPEARE
  (1564-1616)

The author loving these
  homely meals   73
  JOHN DAVIES, OF HEREFORD
  (1565 (?) -1618)

The azured vault   74
  KING JAMES I.
  (1566-1625)

Upon the Death of
  Sir Albert Morton's Wife   75
  SIR HENRY WOTTON
  (1568 (?) -1639)

Twicknam Gardens   76
Witchcraft by a Picture   77
Death be not proud   78
The Apparition   79
The Relic   80
The Will   81
  JOHN DONNE
  (1572-1635)

An Ode: To Himself   82
The Hour-Glass   83
  BEN JONSON
  (1573-1637)

If Music and sweet Poetry agree   84
  RICHARD BARNFIELD
  (1574-1627)

Melancholy   85
  JOHN FLETCHER
  (1579-1625)

A Dirge   86
JOHN WEBSTER
(1580 (?) - 1630 (?))

Fairford Windows   87
Nonsense   88
A Non Sequitur   89
RICHARD CORBETT
(1582 - 1635)

Dear Lord, receive my son   90
SIR JOHN BEAUMONT
(1583 - 1627)

Black itself   91
Black beauty   92
EDWARD, LORD HERBERT
OF CHERBURY
(1538 - 1648)

Saint John Baptist   93
*I know that all beneath the
   moon decays*   94
Sleep, silence' child   95
The Book of the World   96
WILLIAM DRUMMOND
OF HAWTHORNDEN
(1585 - 1649)

*On the Tombs
   of Westmister Abbey*   97
FRANCIS BEAUMONT
(1586 - 1616)

*Epitaph on Mary Herbert,
   Countess of Pembroke*   98
*Epitaph in Obitum M. S.
   X° Maij, 1614*   99
WILLIAM BROWNE
(1588 - 1643)

To Electra   100
Epitaph upon a Child that died   101
ROBERT HERRICK
(1591 - 1674)

Man is a tennis-court   102
FRANCIS QUARLES
(1592 - 1644)

*Being Waked out of my Sleep
   by a Snuff of Candle which
   Offended me, I thus thought*   103
HENRY KING
(1592 - 1669)

Epitaph   104
THOMAS CAREW
(1595 (?) - 1639 (?))

Death the leveller   105
JAMES SHIRLEY
(1596 - 1666)

I saw my Lady weep   106
*Weep you no more,
    sad fountains*   107
   ANONYM
   (from Dowland's Booke
   of Songes 1600/1603)

*On a Gentlewoman walking
    in the snow*   108
   WILLIAM STRODE
   (1602 - ca 1644/45)

Music, thou Queen of Souls   109
   THOMAS RANDOLPH
   (1605 - 1635)

Old Age   110
   EDMUND WALLER
   (1606 - 1687)

On his Blindness   111
   JOHN MILTON
   (1608 - 1674)

A Farewell to love   112
   SIR JOHN SUCKLING
   (1609 - 1642)

In Darkness let me dwell   113
   ANONYM
   (from Dowland jun.'s
   A Musicall Banquet 1610)

*Still do the stars
    impart their light*   114
   WILLIAM CARTWRIGHT
   (1611 - 1643)

*An Epitaph upon Husband
    and Wife*   115
*Death's Lecture and the Funerall
    of a Young Gentleman*   116
   RICHARD CRASHAW
   (1612 - 1649)

Corruption   117
   HENRY VAUGHAN
   (ca 1621/22 - 1695)

*Vpon the Double Murther
    of K(ing) Charles I.: in Answer
    to a Libellous Copy of Rhymes
    by Vavasor Powell*   118
   KATHERINE PHILIPS
   (1631 - 1664)

The sad Day   119
   THOMAS FLATMAN
   (1637 - 1688)

*On Eleanor Freeman
    who died 1650, aged 21*   120
   ANONYM
   (about 1650)

from «Creation»:
  The Digestive System   121
  SIR RICHARD BLACKMORE
  (1652-1729)

A Quiet Soul   122
  JOHN OLDHAM
  (1653-1683)

from «The Art of Cookery»   123
  WILLIAM KING
  (1663-1712)

Description of a Morning   124
*A beautiful young nymph
  going to bed*   125
  JONATHAN SWIFT
  (1667-1745)

*Epigram on a Lady who shed her
  water at seeing the Tragedy of Cato;
  occasioned by an Epigram
  on a Lady who wept at it*   126
  NICHOLAS ROWE
  (1674-1718)

from «The Chase»   127
  WILLIAM SOMERVILLE
  (1675-1742)

An Elegy, To an Old Beauty   128
  THOMAS PARNELL
  (1679-1718)

from «Oppian's Halieutics»   129
  WILLIAM DIAPER
  (1685-1717)

*On a Lady, Preached into a Colic,
  by One of her Lovers*   130
  AARON HILL
  (1685-1750)

Newgate's Garland   131
from «Trivia»   132
  JOHN GAY
  (1685-1732)

from «An Essay on Criticism»   133
from «Epilogue to the Satires»   134
  ALEXANDER POPE
  (1688-1744)

from «The Grave»   135
  ROBERT BLAIR
  (1699-1746)

from «The Country Walk»   136
  JOHN DYER
  (1699-1758)

Solitude 137
*On the Death
 of a particular Friend* 138
Cattle in Summer 139
Robin Redbreast 140
JAMES THOMSON
(1700-1748)

from «The Modern Fine Lady» 141
*from «The Modern Fine
 Gentleman»* 142
Epitaph on Dr Samuel Johnson 143
SOAME JENYNS
(1704-1787)

*from «The Art of Preserving Health»:
 Air Pollution/
 Causes of Old Age* 144
JOHN ARMSTRONG
(1709-1779)

*from «The Gymnasiad»:
 The Boxers* 145
PAUL WITHEHEAD
(1710-1774)

The Nun. A Cantata 146
EDWARD MOORE
(1712-1757)

from «Sickness» 147
WILLIAM THOMPSON
(1712 (?) -1766 (?))

*Ode/ on the Death of a
 Favourite Cat/ Drowned
 in a Tub of Gold Fishes* 148
THOMAS GRAY
(1716-1771)

*On Seeing a Tapestry Chair-Bottom
 Beautifully Worked by His Daughter
 for Mrs. Holroyd. WRITTEN IN
 THE YEAR 1793* 149
RICHARD OWEN CAMBRIDGE
(1717-1802)

from «Of Taste» 150
JAMES CAWTHORN
(1719-1761)

Ode to Evening 151
WILLIAM COLLINS
(1721-1759)

from «Hymn to Science» 152
MARK AKENSIDE
(1721-1770)

from «Jubilate Agno» 153
CHRISTOPHER SMART
(1722-1771)

from «The Deserted Village» 154
OLIVER GOLDSMITH
(1728-1774)

*from «The Pleasures
of Melancholy»* 155
*Prologue/ On The Old
   Winchester Playhouse/ over
   The Old Butcher's Shambles* 156
THOMAS WARTON
(1728-1790)

Retort on the Foregoing 157
JOHN SCOTT OF AMWELL
(1730-1783)

from «The Task» 158
*Motto for a Clock/ sculptured
  by Bacon for George III* 159
On the Neglect of Homer 160
Epigram 161
The Modern Patriot 162
Lines on a late Theft 163
*To Mrs. Throckmorton/ On her
  beautiful Transcript
  of Horace's Ode* 164
An Ancient Prude 165
*Two Inscriptions for Stones erected at
  the Sowing of a Grove of Oaks at
  Chillington, The Seat of
  T. Giffard, Esq., June 1790* 166
*Epitaph on FOP,/ A Dog belonging to
Lady Throckmorton* 167
   WILLIAM COWPER
   (1731-1800)

from «The Shipwreck» 168
WILLIAM FALCONER
(1732-1769)

Epigram 169
SIR WILLIAM JONES
(1746-1794)

The Methodist 170
THOMAS CHATTERTON
(1752-1770)

*from «The Village»:
  The Poor-House* 171
GEORGE CRABBE
(1754-1832)

The Chimney-Sweeper 172
*Long John Brown
  and Little Mary Bell* 173
Holy Thursday 174
Milton. Preface 175
London 176
WILLIAM BLAKE
(1757-1827)

from «Michael.
  A Pastoral Poem»   177
Composed upon
  Westminster Bridge   178
Cranmer   179
With ships
  the sea was sprinkled   180
Twilight   181
It is not to be thought   182
A Grave-stone upon the floor
  in the Cloisters
  of Worcester Cathedral   183
It is a Beauteous Evening   184
If thou indeed derive thy light   185
from «Prelude, or,
  Growth of a Poet's Mind»   186
Composed by the Sea-side,
  near Calais, August, 1802.   187
  WILLIAM WORDSWORTH
  (1770-1850)

The return to Ulster   188
  SIR WALTER SCOTT
  (1771-1832)

Time: real and imaginary.
  An Allegory   189
  SAMUEL TAYLOR COLERIDGE
  (1772-1843)

His Books   190
Winter   191
A Mountain Landscape   192
  ROBERT SOUTHEY
  (1774-1843)

The Old Familiar Faces   193
Composed in
  Hoxton Lunatic Asylum   194
  CHARLES LAMB
  (1775-1834)

Finis   195
  WALTER SAVAGE LANDOR
  (1775-1864)

At Night   196
Echoes   197
  THOMAS MOORE
  (1779-1852)

The Fish, The Man,
  and the Spirit   198
  LEIGH HUNT
  (1784-1859)

Three Men of Gotham   199
  THOMAS LOVE PEACOCK
  (1785-1866)

A Churchyard Scene   200
  JOHN WILSON
  (1785-1854)

The Moon 201
Ozymandias 202
Music, when soft Voices die 203
Sonnet: England in 1819 204
  PERCY BYSSHE SHELLEY
  (1792-1822)

At Hooker's Tomb 205
November 206
  JOHN KEBLE
  (1792-1866)

The Thrush's Nest 207
Written in Northampton
  County Asylum 208
Burthorp Oak 209
  JOHN CLARE
  (1793-1864)

If by dull rhymes 210
When I have fears 211
  JOHN KEATS
  (1795-1821)

Friendship 212
  HARTLEY COLERIDGE
  (1796-1819)

Silence 213
  THOMAS HOOD
  (1798-1845)

Substance and Shadow 214
  JOHN HENRY NEWMAN
  (1801-1890)

The Plough.
  A Landscape in Berkshire 215
  RICHARD HENRY HORNE
  (1803-1884)

The Lamp 216
  CHARLES WHITEHEAD
  (1804-1862)

Grief 217
  ELIZABETH BARRET BROWNING
  (1806-1861)

On Translating the
  Divina Commedia 218
The Phantom Ship 219
Chaucer 220
Excelsior 221
from «Evangeline» 222
Autumn 223
The Old Clock on the Stairs 224
The Cross of Snow 225
Blind Bartimeus 226
The Wreck of the Hesperus 227
The Bells of Lynn 228
  HENRY
  WADSWORTH LONGFELLOW
  (1807-1882)

Letty's Globe   229
*On the Eclipse of the Moon
   of October 1865*   230
   CHARLES TENNYSON TURNER
   (1808 - 1879)

Summer Night   231
   ALFRED TENNYSON,
   LORD TENNYSON
   (1809 - 1892)

Persicos Odi   232
   WILLIAM
   MAKEPEACE THACKERAY
   (1811 - 1863)

The Old Stoic   233
   EMILY BRONTË
   (1818 - 1848)

The Toys   234
   COVENTRY PATMORE
   (1823 - 1896)

Dirge in Woods   235
Lucifer in Starlight   236
   GEORGE MEREDITH
   (1828 - 1909)

Silent Noon   237
Raleigh's Cell in Tower   238
   DANTE GABRIEL ROSSETTI
   (1828 - 1882)

Song   239
Remember me   240
Rest   241
   CHRISTINA GEORGINA ROSSETTI
   (1830 - 1894)

A Church Romance   242
*To the Matterhorn
   (June - July 1897)*   243
At a lunar Eclipse   244
   THOMAS HARDY
   (1840 - 1928)

When You are old   245
Epitaph   246
   WILLIAM BUTLER YEATS
   (1865 - 1939)

Clouds   247
The Soldier   248
   RUPERT BROOKE
   (1887 - 1915)

Nachwort
Anfangszeilen-Register
Autorenverzeichnis

My Second Self
When I Am Gone

1   Now goth sonne under wod:
     Me reweth, Marye, thy faire rode.
     Now goth sonne under Tre:
     Me reweth, Marye, thy sone and thee.

ANONYM (earlier 13th century)
Now goth sonne under wod

Die Sonne geht nun unter hinterm Marterholtz.
Dein holdes Antlitz dauert mich, Maria.
Nun neigt die Sonn sich unters Holz der Pein:
Mich barmt des Sohnes, barmt, Maria, dein.

2   Sing! cuccu, nu.
    Sing! cuccu.
    Sing! cuccu.
    Sing! cuccu, nu.

    Sumer is icumen in—
    Lhude sing! cuccu.
    Groweth sed and bloweth med
    And springth the wude nu—
    Sing! cuccu.

    Awe bleteth after lomb,
    Lhouth after calve cu,
    Bulluc sterteth, bucke verteth,
    Murie sing! cuccu.
    Cuccu, cuccu,
    Well singes thu, cuccu—
    Ne swik thu naver nu!

    ANONYM (earlier 13th century)
    Sing! cuccu, nu. Sing! cuccu.

sing, kukuk nû!
singe nun, kukkû!
singe nun, kukkû!
sing, kukuk nû!

summer ist gezogen în,
lûte sing, kukkû!
gras stêt uf bluomen anger mâd,
das holz in vollem lawbe stêt –
sing, kukuk nû!

schafin bloekt umb ire lamb,
kû brullt umb ire calb,
bull bokkt unde widder springt,
sing wunniclich, kukkû!
kukuk, kukuk,
fein singestû, kukkû –
nun swaige nimmer du!

3   Mirie it is, while sumer ilast,
With fugheles song.
Oc nu necheth windes blast,
And weder strong.
Ey! ey! what this night is long!
And ich, with well michel wrong,
Soregh and murne and fast.

Anonym (earlier 13th century)
Mirie it is, while summer ilast

wunniclich ists weil der summer weilt
mit vogellîn gesang.
doch nun des sturmes winde eilt
mit ungewetter.
ahî! swaz ist die nacht so lang,
daz ich mein michels ungemuot
musz hungers klagen, unde bang.

4   *RICHARD,*
thah thou be ever trichard,
Tricchen shalt thou nevermore.

Sitteth alle stille and herkneth to me!
The King of Alemaigne, by my leaute,
Thritty thousand pound askede he
For to make the pees in the countre—
   And so he dude more.

Richard of Alemaigne, whil that he wes king,
He spende all his tresour upon swiving.
Haveth he nout of Walingford o ferling!
Let him habbe ase he brew—bale to dring—
   Maugre Windesore.

The King of Alemaigne wende do full well:
He saisede the mulne for a castel;
With hare sharpe swerdes he grounde the stel—
He wende that the sailes were mangonel
   To helpe Windesore.

The king of Alemaigne gederede his host,
Makede him a castel of a mulne post,
Wende with his prude and his muchele bost,
Broghte from Alemaigne mony sory ghost
   To store Windesore.

RICHERD!
Zwâr bleibstu stêt ein trichser
Doch tricksen solltu nimmermêr!

Sizt still, hoert zu mir in der rund,
Der allemannen kunic, traun,
Der heischte drîssig tûsend pfund
Um friede in dem land zu baun,
    Und mêre gar.

Richard von tuitsland als kunic er stand,
Verbrûset sein goldschatz uf kebsweiber gnunc,
Keinen farthing bekom er aus wallingfords hand –
Er krieg swaz er brawete: jammer ze trunc,
    Trutz windesor.

Der kunic von tuitsland hat bei sich gedaht
Er sazte ein windmülle als ein kastell,
Mit scarfem geswêrte begrundt er die stell,
Aus den vlügelln ein katapult er auch gemaht,
    Windsor zu hilf.

Der kunic von tuitsland versammlet sein hêr,
Aus einer windmuell ein veste er stellt,
Kam in sein stolze vnd prâlen so lêr,
Brahte aus tuitsland vil jammergestalt,
    Windsor zum fort.

By God that is aboven ous, he dude muche sin
That lette passen over see the Erl of Warin:
He hath robbed Engelond, the mores and the fen,
The gold and the selver, and iboren henne,
   For love of Windesore.

Sire Simon de Montfort hath swore by his chin,
Hevede he now here the Erl of Warin,
Shulde he never more come to his inn,
Ne with sheld, ne with spere, ne with other gin,
   To help of Windesore.

Sire Simon de Montfort hath swore by his top,
Hevede he now here Sire Hue de Bigot,
All he shulde quite here twelfmoneth scot—
Shulde he never more with his fot pot
   To helpe Windesore.

Be thee luef, be thee loth, Sire Edward,
Thou shalt ride sporeles o thy liard
All the righte way to Dovereward—
Shalt thou nevermore breke foreward,
   And that reweth sore.

   EDWARD,
thou dudest ase a shreward,
Forsoke thine eme's lore.

ANONYM (about 1265)
Richard, thah thou be ever trichard

Bei gôt in der hoehe! er tate vil sünd,
Die der earl of warin nur zu gerne mißacht,
Hat england geplundert in sumpf môr vnd sund,
Das gold vnd das silber von hinnen gebraht,
   Windsor zu lîb.

Sir simon de montfort, der swûr bei sin kinn:
Hätt er jezt hier jenen earl of warin,
Käm diser nimmer daheim in sein inn,
Niht mit schild, niht mit spêr, niht mit ander gewinn,
   Windsor zu hilf.

Sir simon de montfort, der swûr bei sin haar:
Hätt er jezt hier den sir hue de bigot,
Solt der bezâlen die zeche ein jâr,
Solt nimmer sein fuosz mêr treten im trot,
   Windsor zu hilf.

Ob ihr wolt oder niht – sire edward:
Ône spôren so reutet uf eurer graw mêr
Geradewegs ab: nach dover ze port!
Solt brechen die abmachung nimmermêr,
   Swaz jammeret sêr.

  EDWARD,
Ihr tatet als ein lumpe:
Versmêt des oheims lêren!

5   Wanne mine eyhnen misten,
      And mine heren sissen,
      And my nose coldet,
      And my tunge foldet,
      And my rude slaket,
      And mine lippes blaken,
      And my muth grennet,
      And my spotel rennet,
      And mine her riset,
      And mine herte griset,
      And mine honden bivien,
      And mine fet stivien—
      Al to late! al to late!
      Wanne the bere is ate gate.
      Thanne I schel flutte
      From bedde to flore,
      From flore to here,
      From here to bere,
      From bere to putte,
      And te putt fordut.
      Thanne lyd mine hus uppe mine nose.
      Of al this world ne give I it a pese!

ANONYM (13th century)
Wanne mine eyhnen misten

wann mine ougen dämmern
vnd mine ôren zischen
vnd mine nas erkaltet
vnd mine zung sich faltet
vnd min gesiht erslaffet
vnd min gelipp sich swartzet
vnd min mund tut grinnen
vnd min spukke rinnen
vnd min haar sich strawbet
vnd min herze rüettelt
vnd min hande schüettelt
vnd min füesz ersteiffen:
ahî, zu spêt! ahî, zu spêt!
wann am tor die bâre stêt:
dann muosz ich gân
vom bett zu boden
vom boden in daz leichentuch
vom leichentuch zur bâre
von der bâre in daz grab
vndes grab slüezzt sih ab.
dann ruot min hûs uf mine nas.
kein heller geb ich uf den ganzen smuosz!

6   Foweles in the frith,
     The fisses in the flod,
     And I mon waxe wod:
     Mulch sorw I walke with
     For beste of bon and blod.

ANONYM (late 13th century)
Foweles in the frith

vogellîn im holze
die fische in dem fluosz
vnd ich muosz werden wirr
wandelnd in grosz wê
vm liebsten fleisch vnd bluotes wegen

7   Now springes the spray,
    All for love I am so seek
    That slepen I ne may.

    Als I me rode this endre day
    O' my pleyinge,
    Seih I whar a litel may
    Began to singe,
    «The clot him clinge!
    Way es him i' love-longinge
    Shall libben ay!»

    Son I herde that mirye note,
    Thider I drogh:
    I fonde hire in an herber swot
    Under a bogh,
    With joye inogh.
    Son I asked, «Thou mirye may,
    Why singes tou ay?»

    Than answerde that maiden swote
    Midde wordes fewe,
    «My lemman me haves bihot
    Of love trewe:
    He chaunges anewe.
    Yiif I may, it shall him rewe
    By this day!»

    ANONYM (about 1300)
    Now springes the spray

Die Zweige schlagen aus im Hag,
Vor Lieb bin ich so krank,
Daß ich an Schlaf nicht denken mag.

Als ich auszog am andern Tag,
Über eine kleine Weil,
Sah ich ein Mägdlein fein
Hub an zu singen:
«Mög die Erde ihn verschlingen!
Unglück ihm das Leben bringen,
Den's nach Lieb verlanget!»

Ich lauschte stracks dem freundlich Klange
Ging ich nach.
Fand sie in einer Laube Schatten
Unter eines Astes Dach:
Glückes genug.
Flugs ich frug: «Du lieblich Kind,
Deut mir dein Singen.»

Da gab zurück die süße Maid
Mit wenig Worten hin:
«Mein Liebster hat geschworen mir
Treu Liebe allezeit.
Er wendete den Sinn.
Wenn ichs vermag, so solls ihn reuen
Diesen Tag!»

8   Mon in the mone stond and strit;
On his bot-forke his burthen he bereth.
It is muche wonder that he na down slit—
For doute leste he falle he shoddreth and shereth.
When the forst freseth muche chele he bid.
The thomes beth kene, his hattren to-tereth.
Nis no wiht in the world that wot when he sit,
Ne, bote it be the hedge, whet wedes he wereth.

Whider trowe this mon ha the wey take?
He hath set his o fot his other toforen.
For non hihte that he hath ne siht me him ner shake:
He is the sloweste mon that ever wes iboren.
Wher he were o the feld pitchinde stake,
For hope of his thornes to dutten his doren,
He mot mid his twibil other trous make,
Other all his dayes werk ther were iloren.

This ilke mon upon heh whener he were,
Wher he were i'the mone boren and ifed,
He leneth on his forke ase a grey frere:
This crokede cainard sore he is adred.
It is mony day go that he was here.
Ichot of his ernde he nath nout isped.
He hath hewe sumwher a burthen of brere,
Tharefore sum hayward hath taken his wed.

Mann-im-Mond steht und stelzt fürbaß;
Trägt an 'ner Zinkenfork sein Rutenbündel.
Ein Wunder ists, daß er nicht runter rutscht –
Aus Furcht vorm freien Fall schwankt er und schaudert,
Und wenn der Frost zwickt, beißt die Kälte ihn.
Scharf sind die Dornen, die die Kleider ihm zerfetzt.
Kein Wicht ist auf der Welt, der wüßt wann er sich setzt,
Und nur die Hecke weiß, welch Rock er trägt.

Wo, glaubt ihr, nahm der Mann wohl seinen Weg?
Den einen Schritt vorm andern hält er inne.
Kein Mühe ficht ihn an, noch etwas das er sähe:
Er ist der trägste Mann, der jemals ward geborn.
Ob er gleich Pfähle auf dem Feld einpflockte,
Aus Hoffnung, Lücken mit den Dornen zu verstopfen,
Muß er doch neue Bündel hacken mit der DoppelAxt,
Sonst wär sein Tagwerk null und nichtig und umsonst.

Der Mann, der dort so hoch da droben,
Ob der wohl auf dem Mond geboren und erzogen?
Auf seiner Forke lehnt er wie ein Franziskaner:
Der krumme Faulpelz ist ganz schön in Furcht.
Schon lang ists her, daß er hier unten war.
Ich weiß, an seinen Wegen war kein Segen.
Einst schnitt er wo ein Bündel Dornenholz,
Dafür gab er dem Heckenwart sich in die Schuld.

Yef thy wed is itake, bring hom the trous,
Sete forth thine other fot, strid over sty.
We shule preye the hayward hom to our hous,
And maken him at eise for the maistry,
Drinke to him derly of god bous,
And oure dame douse shall sitten him by.
When that he is dronke ase a dreint mous,
Thenne we schule borewe the wed ate baily.

This mon hereth me nout, thah ich to him crye:
Ichot the cherl is def—the Del him to-drawe!
Thah ich yeye upon heh, nulle nout hye:
The lostlase ladde con nout o lawe.
Hupe forth! Hubert, hosede pie.
Ichot th'art amarscled into the mawe.
Thah me tene with him that mine teth mye,
The cherl nul nout adown er the day dawe.

ANONYM (later 13th - earlier 14th century)
Mon in the mone stond and strit

Wenn du gepfändet, trag nach Haus dein Bündel,
Voran den andern Fuß! Stapf übern Pfad!
Laßt uns den Heckenwart zum Schmause laden,
Unds ihm so angenehm als möglich machen,
Und auf sein Wohl mit unserm besten Schnapse trinken,
Und unser süßes Fräulein soll an seine Seit sich satzen.
Wenn er dann trunken ist gleich einer Mausekatzen,
Dann wollen wir die Schuld beim Landvogt lösen.

Der Mann, der hört mich nicht, ob ich gleich zu ihm schrei:
Ich weiß, der Kerl ist taub – zur Höll mit ihm!
Obwohl ich – He! – hoch brüll, hat ers nicht eben eilig.
Der träge Bursch weiß nichts vom Bürgerlichen Recht.
Hopp! Los! Hubert, du Hosen-Elster!
Ich weiß, dir ist die Wampe proppenvoll.
Wenn auch die Zähn mir knirschen vor Verdruß –
Der Kerl steigt nicht zur Erd, eh' nicht der Tag aufdämmert.

9   Ich am of Irlaunde,
      And of the holy londe
      Of Irlande.

      Gode sire, pray ich thee,
      For of sainte charite,
      Come and daunce wit me
      In Irlaunde.

ANONYM (earlier 14th century)
Ich am of Irlaunde

Ich bin aus Ireland
Komm von dem Heiligen Irr-
Lande.

Herre GOtt, ich bet zu Dir,
Um des heilig Barmens willen,
Komm & tanz mit mir
In Ireland

Lollay, lollay, little child, why wepestou so sore?
Nedes mostou wepe—it was iyarked thee yore
Ever to lib in sorow, and sich and mourne evere,
As thine eldren did er this, whil hi alives were.
Lollay, lollay, little child, child, lollay, lullow,
Into uncuth world icommen so ertou.

Bestes, and thos foules, the fisses in the flode,
And euch shef alives, imaked of bone and blode,
Whan hi commeth to the world, hi doth hamsilf sum gode,
All bot the wrech brol that is of Adames blode.
Lollay, lollay, little child, to car ertou bemette;
Thou nost noght this worldes wild before thee is isette.

Child, if betideth that thou shalt thrive and thee,
Thench thou wer ifostred up thy moder kne:
Ever hab mund in thy hert of thos thinges thre,
Whan thou commest, what thou art, and what shall com of thee.
Lollay, lollay, little child, child, lollay, lollay,
With sorow thou com into this world, with sorow shalt wend away.

Ne tristou to this world: it is thy ful fo.
The rich he maketh pouer, the pore rich also.
It turneth woe to wel, and ek wel to wo.
Ne trist no man to this world whil it turneth so.
Lollay, lollay, little child, the fote is in the whele:
Thou nost whoder turne, to wo other wele.

Schlafe, schlafe, Kindlein: schlaf; Was weinest du so schwer?
Mußt trauren ja, da dir's bestimmt von alters her,
im Grame stets zu leben, zu seufzen und zu klagen
wie's deine Eltern taten in ihren Erdentagen.
Schlaf, schlaf, Kind – web' dein Traumeshemd,
bist kommen in ein Welt so fremd.

Wild Tiere und die Vogellin, die Fische in dem Fluss,
und alle Kreatur so Odem hat,
ein jedes das zur Welt gekommen, Gutes tut –
Nur nicht die elendige Brut die Adams Stamm entsprossen.
Schlafe, schlafe, Kindlein: schlaf, zu Sorge vorgericht' –
Du kennst, die deiner harrt: die Wildnis, nicht.

Kind, falls dich treffe ein gedeihlich Los,
denk, daß du groß wardst auf der Mutter Schoß:
Der Dinge drei laß dir im Herzen frommen:
Woher du kömmst, und wer du seist, und was nach dir soll kommen.
Schlaf, schlaf, Kind: Kindlein, schlafe schön –
Mit Sorgen kamst du auf die Welt – mit Sorgen sollst du gehn.

Trau nicht der Welt: die ist dein Erzfeind mächtig!
So wie den Reichen arm, macht sie den Armen prächtig.
Sie wendet Weh in Wohl und Wohl in Wehe:
Jedweder argwöhn' weltlich Gunst, da sie sich also drehe!
Schlafe, schlafe, Kindlein: schlaf; dein Fuß steht auf Fortunens Rad –
nimmer weißt du, wie sich's dreht: zu Wohlstand – oder Not?

Child, thou ert a pilgrim in wikedness ibor:
Thou wandrest in this fals world—thou lok thee befor!
Deth shall come with a blast, ute of a well dim horre,
Adames kin dun to cast, himsilf hath ido befor.
Lollay, lollay, little child, so wo thee worp Adam,
In the lond of paradis, throgh wikedness of Satan.

Child, thou nert a pilgrim bot an uncuthe guest:
Thy dawes beth itold, thy jurneys beth icest.
Whoder thou shalt wend, north other est,
Deth thee shall betide with bitter bale in brest.
Lollay, lollay, little child, this wo Adam thee wroght,
Whan he of the apple ete and Eve it him betoght.

ANONYM (earlier 14th century)
Lollay, lollay, little child, why wepestou so sore?

Kind: Du bist ein Pilgersmann, in Sünden schwer geborn;
du wanderst in ein falsche Welt: nun sieh nach vorn!
Tod tritt im Luftzug aus dem düstern Tor
um Adams Stamm zu schlagen, wie jenen selbst zuvor.
Schlafe, Kindlein, schlafe schön: so Adam deinetwillen Leid
im Paradiese litt durch Satans Schlechtigkeit.

Kind – nein! Kein Pilgrim bist – ein fremder Gast!
Dein' Tage sind gezählt, dein Wandern stehet fest;
du magst dich wenden gegen Ost – Nord – West,
Tod pflanzt dir bitter Elend in die Brust.
Schlaf, schlaf, Kind: es ist Schlafenszeit.
Adam trug deinetwillen Leid,
als er vom Apfel aß den Eva ihm gebeut.

11   Why have ye no reuthe on my child?
Have reuthe on me, full of murning.
Taket down on Rode my derworthy child,
Or prek me on Rode with my derling.

More pine ne may me ben don
Than laten me liven in sorwe and shame.
Als love me bindet to my sone,
So lat us deiyen bothen isame.

Anonym (14th century)
Why have ye not reuthe

was barmet euch mein kinde nicht
erbarmt euch meiner voller jammern
vom holz mein liebreich kinde brecht
nein sollt mich mit an cräuzstamm hammern

mehr pein ist nicht als wie die fron
von trauer so mich machet schamen
da lieb mich ziehet zu mein sohn
so lasst uns sterben beid insamen

I am Jesu that cum to fight
Withouten sheld and spere:
Elles were thy deth idight,
Yif my fighting ne were.
Sithen I am comen and have thee brought
A blisful bote of bale,
Undo thin herte, tell me thy thought,
Thy sennes grete and smale.

ANONYM (14th century)
I am Jesu that cum to fight

Bin I. N. R. I., kommen in die Schlacht
ohne Schild noch Speer.
Wenn nicht mein Kämpfen wär,
Wär dir dein Tod vorhergesagt.
Nun ich gekommen und gebracht
Gesegnet Arzenein,
Schließ auf dein Denken mir aus deines Herzens Nacht,
Dein Sünden groß und klein.

13 Ye that pasen by the weiye,
    Abidet a little stounde.
    Beholdet, all my felawes,
    Yef any me lik is founde.
    To the Tre with nailes thre
    Wol fast I hange bounde;
    With a spere all thoru my side
    To mine herte is mad a wounde.

ANONYM (mid 14th century)
Ye that pasen by the weiye

Ihr, die ihr eures Weges wallet,
Haltet eine Weile ein.
Erwäget, meine Brüder alle,
Ob je mir gleich ward einer funden.
Am Kreuze mit der Näglen drei'n
Geheftet häng ich fest gebunden:
Mit einem Speere quer durch meine Seit
Bis an mein Herz ein Wunde ist geschneidt.

14   Of thes Frer Minours me thenkes moch wonder,
That waxen are thus hautein that somtime weren under:
Among men of Holy Chirch thay maken mochel blonder.
Now he that sites us above make ham sone to sonder.
With an O, and an I, thay praisen not Seint Poule,
Thay lyen on Seint Fraunceys, by my fader soule!

First thay gabben on God, that all men may se,
When thay hangen him on hegh on a grene tre,
With leves and with blossemes that bright are of ble—
That was never Goddes son, by my leute!
With an O, and an I, men wenen that thay wede,
To carpe so of clergy—thay can not thair crede!

Thay have done him on a crois fer up in the skye,
And festned in him wyenges as he shuld flye:
This fals, feined belefe shall thay soure bye,
On that lovelich Lord so for to lie.
With an O, and an I, one said full still,
«Armachan destroy ham, if it is Goddes will.»

A cart was made all of fire as it shuld be:
A gray frer I sawe therinne that best liked me.
Wele I wote thay shall be brent, by my leaute!
God graunt me that grace that I may it se!
With an O, and an I, brent be thay all,
And all that helpes therto, faire mot befall.

Das deucht mich ob der MinoritenBrüder wunders:
Dasz izt ein Hochmut sprosz der doch einstmals ganz underst:
Vil Wirrnis sie im Volk der Heilig Kirch gestifft.
Wann doch vns aller HErr sie bald in Stücke schlüge!
Mit nem O und nem I – nicht St. Paul preisen sie,
Bei meines Vadders Seel – : St. Franziskus ist Zielscheib ihrer Lügen!

Zuerst höhnten sie G.O.T.T., wie jeder sehen kann,
Als sie IHn einem grünen Baum hoch hängten an,
Mit Blättern & mit Blüten in leuchtend Farben sehre –
Das war der Heiland nit, bei meiner Ehre!
Mit nem O und nem I – narrisch dünken sie:
Den eignen Glauben kennens nit – und wollen uns belehren!

Sie haben hoch gehefftet IHn an das Marterholtz,
Vnd Flügellin im angetan als wenn er fliegen sollt:
Diß Falschheit, glaubts, soll ihnen sawer fallen:
Von vnserm lieblichen HErrn solch Lügenmär vertellen:
Mit nem O und nem I – sprach einer ganz still:
«Erzbischof, zerschlag sie, wenns so ist GOttes Will'!»

Ein Karren ward gemacht voll Feuer – *so* sollts sein!
Sah einen Grawen Bruder drinnen: tat mich freun.
Glaubts mir, sie sollen brennen, glaubt mirs, ich weiß es wol!
GOtt wies mir solche Gnad, dasz ich diß schawen soll!
Mit nem O und nem I – all werden sie verbrennt!
Vil Glück! dem der da Händ anlegt zu dem verdienten End.

Thay preche all of povert bot that love thay noght;
For gode mete to thair mouthe the town is thurgh soght;
Wide are thair wonninges and wonderfully wroght,
Murdre and whoredome full dere has it boght.
With an O, and an I, for sixe pens er thay faile,
Sle thy fadre and jape thy modre and thay will thee assoile!

ANONYM (later 14th century)
Of thes Frer Minours me thenkes moch wonder

Sie predigen alle von Dürftigkeit – vnd haben der Liebe vergessen;
Umbwalzet die Suche die ganze Stadt nach Essen für ihre Fressen;
Geraumig ihre Heuser sind, gebawet wunderschon! –
Gekauft mit Vnzucht! und mit Mord! Gekauft von Hurenlohn!
Mit nem O und nem I – einst keinen Penny hattens nie;
Für Vatermord & Mutterschand erteilen sie dir Absol'tion.

15   Hide, Absolon, thy gilte tresses clere;
Ester, ley thou thy mekenesse all adown;
Hide, Jonathas, all thy frendly manere;
Penalopee, and Marcia Catoun,
Make of youre wif hode no comparisoun;
Hide ye youre beautes, Isoude and Heleine:
My lady cometh that all this may disteine.

Thy faire body, lat it nat appere,
Lavine, and thou, Lucresse of Rome town;
And Polixene, that boghten love so dere,
And Cleopatre, with all thy passioun,
Hide ye your trouthe of love and your renown;
And thou, Tesbe, that hast of love suche peine:
My lady cometh that all this may disteine.

Hero, Dido, Laudomia, alle ifere,
And Phyllis, hanging for thy Demophoun,
And Canace, espied by thy chere,
Ysiphile, betraysed with Jasoun:
Maketh of your trouthe neither boost ne soun,
Nor Ypermystre or Adriane, ye tweine:
my lady cometh that all this may disteine.

GEOFFREY CHAUCER (1340(?)-1400)
Hide, Absalon

Verhülle, *Absalon*, der goldnen Locken Zier!
Esther: leg ab nur deine Sanftmut schon!
Verbirg doch, *Jonathan*, all deine artige Manier!
Penelope und *Marcia Caton:*
Legt eure Weibeszier nicht auf Vergleichens Thron!
Isolde, Helena: nicht eurer Schönheit prahlt!
: Mein Lady kömmt, die alle überstrahlt.

Den schönen Leib laßt nicht erzeigen hier,
Lavinia, und du, *Lucrezia*, Romae Eidolon,
Polyxena, der Venus Siegs-Panier,
Kleopatra, mit deiner Passion!
Fort euer Ruhm und aller Minne Lohn!
Auch du, *Thisbe*, die ihn mit Leid bezahlt!
: Mein Lady kömmt, die alle überstrahlt.

Hero, Dido, Laodania: Amoris Elixier,
Und *Phyllis*, die du hangest für dein' Demophon,
Und *Canace*, entdeckt für Liebreiz schier,
Hypsipyle, betrogen von Jason:
Laßt Euer Brüsten, eure Exaltation!
Auch *Hypermnestra, Ariadne*, viel-gemalt!
: Mein Lady kömmt, die alle überstrahlt.

16   Nowe welcome, Somor, with sonne softe,
       That hast thes Wintres wedres overeshake,
       And drevine away the lange nightes blake.
       Saint Valentine, that ert full hye alofte,
       Thus singen smal fowles for thy sake.

       Nowe welcome, Somor, with sonne softe,
       That hast thes Wintres wedres overeshake.

       Wele han they cause for to gladen ofte,
       Sethe ech of hem recoverede hathe his make:
       Full blisseful mowe they ben when they wake.

       Nowe welcome, Somor, with sonne softe,
       That hast thes Wintres wedres overeshake,
       And drevine away the lange nightes blake.

GEOFFREY CHAUCER (1340 (?) -1400)
Nowe welcome Somor, with sonne softe

Nun sei willkommen, Lenz, mit sanfter Sonne mild,
Da du das Joch warfst ab der Winterstürme wild,
Und banntest fern der schwarzen Nächte lange Dauer.
Daß hoch im Grase nun die Welt, Sankt Valentin,
Des singen dir zum Preis die kleinen Vogellin.

Nun sei willkommen, Lenz, mit sanfter Sonne mild,
Da du das Joch warfst ab der Winterstürme wild.

Wohl Ursach haben sie der Freuden viel:
Ein jedes, das erwacht, hat sein Gespiel,
Reibt sich die Augen: singt vor Glück.

Nun sei willkommen, Lenz, mit sanfter Sonne mild,
Da du das Joch warfst ab der Winterstürme wild,
Und banntest fern der schwarzen Nächte lange Dauer.

17   To you, my purse, and to noon other wight
Complain I, for ye be my lady dere.
I am so sory now that ye been light,
For, certes, but if ye make me hevy chere,
Me were as leef be laid upon my bere!
For which unto your mercy thus I crye:
Beth hevy ayeine, or elles mot I die.

Now voucheth sauf this day, or it be night,
That I of you the blisful soun may here,
Or see your colour, like the sonne bright,
That of yellownesse hadde never pere.
Ye be my lif! Ye be mine hertis stere!
Quene of comfort, and of good companye!
Beth hevy ayeine, or elles mot I die.

Now, purse, that ben to me my lives light
And saviour, as down in this worlde here,
Oute of this towne helpe me thurgh your might,
Sin that ye wole nat bene my tresorere!
For I am shave as nye as is a frere.
But yet I pray unto your curtesye,
Beth hevy ayeine, or elles mot I die.

L'envoi de Chaucer

O! Conquerour of Brutes Albion,
Whiche that, by line and free eleccion,
Been verray kinge, this song to you I sende:
And ye, that mowen alle mine harme amende,
Have minde upon my supplicacion.

GEOFFREY CHAUCER (1340 (?) -1400)
A Song to his Purse for the King

Euch, meiner Börse, keiner andern Maid
(denn Ihr seid meine Hohe Frouwe), sei's geklagt:
Ich bin so ellend, da Ihr eine Leichte Magd;
denn, traun, wenn Ihr gravide nicht mich freit,
wär ich so froh, als läg ich auf den Tod bereit.
Daher ich Eurem Barmen alse stöhn:
Seid wieder schwer – sonst muß ich schier vergehn.

Schwört, daß ich diesen Tag, noch diese Nacht
vernehme Euer segensreiches KlingGedicht,
und Eure Farbe seh, die wie die Sonne lacht
so hat an geelem Glanz ihrsgleichen nicht.
Mein Leben seid Ihr! Meines Herzens Sternenlicht!
Trostkönigin! Gefährtin, einzig schön!
Seid wieder schwer – sonst muß ich schier vergehn.

Nun, Geldkatz, die Ihr mir mein Lebensschein,
Heilandin in dem Jammerthal: könnt Ihr mich armes Luder
mit Eurer Macht nicht aus der Stadt befrein,
wenn Ihr schon nicht mein Goldschatz wollet sein?
Ich bin ja kahl wie nicht einmal ein Klosterbruder.
Doch Eurer Courteoisie ich mein Ersuchen stöhn:
Seid wieder schwer – sonst muß ich schier vergehn.

L'envoi de Chaucer

*<center>Eroberer von Brutus' Albion!
Der Du qua Abstammung & freier Elektion
Wahrhaftig König bist: Dir will den Sang ich senden.
Und Du, der all mein Ungemach könnt wenden,
Erwäge meine Supplikation!</center>*

18   Of my lady well me rejoise I may!
      Hir golden forheed is full narw and smal;
      Hir browes been lik to dim, reed coral;
      And as the jeet hir yen glistren ay.
      Hir bowgy cheekes been as softe as clay,
      With large jowes and substancial.
      Hir nose a pentice is that it ne shal
      Reine in hir mouth thogh she uprightes lay.
      Hir mouth is nothing scant with lippes gray;
      Hir chin unnethe may be seen at al.
      Hir comly body shape as a footbal,
      And she singeth full like a papejay.

Thomas Hoccleve (1368 - 1450 (?))
Of my lady well me rejoise I may!

Traun, einer Lady darf ich mich erfreun!:
Ihr gülden Vorhaupt ist ganz schmal und klein;
Die Brauen gleichen trübe-rot Korallen;
Und, ja, wie Jett gleißt ihrer Augen Strahlen.
Ihr Beutelwangen sind wie Mörtel weich,
Die Kieferknochen breit & satt im Fleisch. Die
Nas: ein Dach, den Mund weit überspringend,
Daß – hebt sie's Gesicht – kein
Naß des Regens in ihn dringet.
Ihr Mund: ein knappes Nichts. Mit grauen Lippen.
Fast gar kein Kinn sieht man darunter wippen.
Des Fußballs Rund macht ihren Leib erst schön.
Ihr Singen gleicht des Papageys Getön.

Bewar, squier, yeman, and page,
For servise is non heritage!

If thou serve a lord of prise,
Be not too boistous in thine servise:
Damne not thine soule in none wise,
For servise is non heritage.

Winteres wether, and wommanes thought,
And lordes love chaungeth oft:
This is the sothe, if it be sought,
For servise is non heritage.

Now thou art gret, tomorwe shall I,
As lordes chaungen here baly:
In thine welthe werk sekirly,
For servise is non heritage.

Than serve we God in alle wise:
He shall us quiten our servise,
And yeven us yiftes most of prise,
Hevene to ben our heritage.

ANONYM (earlier 15th century)
Bewar, squier, yeman

Hüt' dich, Freisasse, Edelpage, Lanzenknecht!
Denn Ritterdienst vererbt sich nicht.

Dienst einem Herren du von Welt
Üb in dem Dienst nicht viels Gewalt!
Dein Seelenheil sei über Alls gestellt:
Denn Ritterdienst vererbt sich nicht.

Winterwetter wie Weibes Geist
Und Herren Gunst, die wanken meist:
Wahr ists dem man die Wahrheit weist –
Denn Ritterdienst vererbt sich nicht.

Heut bist *du* groß – und morgen *ich*;
Die Herren wechseln ihr Gesicht:
Auf Sicherheit dein Wirken richt!
Denn Ritterdienst vererbt sich nicht.

Dann dien'n wir GOtt auf alle Weis;
Für unser Dienen ER uns speis'
Mit Himmelsmanna. IHm sei Preis:
Da ER den Himmel uns als Erbschaft weist.

20   I have a yong suster,
Fer beyonden the se:
Many be the drowryes
That she sente me.

She sente me the cherye
Withouten ony ston;
And so she dede the dove
Withouten ony bon;

She sente me the brer
Withouten ony rinde;
She bad me love my lemman
Withoute longing.

How shuld ony cherye
Be withoute ston?
And how shuld ony dove
Ben withoute bon?

How shuld ony brer
Be withoute rinde?
How shuld love mine lemmam
Without longing?

Whan the cherye was a flowr
Than hadde it non ston;
Whan the dove was an ey
Than hadde it non bon;

ich hab ein junge schwester
weit übers meer entrückt:
viel sind der liebesgaben
die sie mir zugeschickt.

sie sandte mir die kirsche
die hat nicht einen stein;
sie brachte mir ein täubchen
ganz ohne knöchelein.

sie schenkte mir ein strauchlin
an dem kein äste hangen;
sie bat mich meinen buhlen
zu minnen ohn verlangen.

wie sollte denn die kirsche
ganz ohne kern wohl sein?
wie könnte denn die taube
entbehren ihr gebein?

wo gäb es denn ein strauchel
an dem nicht zweige hangen?
wie sollt ich meinen buhlen
denn minnen ohn verlangen?

wenn denn ein baum die kirsche wär
dann hätt sie keinen stein;
wenn noch ein ei das täubchen
hätt' es kein knöchelein.

Whan the brer was onbred
Than hadde it non rinde;
Whan the maiden hath that she loveth
She is without longing.

ANONYM (earlier 15th century)
I have a yong suster

und wär der strauch ein samenkorn
wär er von zweigen leer:
wenns maidlin meint, es minnet –
dann hat es kein begehr.

I sing of a maiden
That is makeles:
King of alle kinges
To here sone she ches.

He cam also stille
Ther his moder was,
As dew in Aprille
That falleth on the grass.

He cam also stille
To his moderes bowr,
As dew in Aprille
That falleth on the flowr.

He cam also stille
Ther his moder lay,
As dew in Aprille
That falleth on the spray.

Moder and maiden
Was never non but she:
Well may swich a lady
Godes moder be.

ANONYM (earlier 15th century)
I sing of a maiden

von ein jungfraw will singen:
trägt keinen hochzeitsflor.
den höchsten aller küninge
sie sich zum sohn erkor.

der kam alse still
wo sein muotter was,
wie tau im april
fällt auf das gras.

der kam alse still
in sein muotter schoß,
wie tau im april
fällt auf die ros.

der kam alse still
wo sein muotter lag,
wie tau im april
fällt auf den grünen hag.

jungfraw unde muotter
gleich ihr was noch kein:
wol mag ein solche frawe
die muotter gotes sein.

A
celuy que pluys eyme en mounde,
  Of alle tho that I have founde
    Carissima,
Saluz ottreye amour,
  With grace and joye and alle honour,
    Dulcissima.

Sachez bien, pleysant et beele,
  That I am right in good heele,
    Laus Christo!
Et moun amour doné vous ay,
  And also thine owene night and day
    Incisto.

Ma tresduce et tresamé,
  Night and day for love of thee
    Suspiro.
Soyez permenant et leal:
  Love me so that I it fele
    Requiro.

Jeo suy pour toy dolant et tryst;
  Thou me peinest bothe day and night
    Amore.

An
die ich auf der Welt am liebsten hab,
  Von allen die ich noch gefunden
    Die Teuerste:
      Carissima:
Verzeiht, daß Lieb Euch Grüß entbeut
  Mit Anmut, Freud' & Ehrerbötigkeit,
    Holdeste:
      Dulcissima!

Sachez bien, freundlich Schöne,
  Daß ich des besten Wohlseins mich erfreu,
    Gottlob!
      Laus Christo!
Wie tief die Neigung, die entgegen ich Euch bracht,
  So berg ich Eure Liebe Tag & Nacht
    Im Busen:
      Incisto.

Ma tresduce et tresamé,
  Tag & Nacht seufz ich nach Euch,
    So lieb ich,
      Suspiro.
Seid beständig, treu im Schwur,
  Liebt mich nur, daß ichs gewahr,
    Des bitt ich:
      Requiro.

Bin traurig & bekümmert Euretwegen;
  Tag und Nacht macht Ihr mir Pein
    Vor Liebe:
      Amore.

Mort ha tret tost sun espeye:
  Love me well er I deye
    Dolore.

Saches bien, par verité,
  Yif I deye I clepe to thee,
    Causantem;
Et par ceo jeo vous tres ser
  Love me well withouten daunger,
    Amantem.

Cest est ma volunté
  That I mighte be with thee,
    Ludendo.
Vostre amour en moun qoer
  Brenneth hote as doth the fir,
    Cressendo.

Jeo vous pry, par charité,
  The wordes that here wreten be
    Tenete,
And turne thine herte me toward.
  O! à Dieu, que vous gard;
    Valete!

ANONYM (earlier 15th century)
A celuy que pluys eyme en mounde

Schnell hat der Tod sein Schwert gezogen:
　　Seid mir gewogen, eh ich sterb
　　　　Vor Schmerz:
　　　　　　Dolore.

Traun, merket wohl, par verité:
　　Im Fall ich stürbe, hieß ich Euch
　　　　Die Schuldige:
　　　　　　Causantem.
Und weil in Treu ich Euer Knecht,
　　So seid nicht bang und liebt nur recht
　　　　Den Liebenden:
　　　　　　Amantem.

C'est ma volunté:
　　Daß ich bei Euch möchte sein
　　　　In Schnäbelturteltändelein:
　　　　　　Ludendo.
Vostre amour en mon cœur
　　Brennet heiß als wie das Feur,
　　　　Und immer heißer wirds:
　　　　　　Cressendo.

Ich bitte Euch, par charité:
　　Den Worten, die hier aufgeschrieben,
　　　　Seid nur gewogen mild:
　　　　　　Tenete.
Schließt Euer Herz mir auf im Lieben.
　　Ach, GOtt sei Euer Schirm & Schild!
　　　　Lebt wohl!
　　　　　　Valete!

23 DEO GRACIAS, ANGLIA, REDDE PRO VICTORIA

Oure kinge went forth to Normandy
With grace and might of chivalry.
Ther God for him wrought mervelusly:
Wherfore Englonde may calle and cry.
‹Deo gracias›.

He sette a sege, the sothe for to say,
To Harflu towne with ryal array:
That towne he wan and made affray
That Fraunce shall riwe till Domesday.
‹Deo gracias›.

Than went oure kinge with alle his hoste
Thorwe Fraunce, for alle the Frenshe boste:
He spared, no drede, of lest ne moste,
Till he come to Azincourt coste.
‹Deo gracias›.

Than, forsoth, that knight comely
In Azincourt feld he faught manly.
Thorw grace of God most mighty
He had bothe the felde and the victory.
‹Deo gracias›.

There dukis and erlis, lorde and barone,
Were take and slaine, and that well sone,
And summe were ladde into Lundone
With joye and merthe and grete renone.
‹Deo gracias›.

DEO GRATIAS, ENGELLANT,
REDDE PRO VICTORIA

Vns Kûnic zog in die Normanney
Mit mâchtig-glânzend Reutterei.
Da stritt mit Pracht vor ihn der HErr:
Darob tôn' Engellants Jubel-Schrei:
‹Deo Gratias›

Umb Harfleur sein Belagrung stund
In kûniclicher Schlacht-Command:
Nahm ein die Stadt & ritt Attack,
Deß klage Frankreich bis zum Jûngsten Tag.
‹Deo Gratias›

Durchs Land zog er mit seinem gantzen Trosz;
Ob der Franzosen Prahlen zweifellos
Verschonte er nicht Klein noch Groß
Bis er zur Kûste kam von Azincourt.
‹Deo Gratias›

Da, traun, der Ritter wolgestalde
Stritt mannhaft auff Azincourts Felde.
Dank GOtt deß Schlacht-Herrn in dem Krieg
Hielt er das Feld wie auch den Sieg.
‹Deo Gratias›

Flugs Hertzoge, der Adelleute Macht,
Barone, Grafen, wurden hingeschlacht',
Nach Londen reiche Beut gebracht
Mit Freuden-Pomp & Wûrden-Pracht.
‹Deo Gratias›

Now gracious God he save oure kinge,
His peple and alle his well-willinge:
Yef him gode life and gode ending,
That we with merth mowe safely singe,
‹Deo gracias›.

ANONYM (1415 (?))
The Azincourt Carol

Nun, gnådig GOtt, wahr unsern Kůnic,
Sein Volck & alle seine Freund:
Gib ime gut Leben vnd ein gutes End,
Dasz wir, trutz Feind!, mit Freude singen können:
‹Deo Gratias›

I have a gentle cock,
Croweth me day:
He doth me risen erly
My matins for to say.

I have a gentle cock,
Comen he is of gret:
His comb is of red coral,
His tail is of jet.

I have a gentle cock,
Comen he is of kinde:
His comb is of red coral.
His tail is of inde.

His legges ben of asor,
So gentle and so smale;
His spores arn of silver whit
Into the wortewale.

His eynen arn of cristal,
Loken all in aumber:
And every night he percheth him
In mine ladye's chaumber.

ANONYM (earlier 15th century)
I have a gentle cock

Ich habe einen edlen Hahn,
Kräht ein mir meine Tagen:
Er läßt mich in der Früh aufstahn
Die Matin aufzusagen.

Ich habe einen edlen Hahn,
Sein Abkunft ist von fürnehm Ahn':
Sein Kamm, der ist von rot Korall,
Sein Schwanz, der ist von Jett.

Ich habe einen edlen Hahn,
Der kommt aus einem guten Stall,
Sein Kamm, der ist von rot Korall,
Sein Schwanz von Indigo.

Die Beine sind wie aus Azur,
So fein, so zart ist ihre Spur:
Die Sporen sind von Silber hell
Bis an der Zehen Krallgestell.

Die Augen sind wie von Kristall,
Fein eingelegt in Amber:
Und nächtens wählt er sich zum Stall
Stets meiner Lady Kammer.

25   Kyrie, so kyrie,
     Jankin singeth merye,
     With Aleison.

     As I went on Yol Day
     In oure prosession,
     Knew I joly Jankin
     By his mery ton,
     Kyrieleyson.

     Jankin began the offis
     On the Yol Day,
     And yit me thinketh it dos me good
     So merye gan he say,
     «Kyrieleyson».

     Jankin red the Pistle
     Full faire and full well,
     And yit me thinketh it dos me good
     As evere have I sel,
     Kyrieleyson.

     Jankin at the Sanctus
     Craketh a merye note,
     And yit me thinketh it dos me good—
     I payed for his cote,
     Kyrieleyson.

Kyrie, ja, Kyrie:
Jenkins singt mit Lust,
Mit Alison.

Als ich am Jultag auszog
In unsrer Prozession,
Erkannt ich den Jolly Jenkins schon
An seinem lustigen Ton.
Kyrieleison.

Jenkins begann das Offizium
Zu den Julfesttagen,
Und schon deuchts mich angenehm,
So lustig begann er zu sagen
«Kyrieleison».

Jenkins las die Epistel
Gewinnend & gar fein,
Und schon deuchts mich angenehm,
Hoff, glücklich stets zu sein.
Kyrieleison.

Jenkins bei dem Sanctus
Trillerte so nett,
Und schon deuchts mich angenehm –
Ich zahlte für sein Bett.
Kyrieleison.

Jankin craketh notes
An hundered on a knot,
And yit he hacketh hem smallere
Than wortes to the pot,
Kyrieleyson.

Jankin at the Agnus
Bereth the pax-brede:
He twinkled but said nowt,
And on my fot he trede,
Kyrieleyson.

Benedicamus Domino,
Christ fro shame me shilde:
Deo gracias, therto—
Alas! I go with childe,
Kyrieleyson.

Anonym (earlier 15th century)
Kyrie, so kyrie

Jenkins trillert Noten
Wohl hundert auf ein Lot,
Und noch kleiner hackt er sie
Als Grünzeug für den Pott.
Kyrieleison.

Jenkins bei dem Agnus
Beut den Friedenskuss:
Zwinkerte, doch sagte nix,
Und trat mir auf den Fuß.
Kyrieleison.

Benedicamus Domino.
Jesus, verbirg die Schande mein!
Dank sei dem Herrn, stimmt alle ein!
Weh, mit nem Kind ich schwanger geh.
Kyrie, Alison!

Tutivillus, the devil of hell,
He writeth har names, sothe to tell,
Ad missam garulantes.

Better wer be at home for ay
Than her to serve the Devil to pay,
Sic vana famulantes.

Thes women that sitteth the church about,
Thay beth all of the Develis rowte,
Divina impedientes.

But thay be still he will hem quell,
With kene crokes draw hem to hell,
Ad puteum autem flentes.

For his love that you der boght
Hold you still and jangle noght,
Sed prece deponentes.

The bliss of Heven than may ye win.
God bring us all to his in,
«Amen, amen,» dicentes.

ANONYM (15th century)
Tutivillus, the devil of hell

Der Höllen Teufel Tutivill
Notiert die Nam' – drauf mein Sigill! –
Der, die zur Messe schwatzen.

Die sollten besser heimwärts bleiben
Als hier dem Satanas Genüge tun
Vnd eitel Dinge treiben.

Die Vetteln hocken in der Kirch herumb,
Sie all sind von des Teufels Rott:
Steine auf dem Weg zu GOtt.

Wenn sie nicht still, wird er sie twingen
Ins Hellenloch mit scharffen Haken
Nicht achtend ihrer Weheklagen.

Umb SEiner Liebe willen, die ER für euch hegt:
Seid still & keinen Muckser gebt;
Legt ab nur das Gebet.

Dann könnt des Himmels Glücke ihr gewinnen,
GOtt mög uns all in SEine Wohnstatt bringen,
Uns so wir «Amen, Amen» singen.

27   Go! hert, hurt with adversite,
      And let my lady thy wondis see,
      And say hir this, as I say thee,
      ‹Farwell! my joy, and welcom paine,
      Till I see my lady againe.›

ANONYM (15th century)
Go! hert, hurt with adversite

Schlag hurtig, Herz, verwundt von Mißgeschehn,
Laß meine Lady deine Wunden sehn,
Und sag ihr dies, wie ich dir's sag:
‹Leb wohl, mein Freud' – Willkommen, Weh!,
Bis ich mein Lady wiederseh'.›

28 All ye that passe by this holy place,
    Both spiritual and temporal of every degre,
    Remember yourselfe well during time and space:
    I was as ye are nowe, and as I ye shall be.
    Wherfore I beseche you, of youre benignite,
    For the love of Jesu and his mother Mare,
    For my soule to say a Pater Noster and an Ave.

ANONYM (15th century)
All ye that passe by this holy place

All die ihr kreuzt die fromme Stätte hier/
Gleich ob ihr geistlichen, ob weltlich' Standes/
Gedenkt des Raumes und der Zeit wohl ein:/
Ich war/ wie ihr itzt seid/ und wie ich/ sollt ihr sein/
Daher ich euch um eurer Güte willen bitte/
Und um der Liebe Jesu und Mariæ wegen:/
Sprecht meiner Seel ein Vaterunser und ein Ave.

29   O! Mankinde,
     Have in thy minde
     My Passion smert,
     And thou shall finde
     Me full kinde—
     Lo! here my hert.

ANONYM (15th century)
O! Mankinde

Oh Menschenheit!
Laß dir begründen
Mein Schmerz vnd Leid:
So wirst du finden mich
Voll Freundlichkeit.
Hier, sieh: mein Herz!

30   It semes white and is red;
      It is quike and semes dede;
      It is fleshe and semes bred;
      It is on and semes too;

      It is God body and no mo.

ANONYM (15th century)
It semes white

Es scheinet weiß – und ist doch rot;
Es ist lebendig – scheint doch tot;
Es ist Fleisch und scheint doch Brot;
Es ist Eins und scheinet Zwei'n:

   Wohl muß dies GOttes Körper sein.

ALANUS CALVUS
IACET HIC SUB MARMORE DURO:
UTRUM SIT SALVUS
NON CURAVIT NECQUE CURO.

HERE LIETH UNDER THIS MARBLE STON
RICHE ALANE, THE BALLED MAN:
WHETHER HE BE SAFE OR NOGHT
I RECKE NEVER FOR HE NE ROGHT.

Anonym (15th century (?))
Epitaph

ALANUS CALVUS
IACET HIC SUB MARMORE DURO;
UTRUM SIT SALVUS
NON CURAVIT NECQUE CURO.

HIER UNTER DIESEM MARMORKLOTZ
LIEGT KAHLKOPF-ALLAN'S SCHEDL-GLATZ:
OB ER HIER SICHER ODER NICHT?
DA'S IHN NIE SCHERT', SCHERTS AUCH NICHT MICH.

At a springe wel under a thorn
Ther was bote of bale a litel here aforn.
Ther beside stant a maide,
Fulle of love ibounde:
Whoso wol seche true love,
In hir it shall be founde.

ANONYM (15th century)
At a springe wel under a thorn

An einem Heilquell, unterm Schlehendorn,
Ward unlängst Arzenei gewonnen.
Dort an der Seit steht eine Maid
In Liebe ganz versponnen:
Wer hier um wahre Liebe freit:
In Ihr fänd er der Liebe tiefen Bronnen.

33   I shall say what inordinat love is:
     The furiosite and wodness of minde,
     A instinguible brenning fawting blis,
     A gret hungre, insaciat to finde,
     A dowcet ille, a ivell swetness blinde,
     A right wonderfulle, sugred, swete errour,
     Withoute labour rest, contrary to kinde,
     Or withoute quiete to have huge labour.

Anonym (15th century)
I shall say what inordinat love is

Werd sagen euch, was Liebe sonder Maßen sei:
Tollheit; des Geistes Raserei;
Unlöschbar Brand der sich im eignen Glück verzehrt;
Unstillbar grimmen Hungers Pein;
Süß Unheil; übel-blinde Süße;
Des Irrtums Honigzuckerlein;
Ruh ohne Arbeit, wider die Natur verkehrt.
(Man kanns auch umdrehn: Mühsal ohne Muße.)

34

Swarte-smeked smethes, smatered with smoke,
Drive me to deth with den of here dintes:
Swich nois on nightes ne herd men never,
What knavene cry and clatering of knockes!
The cammede kongons cryen after «Col! col!»
And blowen here bellewes that all here brain brestes.
«Huf, puf,» seith that on, «Haf, paf» that other.
They spitten and sprawlen and spellen many spelles,
They gnawen and gnacchen, they grones togidere,
And holden hem hote with here hard hamers.
Of a bole hide ben here barm-felles,
Here shankes ben shakeled for the fere-flunderes.
Hevy hameres they han that hard ben handled,
Stark strokes they striken on a steled stocke.
«Lus, bus, las, das,» rowten by rowe.
Swiche dolful a dreme the Devil it todrive!
The maister longeth a litil and lasheth a lesse,
Twineth hem twein and toucheth a treble.
«Tik, tak, hic, hac, tiket, taket, tik, tak,
Lus, bus, lus, das». Swich lif they leden,
Alle clothemeres, Christ hem give sorwe!
May no man for brenwateres on night han his rest.

ANONYM (mid 15th century)
Swarte-smeked smethes, smatered with smoke

Schwarzschlackiger Schmiede – schuftend in schmierigem Schmauch –
Schnaufendes Tosen treibt mich zu Taubheit & Tod:
Nimmer vernahm solchen Lärm noch niemand zur Nacht;
Welch Kumpels Krakeelen und klappernd-knatternder Krach!
Krummnäsige Bälger kreischen nach «Kohlen her, Kohlen!»
Und blasen die Bälge bis schier ihre Brägen zerbersten.
«Haff, paff» sagt der eine, «Heff, peff» tönt der andre.
Sie speien & spreizen sich, schwatzen Geschichten sogar,
Sie knabbern & knirschen, wimmern wohl gar um die Wett,
Mit harten Hämmern halten & hüten die Hitz sie.
Von Bullenhaut sind ihre ledernen Schürzen,
Ihre Schenkel geschützt gegen flammende Funken des Feuers.
Hart zu handhaben sind ihre horrend schweren Hämmer;
Starke Schläge auf stählernen Amboß sie schmettern.
«Lass, bass, less, dess,» so tönts reihum.
Mög der Leibhaftige enden das elend Spektakel!
Hier zerrt – dort zwackt der Meister ein Stück,
Zwirbelt die zwei Stück zum Zwickel zusammen.
«Tick, teck, hick, heck, ticket, tecket, hick, heck,
Lass, bass, lass, dess.» –
Das ist ihr Leben. –
Gott strafe alle, die eisernes Rüstzeug für Pferde
Pfauchend ins Kühlwasser tauchen –
Niemand kann schlafen
Alsdann zur Nacht!

35   Whan netilles in winter bere roses rede,
And thornes bere figges naturally,
And bromes bere appilles in every mede,
And lorelles bere cheris in the croppes so hie,
And okes bere dates so plentuosly,
And lekes geve honey in ther superfluence—
Than put in a woman your trust and confidence.

Whan whiting walk in forestes, hartes for to chase;
And heringes in parkes hornes boldly blowe,
And flownders more-hennes in fennes enbrace,
And gornardes shote rolyons out of a crosse-bowe,
And grengese ride in hunting the wolf to overthrowe,
And sperlinges rone with speres in harness to defence—
Than put in a woman your trust and confidence.

Whan sparowes bild chirches and stepulles hie,
And wrennes cary sackes to the mille,
And curlews cary clothes horses for to drye,
And se-mewes bring butter to the market to sell,
And wod-doves were wod-knives theves to kill,
And griffons to goslinges don obedience—
Than put in a woman your trust and confidence.

Whan crabbes tak wodcokes in forestes and parkes,
And hares ben taken with swetness of snailes,
And camelles with ther here tak swalowes and perches,
And mice mowe corn with waveying of ther tailes,
Whan duckes of the dunghill sek the Blod of Hailes,
Whan shrewed wives to ther husbondes do non offence—
Than put in a woman your trust and confidence.

ANONYM (later 15th century)
Whan netilles in winter bere roses rede

Wenn Brennesseln im Winter rote Rosen tragen,
Und Schwarzdorn Feigen trägt ganz artgemäß,
Ginster mit Äpfeln wächst auf jeder Wies,
Die Kirsch sich in dem Lorbeer-Wipfel wiegt,
Die Eiche Datteln trägt in Hüll und Fülle,
Und Schnittlauch Honigseim im Überflusse gibt – :
Dann kannst getrost den Frau'n vertrauen wagen!

Wenn Weißlinge im Walde Hirsche jagen,
Und Heringe im Park das Hifthorn blasen kühn,
Und Flundern Moorhennen im Fenn zusammentreiben,
Und Gurnards Rolyons schießen mit der Armbrust Pfeilen,
Das Gänschen im Galopp zur Wolfsjagd hetzt,
Der Spatz im Harnisch mit dem Speer zur Wehr sich setzt – :
Dann bau nur zutraulich auf Treu der Frauen!

Wenn Spatzen Kirchentürme bauen,
Zaunkönige zur Mühle Säcke schleppen,
Und Brachvögel zum Gäuletrocknen Tücher bringen,
Seemöw wohlfeile Butter auf dem Markte zeigt,
Waldtaub den Jagddolch trägt, die Dieb zu töten,
Vorm Gänschen sich der Greif erbötig beugt – :
Dann trau den Frau'n treuherzig ohne Bangen!

Wenn Krabben Schnepfenhappen sich im Waldpark fangen,
Und Schnecken sich die leckern Hasen schnappen,
Unds zottige Kamel sich Barsche grabscht und Schwalben,
Die Maus das Korn drischt mit dem Schwanze auf der Tenn',
Wenn Enten auf dem Dunghauf nach dem Heilsblut schnabeln,
Das zänkisch Weib der Worte mangelt wider ihren Mann – :
Dann, traun, vertrau den Frau'n auf Treu und Glauben!

To my trew love and able—
As the wedir cock he is stable—
This letter to him be delivered.

Unto you, most froward, this letter I write
Which hath caused me so longe in despaire.
The goodlinesse of your persone is esye to endite,
For he leveth nat that can youre persone appaire,
So comly best shapen, of feture most faire,
Most fresh of contenaunce, even as an owle
Is best and most favored of ony oder fowle.

Youre manly visage, shortly to declare,
Your forehed, mouth and nose so flatte,
In short conclusion best likened to an hare,
Of alle living thinges, save only a catte.
More wold I sey if I wist what.
That swete visage full ofte is beshrewed
Whan I remember of som bawd so lewd.

The proporcion of your body comende welle me aught,
Fro the shuldre down, behinde and beforn.
If alle the peintours in a land togeder were soght
A worse coude they not portrey, thogh alle they had it sworn.
Kepe welle your pacience, thogh I sende you a scorne!
Your garmentes upon you full gayly they hinge,
As it were an olde gose had a broke winge.

An meinen treu-liebreizenden Galan
so standhaft wie der Wetterhahn
soll dies Süßbriefchen gân

Epistolarisch Gruß! dir, so verdrießlich meist,
was mir gebracht gar viel der Leidsgewalt.
Leicht auszudrücken ist, wie *exquisit* du seist,
denn den gibts nicht, der dem Vergleich standhalt:
So hübsch geformt! Von edelster Gestalt!
Und frischster *Contenaunce,* so wie der Eulenvogel
stets Favorit ist unter anderem Geflügel.

Dein mannhafte Visage – in einem kurzen Satz:
dein Maul, dein Vorhaupt, deine flache Nasen –
gleicht, pointirt, am eh'sten einem Hasen
von allem was da kreucht. Vielleicht noch einer Katz.
(Würd mehr noch sagen, wenn ich wüsste, waz.)
Dies lieb Gesichtchen wird so oft verflucht
wie, meines Wissens, nur des Hurenbocks Unzucht.

Deins Leibes *Proporcion* sollt sunders mir gefalen
von Schultern abwärts, hinden gleichwie vorn.
Sucht alle Konterfeiter eines Landes, dich zu malen:
sie fänden Schlimmres nicht, wie sie sich auch verschworn.
(Bewahre *Pacience* trotz meines Schmälens Zorn!)
Dein Rock hängt dir so niedlich überm Knochenbügel,
als wärs 'ne alte Gans mit 'nem gebrochnen Flügel.

Your thighes misgrowen, youre shankes mich worse,
Whoso beholde youre knees so croked,
As ich of hem bad oder Christes curse,
So go they outward; youre hammes ben hoked;
Such a peire chaumbes I never on loked;
So ungoodly youre heles ye lifte,
And youre feet ben croked, with evil thrifte.

Who might have the love of so swete a wight
She might be right glad that ever was she born.
She that onis wold in a dark night
Renne for your love, till she had caught a thorn,
I wolde her no more harme but hanged on the morn,
That hath two good eyen and ichese here suche a make
Or onis wold lift up here hole for youre sake!

Youre swete love
with blody nailes,
Whiche fedeth mo lice than quailes.

ANONYM (15th century)
To my trew love

Die schiefen Schenkel und die Waden sind betörend!
Wer da betrachtete die mißgeformten Knie:
Als wollten sie eins auf das andre schwören,
so krumb sind sie. Und dieses Schinkens Bogen!
So ein Sitzbackenpaar schien mir bis jetzt erlogen.
Du hebst so ungut deine Fersen auf
mit einem Klumpfuß: Belial, nun lauf!

Wer da die Lieb gewönne von so süßem Wicht,
die wäre richtig froh, daß ihr das Leben klinge,
ihr, die einst deiner Lieb in dunkler Nacht
war hinterhergejagt – und bloß ein' Dorn sich finge:
Mehr Leid wünsch ich der nicht, als daß sie morgen hinge
der ein gut Augenpaar vermacht, und so'nen Koofmich kor
und einst um deinetwillen hielt ihr Loch empor!

Dein Buhle hold
mit blut'gen Fingernägeln
(: von Läusen eher denn von Wachtelschlegeln)

Continuaunce
Of remembraunce,
Withoute ending,
Doth me penaunce
And grete grevaunce,
For your partinge.

So depe ye be
Gravene, parde,
Within mine hert,
That afore me
Ever I you see,
In thought covert.

Though I ne plain
My woful pain,
But bere it still,
It were in vain
To say again
Fortune's will.

ANONYM (later 15th century)
Continuaunce

Ewigen
Erinnerns Pein,
Ohne End,
Leiden macht
Und großen Schmerz
Mir dein Scheiden.

Bist so tief
Eingewebt
In mein Herz,
Daß vor mir
Stets dein Bild
In Gedanken schwebt.

Klag doch nicht
Mein wehes Leid,
Trag es still.
Eitelkeit
Wärs, sprechen gen
Fortunens Will'.

38   For a man that is almost blind,
      Lat him go barhed all day agein the wind,
      Till the sonne be set.
      At even wrap him in a cloke
      And put him in a hous full of smoke,
      And loke that every hol be well shet.

      And when his eyen begine to rope,
      Fill hem full of brimstone and sope,
      And hill him well and warm:
      And if he see not by the next mone,
      As well at midnight as at none,
      I shall lese my right arm!

ANONYM (later 15th century)
For a man that is almost blind

Einen Mann, der fast blind,
Laß barhaupt gehen gen den Wind,
Täglich, bis die Sonn verschwindt.
Dazu pack ihn in eine Deck
Und in ein Haus voll Rauch ihn steck,
Gib acht, daß jeder Schlupf verstopft.

Und wenn dann zu tränen anheben die Augen,
Dann füll sie mit Weichbrod und Schwefellaugen,
Und hüll ihn & deck ihn recht artig warm:
Sollt er dann nichts sehn zum nächsten Mond
Um Mitternacht, wie auch zur Non',
Dann soll mir abfallen der rechte Arm!

My ghostly fader, I me confess,
First to God and then to you,
That at a window, wot ye how,
I stale a kosse of gret swetness,
Which don was out avisiness—
But it is doon, not undoon, now.

My ghostly fader, I me confess,
First to God and then to you.

But I restore it shall, doutless,
Agein, if so be that I mow;
And that to God I make a vow,
And elles I axe foryefness.

My ghostly fader, I me confesse,
First to God and then to you.

CHARLES OF ORLEANS (?) (mid 15th century)
My ghostly fader, I me confess

Mein geistlich Vater, mit Verlaub – :
Ich beicht erst GOtt, dann Euch,
Daß an nem Fenster, wie Euch deucht,
Ein Kuss von groszer Sůsse ich geraubt;
Das war getan ohne jed Bedåchtigkeit –
Und doch getan, nicht ungeschehen, heut.

Mein geistlich Vater, muß gestehen,
Zuerst vor GOtt und dann vor Euch.

Doch zweifelt nicht, bei 'ner Gelegenheit
Werd ich die Diebsbeut wieder retournieren.
Und das gelob ich hier vor GOtt,
Und Ellen Holz hack ich zur Poenitenz.

Mein geistlich Vater, ich bekenns
Zuerst vor GOtt und dann vor Euch.

For dedy liif, my livy deth I wite;
For ese of paine, in paine of ese I die;
For lengthe of woo, woo lengteth me so lite
That quik I die and yet as ded live I.
Thus nigh, afer, I fele the fer is nigh,
Of thing certeine that I, uncerteine, seche,
Which is the Deth, sith Deth hath my lady.
O! woful wretche! O! wretche, lesse ones thy speche!

O! ghost formatt, yelde up thy breth att ones!
O! carcas faint, take from this liif thy flight!
O! bolled hert, forbrest thou with thy grones!
O! mested eyen, why faile ye not youre sight?
Sin Deth, alas! hath tane my lady bright,
And left this world without on to her leche,
To lete me live ye do me gret unright.
O! woful wretche! O! wretche, lesse ones thy speche!

What is this liif?—a liif or deth I lede?
Nay! certes, deth in liif is likliness.
For though I faine me port of lustihede,
Yet, inward, lo! it sleth me, my distress.
For from me fledde is joy and all gladness,
That I may say, in all this world so reche
As I is noon of paine and heviness.
O! woful wretche! O! wretche, lesse ones thy speche!

Ther nis no thing sauf Deth, to do me day,
That may of me the wooful paines leche.
But wolde I day, alas! yet I ne may.
O! woful wretche! O! wretche, lesse ones thy speche!

CHARLES OF ORLEANS (?) (mid 15th century)
For dedy liif, my livy deth I wite

Um toten Lebens wegen weiß ich um mein lebend Tod;
Für leichtes Leid sterb ich im Leiden an Beiläufigkeit;
Vor langem Schmerz verlängert mir der Schmerz mein Leben kaum:
So sterb lebendig ich und lebe schon wie tot.
So nah – doch fern! – ich fühl die Ferne nah.
Ein fester Halt ists, den ich, haltlos, suche:
Das ist der Tod, da er mein Lady hat genommen.
Weh, Elend! Weh, laß einmal doch dein Wort verstummen.

Ach, Geist: schachmatt besiegt, halt an den Atem flugs!
Ach, schwacher Leib, lenk dieses Lebens Flug zur Erd!
Ach, schwellend Herz, brich ganz entzwei mit deinem Seufzen!
Ach, ihr zwei dämmernd Augenstern, was darbt ihr der Gesichte nicht?,
Da mir der Tod nahm meine Lady freudenhelle – Weh,
Und sie, ohngleichen, schied aus dieser Welt;
Welch Unrecht tust mir an: mich leben lassen!
Ach, Elend! Weh, laß einmal doch dein Wort vergessen.

Was ist dies Leben? – Leb ich ein Leben oder einen Tod?
Neinnein, gewiß, ein Tod-im-Leben ists wahrscheinlich.
Denn wenn der Heiterkeit Manieren ich auch pflege,
So mordet mich im Innern doch die Schmerzenspein.
Denn Freud' und alle Lustbarkeiten flohen mich,
Daß ich wohl sagen darf, auf all der reichen Welt
Sei niemand so wie ich mit Trauer-Leid beladen.
Weh, Elend! Ach, laß einmal doch dein Reden enden.

Kein Ding ist auf der Welt, zu töten mich,
Bis auf den Tod, der mir die Wunden könnt kuriern.
Würd ich doch sterben! weh, doch kann ichs nicht.
Ach, Elend! Ach, laß einmal doch die Sprache schweigen.

41 Done is a battell on the dragon blak!
Our campioun, Christ, confoundit thes his force;
The yettis of hell brokin with a crak;
The signe triumphall rasit is of the Croce;
The divillis trimmillis with hiddous voce;
The saulis ar borrowit and to the blis can go:
Christ with his blud our ransonis dois indoce.
Surrexit Dominus de sepulchro.

Dungin is the deidly dragon, Lucifer,
The crewall serpent with the mortall stang,
The auld, kene tegir with his teith on char,
Whilk in a wait hes line for us so lang,
Thinking to grip us in his clows strang:
The mercifull Lord wald nocht that it wer so—
He maid him for to felye of that fang.
Surrexit Dominus de sepulchro.

He for our saik that sufferit to be slane,
And lik a lamb in sacrifice wes dicht,
Is lik a lione rissin up agane,
And as gyane raxit him on hicht.
Sprungin is Aurora radius and bricht;
On loft is gone the glorius Appollo;
The blisfull day depairtit fro the nicht.
Surrexit Dominus de sepulchro.

Auffs Haubt geschlagen ist der schwarze Drachen!
Durch Christum, unsern Held, zuschanden ward sein Macht!
Der Hellen Tor zerschmettert mit ein Krachen!
Vom Kreuze weht die Siegesfahn der Schlacht
So kreischend Beelzebuben schütteln macht!
Die Seelen sind erlöst und heischen Segen – oh!
Zu unserm Lösegeld hat ER SEin Blutt gebracht!
Surrexit Dominus de sepulcro.

Nun ist der alte Mord-Drach, Lucifer, gerochen,
Die grausam Schlange mit dem Todes-Stachel,
Der scharffe Tiger mit dem Meuchel-Rachen,
Der uns gelauert hat so lang,
Dacht vns mit sein stark Klawn zur Beut zu machen,
Des wollt der HErre GOtt nit leiden – oh!
Ließ ihn seins Fanges werden bang.
Surrexit Dominus de sepulcro.

Der für uns' Heil geschlachtet werden litt
Und als ein Lamb zum Opfer ward getwungen,
Ist auferstanden als ein Leu,
Reckt sich als Riese in die Höh.
Aurora kömmt aus Strahlenglanz entsprungen,
Zuhöchst der ruhmreiche Apoll gegangen – oh!
Der Segenstag hat sich der Nacht entrungen!
Surrexit Dominus de sepulcro.

The grit victour agane is rissin on hicht,
That for our querrell to the deth wes woundit;
The sone that wox all paill now shinis bricht,
And, dirknes clerit, our faith is now refoundit;
The knell of mercy fra the Hevin is soundit;
The Christin ar deliverit of thair wo;
The Jowis and thair errour ar confoundit.
Surrexit Dominus de sepulchro.

The fo is chasit, the battell is done ceis;
The presone brokin, the jevellouris fleit and flemit;
The weir is gon, confermit is the peis;
The fetteris lowsit and the dungeoun temit;
The ransoun maid, the presoneris redemit;
The feild is win, ourcumin is the fo,
Dispulit of the tresur that he yemit.
Surrexit Dominus de sepulchro.

WILLIAM DUNBAR (about 1500)
Done is a battell on the dragon blak!

Nun ist der große Sieger wieder aufgericht'
So unsers Falles wegen auf den Todt verwundt.
Die finsterbleiche Sunnen, sie leuchtet nun im Licht,
Das Tunckel weicht – der Glaube new vns grünt,
Die Gnadenglocke auß dem Himmel tönt,
Die Christen sind entledigt ihrer Quaalen – oh!
Der Jud und seine Irrthat sind verhöhnt.
Surrexit Dominus de sepulcro.

Der Feind verjagd! Die Schlacht ist auß hienieden!
Die Wärter sind verheert! Der Kerker aufgebracht!
Der Krieg ist auß! Gefestigt steht der Frieden!
Geleeret das Verließ! Die Fesseln abgemacht!
Gezahlt das Lösegeld! Die Sassen frei entdacht!
Das Feld gewunnen vnd der Feind versehret – oh!
Entrissen ihm der Schatz, den er bewacht!
Surrexit Dominus de sepulcro.

42   Most soveren lady, comfort of care,
A next in my hert, most in my minde,
Right welth and cause of my welefare,
Gentle trulove, special and kinde,
Eey pinacle, pight with stidfasteness,
Right tristy, and truth of my salace,
Ever well-springinge stillatorye of sweteness,
Tresore full dere, gronded with grace.

Anonym (about 1500)
MARGERET (Akrostichon)

Mein höchstedle Frawe, Trost im Kummer,
Allernächst meinem Herz, zutiefst in meinem Gemüth,
Reichtum der Seele & Ursach meiner Wolfarth,
Geneigte Trewe, hochherzig ohngleichen,
EdelweibBerg, des Gipfel heißt Beständigkeit,
Ruhe im Trost verheißt Ihr mir werth des Vertrauens,
Ewigüberquellendes Manna der Holdsäligkeit,
Tresor voller Liebe, auf Grazie gegründet!

43   My lefe is faren in a lond—
       Alas! why is she so?
       And I am so sore bound
       I may nat com her to.
       She hath my hert in hold,
       Where-ever she ride or go,
       With trew love a thousandfold.

ANONYM (about 1500)
My lefe is faren in a lond

Mein Lieb ist fahren in ein Land –
Warum tat sie das mir?
Und ich in Trauer bin gebannt:
Nicht gehen darf zu ihr.
Sie halt mein Herz gefangen, ach!
Wo sie auch fahre oder geh
In treuer Liebe tausendfach.

44   I must go walke the woed so wild
And wander here and there
In dred and dedly fere,
For where I trusted I am begild,
And all for one.

Thus am I banished from my blis
By craft and false pretens,
Fautless, without offens,
As of return no certen is,
And all for fer of one.

My bed shall be under the grenwod tree,
A tuft of brakes under my hed,
As one from joye were fled.
Thus from my lif day by day I flee,
And all for one.

The ronning stremes shall be my drinke,
Acorns shall be my fode:
Nothing may do me good,
But when of your bewty I do think,
And all for love of one.

ANONYM (about 1500)
I must go walke the woed so wild

Muß irren durch den Wald so wild
Und hin und wider wandern
In schrecklich Todesbangen,
Denn wo ich glaubte, fand ich Trug,
Und alls der Einen wegen.

Verbannt bin ich von meinem Glück
Durch kunstvoll falschen Schein,
Schuldlos und ohne Missetat;
Kein Sicherheit beut ein Zurück,
Alls aus der Sorg um Eine.

Mein Bett sei unterm Laubengrün,
Mein Kopf auf einem Kissen Farn,
Gleich einem, den die Freude floh.
So flieh ich Tag um Tag von meinem Lebens-
Liebes-Bronn, und alls der Einen wegen.

Mein Trank sei aus dem Stromeslauf,
Bucheckern meine Speise:
Nichts kann mir helfen, es wär denn,
An Deine Schönheit dächt ich
Alls aus der Lieb um Eine wegen.

45 Westron winde, when will thou blow,
    The smalle raine downe can raine?
    Christ if my love were in my armes,
    And I in my bed againe.

ANONYM (earlier 16th century)
Westron winde, when will thou blow

Westlich Wind, wann wirst du wehen,
Daß sich der zarte Regen abestürzen kann?
Jesus, wenn ich mein Lieb in Armen hätt
Und wieder läg in meinem Bett.

46   Burgeis, thou haste so blowen atte the cole,
That alle thy rode is from thine face agoon,
And haste do so many shotte and istoole,
That fleesh upon thy carkeis is there noon:
There is nought lefte but empty skinne and bone.
Thou were a trewe swinkere, atte the fulle,
But nowe thy chaumbre toukes been, echon,
Peesed and fleedde, and of her laboure dulle.

Thy warderer, that was wonte for to be
Mighty and sadde and grene in his laboure,
So wery is of superfluite
He wolle no more be none ratoure.
Himselfe he is thy verrey accusoure,
For so sayne they that knowe his impotence
As welle as ye, my maister reveloure.
Nowe been ye apte to lye in continence!

Thy pilers of thine body in apparence
Been sufficiaunt to utwarde juggement,
But they been feint and weike in existence,
For that her stuffe iwastede is and spente.
And yette thou haste a desirous talente
For to fullefille that that wol not be.
For love of God, be nat impaciente,
But what that I shalle say, nowe herken me.

ANONYM (earlier 16th century)
Burgeis, thou haste so blowen

Bürger, Ihr habt so rotgepust't die Kohlen der Passion,
daß Euch schon alle Röte schwand aus dem Gesicht;
und habt geschweinigelt, und es so wüst getrieben
daß Eur Kadaver kennt der Fleisches Fülle nicht:
Nur eitel Haut & Knochen sind Euch blieben.
Ihr wart ein Rammbock, der zwar etwas taugt,
doch sind Eurs Bettes *zwiefach Waffen* schon
von ihrer öden Rammelei geschrumpft & ausgelaugt:

Eurm *Prügel*, der gewöhnlich bei der Plackerei
strammstrotzend, resch und lebensfrisch gewesen,
ist nun sein Überfließen derart einerlei,
daß man zur Lust ihn schwerlich noch mag kiesen.
Er selber klagt Euch itzo wohlfeil an:
so sagen die, die Eure Impotenz gut kennen
gleichwie Euch selbst, mein Meister-Seladon!
Jetzt könnt Ihr trefflich Euch zur Castitas bekennen.

Und *äußerlichem* Urteil scheint
Eurs Leibes *DoppelMorgenstern* vollauf zu reichen.
Doch ist *de fuckto* er nun welk & weiche
weil all sein Stoff verschleudert ward, verschweint.
Doch habt Ihr nach wie vor den leckern Appetite
das zu vollziehen, was nicht sein gesollt.
Um Gottesliebe, übt Euch in Geduld
und lauscht, was ich zu sagen mich bemühte.

47   With, «Lullay! lullay!» like a childe
Thou slepest too long, thou art begilde!

«My darling dere, my daisy floure,
Let me», quod he, «ly in your lap.»
«Ly stil», quod she, «my paramoure,
Ly still, hardely, and take a nap.»
His hed was hevy, such was his hap!
All drowsy, dreming, drownd in slepe,
That of his love he toke no kepe.

With, «Ba! ba! ba!» and, «bas! bas! bas!»
She cherished him both cheke and chin,
That he wist never where he was,
He had forgoten all dedely sin.
He wanted wit her love to win!
He trusted her payment and lost all his pray,
She left him sleping and stale away.

The rivers rowth, the waters wan,
She spared not to wete her fete.
She waded over, she found a man
That halsed her hartely and kist her swete.
Thus after her cold she cought a hete!
«My lefe», she said, «rowteth in his bed.
Iwis, he hath an hevy hed!»

Mit Lullay-Kinderschlafgesang
schläfst du zu lang – bist du bestrickt!

«Mein Tausenschön, mein Veilchen in der Vase,
in deinem Schoße», sprach er, «such ich meine Ruh.»
«Lieg still,» sprach sie, «mein Schlummerhase,
lieg ernstlich still, und mach die Augen zu.»
Schwer wog sein Kopf wie sein Geschick:
so bräsig – drömelig – schlafdösig dick,
daß er sein Lieb nicht würdigt' mehr mit einem Blick.

Mit «Ba, ba, ba» und «Bas, bas, bas»
liebkoste sie ihm Wang und Haar
bis daß er nimmer wußte, wo er war,
und aller Todsünde alsbald vergaß.
Schnell floh der Minne-Witz den Bacchussohn:
Er baut' auf ihr Löhnen und verlor seinen Lohn –
Sie ließ ihn im Schlummer und stahl sich davon.

Die Wasser schwarz ... die Flüsse rauh ...
mit Nässe schont' sie nicht die Füß:
Sie watete hindurch. Ein Mannsbild fand die Frau,
das halste sie herzlich und küßte sie süß:
so kam sie erst zum Schnupfen, dann zur Hitzen.
«Mein Friedel schnarcht,» sprach sie. «Je nun,
sein Haupt ist schwer. Er hat wohl einen sitzen.»

What dremest thou, drunchard, drowsy pate,
Thy lust and liking is from thee gone!
Thou blinkerd blowboll, thou wakest too late!
Behold! thou lyeste, luggard, alone.
Well may thou sigh, well may thou grone,
To dele with her so cowardly.
Iwis, powle-hachet, she blered thine I!

JOHN SKELTON (earlier 16th century)
With «lullay! lullay!» like a childe

Was träumelst du Tranfunzel, Trinkerpatron?
Dein Wollustvergnügen, es hat dich geflohn;
du erwachest zu spät, du versoffenes Schwein:
schau her, du Triefauge, nun liegst du allein.
Da magst du nun winseln, da magst du nun grein'n
daß du als eine Memme um sie nur konntest frei'n.
Betracht', gehörntes Vieh, die Blindenkappe dein!

48   My galley, charged with forgetfulness,
Thorough sharp seas in winter nights doth pass
'Tween rock and rock; and eke my foe, alas,
That is my lord, steereth with cruelness;
And every oar a thought in readiness,
As though that death were light in such a case;
An endless wind doth tear the sail apace.
Of forced sighs, and trusty fearfulness;
A rain of tears, a cloud of dark disdain,
Hath done the wearied cords great hinderance;
Wreathed with error and eke with ignorance,
The stars be hid that led me to this pain.
Drowned is reason that should me comfort,
And I remain, despairing of the port.

SIR THOMAS WYATT (1503-1542)
My galley, charged with forgetfulness

Meine Galeere kreuzt, befrachtet mit Vergessenheit,
In Winters Nächten durch die rauhe See
Von Riff zu Fels – und auch mein Feind, ach weh!
Nemlich mein Lord, lenkt's Steuer voller Grausamkeit:
Und jedes Ruderblatt folgt des Gedankens Drange
Daß doch der Tod Erleichtrung wäre in dem Fall.
Ein Wind ohn End strafft aus das Segel: prall
Von kräftgen Seufzern & wahrhaftgem Bangen.
Ein Thränenregen & ein dunckler Dunst: Verachtung
Hat das erschlaffte Takelwerck gemacht zu Hindernissen.
Verstrickt in Irrtum und in Nimmerwissen:
Versteckt euch, Sterne, die ihr mich auf solchen Kurs gebracht!
Ertrunken ist Vernunft, die mich getröstet hieße schlafen –
Zurück, alleine, *ich!* verzweifelnd nach dem Hafen.

49   They flee from me that sometime did me seek,
     With naked foot stalking in my chamber:
     I have seen them gentle, tame, and meek,
     That now are wild, and do not once remember
     That sometime they have put themselves in danger
     To take bread at my hand; and now they range,
     Busily seeking with a continual change.

     Thanked be fortune, it hath been otherwise
     Twenty times better; but once, in special,
     In thin array, after a pleasant guise,
     When her loose gown from her shoulders did fall,
     And she me caught in her arms long and small,
     Therewith all sweetly did me kiss,
     And softly said, «Dear heart, how like you this?»

     It was no dream; I lay broad waking:
     But all is turned, thorough my gentleness,
     Into a strange fashion of forsaking;
     And I have leave to go, of her goodness;
     And she also to use new-fangleness.
     But since that I unkindely so am served,
     «How like you this?»—what hath she now deserved?

SIR THOMAS WYATT (1503 -1542)
Vixi Puellis Nuper Idoneus . . .

Die fliehn mich nun, die einst auf nackten Sohlen
Um meiner wegen in mein Zimmer sich gestohlen;
Ich durft sie sanft & zahm & zärtlich wissen,
Die itzt so wild, und schon vergessen,
Daß sie sich selbst einst in Gefahr gebracht, das Brot
Mir aus der Hand zu essen; nun irren sie verstohlen
Geschäftig in beständgen Wechsels Noth.

Dem Schicksal Dank! – : es war ja einmal anders,
Zwanzigmal besser; ganz besonders,
Nachdem ihr Umhang reizend in einer dünnen Hüll'
Und das Gewand ihr locker von den Schultern fiel,
Als sie mich mit den Armen lang & schlank umfing,
Mich auch noch küsst ganz süß,
Sanft sprach «Herzliebster, wie gefällt dir das?»

Das war kein Traum! – ich lieg hellwach;
Das Blatt hat sich gewendet, zu meinem Ungemach,
In eine eigenartge Mode von Verlassenwollen;
Bin dispensiert dank ihrer Güte, mich zu trollen,
Und ihr ist neues Gift im Zähnchen so geronnen.
Doch da so freundlich man mich abserviert –
«Gefällt dir das?» – Was hat sie nun gewonnen?

50

What menethe this? When I lye alone
I tosse, I turne, I sighe, I grone;
My bed me semes as hard as stone:
What menes this?

I sighe, I plaine continually;
The clothes that on my bed do lie
Always, methinks, they lie awry:
What menes this?

In slumbers oft for fere I quake,
For hete and cold I burne and shake,
For lake of slepe my hede dothe ake:
What menes this?

A morninges then when I do rise
I torne unto my wonted gise,
All day after muse and devise:
What menes this?

And if perchance by me there passe
She unto whome I sue for grace,
The cold blood forsakethe my face:
What menethe this?

But if I sitte nere her by
With loud voice my hart dothe cry,
And yet my mouthe is dome and dry:
What menes this?

Was will denn dies? Lieg ich allein,
wühlstöhn' ich – wälz mich – könnte schrein –
dünkt mich mein Bette hart wie Stein:
Was will denn dies?

Ich seufz und klag, bin ganz verstört;
das Tuchzeug, das den Leib mir schwert,
liegt immer irgendwie verkehrt:
Was will denn dies?

Im Schlummer schüttelt mich der Schweiß;
vor Furcht brenn' kalt ich – friere heiß;
das Kopfweh kühlt ein Beutel Eis:
Was will denn dies?

Des Morgens früh, wenn ich mich rühr,
nehm gleich ich die gewohnt' Manier,
heft mir die Grillen ans Panier:
Was will denn dies?

Führt SIE der Zufall mir vorbei,
('hoff, daß sie mir gewogen sey)
wird mir das Antlitz weiß wie Ey:
Was will denn dies?

Doch sitze ich ihr nahe bey,
ruft mir mein Herz mit lautem Schrei –
mein Mund jedoch scheint voller Brei:
Was will denn dies?

To aske for helpe no hart I have,
My tong dothe faile what I shuld crave;
Yet inwardly I rage and rave:
What menes this?

Thus have I passed many a yere
And many a day, tho nought appere,
But most of that that most I fere:
What menes this?

SIR THOMAS WYATT (1503-1542)
What menethe this?

Um Hülfe flehn, fehlt mir Courage;
die Zung' macht mir, statt Frawenlob, Blamage;
doch mir im Innern raast & peitscht die Rage:
Was will denn dies?

So bracht ich viele Jahre hin
und viele Tage, ohne Sinn
bis auf, wes ich höchst furchtsam bin:
Was will denn dies?

51

The soote season, that bud and bloom forth brings,
With green hath clad the hill and eke the vale,
The nightingale with feathers new she sings;
The turtle to her make hath told her tale.
Summer is come, for every spray now springs;
The hart hath hung his old head on the pale;
The buck in brake his winter coat he flings;
The fishes flete with new-repaired scale;
The adder all her slough away she slings;
The swift swallow pursueth the flies smale;
The busy bee her honey now she mings;
Winter is worn that was the flowers' bale.
And thus I see among these pleasant things
Each care decays, and yet my sorrow springs.

HENRY HOWARD, EARL OF SURREY (1517 (?) -1547)
The soote season, that bud and bloom forth brings

Die süsse Frühlingszeit, die Blüt und Knospen bringt,
hat grün gekleidt den Hügel und das Thal.
Die Nachtegal in nevvem Federwamse singt,
die Taub hat was geflustert dem Gemahl.
Lenz ist nun kommen: iedes Zweiglin springt,
nun hängt der Hirsch sein alte Stangen an den Pfahl,
ab streift der Widderbock den Winterrock im Dikkicht flink;
Die Fische werfen sich, ganz nevv geschuppt, in Schal' –
Die Otter sich aus ihrer Häutung schlingt –
Der flinken Schwalb entfleucht die Mucke grad nochmal.
Die Imme emsig ihren Seim zur Honig-Gärung zwingt.
Ganz schal ist nun der Winter, der aller Blumen Quaal.
So seh ich nun in allen Ding so süssen,
wie Frühling Lieder singt – doch meine Leiden spriessen.

One day I wrote her name upon the strand,
But came the waves and washed it away:
Again I wrote it with a second hand,
But came the tide and made my pains his prey.

Vain man (said she), that dost in vain assay
A mortal thing so to immortalise;
For I myself shall like to this decay,
And eke my name be wiped out likewise.

Not so (quod I); let baser things devise
To die in dust, but you shall live by fame;
My verse your virtues rare shall eternise,
And in the heavens write your glorious name:
Where, whenas death shall all the world subdue,
Our love shall live, and later life renew.

EDMUND SPENSER (1552 (?) -1599)
One day I wrote her name upon the strand

Ich schrieb ihren Namen in den Strand,
Da kamen die Wellen und wuschen ihn fort.
Noch einmal senkt ich zum Schreiben die Hand,
Doch die Flut macht' zum Raube sich meinen Tort.

Du Tor, sprach Sie da, der du suchst ohne Sinnen
Unsterblich zu machen ein sterbliches Sein,
Ich muß ja vergehen, auch ich soll verrinnen,
So muß auch mein Name zerrieben sein.

Niemals! sprach ich; denk': Laß niederen Dingen
Im Staube ein Tod – doch Du lebe im Ruhme,
Mein Dichten soll ewig dein Tugendlob singen,
Dem Himmel einschreiben den herrlichen Namen,
Wo /: sollte auch die ganze Welt vorm Todesnahen beben: /
Soll leben unsre Liebe, stets erneuen künftges Leben.

52B *Song! made in lieu of many ornaments,*
With which my love should duly have been dect,
Which cutting off through hasty accidents,
Ye would not stay your dew time to expect,
But promist both to recompens;
Be unto her a goodly ornament,
And for short time an endlesse moniment.

Ye learnèd sisters, which have oftentimes
Beene to me ayding, others to adorne,
Whom ye thought worthy of your gracefull rymes,
That even the greatest did not greatly scorne
To heare theyr names sung in your simple layes,
But joyèd in theyr praise;
And when ye list your owne mishaps to mourne,
Which death, or love, or fortunes wreck did rayse,
Your string could soone to sadder tenor turne,
And teach the woods and waters to lament
Your dolefull dreriment:
Now lay those sorrowfull complaints aside;
And, having all your heads with girlands crownd,
Helpe me mine owne loves prayses to resound;
Ne let the same of any be envide:
So Orpheus did for his owne bride!
So I unto my selfe alone will sing;
The woods shall to me answer, and my Eccho ring.

Mein Lied! das du, erdacht statt Goldgeschmeid
Mit dem mein Lieb gezieret werden sollt
Doch durch ein jäh Geschick in Stück zerbrochen,
Auf rechte Zeit zu warten nicht gewollt,
Nein, Beides zu ersetzen du versprochen:
Sei ihr für unsre kurze Zeit
Ein Diadem & Dokument der Ewigkeit!

Gelehrte *Schwestern*! die ihr oft zur Seite mir,
Zu rühmen Andre mannigfalt
Die ihr für wert befunden eurer Reime Zier,
Daß noch der Größte gar nicht gröblich schalt
In euren schlichten Liedern seines Namens Klang –
Nein, trank den Preisgesang!
Und die ihr eures Unglüks Klage lauscht
Das Liebe, Tod und Schicksals Wrack entband,
Die frohen Saiten strack mit trübem Ton vertauscht
Und lehret alle Wasser, Wälder gar am End
Eur trauriges Lament:
Nun legt die schmerzensvolle Klag beiseit
Und, da ein jedes Haupt mit Lorber sey bekrönt,
Helft daß mein Liebesruhm-Lied nun ertönt;
Bereite es doch Niemandem, ach, Neid!
Gleichwie *Orfeo* tat für seine Braut
So will ich zu mir selber jetzo singen:
Die Wälder solln mir widerhalln, mein Echo klingen!

Early, before the worlds light-giving lampe
His golden beame upon the hils doth spred,
Having disperst the nights unchearefull dampe,
Doe ye awake; and, with fresh lusty-hed,
Go to the bowre of my belovèd love,
My truest turtle dove;
Bid her awake; for Hymen is awake,
And long since ready forth his maske to move,
With his bright Tead that flames with many a flake,
And many a bachelor to waite on him,
In theyr fresh garments trim.
Bid her awake therefore, and soone her dight,
For lo! the wishèd day is come at last,
That shall, for all the paynes and sorrowes past,
Pay to her usury of long delight:
And, whylest she doth her dight,
Doe ye to her of joy and solace sing,
That all the woods may answer, and your eccho ring.

Frühauf, noch eh die Leuchte, die der Welten Schein
Mit güldnen Strahlen um die Hügel webt,
Den düstern Dunst der Nebelnacht zerstiebt,
Erwachet ihr – und mit frischlustgem Sinn
Geht zu der Laube meiner Liebsten hin,
Der Turteltaube mein;
Weckt sie ganz sacht – denn *Hymen* ist erwacht
Und lange schon bereit zu seinem Masquenspiel
Mit seiner Leuchte-Fakel der die Flamme lacht
Und, aufzuwarten ihm, der jung Gesellen viel
In frisch Gewänderpracht.
Heißt sie: Erwacht! und: Schmückt Euch fein!
Denn sieh, gekommen ist der hocherwünschte Tag
Der für vergangnen Kummer, Schmerz und Plag
Ihr zollt, daß ewge Wonne sie entzückt.
Und, da sie sich jezt schmückt,
Macht, daß die Freud, der heitre Sinn ihr singe,
Daß alle Wälder widerhalln, eur Echo klinge.

Bring with you all the Nymphes that you can heare
Both of the rivers and the forrests greene,
And of the sea that neighbours to her neare:
Al with gay girlands goodly wel beseene.
And let them also with them bring in hand
Another gay girland
For my fayre love, of lillyes and of roses,
Bound truelove wize, with a blew silke riband.
And let them make great store of bridale poses,
And let them eeke bring store of other flowers,
To deck the bridale bowers.
And let the ground whereas her foot shall tread,
For feare the stones her tender foot should wrong,
Be strewed with fragrant flowers all along,
And diapred lyke the discolored mead.
Which done, doe at her chamber dore awayt,
For she will waken strayt;
The whiles doe ye this song unto her sing,
The woods shall to you answer, and your Eccho ring.

Bringt mit euch alle Nymphen, die belauscht
In Flüssen, Hainen und in Wäldern grün
Und in der See, die nahebei ihr rauscht,
Umrankt mit heiteren Guirlanden schön.
Heißt sie, daß jede nehme sich zur Hand
Ein heitere Guirland
Von Lilien, Rosen, für mein holdes Lieb
Zu treuem Bund umwunden mit blauem Seidenband.
Heißt sie, daß jed' in bräutlicher Statur sich üb',
Heißt sie viel mehr der Blumen noch zu pflücken,
Das Brautgemach zu schmücken,
Und sorgt, es sey der Grund, den sie beschreit't,
Daß nicht den zarten Fuß der Stein verletzt,
Mit duftend Blüten allerwegs bestreut
Der Wiese gleich, die blumenbunt benetzt.
Ist das getan, harrt ihrer an der Kammertür –
Denn gleich tritt sie herfür.
Derweilen eur Gesang ihr singe,
Solln euch die Wälder widerhalln, eur Echo klingen.

Ye Nymphes of Mulla, which with carefull heed
The silver scaly trouts doe tend full well,
And greedy pikes which use therein to feed;
(Those trouts and pikes all others doo excell;)
And ye likewise, which keepe the rushy lake,
Where none doo fishes take;
Bynd up the locks the which hang scatterd light,
And in this waters, which your mirror make,
Behold your faces as the christall bright,
Then when you come whereas my love doth lie,
No blemish she may spie.
And eke, ye lightfoot mayds, which keepe the deere,
That on the hoary mountayne used to towre;
And the wylde wolves, which seeke them to devoure,
With your steele darts doo chace from comming neer;
Be also present heere,
To helpe to decke her, and to help to sing,
That all the woods may answer, and your eccho ring.

Ihr Mullas Nymphen die ihr achtsam wacht
Der silberschuppichten Forelle, hütet in der Flut
Auch den gefräßgen Hecht der gute Mahlzeit macht
(Ach diese Hechte & Forellen sind so gut);
Gleichweis ihr Teiches Wächter, wo die Binse schwimmt
Und Niemand Fische nimmt:
Steckt auf der Lockenfüll' zerzauste Pracht;
In seinem Wasser das euch spiegeln macht
Seht euer Antlitz hell wie Crystall-Schnee,
Daß, wenn ihr naht, wo mein Herzlieb erwacht,
Sie keinen Makel seh.
Ihr leichtfüszigen Maiden, Hüterin der Hirschen,
Des gräulichen Gebürges Gipfelthier,
Die wilden Wölf' die ihn zu schlingen pirschen
Mit stählern Pfeilen jagt, vereitelt ihre Gier:
Seid auch willkommen hier!
Helft, sie zu zieren, helft daß sie singe:
Daß alle Wälder widerhalln, eur Echo klinge.

Wake now, my love, awake! for it is time;
The Rosy Morne long since left Tithones bed,
All ready to her silver coche to clyme;
And Phœbus gins to shew his glorious hed.
Hark! how the cheerefull birds do chaunt theyr laies
And carroll of Loves praise.
The merry Larke hir mattins sings aloft;
The Thrush replyes; the Mavis descant playes;
The Ouzell shrills; the Ruddock warbles soft;
So goodly all agree, with sweet consent,
To this dayes merriment.
Ah! my deere love, why doe ye sleepe thus long?
When meeter were that ye should now awake,
T' awayt the comming of your joyous make,
And hearken to the birds love-learnèd song,
The deawy leaves among!
Nor they of joy and pleasance to you sing,
That all the woods them answer, and theyr eccho ring.

Wach nun, mein Lieb, erwach! Denn es ist Zeit;
Der Rosenmorgen kroch aus *Tithons* Bett, im Glanz
Den Silberwagen zu besteigen froh bereit;
Und *Phoebes* Haupt zeigt sich im Ruhmeskranz.
Horch, wie die heitern Vögel flöten Lais
Im Chor zum Liebes-Preis:
Die lustge Lerche hochauf intonirt;
Die Drossel zwitscht; der Zeisig warbelt leis;
Die Amsel gurrt; die Grasmück diskantirt;
So ist sich jedes gut, vereint sich heut
Mit unsrer Seligkeit.
Ach Liebste mein, was schläfest du so lang?
Wenns richtger wär, daß du erwachtest nun,
Und harrtest auf dein Freuden-Theil zu tun
Und lauschtest auf der Vögel liebesklugen Sang
In taufeucht Blattbehang.
Solln sie von Lust & Jubel dir nicht singen,
Daß alle Wälder widerhalln, dir Echo klingen?

My love is now awake out of her dreames,
And her fayre eyes, like stars that dimmèd were
With darksome cloud, now shew theyr goodly beams
More bright then Hesperus his head doth rere.
Come now, ye damzels, daughters of delight,
Helpe quickly her to dight:
But first come ye fayre houres, which were begot
In Joves sweet paradice of Day and Night;
Which doe the seasons of the yeare allot,
And al, that ever in this world is fayre,
Doe make and still repayre:
And ye three handmayds of the Cyprian Queene,
The which doe still adorne her beauties pride,
Helpe to addorne my beautifullest bride:
And, as ye her array, still throw betweene
Some graces to be seene;
And, as ye use to Venus, to her sing,
The whiles the woods shal answer, and your eccho ring.

Nun ist mein Lieb aus ihrem Traum erweckt:
Ihr schönes Aug, gleich Sternen welche eingewebt
In dunkle Wolken waren, jetzo Strahlen schickt
Heller denn *Hesperus* sein Haupt erhebt.
Herbei nun, Jungfraun, Töchter des Entzücken,
Helft ihr, sich rasch zu schmücken –
Doch kommt erst, schöne *Horen*, ihr! gezeugt
Von Tag und Nacht in *Jovis*' Paradeis,
Die ihr die Jahreszeit der Zeit anweist,
Und alls was nur in dieser Welt ist fein,
Schmück sich und kehre ein;
Und ihr, der *Kyprischen Regentin* Zofen drei'n,
Die ihr vor jener Schönheit Stolz euch beugt,
Helft meine Herrlichste mit Grazie zu bestreun,
Wenn eure Hand ihr Kleiderzier anneigt,
Daß sich ihr Reiz erzeigt;
Wer hier zu *Venus* singt, zu *Ihr* auch singe,
Dieweil die Wälder widerhalln, eur Echo klinge!

Now is my love all ready forth to come:
Let all the virgins therefore well awayt:
And ye fresh boyes, that tend upon her groome,
Prepare your selves; for he is comming strayt.
Set all your things in seemely good aray,
Fit for so joyfull day:
The joyfulst day that ever sunne did see.
Faire Sun! shew forth thy favourable ray,
And let thy lifull heat not fervent be,
For feare of burning her sunshyny face,
Her beauty to disgrace.
O fayrest Phœbus! father of the Muse!
If ever I did honour thee aright,
Or sing the thing that mote thy mind delight,
Doe not thy servants simple boone refuse;
But let this day, let this one day, be myne;
Let all the rest be thine.
Then I thy soverayne prayses loud wil sing,
That all the woods shal answer, and theyr eccho ring.

Schon ist mein Lieb hinanzukomm'n bereit:
Drum laßt aufwarten alle Jungfraun ihr;
O frische Knaben, Bräutigams Geleit,
Bereitet euch, denn gleich tritt er herfür.
In artger Zier sich jedes schmücken mag
Schicklich so frohem Tag,
Dem frohsten Tag den ie die Sonn beschien.
O schöne Sonn! Die Gnadenpfeile richt,
Doch laß die scharfe Glut nicht glühend sein,
Auf daß dein Brand ihr Sonnenscheingesicht
Im Rang verdunke nicht!
O schönster *Phöbus*! Musen-Vater! macht
Ich dir ie mein Ehrerbieten recht
Und sang, was deinem Sinn Entzücken bracht,
Verschmäh die schlichte Gabe nicht von deinem Knecht;
Mach, daß der Tag, nur dieser Tag, sey mein;
Was du sonst wilt, sey dein.
Deins Herrschafts Loblied ich dann freudig singe,
Daß alle Wälder widerhalln, sein Echo klinge.

Harke! how the Minstrils gin to shrill aloud
Their merry Musick that resounds from far,
The pipe, the tabor, and the trembling Croud,
That well agree withouten breach or jar.
But, most of all, the Damzels doe delite
When they their tymbrels smyte,
And thereunto doe daunce and carrol sweet,
That all the sences they doe ravish quite;
The whyles the boyes run up and downe the street,
Crying aloud with strong confusèd noyce,
As if it were one voyce,
Hymen, ïo Hymen, Hymen, they do shout;
That even to the heavens theyr shouting shrill
Doth reach, and all the firmament doth fill;
To which the people standing all about,
As in approvance, doe thereto applaud,
And loud advaunce her laud;
And evermore they Hymen, Hymen sing,
That al the woods them answer, and theyr eccho ring.

Horch auf der Spielleut' Tönen laut & klar,
Wie so von fern ihr Klingen widerhallt
Mit Pfeife, Tambour, in der Sänger Schar
Nicht Streit noch Mißton in die Harmonieen schallt;
Indes am lieblichsten der Mädchen Sang
Mit ihrer Schellen Klang
Dazu im Tanz mit Liedern hold verweilen,
Daß jedem Sinn vor Taumel-Lust wird bang,
Dieweil die Straßen auf & ab die Knaben eilen
In wirrer Stimmen Schall laut rufen, und
Als wärs aus *einem* Mund,
Der Schrei *Hymen, ïo, Hymen, Hymen* aufschwillt,
Daß bis zum Himmel gar ihr Rufen dringt,
Das ganze Firmament mit Jubel füllt,
Mit Vivat & Applauso heiß umringt
Von großer Menge Schaar, die Beyfall gellt
Und lauthals *Laudes* bringt,
Und immer wieder *Hymen, Hymen* singet,
Daß alle Wälder widerhalln, ihr Echo klinget.

Loe! where she comes along with portly pace,
Lyke Phœbe, from her chamber of the East,
Arysing forth to run her mighty race,
Clad all in white, that seemes a virgin best.
So well it her beseemes, that ye would weene
Some angell she had beene.
Her long loose yellow locks lyke golden wyre,
Sprinckled with perle, and perling flowres atweene,
Doe lyke a golden mantle her attyre;
And, being crownèd with a girland greene,
Seeme lyke some mayden Queene.
Her modest eyes, abashèd to behold
So many gazers as on her do stare,
Upon the lowly ground affixèd are;
Ne dare lift up her countenance too bold,
But blush to heare her prayses sung so loud,
So farre from being proud.
Nathlesse doe ye still loud her prayses sing,
That all the woods may answer, and your eccho ring.

Sieh! Wo sie kömmt mit würdevollem Schritt,
Wie *Phoebe* aus der Kammer sich im Osten
Erhebt, zu mächtgem Laufe sich zu rüsten,
In Weiß gekleidet, die schönste Jungfrau mit
So herrlicher Gewandung: man sollt wähn'n
Ein *Engel* gar zu sehn:
Die langen Locken blond wie Goldgeschmeid
Mit Perlbesatz, Perlblumen mittenin,
Sich wie ein güldner Mantel um sie breit'
Annoch gekrönet mit Guirlanden grün
Wie *Oriana Queen*.
Das scheue Aug, zu schamhaft zu erschaun
Wie tausend Augen sich verehrend auf sie richten,
Ist auf den Boden fest gebannt, zu traun
Sich allzu kühner Contenance mag sie mitnichten –
Nein, sie errötet bei des Preislieds Harmonie,
So wenig stolz ist sie.
Doch wollt ihr weiter laut ihr Loblied singen,
Daß alle Wälder widerhalln, ihr Echo klingen.

Tell me, ye merchants daughters, did ye see
So fayre a creature in your towne before;
So sweet, so lovely, and so mild as she,
Adorned with beautyes grace and vertues store?
Her goodly eyes lyke Saphyres shining bright,
Her forehead yvory white,
Her cheekes lyke apples which the sun hath rudded,
Her lips lyke cherryes charming men to byte,
Her brest like to a bowle af creame uncrudded,
Her paps lyke lyllies budded,
Her snowie necke lyke to a marble towre;
And all her body like a pallace fayre,
Ascending up, with many a stately stayre,
To honors seat and chastities sweet bowre.
Why stand ye still ye virgins in amaze,
Upon her so to gaze,
While ye forget your former lay to sing,
To which the woods did answer, and your eccho ring?

Sprecht, o ihr Kaufmannstöchter, saht ihr ie
In eurer Stadt ein Wesen alse schön:
So hold, so lieblich und so mild wie sie
Mit Anmuths Reiz so tugendreich zu sehn?
Die Augen gleich des Saphirs hellem Schein,
Die Stirne elfenbein,
Die Wangen Äpfeln gleich, gerötet in der Sonn,
Die Lippen Zauberkirschen (gern beißt er hinein),
Der Busen beut alswie die Sahneschale Wonn',
Die Brüstchen lilienfein,
Der Hals gleich einem Marmel-Turm schneeweiß,
Der ganze Leib gleichwie des Lust-Palais
Herrschaftlich Treppe führet in die Höh
Zur Ehre Sitz, zu Keuschheits Thron & Preis.
Was wollt ihr innehalten, o ihr jungen Fraun,
Verzaubert sie zu schaun;
Habt ihr vergessen nun den alten Sang,
Dem alle Wälder widerhallten und eur Echo klang?

But if ye saw that which no eyes can see,
The inward beauty of her lively spright,
Garnisht with heavenly guifts of high degree,
Much more then would ye wonder at that sight,
And stand astonisht lyke to those which red
Medusaes mazeful hed.
There dwels sweet love, and constant chastity,
Unspotted fayth, and comely womanhood,
Regard of honour, and mild modesty;
There vertue raynes as Queene in royal throne,
And giveth lawes alone,
The which the base affections doe obay,
And yeeld theyr services unto her will;
Ne thought of thing uncomely ever may
Thereto approch to tempt her mind to ill.
Had ye once seene these her celestial threasures,
And unrevealèd pleasures,
Then would ye wonder, and her prayses sing,
That al the woods should answer, and your echo ring.

Doch säht ihr, was kein *Auge* ie entzükt,
Ihrs Lebenshauches *innre* Schönheit gar
Mit Himmelsgaben hohen Grads geschmückt,
Mit weit mehr Staunen nähmt ihr wahr
Mit mehr Erstarrn, als jene die entrückt
Von *Gorgos* Schlangenhaar:
Die Liebe selbst, inständge Keuschheit wohnt
Hier, reiner Glaube, schönste Weiblichkeit,
Ehr-Würdigkeit & mild Bescheiden, thront
Als Queen die *Tugend* in royaler Pracht,
Allein Gesetze macht,
Die niedren Leidenschaften setzen ihre Schranke,
Nur ihrem Willen ihre Dienste anbefehlen,
Auf daß sich nahe ja kein unziemlich Gedanke
Mit bös Verführen ihren Sinn zu quälen:
Wollt ihr *den* Himmels-Schatz betrachten nur einmal,
Die Freuden sonder Zahl,
Dann mögt ihr staunen, und ihr Preislied singen,
Daß alle Wälder widerhalln, eur Echo klinge.

Open the temple gates unto my love,
Open them wide that she may enter in,
And all the postes adorne as doth behove,
And all the pillours deck with girlands trim,
For to receyve this Saynt with honour dew,
That commeth in to you.
With trembling steps, and humble reverence,
She commeth in, before th' Almighties view;
Of her ye virgins learne obedience,
When so ye come into those holy places,
To humble your proud faces:
Bring her up to th' high altar, that she may
The sacred ceremonies there partake,
The which do endlesse matrimony make;
And let the roring Organs loudly play
The praises of the Lord in lively notes;
The whiles, with hollow throates,
The Choristers the joyous Antheme sing,
That al the woods may answere, and their eccho ring.

Macht auf die Tempelpforten für die Liebste mein,
Öffnet sie weit, daß sie eintrete lind,
Und alle Pfeiler sein umwunden fein
Und jede Säule sey umrankt mit Kranzgewind,
Die Heilge würdig zu empfangen, wie's ihr frommt,
Die nunmehr zu euch kommt:
Mit zagem Schritt, und voll Ergebenheit
Tritt sie vor des Allmächtigen Gesicht,
Und ihr, o Jungfern, lernt Gehorsam heut:
An heilgem Ort dereinst die heilge Pflicht erfüllen,
Den Stolz euch zu verhüllen.
Führt sie zum Hochaltar, daß sie itzund
Den andachtsvollen Zeremonien mag frönen
Zum ewgen Hochzeitsbund,
Und laßt die Orgelpfeifen herrlich dröhnen
Dem Herrn in frohen Tönen Hymnen, und
Dazu aus tiefem Schlund
Die *Choristers* das Freuden-*Anthem* singen,
Dem alle Wälder widerhalln, ihm Echo klingen.

Behold, whiles she before the altar stands,
Hearing the holy priest that to her speakes,
And blesseth her with his two happy hands,
How the red roses flush up in her cheekes,
And the pure snow, with goodly vermill stayne
Like crimsin dyde in grayne:
That even th' Angels, which continually
About the sacred Altare doe remaine,
Forget their service and about her fly,
Ofte peeping in her face, thet seems more fayre,
The more they on it stare.
But her sad eyes, still fastened on the ground.
Are governèd with goodly modesty,
That suffers not one looke to glaunce awry,
Which may let in a little thought unsownd.
Why blush ye, love, to give to me your hand,
The pledge of all our band!
Sing, ye sweet Angels, Alleluya sing,
That all the woods may answere, and your eccho ring.

Seht her, wie sie vor dem Altare steht,
Dem Priester lauschet, der sich zu ihr wendet,
Ihr aus geweihten Händen Segen spendet,
Daß ihre Wangenrose hold sich röt',
Und Scharlachröte sich mit Schnee darein
Verwebt zu Karmesin:
Daß gar die Engel, die sonst eben
Nur hoch auf dem geheiligten Altare sein,
Der Pflicht mißachtend, ihr Gesicht umschweben
Des Züge, fürwitzig beguckt, so mehr beglüken
Je öfter sie's erblicken.
Doch bleibt ihr Auge schatticht zu der Wangenröte
Und auf den Boden in *Bescheidenheit* gesenkt
Die keinen Blick vom Pfade seitwärts lenkt
Der einem kleinen unreinen Gedanken Einlaß böte.
Was rötest du, mein Lieb? Reich mir die Hand:
Der Gattenliebe Pfand.
Singt, süße Engel, Alleluja singet,
Daß alle Wälder widerhalln, eur Echo klinge.

Now all is done: bring home the bride againe;
Bring home the triumph of our victory:
Bring home with you the glory of her gaine;
With joyance bring her and with jollity.
Never had man more joyfull day then this,
Whom heaven would heape with blis,
Make feast therefore now all this live-long day;
This day for ever to me holy is.
Poure out the wine without restraint or stay,
Poure not by cups, but by the belly full,
Poure out to all that wull,
And sprinkle all the postes and wals with wine,
That they may sweat, and drunken be withall.
Crowne ye God Bacchus with a coronall,
And Hymen also crowne with wreathes of vine;
And let the Graces daunce unto the rest,
For they can doo it best:
The whiles the maydens doe theyr carroll sing,
To which the woods shall answer, and theyr eccho ring.

Nun ists getan – die Braut bringt wieder heim!
Bringt unsers Sieges Hoch-Triumph nach Haus,
Bringt mit euch heim ihres Gewinnes Ruhm,
Bringt sie zu Freudentanz & Trank & Schmaus!
Nie ward zuvor dem Mann ein Freudentag gleich dem
Behäuft mit Himmels-Preis:
Derhalben feiert nun den lebens-langen Tag,
Den Tag der mir auf ewig heilig sei.
Schenkt aus den Wein ohn Zaudern noch Beschlag!
Schenkt nicht aus Tassen, nein, aus Schläuchen frei;
Schenkt jedem ein, der mag!
Besprüzt die Säulen und die Wänd' mit Wein
Auf daß sie dampfen und betrunken sein;
Bekränzt des Gottes Bacchus Stirn, Epheben!
Auch Hymen kränzet mit dem Laub der Reben!
Und laßt die Grazien tanzen zu dem Feste –
Sie könnens ja am besten.
Derweil der Mädchen Schar ihr Loblied singe,
Dem alle Wälder widerhalln, sein Echo klinge.

Ring ye the bels, ye yong men of the towne,
And leave your wonted labors for this day:
This day is holy; doe ye write it downe,
That ye for ever it remember may.
This day the sunne is in his chiefest hight,
With Barnaby the bright,
From whence declining daily by degrees,
He somewhat loseth of his heat and light,
When once the Crab behind his back he sees.
But for this time it ill ordainèd was,
To chose the longest day in all the yeare,
And shortest night, when longest fitter weare:
Yet never day so long, but late would passe.
Ring ye the bels, to make it weare away,
And bonefiers make all day;
And daunce about them, and about them sing,
That all the woods may answer, and your eccho ring.

Läutet vom Turm die Glocken, Jünglinge zuhauf!
Laßt ruhen eure Arbeit diesen Tag:
Er ist geweiht; geht, schreibt es auf,
Daß man auf immer sich erinnern mag.
Heut klimmt der Sonne Lauf auf den Zenith,
'S ist *Barnabas*' Tag heut,
Von wo ab, stufenweis im Niedersteigen,
Sich ihre Hitze und das Licht allmählich neigen
Wenn erst der *Krebs* sich hintern Rücken sieht.
Traun, schlecht erkoren war die Sonnenwende,
Den längsten Tag im ganzen Jahr zu wähln,
Die kürzte Nacht, wo doch die längsten besser zähln.
Doch ist kein Tag so lang, daß er nicht doch sich rûnde;
Läutet die Glocken, daß die Stunden schwinden,
Laßt Freudenfeuer zünden,
Umtanzet sie, laßt freudenfeurig singen,
Daß alle Wälder widerhalln, eur Echo klinge!

Ah! when will this long weary day have end,
And lende me leave to come unto my love?
How slowly do the houres theyr numbers spend!
How slowly does sad Time his feathers move!
Hast thee, O fayrest Planet, to thy home,
Within the Westene fome:
Thy tyrèd steedes long since have need of rest.
Long though it be, at last I see it gloome,
And the bright evening-star with golden creast
Appeare out of the East.
Fayre childe of beauty! glorious lampe of love!
That all the host of heaven in ranks doost lead,
And guydest lovers through the nights sad dread,
How chearefully thou lookest from above.
And seemest to laugh atweene thy twinkling light,
As joying in the sight
Of these glad many, which for joy doe sing,
That all the woods them answer, and their echo ring!

Ach wann will dieser müde Tag denn enden
Und die Geliebte endlich zu mir bringen?
Wie träge will das Stundenblatt sich wenden,
Wie schleichend rührt die trübe Zeit die Schwingen!
Eil doch, du schönster Stern, den Flug ins Nest
Gen Horizont im West,
Denn deine Rosse haben Ruhe not.
Doch seh ich endlich dann im Dämmerrot
Den hellen Abendstern mit goldner Kron
Im Osten auferstehn.
Du Liebesfakel, Schönheit selbst gebar
Dich ruhmreich anzuführn die Himmels-Schar:
Du leitst die Liebenden durch nächtliche Geschicke,
Wie heiter schaust du jezt von oben drein,
Scheinst gar zu lächeln durch den Zwinkerschein,
Zu freuen dich am Blicke
Der vielen Frohen, die vor Freude singen
Daß alle Wälder widerhalln, ihr Echo klingen.

Now ceasse, ye damsels, your delights fore-past;
Enough it is that all the day was youres:
Now day is doen, and noght is nighing fast,
Now bring the Bryde into the brydall boures.
The night is come, now soon her disaray,
And in her bed her lay;
Lay her in lillies and in violets,
And silken courteins over her display,
And odourd sheetes, and Arras coverlets.
Behold how goodly my faire love does ly,
In proud humility!
Like unto Maia, when as Jove her took
In Tempe, lying on the flowry gras,
Twixt sleepe and wake, after she weary was,
With bathing in the Acidalian brooke.
Now it is night, ye damsels may be gon,
And leave my love alone,
And leave likewise your former lay to sing:
The woods no more shall answere, nor your echo ring.

Nun endet, Mädchen, des Vergnügens Pracht,
Daß euch der Tag gehörte, sei anjetzt genu',
Vorüber ist der Tag, rasch naht die Nacht:
Nun sey die Braut ins bräutliche Gemach gebracht.
Die Nacht ist da, entkleidet sie ganz sacht
Und bettet sie zur Ruh.
Wollt sie auf Lilien und auf Veilchen betten
Und seidne Schleier um sie breiten,
Duftenden Laken & gewirkte Linnen spreiten:
Seht, wie so reizend die Geliebte gut
In stolzer Demut ruht
Gleich *Maja*, da ihr *Jupiter* stellt' nach
Im Tempe-Thal, auf blumenbuntem Hag
Halb wach, halb schlafend, müde lag
Nach ihrem Bad im Akydel'schen Bach.
Die Nacht ist da. Laßt itzo gut es sein,
Und laßt mein Lieb allein,
Und endet gleicherweise euer Singen.
Nicht soll der Wald mehr widerhalln, euch Echo klingen.

Now welcome, night! thou night so long expected,
That long daies labour doest at last defray,
And all my cares, which cruell Love collected
Hast sumd in one, and cancellèd for aye:
Spread thy broad wing over my love and me,
That no man may us see;
And in thy sable mantle us enwrap,
From feare of perrill and foule horror free.
Let no false treason seeke us to entrap,
Nor any dread disquiet once annoy
The safety of our joy;
But let the night be calme, and quietsome,
Without tempestuous storms or sad afray:
Lyke as when Jove with fayre Alcmena lay,
When he begot the great Tirynthian groome:
Or lyke as when he with thy selfe did lie
And begot Majesty.
And let the mayds and yong men cease to sing;
Ne let the woods them answer nor theyr eccho ring.

Nun sey willkommen, Nacht: so lang entbehrt!
Wollst mir des langen Tages Mühen widerzahlen
Und meine Sorgen, angehäuft von Liebes-Qualen,
Ineins summirn, und annullirn den Wert.
Spreit deine weiten Fittiche ob Weib und Mann,
Daß Keins uns sehen kann.
Hüll uns in deinen zobelschwarzen Mantel ein
Auf daß wir frei von Furchten & Gefahren sein,
Daß kein Verrat uns falsche Fallen stelle
Und keine unmutsvolle Unruh drohe, wenn wir schlafen
In unserm Freuden-Hafen.
Mach, daß die Nacht sey friedevoll & stille
Ohn Ungewetter oder Trauer-Schlag,
Wie als einst *Iovis* bey *Alkmene* lag
Und zeugt' den Helden von Tiryns aus seinem Blute,
Alswenn *Zeus* bey dir selbsten ruhte
Und zeugte Majestät.
Und laß die Koren & Epheben nicht mehr singen,
Auch nicht die Wälder widerhalln, ihr Echo klingen.

Let no lamenting cryes, nor dolefull teares,
Be heard all night within, nor yet without:
Ne let false whispers, breeding hidden feares,
Breake gentle sleepe with misconceivèd dout.
Let no deluding dreames, nor dreadfull sights,
Make sudden sad affrights;
Ne let house-fyres, nor lightnings helpelesse harmes,
Ne let the Pouke, nor other evill sprights,
Ne let mischivous witches with theyr charmes,
Ne let hob Goblins, names whose sence we see not,
Fray us with things that be not:
Let not the shriech Oule nor the Storke be heard,
Nor the night Raven, that still deadly yels;
Nor damnèd ghosts, cald up with mighty spels,
Nor griesly vultures, make us once affeard:
Ne let th' unpleasant Quyre of Frogs still croking
Make us to wish theyr choking.
Let none of these theyr drery accents sing;
Ne let the woods them answer, nor theyr eccho ring.

Laß uns nicht Klageschreie oder Schmerzensthränen
Die Nacht durch Innen oder Außen hören,
Nicht angstvoll brütend Flüstern, spukhaft Wähnen
Den sanften Schlaf mit trüben Zweifeln stören,
Laß uns im Traum kein Trug-Gesichte schrecken
Und unversehens wecken.
Laß weder Feur noch hülflos Harm von Blitzen,
Laß nicht den Puck noch andre üble Wesen
Wie Circen-Hexen die auf Zauberbesen,
Kobolde, namenlose Schrate, mit Entsetzen
Das was nicht ist, aushecken.
Laß nicht der Leichenvögel Schar die Schnäbel wetzen,
Den nächtgen Raben, der so tödlich knarrt,
Verdammte Seelen derer, die da eingescharrt,
Grässliche Geier uns in Angst versetzen.
Mach, daß den Fröschen wir dem Zwange widerstehn
Die Hälse abzudrehn.
Mach, daß von diesen Keines düster singe,
Und daß der Wald nicht widerhall', kein Echo klinge.

But let stil Silence trew night-watches keepe,
That sacred Peace may in assurance rayne,
And tymely Sleep, when it is tyme to sleepe,
May poure his limbs forth on your pleasent playne;
The whiles an hundred little wingèd loves,
Like divers-fethered doves,
Shall fly and flutter round about your bed,
And in the secret darke, that none reproves,
Their prety stealthes shal worke, and snares shal spread
To filch away sweet snatches of delight,
Conceald through covert night.
Ye sonnes of Venus, play your sports at will!
For greedy pleasure, carelesse of your toyes,
Thinks more upon her paradise of joyes,
Then what ye do, albe it good or ill.
All night therefore attend your merry play,
For it will soone be day:
Now none doth hinder you, that say or sing;
Ne will the woods now answer, nor your Eccho ring.

Bestimm zur treuen Nachtwache nur *Schweigen* mild,
Laß Weihefrieden unsrer Traulichkeit nur frommen,
Daß Schlaf beizeiten, wenn die Zeit gekommen,
Die Glieder strecke auf dein schön Gefild,
Und hunderte geschwingte Amoretten
In taubenzart Gefieder
Umschwirren & umflattern unsre Betten
In heimlich Dunkel – wer wollts schmälen? –
Verspielte Listen hegen, Schlingen legen
Um süße Bissen des Entzückens sich zu stehlen
In dichte Nacht gehüllt:
Treibt, Venus-Kinder, Kurzweil wie ihr willt!
Lust ist bey eurem Spiel nicht auf der Hut –
Die gibt ja auf *ihr* Freuden-Paradeis nur acht –
Nicht euer Tun, seis böse oder gut.
Behagt euch dieses Spiel in tiefer Nacht?
Es tagt schon bald.
Euch hindert Keins – kein Sprechen oder Singen –
Kein Wald wird euch jezt widerhalln, kein Echo klingen.

Who is the same, which at my window peepes?
Or whose is that faire face that shines so bright?
Is it not Cinthia, she that never sleepes,
But walkes about high heaven al the night?
O! fayrest goddesse, do thou not envy
My love with me to spy:
For thou likewise didst love, though now unthought,
And for a fleece of wooll, which privily
The Latmian shepherd once unto thee brought,
His pleasures with thee wrought.
Therefore to us be favorable now;
And sith of wemens labours thou hast charge,
And generation goodly dost enlarge,
Encline thy will t'effect our wishfull vow
And the chast wombe informe with timely seed
That may our comfort breed:
Till which we cease our hopefull hap to sing;
Ne let the woods us answere, nor our Eccho ring.

Wer wagt's, durch meine Fenster scheu zu spähn?
Wes ist das Schimmer-Antlitz, das so licht?
Ist es nicht *Cynthia*, die immer wacht,
Durch hohe Himmel wandelt in der Nacht?
O schönste Göttin, neide mir doch nicht
Die Liebste Frau zu sehn:
Auch Du hast doch geliebt, woran du nicht gedacht,
Und für das *Goldne Fließ*, das unbewußt
Latmions Schäfer einstens dir gebracht,
Gabst du ihm deine Lust.
Darum beschenk uns jezt mit deiner Huld,
Und da der Weiber Kindbett deine Schuld
Und dir obliegt, Geschlechter zu vermehren,
Öffne die Sinne unserm Wunsch-Gelübde frei,
Den keuschen Schoß mit reicher Saat zu ehren:
Was unsre Tröstung sey.
Laß uns auf dieses hoffen, doch nicht singen –
Der Wald soll uns nicht widerhalln, kein Echo klingen.

And thou, great Juno! which with awful might
The lawes of wedlock still dost patronize;
And the religion of the faith first plight
With sacred rites hast taught to solemnize;
And eeke for comfort often callèd art
Of women in their smart;
Eternally bind thou this lovely band,
And all thy blessings unto us impart.
And thou, glad Genius! in whose gentle hand
The bridale bowre and geniall bed remaine,
Without blemish or staine;
And the sweet pleasures of theyr loves delight
With secret ayde doest succour and supply,
Till they bring forth the fruitfull progeny;
Send us the timely fruit of this same night.
And thou, fayre Hebe! and thou, Hymen free!
Grant that it may so be.
Til which we cease your further prayse to sing;
Ne any woods shall answer, nor your Eccho ring.

Du große *Juno*! die mit hehrer Macht
Der Eh' Gesetze stets noch überwacht,
Und unsers Glaubens Treueschwur verehrt
Mit heilgen Riten uns zu feiern hast gelehrt,
Und oft herbeigerufen uns zum Trost
Der Weiber List:
Verknüpfe ewig unser holdes Band,
Gieß über uns dein' reiche Seegens-Flut.
Du heitrer *Amor*! In des sanfter Hand
Das Brautgemach wie Liebeslager ruht
Ohn Makel oder Schand,
Der unsrer Freuden lieblichem Entzücken
Mit insgeheimem Beistand Hülf gebracht
Bis sie die Nachkomms-Früchte schicken:
Bring uns die zeitgen Früchte dieser Nacht.
Du, schöne *Hebe*! Und du, *Hymen* frei!
Versprecht, daß es so sey.
Bis dann wolln wir kein weiter Preislied singen,
Nicht soll der Wald uns widerhalln, kein Echo klingen.

And ye high heavens, the temple of the gods,
In which a thousand torches flaming bright
Doe burne, that to us wretched earthly clods
In dreadful darknesse lend desirèd light
And all ye powers which in the same remayne,
More then we men can fayne!
Poure out your blessing on us plentiously,
And happy influence upon us raine,
That we may raise a large posterity,
Which from the earth, which they may long possesse
With lasting happinesse,
Up to your haughty pallaces may mount;
And, for the guerdon of theyr glorious merit,
May heavenly tabernacles there inherit,
Of blessèd Saints for to increase the count.
So let us rest, sweet love, in hope of this,
And cease till then our tymely joyes to sing:
The woods no more us answer, nor our eccho ring!

EDMUND SPENSER (1552 (?) -1599)
Epithalamion

Ihr hohen Himmel, großer Götter Schoß,
Die ihr von tausend Fakeln luminirt
Mit hellem Brand, leiht auch uns armem Erdenkloß
Im grausen Dunkel Licht, das wir ersehnen.
Und all ihr Mächte, die ihr dort regiert
Mehr als wir Menschen wähnen:
Gießt euren Segen reichlich auf uns aus,
Laßt gnädiges Geschicke auf uns fallen,
Daß große Nachkommschaft entspringe unserm Haus,
Die von der Erd, auf der sie lange wallen
Mög, allen Glückes voll,
Zu euren ragenden Palästen steigen soll,
Und auf gerecht verdientem Ruhmesthron
Des Himmels Tabernakel erben mag
Aus Händen aller Heiligen zum Lohn.
So laß uns ruhn. Bis wir, mein Lieb, am letzten Tag
Dann enden unsern zeitlichen Gesang
Dem einst die Wälder widerhallten und sein Echo klang.

53 A secret murder hath been done of late—
Unkindness found to be the bloody knife;
And she that did the deed a dame of state,
Fair, gracious, wise, as any beareth life.

To quit herself, this answer did she make:
Mistrust (quoth she) hath brought him to his end,
Which makes the man so much himself mistake,
To lay the guilt unto his guiltless friend.

Lady, not so. Not feared I found my death,
For no desert thus murdered is my mind.
And yet before I yield my fainting breath,
I quit the killer, though I blame the kind.
You kill unkind; I die, and yet am true—
For at your sight my wound doth bleed anew.

SIR WALTER RALEGH (1552 (?) -1618)
A secret murder hath been done of late

Geheimer Mord ward unlängst jüngst vollstreckt:
Als blutges Messer man *Ungnädigkeit* da fand;
Die Lady, die die Tat geheckt (sie ist von Stand
Und schön & artig-weis, wie nur was irgend lebt)
Sich selbst zum Freispruch sie die Antwort gibt:

Mißtraun, sagt sie, hat ihn zu solchem Schluß geführt,
Daß sich der arme Mann so in sich selbst verirrt,
Daß er schuldloser Freundin die Schuldbürd aufgeschirrt.

Falsch, gnädge Frau! Furchtlos fiel ich anheim dem Tode,
Für kein Verdienst gemordet liegt mein Geist –
Doch eh ich aushauch meinen letzten Odem,
Sprech ich den Mörder frei, klag an die Art & Weis:
Weißt', *Ungnädigkeit* tötet. Ich sterb – und bin doch treu:
Denn auf bricht meine Wunde / : wenn sie dich sieht : / aufs neu.

54   What is our life? a play of passion.
Our mirth the music of division.
Our mothers' wombs the tiring houses be,
Where we are dressed for this short Comedy.
Heaven the judicious sharp spectator is,
That sits and marks still who doth act amiss.
Our graves, that hide us from the searching sun,
Are like drawn curtains when the play is done.

Thus march we, playing, to our latest rest;
Only we die in earnest, that's no jest.

Sir Walter Ralegh (1552 (?) - 1618)
What is our life? a play of passion

Was unser Leben ist? – : Ein Schauerspiel,
wo unsre Freuden sind nur Entreact-Musicken,
und unsrer Mütter Schöße sind die Schmink-Budiken,
wo man uns costumirt für den Comoedienflitter.
Der Himmel ist das Publicum: das sitzt mit Richterblicken
und stiert und merkt auf jeden Schnitzers Blöße.
Das Grab, das uns beschützt vorm SonnenBlitzlicht-Glitter,
gleicht / : Finis Ludi : / dem geschlossnen Vorhang.

So unser Aufzug: *spielend,* zum letzten Port der Welt.
Doch wenn die Masque fällt: Wie wird der Tod uns bitter!

My body in the walls captived
Feels not the wounds of spiteful envy;
But my thrall'd mind, of liberty deprived,
Fast fettered in her ancient memory,
Doth nought behold but sorrow's dying face.

Such prison erst was so delightful
As it desired no other dwelling place,
But time's effects and destinies despiteful
Have changed both my keeper and my fare.
Love's fire and beauty's light I then had store;
But now, close kept, as captives wonted are,
That food, that heat, that light, I find no more.

Despair bolts up my doors, and I alone
Speak to dead walls, but those hear not my moan.

SIR WALTER RALEGH (1552 (?) -1618)
My body in the walls captived

Mein Leib, gefangen zwischen Wänden,
fühlt der Ranküne Wunden nicht, die Schnitte –
doch mein versklavter Geist, des Freiheit liegt in Banden,
an ihrs Erinnerns langer FesselKette,
betrachtet einzig noch des Kummers Sterbensantlitz.

Erst war solch Kerker ja ein angenehmer Platz:
da kam kein Wunsch, an anderm Sitz zu wohnen.
Allein der Zeiten Wirken und des Schicksals Trotz
verändert' meinen Wärter und meine Kerkerkost.
Einst hatt ich Liebes Feuer noch und Schönheits Licht im Zimmer –
Doch itzt in diesem Loch (wie's halt der Brauch in solchem Knast)
find ich das Licht, die Wärme, und die Speisen nimmer.

Verzweiflung riegelt meine Türen ein, und ich, allein, verloren,
red' toten Wänden zu, die doch mein Stöhnen ja nicht hören.

Like to a hermit poor, in place obscure,
I mean to spend my days of endless doubt,
To wail such woes as time cannot recure,
Where none but Love shall ever find me out.
My food shall be of care and sorrow made;
My drink nought else but tears fall'n from mine eyes;
And for my light, in such obscured shade,
The flames shall serve which from my heart arise.
A gown of grief my body shall attire;
My staff of broken hope whereon I'll stay;
Of late repentance linked with long desire
The couch is framed whereon my limbs I'll lay.
And at my gate Despair shall linger still,
To let in Death when Love and Fortune will.

Sir Walter Ralegh (1552 (?) -1618)
Like to a hermit poor, in place obscure

Gleich einem armen Eremit, an düsterm Ort
(mich dünkt) verbring ich meine Tage endlosen Zweifels voll,
um (was auch Zeit nicht heilen kann) zu klagen solchen Tort,
wo niemand / : einzig Liebe / : mich jemals finden soll.
Gram sei und Sorge meiner Speisen Koch,
mein Trank sei'n Thränen die aus meinen Augen rinnen,
und als mein Licht in diesem Dämmerloch
solln jene Flammen dienen, die meinem Herz entbrennen.
Ein Schmerzenskleid soll meinen Leib bedecken.
Worauf ich lehn'? – : gebrochner Hoffnung Stecken.
Aus Stangen später Reue verschränkt mit lang Verlangen
gezimmert sei die Liege, auf die ich meine Glieder strecke.
Verzweiflung lungere an meines Tores Schwelle,
dem Tod die Tür zu öffnen: wenn's *Amors & Fortunens* Wille.

57   Three things there be that prosper up apace
And flourish, whilst they grow asunder far;
But on a day, they meet all in one place,
And when they meet they one another mar:
And they be these—the wood, the weed, the wag.
The wood is that which makes the gallows tree;
The weed is that which strings the hangman's bag;
The wag, my pretty knave, betokeneth thee.
Mark well, dear boy, whilst these assemble not,
Green springs the tree, hemp grows, the wag is wild;
But when they meet, it makes the timber rot,
It frets the halter, and it chokes the child.
Then bless thee, and beware, and let us pray
We part not with thee at this meeting day.

SIR WALTER RALEGH (1552 (?) -1618)
To his Son

Der Dinge drei sind's, die gedeihen schnell
und blühn, zwar erst einander weit geschieden;
Doch eines Tages – eines Orts – begegnen sie hienieden,
und kommen sie zusamm': bereiten sie einand die Höll!
Und das sind folgende: Holz; Hanf; und Hitzkopf stolz.
Von Holz gezimmert ist der Galgen bang,
Aus Hanf gedrehet ist des Henkers Strang,
Und Heißsporn hat von dir, du hübscher Bursch, Besitz ergriffen.
Merk wohl, mein guter Jung, so diese *nicht* sich treffen,
grünt Baum – blüht Hanf – ist Schalk bloß Wirbelwind;
Doch kommen sie zusamm': zermorschts das Holz geschwind,
zerfrißts den Strick, und würget ab das Kind.
GOtt sei mit dir! Und sieh dich für! Laßt uns Gebete sagen,
daß wir nicht von dir scheiden an dieses Treffens Tage.

58   Even such is tyme that takes in Trust
Our Youth, our Joyes, our all we have,
And payes us but with Earth and Dust;
Who, in the darke and silent Grave,
When we have wandered all our wayes
Shutts up the Story of our Dayes.
But from this Earth, this Grave, this Dust,
My God shall rayse me up I trust.

SIR WALTER RALEGH (1552 (?) - 1618)
Last Verse

Ja! das ist *Zeit:* die nimmt getrost
Unsere Jugend – Freuden – alle unsre Habe
Zu treuer Hand – zahlt uns nur Erd und Staub;
Die, in dem duncklen stillen Grab
Wenn wir zu End mit unserm Wanderstabe,
Das Märchen unsrer Erdentage schleußt.
Doch aus der Erd empor – dem Staub – dem Grabe
Bin ich getrost dasz GOtt mich zu sich reißt.

Here lieth, hidden in this Pitt,
The Wonder of the World for Witt.
It to small purpose did him serve;
His Witt could not his Life preserve.
Hee living, was belov'd of none,
Yet in his death all did him moane.
Heaven hath his Soule, the world his Fame,
The grave his Corps; Stukley his shame.

ANONYM (ca 1618)
Epitaph on Sir Walter Ralegh

Hier ruht/ in dieser Grub' verborgnen Bahre
Der Welt Miraculum an Witz
So ihm gedient zu wenig Nutz/
Sein Witz konnt nicht sein Leben ihm bewahren.
Er / : lebend : / ward geliebt von keinem/
Doch alle weinen da sein Todt bekannt.
Der Himel hat sein Seel/
Die Welt sein Ruhm so reich/
Das Grab die Leych/ und STUKLEY seine Schand.

In night when colours all to black are cast,
Distinction lost, or gone down with the light;
The eye a watch to inward senses plac'd,
Not seeing, yet still having power of sight,

Gives vain alarums to the inward sense,
Where fear stirr'd up with witty tyranny,
Confounds all powers, and thorough self-offence,
Doth forge and raise impossibility:

Such is in thick depriving darknesses,
Proper reflections of the error be,
And images of self-confusednesses,
Which hurt imaginations only see;

And from this nothing seen, tells news of devils,
Which but expressions be of inward evils.

FULKE GREVILLE, LORD BROOKE (1554 - 1628)
In night when colours all to black are cast

Wenn alle Farben nachts in *Schwarz* gefaßt,
Jed Unterschied versunken hinunter mit dem Licht,
Dann auf die innern Sinne das wache Auge paßt
Des Sehns zwar mächtig noch, doch sehend nicht,

Blinden Alarm der Innenwelt dann schlägt,
Wo aufgerührte Angst, des Irrwitz Zwangsherrschaft
Die Kräfte ganz verwirrt, mit Selbstzerstörung hegt
Und schafft & schmiedet die Unmöglichkeit,

Daß noch in lichtberaubter dichter Dunkelheit
Sorgfältge Einschätzung des Irrens möchte sein,
Ein Abbild von der Selbstverworrenheit,
Die nur Einbildungskraft, gestört, kann sehn,

Und kann aus Nichtsehn ein satanisch Flüstern lösen,
Was nichts als Ausdruck ist des inwendigen Bösen.

61   With how sad steps, O Moon, thou climb'st the skies!
How silently, and with how wan a face!
What, may it be that even in heavenly place
That busy archer his sharp arrows tries?
Sure, if that long-with-love-acquainted eyes
Can judge of love, thou feel'st a lover's case;
I read it in thy looks; thy languisht grace
To me that feel the like, thy state descries.
Then, even of fellowship, O Moon, tell me
Is constant love deemed there but want of wit?
Are beauties there as proud as here they be?
Do they above love to be loved, and yet
Those lovers scorn whom that love doth possess?
Do they call virtue there ungratefulness?

SIR PHILIP SIDNEY (1554 - 1586)
With how sad steps, o moon

Mit welch betrübten Schritten, Mond! klimmst du den Himmel dort.
Wie still; und mit welch blassem Angesicht.
Wie? Kann das sein, daß gar am Sternenort
der umtriebige Schütze seine scharfen Pfeile richt't?
Ja, wenn solch lang mit Lieb vertraute Augen
ob Liebe urteiln können, fühlst *du* eines Verliebten Fall:
In deinem Blick les ich's. An deines sehnsüchtigen Liebreiz' Ball
kann, der das Gleiche fühlt, ich deinen Zustand schaugen.
So sag mir, Mond! da nun verbrüdert wir:
Hält man Beständigkeit für Torheit auch bei euch?
Sind Schönheiten dort auch so stolz wie hier?
Liebt man dort um geliebt zu sein – zugleich
verachtet man die Liebenden in ihrem Leid?
Nennt man auch «Tugend» dort – Undankbarkeit?

Thou blind man's mark, thou fool's self-chosen snare,
Fond fancy's scum, and dregs of scattered thought;
Band of all evils, cradle of causeless care;
Thou web of will, whose end is never wrought:

Desire! Desire! I have too dearly bought,
With price of mangled mind, thy worthless ware;
Too long, too long, asleep thou hast me brought,
Who shouldst my mind to higher things prepare.

But yet in vain thou hast my ruin sought,
In vain thou mad'st me to vain things aspire,
In vain thou kindlest all thy smoke fire,
For Virtue hath this better lesson taught:

Within myself to seek my only hire,
Desiring nought but how to kill Desire.

Sir Philip Sidney (1554 - 1586)
Thou blind man's mark, thou fool's self-chosen snare

Du Blindenstock! Du selbsterkorne Narrenschelle!
Du Abschaum stolzen Blähns, zerstreuten Denkens Bodensatz,
Grundloser Sorge Wieg' und allen Übels Latz,
Du niemals endlich aufgerollte Willenszwille:

Ach *Sehnsucht*! Ach Begehren! Zu teuer ausgepreist
Hab um zermürbten Geist ich deinen Ramsch erstanden;
Zu lang hast du gelähmt mich mit des Schlafes Banden
Der du doch höher spannen solltest meinen Geist;

Und hast vergeblich doch versucht mein Ende,
Daß ich nach Nichtgem strebe, mich zu nöten,
Umsonsten sollst du mir dein Räucherblendwerk zünden,
Denn eine bessre Lehre gab Tugend mir zu Händen:

Ich kann die Ehre einzig nur in mir selber finden
Sehnsüchtiglich begehrend, die Sehnsucht abzutöten.

63   Come Sleep, O Sleep! the certain knot of peace,
The baiting-place of wit, the balm of woe,
The poor man's wealth, the prisoner's release,
The indifferent judge between the high and low;
With shield of proof shield me from out the prease
Of those fierce darts Despair at me doth throw:
Oh, make in me those civil wars to cease!
I will good tribute pay if thou do so.
Take thou of me smooth pillows, sweetest bed,
A chamber deaf to noise and blind of light,
A rosy garland and a weary head:
And if these things, as being thine by right,
Move not thy heavy grace, thou shalt in me
Livelier than elsewhere Stella's image see.

Sir Philip Sidney (1554 - 1586)
Come, Sleep; O Sleep!

Komm Schlaf/ o Schlaf! du fest vertäuter Frieden/
des Witzes Imbiß-Stand/ du Balsam aller Pein/
des Armen Reichtum/ des Gekerkerten Befrein/
Indifferenter Richter zwischen hoch und nieden:/
schirm' mich mit undurchdringlich Schilde vorm Verschwenden/
der grausen Pfeile/ die Verzweiflung nach mir schmeißt!/
O laß den innren Bürgerkrieg mir enden!/
Erfüllung meiner Bitte dir guten Lohn verheißt:/
Nimm hin von mir glatt Linnen/ süßest Bettestatt/
die Kammer: lärmgedämpft & lichtesmatt/
ein Rosen-Angebind/ ein Haupt das sehnt zur Ruh/
und sollte diß/ das ja mit vollem Rechte dein/
dir nicht die ernste Gnad bewegen/ dann sollstu
lebendiger denn sonstwo Stellas Imago in mir sehn!/

64 When as the rye reach to the chin,
  And chopcherry, chopcherry ripe within,
  Strawberries swimming in the cream,
  And school-boys playing in the stream;
  Then O, then O, then O my true love said,
  Till that time come again,
  She could not live a maid.

GEORGE PEELE (1558 (?) -1597)
A Summer Song

Wenn erst der Roggen wieder reicht ans Kinn,
Und Schnittkirschen, Schnittkirschen reifen darin,
Schulbuben schwimmen in dem Strom,
Erdbeeren treiben in der Crem'....
Ach dann, ach dann, Feinsliebchen sprach,
Ach bis *die* Zeit erst wiederkäm,
So lang wollt sie nicht Mägdlein bleiben.

65 What meant the poets in invective verse
   To sing Medea's shame, and Scylla's pride,
   Calypso's charms by which so many died?
   Only for this their vices they rehearse:
   That curious wits which in the world converse,
   May shun the dangers and enticing shows
   Of such false sirens, those home-breeding foes,
   That from their eyes their venom do disperse.
   So soon kills not the basilisk with sight;
   The viper's tooth is not so venomous;
   The adder's tongue not half so dangerous,
   As they that bear the shadow of delight,
   Who chain blind youths in trammels of their hair,
   Till waste brings woe, and sorrow hastes despair.

   ROBERT GREENE (1560 - 1592)
   What meant the poets in invective verse

Was wollten Dichter mit des Schmälens Zeilenlauf
Medeas Schande, Scyllas Stolz besingen,
Kalypsos Charme, durch den so viele untergingen?
Wohl darumb zähln sie deren Bosheit auf:
daß weltgewandter Umgang, mit Neugier und gewitzt,
könnt die Gefahren und VerführungsShows vermeiden
falscher Sirenen gleich der wolbekannten Feinden
die da ihr Gift aus ihrem Auge sprüzt.
So strack töt't nicht des Basilisken Blicken,
der Viper Zahn ist ja so tückisch nicht,
der Otter Zung nicht halb so voll Gefahr
als die, die prätendirn ihr Schein-Entzücken
und blinde Jugend fang'n im Netze ihrer Haar,
bis Unheil Weh bringt & Verzweiflung sich in Leiden flicht.

66

My lady's presence makes the roses red,
Because to see her lips they blush for shame:
The lily's leaves, for envy, pale became,
And her white hands in them this envy bred.
The marigold abroad her leaves doth spread,
Because the sun's and her power is the same;
The violet of purple colour came,
Dyed with the blood she made my heart to shed.
In brief, all flowers from her their virtue take:
From her sweet breath their sweet smells do proceed,
The living heat which her eye-beams do make
Warmeth the ground, and quickeneth the seed.
The rain wherewith she watereth these flowers
Falls from mine eyes, which she dissolves in showers.

HENRY CONSTABLE (1562 - 1613)
Of his mistress, upon occasion of her walking in a garden

Rot wird die Ros bey meiner Dame Schreiten:
denn *ihre* Lippen sehn, läßt sie vor Scham erröthen.
Bleich sind vor Eifersucht der Lilgen Blüten:
da *ihre* weißen Hände Neid bereiten.
Aus ihrem Blattgehäus die Dotterblum will sprießen,
denn *ihre* Stärk und die der Sonn sind gleich.
Das Veilgen kömmt gefärbt in Purpur: reich
vom Herzblut das um *sie* ich mußt vergießen.
Ja, alle Blumen sich aus *ihr* die Zier beziehen:
Ihr Duft steigt auf aus *ihrem* süßen Odem;
die Lebenswärm' so *ihre* AugStern sprühen,
erquickt die Saat, erwärmt den Grund, den Boden.
Der Regen, mit dem *sie* diese Blumen geußt,
fließt aus den Augen mir die *sie* in Schauer löst.

67 Give pardon blessèd soul, to my bold cries,
   If they, importune, interrupt thy song,
   Which now with joyful notes thou sing'st among
   The angel-quiristers of th' heavenly skies.
   Give pardon eke, sweet soul, to my slow eyes,
   That since I saw thee now it is so long,
   And yet the tears that unto thee belong
   To thee as yet they did not sacrifice.
   I did not know that thou wert dead before;
   I did not feel the grief I did sustain;
   The greater stroke astonisheth the more;
   Astonishment takes from us sense of pain;
   I stood amazed when others' tears begun,
   And now begin to weep when they have done.

HENRY CONSTABLE (1562 -1613)
On the death of Sir Philip Sidney

Verzeih, gepriesne Seel, der Zähren frechen Wust,
wenn sie unzeitig den Gesang dir stören
den du mit Freudentönen nun in Engel-Chören
der himmlischen Gewölbe intonieren tust.
Wollst meinem trägen Auge, hohe Seele, auch nicht grollen,
weil, lange her schon, da es dich erblickt,
es doch die Thrän-Flut, die vor dich sich schickt,
dir bis anjetzt noch nicht konnt opffern wollen.
Daß du nun tot: begreifen konnt ich's nit;
ich spürte nicht den Schmerz, den ich erlitt;
so großer Schlag macht staunen ja vielmehr:
Erstaunen raubt das Schmerzgefühl, macht leer.
Ich stand im Stupor, da die andern weinten; stand so lang
bis, als ihr' Thrän-Flut leer, jäh, fassungslos, die meine sprang.

68   Care-charmer Sleep, son of the sable Night,
Brother to Death, in silent darkness born,
Relieve my languish, and restore the light;
With dark forgetting of my care return,
And let the day be time enough to mourn
The shipwreck of my ill-adventured youth:
Let waking eyes suffice to wail their scorn,
Without the torment of the night's untruth.
Cease, dreams, the images of day-desires,
To model forth the passions of the morrow;
Never let rising Sun approve you liars,
To add more grief to aggravate my sorrow:
Still let me sleep, embracing clouds in vain,
And never wake to feel the day's disdain.

SAMUEL DANYEL (1563 - 1619)
Care-charmer sleepe

SorgenBesänft'ger SCHLAF! Sohn zobelpelzger Nacht!
Aus Schweigens Düsternis ensprung'n, des Todes Gegenstück:
Leichtre mein Sehnen! Licht sei neu entfacht!
Mit schwarz Vergessen meiner Sorgen kehr zurück!
Laß nur dem Tag getrost den Platz für Kummer
ob meines Kenterwracks der Jugendzeit –
dem wachen Auge sei's genug: Verachtens Jammer,
ohne die Folter nächtger Traumarbeit.
Laßt, Träum', das Schilderwerk von unsrer Tage Sehnen!
Laßt, die Passion des morgen fortzumodelliern!
Laßt nie euch von der Sonne ‹Lügner› höhnen:
mit noch mehr Schmerz mein Leid noch zu beschwern.
Husch! Laßt mich schlafen, wolk-umarmt, mit Wolken spielen –
laßt nie erwachen mich, des Tages Schmach zu fühlen.

How many paltry, foolish, painted things,
That now in coaches trouble every street,
Shall be forgotten, whom no poet sings,
Ere they be well wrapped in their winding-sheet?
Where I to thee eternity shall give,
When nothing else remaineth of these days,
And Queens hereafter shall be glad to live
Upon the alms of thy superfluous praise.
Virgins and matrons, reading these my rhymes,
Shall be so much delighted with thy story,
That they shall grieve they lived not in these times,
To have seen thee, their sex's only glory.
So shalt thou fly above the vulgar throng,
Still to survive in my immortal song.

MICHAEL DRAYTON (1563 - 1631)
How many paltry, foolish, painted things

Wie viele nichtswürdige, lachhaft angetünchte Viecher,
was jetzt in Droschken jede Straße stört,
sind schon vergessen (vom Dichter ungehört),
noch eh sie hübsch verpackt in ihre Leichentücher?
Hingegen *Dir* will Ewigkeit ich geben,
dieweil nichts bleibet sonst von dieser Zeit.
Hernach solln Königinnen froh sein, so zu leben:
von den Almosen Deiner HochGroßartigkeit.
Virginen und Matronen, die diese Zeilen lesen,
solln so entzückt sein über Dein Geschehn,
daß sie beklagen solln, in diesen Tagen nicht gewesen
zu sein, und ihrs Geschlechtes einzge Zierde nicht gesehn.
So sollst Dich weit ob die vulgäre Schar erheben:
in meinem unsterblichen Liede fortzuleben.

Look how the pale queen of the silent night
Doth cause the Ocean to attend upon her,
And he, as long as she is in his sight,
With his full tide is ready her to honour;
But when the silver waggon of the Moon
Is mounted up so high he cannot follow,
The sea calls home his crystal waves to moan,
And with low ebb doth manifest his sorrow.
So you, that are the sovereign of my heart,
Have all my joys attending on your will,
My joys low-ebbing when you do depart—
When you return, their tide my heart doth fill:
So as you come, and as you do depart,
Joys ebb and flow within my tender heart.

CHARLES BEST (? - ?)
To the moon

Sieh, wie die blasse Königin der stillen Nacht
die See in Aufwartung sich lässt verzehren,
daß sie, so lange ihr der Anblick wacht,
sich anschickt, sie mit *HochFlut* zu verehren.
Doch wenn so hoch des Mondes Silberwagen
am Himmel steht, daß sie nicht folgen kann,
ruft heim die See ihre crystallnen Wogen:
dann zeigt die *Ebbe* seufzend ihre Schwermut an.
So heißt du mich, o Herzens Herrscherin apart,
mit Freuden aufzuwarten deinem Willen:
In meiner Freud ist Ebbe, wenn dich davonnimmt deine Fahrt –
doch deine Heimkehr läßt mein Herz mit Flut sich füllen.
So: wie du ankömmst – wie dich fortträgt deine Fahrt,
spieln *Ebb & Fluth* mit meinem Herzen zart.

71

Tired with all these, for restful death I cry,—
As, to behold Desert a beggar born,
And needy Nothing trimm'd in jollity,
And purest Faith unhappily forsworn,
And gilded Honour shamefully misplaced,
And maiden Virtue rudely strumpeted,
And right Perfection wrongfully disgraced,
And Strength by limping Sway disabled,
And Art made tongue-tied by Authority,
And Folly, doctor-like, controlling Skill,
And simple Truth miscall'd Simplicity,
And captive Good attending captain Ill:

Tired with all these, from these would I be gone,
Save that, to die, I leave my love alone.

WILLIAM SHAKESPEARE (1564 - 1616)
Tired with all these, for restful death I cry

Ich bin das all's so leid, nach Todesruh ich schrei –
Wenn ich Verdienst als Bettler seh geboren,
Und läppisch Nichtigkeiten im Kleid der Drolerei,
Und reinste Lauterkeit meineidig sich verschworen,
Der Ehre güldne Ketten beschämend mißplacirt,
Der Mädchen Zierde rüd prostituiert,
Und rechte Perfektion durch Schlamperei entehrt,
Und Kraft durch schlaffes Schwanken schwer versehrt,
Und Kunst kriegt einen Maulkorb vorgesetzt,
Talent geprüft von Dummheit unterm Doktorhut,
Und schlichte Wahrheit wird als Simpelei verpetzt,
Und Schächer *Böse* hält in Schach das mattgesetzte *Gut*:

Die Welt verließ ich gern, so müd in meinem Hassen –
Würd meine Liebste nicht mein Tod alleine lassen.

Spring:
When daisies pied and violets blue,
And lady-smocks all silver-white,
And cuckoo-buds of yellow hue
Do paint the meadows with delight,
The cuckoo then, on every tree,
Mocks married men; for thus sings he,
  Cuckoo!
Cuckoo, cuckoo!—O word of fear,
Unpleasing to a married ear!

When shepherds pipe on oaten straws,
And merry larks are ploughmen's clocks,
When turtles tread, and rooks, and daws,
And maidens bleach their summer smocks
The cuckoo then, on every tree,
Mocks married men; for thus sings he,
  Cuckoo!
Cuckoo, cuckoo!—O word of fear,
Unpleasing to a married ear!

Winter:
When icicles hang by the wall,
And Dick the shepherd blows his nail.
And Tom bears logs into the hall,
And milk comes frozen home in pail,
When blood is nipp'd and ways be foul,
Then nightly sings the staring owl,
  To-whit!
To-who!—a merry note,
While greasy Joan doth keel the pot.

Frühling:
Wenn Maßliebchen gescheckt mit Veilchen schmust,
und Damenblusen *(Kresse)* weiß und silber
mit Kuckucksblumen *(Schaumkraut)* geel um gelber
die Wiesen sprenkeln voller Lust:
Auf jedem Baum der Kuckuck dann
singt *Kuckuck!* Spott dem Ehemann:
   Kucku!
Kucku! Kucku! – singt Wehe zu!
Das Ehe-Ohr ist *not amused.*

Wenn Schäfer rohrblattblasen nun aus voller Brust,
die Lerchen früh aufs Feld den Pflüger holen,
wenn Tauben vögeln, Krähen *(Pfaffen)*, Dohlen,
und Mädgen bleichen ihre Linnen, fein beblust:
Der Gauch auf jedem Baume dann
singt Spott *Kuckuck!* dem Ehemann:
   Kucku!
Kucku! Kucku! – singt Unruh zu!
Das Ehe-Ohr ist *not amused.*

Winter:
Wenn vom Gesimse Eis in Zapfen starrt,
und Schäfer Dick sich eins ins Fäustchen fiept,
die Milch friert in der Kanne steif und hart,
und Tom das Langholz in die Halle schiebt,
und's Blut erstarrt und Weg & Steg verrotten:
Dann heult die Nacht-Eul runden Auges *Huh!*
   Tuhuh!
Tuwitt! Tuhuh! – singt lustig zu!
Die Schmuddel-Hanne rührt im Potte.

When all aloud the wind doth blow,
And coughing drowns the parson's saw,
And birds sit brooding in the snow,
And Marian's nose looks red and raw,
When roasted crabs hiss in the bowl,
Then nightly sings the staring owl,
   To-whit!
To-who!—a merry note,
While greasy Joan doth keel the pot.

WILLIAM SHAKESPEARE (1564 - 1616)
from «Love's Labour's Lost»

Wenn weit herum die Windsbraut jagend keift,
des Pastors Suada *(Bürzel)* hustend stockt,
das Vögelvolk im Schnee sich plusternd hockt,
und Mariandels Nase rot bereift,
im Kessel zischend Krebsenfleisch gesotten:
Dann kwarzt der Nachtkauz runden Auges *Huh!*
 Tuhuh!
Tuwitt Tuhuh! – singt lustig zu!
Die Schmuddel-Hanne rührt im Potte.

*The author loving these homely meats specially, viz.:
cream, pancakes, buttered pippin pies (laugh, good people)
and tobacco; writ to that worthy and virtuous gentlewoman,
whom he calleth mistress, as followeth*

If there were, oh! an Hellespont of cream
Between us, milk-white mistress, I would swim
To you, to show to both my love's extreme,
Leander-like,—yea! dive from brim to brim.
But met I with a buttered pippin-pie
Floating upon 't, that would I make my boat
To waft me to you without jeopardy,
Though sea-sick I might be while it did float.
Yet if a storm should rise, by night or day,
Of sugar-snows and hail of caraways,
Then, if I found a pancake in my way,
It like a plank should bring me to your kays;
Which having found, if they tobacco kept,
The smoke should dry me well before I slept.

JOHN DAVIES, OF HEREFORD (1565 (?) - 1618)
The author loving these homely meats

Des Authoris heiß Verlangen/ nach ienen hausbacken göttlich Speiß/ als da sind zumal/ Sahne Pfannkuch gebuttert Apfelpasteten/ (lacht nur, ihr Guten)/ und Taback/ zugeeignet der edlen und tugendreichen Dame/ die er Mistress nennet/ wie folgt

Oh wenn uns trennt' ein Hellespont von Crem,
milchweißes Weib!, ich taucht im Schwimmgewand
Euch beid zu zeigen meiner Lieb' Extrem,
gleich dem Leander, ja, von Rand zu Rand.
Doch träfs, daß unterwegs 'ne ButterapfelBemme
ich fänd, ich macht's zu meinem Boot
und flög zu Euch ganz ohn Gefahr und Not,
wiewohl ich seekrank möchte werden, da es schwämme.
Doch falls ein Sturm sich höb, bei Nacht oder bei Tage,
aus Zuckerschnee & KümmelkarbenHagel,
dann, fänd 'nen Pfannkuch ich auf meinem Wege,
solls gleich der Plank' mich tragen an Eure Uferstege
die, käm ich an, falls sie auch Toback hätten,
könnt ich, vom Rauch getrocknet, getrost zur Ruh mich betten.

74 The azured vault, the crystal circles bright,
The gleaming fiery torches powdered there,
The changing round, the shining beamy light,
The sad and bearded fires, the monsters fair,
The prodigies appearing in the air,
The rearding thunder, and the blustering winds,
The fowls in hue, in shape and nature rare,
The pretty notes that winged musicians finds,
In earth the savoury flowers, the metalled minds,
The wholesome herbs, the haughty pleasant trees,
The silver streams, the beasts of sundry kinds,
The bounded roars and fishes of the seas;

All these for teaching man the Lord did frame,
To do His will whose glory shines in them.

King James I. (1566 - 1625)
The azured vault, the crystal circles bright

Die Kupel aus Azur/ die Cirkel von Crystallen/
Der Fakel asch- & funkenfeurig Glühn/
Der Cyclen Wechselrund/ deß Scheinens lichte Stralen/
Die gram-gesträhnten Flam̃en/ die Ohngehewer schön/
Der Lufft Erscheynungen & Wunderzeichen/
Des Donners Raasen & der Winde Brüllen/
Die Vögel: in Farbe/ Form/ Natur ohngleichen/
Der Fittichmusicanten Noten-trillen/
Die Würzig Blum auff Erden/ und der Metalle Schacht/
Die heilsam Kräuter & die artig-stolzen Bäume/
Die Silberströme/ die Thiere mannigfacht/
Die Seefisch & der brüllnden Brandung Schäumen/

Dasz IHm der Mensch zu Willen/ tat GOtt zur Lehr ersinnen
All dies worauß SEyn Ruhm erglänzt als Widerschein von innen.

75   He first deceased; she for a little tried
      To live without him, liked it not, and died.

SIR HENRY WOTTON (1568 (?) - 1639)
Upon the Death of Sir Albert Morton's Wife

ER ging zuerst voran. SIE ohne ihren Mann
Versucht zu leben, fands nich doll, starb dann.

Blasted with sighs, and surrounded with teares,
    Hither I come to seeke the spring,
    And at mine eyes, and at mine eares,
Receive such balmes, as else cure every thing;
    But O, selfe traytor, I do bring
The spider love, which transubstantiates all,
    And can convert Manna to gall,
And that this place may thoroughly be thought
    True Paradise, I have the serpent brought.

'Twere wholsomer for mee, that winter did
    Benight the glory of this place,
    And that a grave frost did forbid
These trees to laugh, and mocke mee to my face;
    But that I may not this disgrace
Indure, nor yet leave loving, Love let mee
    Some senslesse peece of this place bee;
Make me a mandrake, so I may groane here,
    Or a stone fountaine weeping out my yeare.

Hither with christall vyals, lovers come,
    And take my teares, which are loves wine,
    And try your mistresse Teares at home,
For all are false, that tast not just like mine;
    Alas, hearts do not in eyes shine,
Nor can you more judge womans thoughts by teares,
    Than by her shadow, what she weares.
O perverse sexe, where none is true but shee,
    Who's therefore true, because her truth kills mee.

JOHN DONNE (1572 - 1635)
Twicknam Gardens

Vom Seufzen verdorret, von Thränen versengt,
  komm ich hierher – wo Frühling mir klingt –
  und meinem Auge träuft, und meinem Ohre singt
solch Balsam, der ein jedes Ding
  sonst heilt. Doch ach, ich Selbstverräter bring
die Spinne *Lieb'*, die alles transsubstantiiert,
  die Manna ja in Galle überführt;
Und daß der Ort vollständig sei gedacht
  ein wahres Paradies: hab ich die Schlange bracht.

'S wär heilsamer für mich, der Winter macht'
  die Pracht des Orts mit Nächtigkeit zunicht;
  und daß ein barscher Frost versagt'
dem Baum zu spotten in mein Angesicht:
  Damit ich diese Ungnad nicht
ertrag (auch nicht von Liebe laß): laß, Liebe, mich
  dem Ort ein sinnlos Stücke sein,
eine Mandragora, die stöhnt; oder die Stein-
  Fontän, als die heraus mein Jahr ich wein'.

Hierher: Kristall-Phiolen; ihr, die liebt:
  Nehmt meine Thränen, die der Liebe Wein!
  Dann probt die Zähren, die euch die Geliebte gibt:
'S ist alles falsch, was nicht so schmeckt wie meine!
  Ach, Herzen nicht aus Augen scheinen!
An Zähren läßt sich grad so wenig schauen, was die Frau bewegt,
  wie an ihrm Schatten, was sie trägt.
Pervers Geschlecht: wo, außer ihr, kein wahres Wort! –
  sie: wahr insofern, als ihr Wahrsein mich ermordt.

77   I fixe mine eye on thine, and there
Pitty my picture burning in thine eye,
My picture drown'd in a transparent teare,
When I looke lower I espie;
Hadst thou the wicked skill
By pictures made and mard, to kill,
How many wayes mightst thou performe thy will?

But now I have drunke thy sweet salt teares,
And though thou poure more I'll depart;
My picture vanish'd, vanish feares,
That I can be endamag'd by that art;
Though thou retaine of mee
One picture more, yet that will bee,
Being in thine owne heart, from all malice free.

JOHN DONNE (1572-1635)
Witchcraft by a Picture

Nah fokussiert mein Aug auf deines: da
barmt mich mein Abbild, das in deinem Auge loht;
Dies Bild ertränkt in transparenter Thräne
erspäh ich, wenn ich tiefer schau'.
Hättst du den Bösen Blick,
mit Abbildung (gebildert wie entstellt) zu töten – :
Auf welche mannigfache Weise zeigte sich dein Hexentrick?

Doch hab ich nun die süßen-salzgen Thränen abgetrunken,
und ob du mehr vergießest gleich, werd ich jezt scheiden.
Mit den geschwundnen Bildern schwindet auch mein Bangen
daß mir Gefahr könnt werden von der Zauberkunst.
Magst du von mir behalten
auch noch ein Bild, es wird ja doch
in deinem eignen Herzen sein: frei von arglistig-dunkelen Gewalten.

78   Death, be not proud, though some have called thee
Mighty and dreadful, for thou art not so;
For those whom thou think'st thou dost overthrow
Die not, poor Death; nor yet canst thou kill me.
From rest and sleep, which but thy pictures be,
Much pleasure: then from thee much more must flow;
And soonest our best men with thee do go—
Rest of their bones and souls' delivery!
Thou'rt slave to fate, chance, kings and desperate men,
And dost with poison, war, and sickness dwell;
And poppy or charms can make us sleep as well,
And better than thy stroke. Why swell'st thou then?
One short sleep past, we wake eternally,
And death shall be no more: Death, thou shalt die.

JOHN DONNE (1572 - 1635)
Death be not proud

Tod: brüst' dich nicht! Auch wenn dich manche nennen
mächtig & grauenvoll. Denn dies bist du mit nichten;
denn die du glaubst mit Macht zu überrennen,
stehn wieder auf. Fy, Tod! auch mich kannst du nicht richten.
Aus Ruhe und aus Schlaf, die nur dein Abbild sind,
weit mehr Vergnügen als aus dir entsprießt.
Und unsre besten Männer: gehn mit dir allerfrühst,
ruhn ihre Knochen auß – frei sich die Seel entbindt!
Du Sklav von Räubern, Königen, Schicksal gleichwie Zufall,
du tust bei Gift & Krieg & Kranckheit wohnen;
wir schlummern doch auch gut mit Schlaftrünk und mit Mohnen
besser denn durch dein' Hieb. Was dann dein Brüsten soll?
Wenn kleiner Schlaf ist üm: so wachen wir allzeit!
Tod, heißts dann, sey nicht mehr!: zum Sterben dich bereit'!

When by thy scorn, O murd'ress, I am dead,
And that thou thinkst thee free
From all solicitation from me,
Then shall my ghost come to thy bed,
And thee, feign'd vestal, in worse arms shall see;
Then thy sick taper will begin to wink,
And he, whose thou art then, being tir'd before,
Will, if thou stir, or pinch to wake him, think
Thou call'st for more,
And in false sleep will from thee shrink;
And then, poor aspen wretch, neglected thou
Bath'd in a cold quicksilver sweat wilt lie,
A verier ghost than I:
What I will say, I will not tell thee now,
Lest that preserve thee; and since my love is spent,
I had rather thou shouldst painfully repent,
Than by my threat'nings rest still innocent.

JOHN DONNE (1572 - 1635)
The Apparition

O Mörderin: bin ich erst tot durch dein Verachten,
und du bedünkst dich frei
von meinem eklen Schmachten –
: Dann tret mein Geist dir an das Bett, sacht nahebei,
und seh' die ScheinVestalin dort in schlimmern Armen –
: Dann blakt dein fahles Wachslicht gleich als wollt es enden –
und er, dem du gehörst, müd zum Erbarmen,
denkt dann, wenn du dich rührst, ihn zu erwecken zwackst, es sey
    weil du ‹noch mal› verlangst,
und wird in vorgetäuschtem Schlaf sich von dir wenden.
Und dann, arm Espenweib, wirst du, vor Angst,
vernachlässigt, in kalt QuecksilberSchweiß gebadet liegen
    : weit mehr Gespenst denn ich –
Was ich dann flüstere? – Das sei jetzt noch verschwiegen,
sonst wärst du ja gefeit. Da meine Huld zerflossen nun,
säh's lieber ich, du würdest peinvoll Buße thun
als auch noch unschuldig mit meiner Drohgebärd' zu ruhn.

80   When my grave is broke up againe
       Some second ghest to entertaine,
       (For graves have learn'd that woman-head
       To be to more than one a Bed)
       And he that digs it, spies
       A bracelet of bright haire about the bone,
       Will he not let'us alone,
       And thinke that there a loving couple lies,
       Who thought that this device might be some way
       To make their soules, at the last busie day,
       Meet at this grave, and make a little stay?

       If this fall in a time, or land,
       Where mis-devotion doth command
       Then, he that digges us up, will bring
       Us, to the Bishop, and the King,
       To make us Reliques; then
       Thou shalt be a Mary Magdalen, and I
       A something else thereby;
       All women shall adore us, and some men;
       And since at such time, miracles are sought,
       I would have that age by this paper taught
       What miracles wee harmlesse lovers wrought.

Wenn mein Grab neu aufgebrochen
Ein zweiter Gast kommt neingekrochen
(Denn Gräber lernten wohl von Frauen fein,
Für mehr als Einen nur ein Bett zu sein),
Und der es gräbt (er kanns nicht fassen)
Sieht einen Reif aus hellem Haar rund um das Totenbein:
Wird er uns nicht alleine lassen
Und glauben, daß ein liebend Paar hier liegt
Das dacht, ein solch Emblem wär wohl ein Weg,
Daß an dem letzten wirren Tag sich seine Seelen
An diesem Grab zu einer Schäferstund beiseite stehlen?

Wenn dies in eine Zeit fällt, in ein Land
Wo falscher Glaube führt des Szepters Hand,
Dann wird, wer uns hier ausgegraben,
Zum Bischof & zum König tragen,
Aus uns Reliquien zu machen; dann
Sollst eine zweite Magdalena sein, und ich
ein Irgendwas daneben;
Anbeten solln uns alle Frauen, manch ein Mann;
Und da in solchen Zeiten auf Wunder man erpicht,
Will ich mit meinen Zeilen die Zeiten unterrichten,
Was durch uns harmlos Liebende für Wunder doch geschicht.

First, we lov'd well and faithfully,
Yet knew not what wee lov'd, nor why,
Difference of sex no more wee knew,
Than our Guardian Angells doe;
Comming and going, wee
Perchance might kisse, but not between those meales;
Our hands ne'r toucht the seales,
Which nature, injur'd by late law, sets free:
These miracles wee did; but now alas,
All measure, and all language, I should passe,
Should I tell what a miracle shee was.

JOHN DONNE (1572 - 1635)
The Relic

Erst liebten wir uns treu und echt,
Doch wußten nicht, warum und was;
Und kannte Keines sein Geschlecht,
Nicht mehr als unsre HüteEngel;
Im Kommen-Gehen mochten wir
Wohl küssen uns, doch zwischen solchen Mahlen nicht;
Nie rührten unsre Hände ans Sigill, das freigesetzt
Natur, vom späteren Gesetz verletzt:
Solch Wunder taten wir; doch ach! anjetzt
Müßt übersteigen ich jed Maß, all Sprach und Lesen,
Wollt ich beschreiben welch ein Wunder S$_\text{IE}$ gewesen.

81 Before I sigh my last gaspe, let me breath,
    Great love, some Legacies; Here I bequeath
    Mine eyes to *Argus*, if mine eyes can see,
    If they be blinde, then Love, I give them thee;
    My tongue to Fame; to'Embassadours mine eares;
    To women or the sea, my teares.
    Thou, Love, hast taught mee heretofore
    By making mee serve her who'had twenty more,
    That I should give to none, but such, as had too much before.

    My constancie I to the planets give;
    My truth to them, who at the Court doe live;
    Mine ingenuity and opennesse,
    To Jesuites; to Buffones my pensivenesse;
    My silence to'any, who abroad hath beene;
    My mony to a Capuchin.
    Thou Love taught'st me, by appointing mee
    To love there, where no love receiv'd can be,
    Onely to give to such as have an incapacitie.

    My faith I give to Roman Catholiques;
    All my goods works unto the Schismaticks
    Of Amsterdam: my best civility
    And Courtship, to an Universitie;
    My modesty I give to souldiers bare;
    My patience let gamesters share.
    Thou Love taughtst mee, by making mee
    Love her that holds my love disparity,
    Onely to give to those that count my gifts indignity.

Bevor ein letztesmal ich Atem hol, laß mich dir, Große Lieb,
ausflüstern einige Vermächtnisse. Und so vererbe
ich *Argus* meine Augen (falls sie nicht blind) –
doch sind sie blind, dann, Liebe, sei'n sie dein.
Und *Fama* meine Zunge, Ambassadoren meine Ohren,
und meine Thrän dem Meere; oder Frau'n.
Du, Liebe, hast mich ja gelehrt,
der ich gehuldigt einer, die schon zwanzig mehr gehabt,
nur dem zu geben – der *vor*dem schon zuviel besaß.

Meine Beständigkeit vermach ich den Planeten,
meine Wahrhaftigkeit dem, der bei Hofe weilt;
Die Offenheit, und meines Scharfsinns Kraft
den Jesuiten. Buffonen die Nachdenklichkeit.
Mein Schweigen jedem, der im Ausland war,
und meine Baarschaft einem Kapuziner.
Du, Liebe, hast mich ja gelehrt,
der ich da liebt', wo Liebe nicht erwidert ward,
nur dem zu geben – der des Vermögens schwer entbehrt.

Und meinen Glauben gebe ich den Katholiken;
All meine guten Werke den Schismatikern
von Amsterdam. Und meine beste *Educazion*
und Höflichkeit den Universitäten.
Meine Bescheidenheit geb ich den Söldnern hin;
und mein Gedulden sollen sich die Spieler teilen.
Du, Liebe, hast mich ja gelehrt,
der ich die lieb', die meine Liebe von sich weist,
nur dem zu geben – den meine Gaben *indigniren*.

I give my reputation to those
Which were my friends; Mine industrie to foes;
To Schoolemen I bequeath my doubtfulnesse;
My sicknesse to Physitians, or excesse;
To Nature, all that I in Ryme have writ;
And to my company my wit.
Thou Love, by making mee adore
Her, who begot this love in mee before,
Taughtst me to make, as though I gave, when I did but restore.

To him for whom the passing bell next tolls,
I give my physick bookes; my writen rowles
Of Morall counsels, I to Bedlam give;
My brazen medals, unto them which live
In want of bread; To them which passe among
All forrainers, mine English tongue.
Thou, Love, by making mee love one
Who thinkes her friendship a fit portion
For yonger lovers, dost my gifts thus disproportion.

Therefore I'll give no more; But I'll undoe
The world by dying; because love dies too.
Then all your beauties will be no more worth
Than gold in Mines, where none doth draw it forth;
And all your graces no more use shall have
Than a Sun dyall in a grave.
Thou Love taughtst mee, by making mee
Love her, who doth neglect both mee and thee,
To'invent, and practise this one way, to'annihilate all three.

JOHN DONNE (1572 - 1635)
The Will

Den Guten Ruf vermach ich denen,
die meine Freunde einst; den Fleiß: den Feinden.
Schulmeistern hinterlaß ich meinen Zweifelsinn.
Die Krankheit meinen Ärzten, nein, besser noch: dem Rausch.
Und der Natur alls, was in Verse ich gefaßt;
und meiner Tafelrunde meinen Witz.
Du, Liebe, hast mich ja gelehrt,
der ich die anbete, die in mir Lieb' entfacht,
zu tun, als *gäb* ich – der ich doch *zurück* nur geb.

Ihm, dem die Sterbeglocke nächstens läutet,
geb meine medizin'schen Bücher ich; und meine Schriften
moralischer Erbauung geb ich dem Narrenhaus;
vermach die Messing-Orden denen, die
des Brotes mangeln – denen, die da wandeln
nur unter Fremden, meine englisch Zung'.
Du, Liebe, hast mich ja gelehrt,
der *jüngeren* Galanen ihre Freundschaft ich empfehl,
daß meine Gaben *disproportioniret* sei'n.

Deshalb vermach ich weiter nichts. Sondern die Welt
mach ich – da Liebe stirbt – durch Sterben ungeschehn.
Dann wird all eure Schönheit nicht mehr wert sein
als Gold in Minen, wo nicht einer gräbt.
Und eure Anmut soll genau so nützen
wie eine Sonnenuhr im Grab.
Du, Liebe, hast mich ja gelehrt, der ich
die liebt', die dich und mich verschmäht, in Plan
und Ausführung also *uns alle drei zu nihiliren*.

Where dost thou careless lie,
Buried in ease and sloth?
Knowledge that sleeps, doth die;
And this security,
It is the common moth,
That eats on wits, and arts, and . . . destroys them both.

Are all th' *Aonian* springs
Dri'd up? Lies *Thespia* waste?
Doth *Clarius*' harp want strings,
That not a nymph now sings?
Or droop they as disgrac'd,
To see their seats and bowers by chatt'ring pies defac'd?

If hence thy silence be,
As 'tis too just a cause,
Let this thought quicken thee:
Minds that are great and free
Should not on fortune pause;
'Tis crown enough to virtue still her own applause.

What though the greedy frie
Be taken with false baits
Of worded balladry,
And think it poesy?
They die with their conceits,
And only pitious scorn upon their follies waits.

Was liegst in seichtem Trott
flott in Bequemlichkeit?
Wissen, das schläft, ist tot!
Und diese Wohligkeit
ist die commune Mott'
die löchert Witz und Künste und . . . zerfrißt sie beid'.

Ist der *Äonisch Bach*
versiegt? Liegt *Thespia* brach?
Hat des *Clarion* Leyer, ach,
nicht Saiten, für Gesang
der Nymphen die ihr Ungemach
betrübt, daß ihren Lauben tönt nur Elsternschwatzens Klang?

Falls darum dein Verstummen sey
(ein guter Grund wärs, meiner Treu!)
laß dich enthusiasmieren:
Ein Geist, der groß und frei,
soll auf den Lohn nicht stieren;
Es ist der Tugend schönste Kron', sich selbst zu applaudiren.

Was solls, wenn man verstockt
von Ködern falsch gelockt
geschwätziger Balladerie –
und hält's für Poesie?
Das stirbt ja aus mit der Concept-Idee,
und ihrer Narrheit harrt nur mitleidiger Schmäh.

Then take in hand thy lyre,
Strike in thy proper strain,
With *Japheth's* line, aspire
Sol's chariot for new fire
To give the world again:
Who aided him will thee, the issue of Jove's brain.

And since our dainty age,
Cannot endure reproof,
Make not thyself a page
To that strumpet the stage,
But sing high and aloof,
Safe from the wolf's black jaw and the dull ass's hoof.

BEN JONSON (1573 -1637)
An Ode to himself

So sei nun recht gesungen,
die Saite straff getwungen:
Mit *Japhets* Abkömmling sollst du
Sols Himmelswagen lenken zu
der Welt new Feuer bringen.
Die ihm half, hülft auch dir: die *Jovis* Haupt entsprungen.

Da unser feinsinniger Chor
verträgt den Vorwurf schlecht,
mach dich nicht selbst zum Knecht
der Bühne, dieser Hur!
Sing fern und unabhängig nur,
frei von des Wolfs schwarz Mäul – des Asinus lang Ohr.

Do but consider this small dust,

Here running in the glass,

By atoms mov'd;

Could you believe, that this

The body was

Of one that lov'd?

And in his mistress' flame playing like a fly

Turn'd to cinders by her eye?

Yes; and in death, as life, unbless'd,

To have't express'd:

Even ashes of lovers find no rest.

BEN JONSON (1573-1637)
The Hour-Glass

Erwäge nur/ wie dieser Staubesand/

Der in dem Stundenglas hier rinnt

In sich bewegt/ doch unteilbar

Kannst du glauben/ dieses war

Von einem einst der Leib

der liebte

Und wie die Fliege blind

In seiner Dame Flammen tanzte?

Und ward zu Asch gebrannt von ihrem Aug?

Ja/ und im Tod/ gleichwie im Leben ohne Segen/

Will sagen: daß selbst als Asche Liebende nicht Ruhe finden.

84   If Music and sweet Poetry agree,
As they must needs, (the sister and the brother),
Then must the love be great 'twixt thee and me,
Because thou lovest the one and I the other.
Dowland to thee is dear, whose heavenly touch
Upon the lute doth ravish human sense;
Spenser to me, whose deep conceit is such
As, passing all conceit, needs no defence.
Thou lovest to hear the sweet melodious sound
That Phoebus' lute, the Queen of Music, makes;
And I in deep delight am chiefly drowned
Whenas himself to singing he betakes.
One god is god of both, as poets feign;
One knight loves both, and both in thee remain.

RICHARD BARNFIELD (1574-1627)
If Music and sweet Poetry agree

Wenn denn Musik und Poesie sind überein,
sind ja fürwahr wie Schwester-Bruder ineinander,
dann muß die Liebe zwischen mir und dir groß sein,
da du die eine liebst, und ich die ander'.
Du huldigst DOWLAND, dessen SphärenGriff
auf seiner Laute das Humanum webt –
ich SPENSER, dessen Bilderscharfsinn tief
den Concettismo übertrifft, sich über jedes Lob erhebt.
Du lauschest gern dem melodiösen süßen Klang,
den Phöbus' Laute, *Queen of Music,* schlägt –
und ich bin hingerissen, tief bewegt
von einer Sprache, transcendirt in reinen Sang.
Ein Gott ist *beider* Gott (wie Dichter schreiben) –
Ein Ritter liebet *beide*: und beid' in *dir* verbleiben.

Hence, all you vain delights,
As short as are the nights
Wherein you spend your folly!
There's naught in this life sweet,
If men were wise to see't,
  But only melancholy—
  O sweet melancholy!
Welcome, folded arms and fixèd eyes,
A sight that piercing mortifies,
A look that's fasten'd to the ground,
A tongue chain'd up without a sound!

Fountain-heads and pathless groves,
  Places which pale passion loves!
Moonlight walks, when all the fowls
  Are warmly housed, save bats and owls!
A midnight bell, a parting groan—
  These are the sounds we feed upon:
Then stretch our bones in a still gloomy valley,
Nothing's so dainty sweet as lovely melancholy.

JOHN FLETCHER (1579 - 1625)
Melancholy

Zeuch weg, eitles Genießen
so kurz nur wie die Nacht
in der ihr eure Albernheit verbracht!
Das Leben kann versüßen
(wollt's Gott, man säh es ein)
  Melancholie allein!
  Melancholie so fein!
Hierher!: verschränkte Arme; Mien' wie Stein;
Der Blick, der selber sich kasteit;
Das Aug, das stier zu Boden schaut;
Die Zunge lahm, und ohne Laut!

SteinBrunnenköpfe; Wäldchen, von Menschen unberührt
  : das lieben wir so bleich charmiert!
Sub luna Gäng', wenn alle Vögel warm zuhaus
  – nur nicht der Kauz, die Fledermaus!
Ein ZwölfUhrschlag, ein Abschiedsstöhnen
  : hach, das sind Töne, den' wir frönen!
Unser Gebein gestrecket in düsterstillem Thal:
So wird Melancholie zu unserm Leckermahl.

86   Call for the robin-redbreast and the wren,
         Since o'er shady groves they hover,
         And with leaves and flowers do cover
      The friendless bodies of unburied men.
      Call unto his funeral dole
         The ant, the field-mouse, and the mole,
      To rear him hillocks that shall keep him warm,
         And (when gay tombs are robb'd) sustain no harm;
      But keep the wolf far thence, that's foe to men,
      For with his nail he'll dig them up again.

JOHN WEBSTER (1580 (?) - 1630 (?))
A Dirge

Ans Rotkehlgen/ den Zawnkonig/ dich wend/
  die über Schattenhainen brüten/
  vnd decken recht mit Blattwerck vnd mit Blüten/
des Unbegrabnen Leichnam ohne Freund./
Und ruf zu seinem Leichenschmaus/
  die Ämse/ Maulwurff/ vnd Feld-mauß:/
die häufeln Hügel ihm/ der halt ihn warm/
  bereit'/ da man nur Luxusgruften räubert/ ihm kein Harm./
Doch halt den Wolf ihm fern/ des Menschen Graus:/
Mit seinen Nägeln scharrt er wieder ihn herauß./

87 Tell me, you Anti-Saints, why glass
With you is longer liv'd then brass?
And why the saints have 'scap'd their falls
Better from windows than from walls?
Is it because the Brethrens' fires
Maintain a glass-house at Blackfriars?
Next which the church stands North and South,
And East and West the preacher's mouth.
Or ist because such painted ware
Resembles something what you are,
So pied, so seeming, so unsound
In manners, and in doctrine, found
That, out of emblematic wit,
You spare yourselves in sparing it?
If it be so, then, Fairford, boast
Thy church hath kept what all have lost;
And is preserved from the bane
Of either war or Puritan;
Whose life is colour'd in thy paint:
The inside dross, the outside saint.

RICHARD CORBETT (1582 - 1635)
Fairford Windows

Ihr Heil'gen-Stürmer, sagt doch mal, warum
laßt *Glas* ihr dauern – doch Metalle enden?
Warum die Heiligen entgingen irem Falle
auß Fenstern eher denn von Wänden?
Ists, weil bei Blackfriars das Puritanertum
ein glaubensfewrig Glaß-Hütt unterhalt,
nah bei der Kürchen, so nord-südwärts fingert,
in der west-östlich schallt des Pred'gers Maulgewalt?
Oder, ist's weil des Malers Dinge
an das gemahnen, was ihr seid:
so scheckig-scheinhaft-ungescheut
in Ethik & Doktrin befunden,
daß dem entbunden emblematisch Witz & Hohn:
‹Wenn ihr sie schont – ihr euch dann selbst verschont?›
Ist's so, dann, Fairford, wirf dich in die Brust:
Dein Kürchen hat gerett, was anderer Verlust,
vnd ist bewahret vor dem Bann
des Krieges, vnd vorm Puritanermann
des Leben ist in deiner Buntheit luminirt:
Das Innre: stumpf – das Äußre: heilig-koloriert.

88   Like to the thund'ring tone of unspoke speeches,
Or like a lobster clad in logic breeches,
Or like the gray freeze of a crimson cat,
Or like a moon-calf in a slipshoe hat,
Or like a shadow when the sun is gone,
Or like a thought that ne'er was thought upon,
    Even such is man, who never was begotten
    Until his children were both dead and rotten.

Like to a fiery touchstone of a cabbage,
Or like a crablouse with his bag and baggage,
Or like th'abortive issue of a fizzle,
Or like the bag-pudding of a plowman's whistle,
Or like the four-square circle of a ring,
Or like the singing of hey down a ding,
    Even such is man, who, breathless without doubt,
    Spake to small purpose when his tongue was out.

Like to the green fresh fading withered rose,
Or like to rhyme or verse that runs in prose,
Or like the mumbles of a tinder-box,
Or like a man that's sound, yet hath the pox,
Or like a hobnail coin'd in single pence,
Or like the present preterperfect tense,
    Even such is man, who died and then did laugh
    To see such strange lines writ on's epitaph.

RICHARD CORBETT (1582 - 1635)
Nonsense

Gleich ungesprochner Reden Donner-laut; oder:
Gleich wie der Hummer sich in Logik-Hosen kleidt; oder:
Gleichwie der Graupelz einer roten Katz; oder:
Gleichwie das Mondkalb in 'ner Schlappenmütz; oder:
Gleich einem Schatten, wenn statt Sonne Nacht; oder:
Gleich dem Gedanken, der nie nachgedacht:
  So ist der Mensch; der kam nie auf die Welt,
  eh seine Kinder nicht stocktot im Grab verfault.

Gleichwie des Kohls Prüf-Feuerbrocken; oder:
Gleichwie die Filzläuse mit Sack & Packen; oder:
Gleich dem Abortus, der da fisselt-keift; oder:
Gleich wie den Sackpudding der Pflüger pfeift; oder:
Gleich einem Viereck-Circel von 'nem Ring; oder:
Gleich wie man singt *Heydownading*:
  So ist der Mensch; der, außer Atem (zweifle nicht!),
  wenn seine Zung er bleckt, kaum mit viel Nutzen spricht.

Gleichwie die grün frisch dürr verwelkte Rose; oder:
Gleich einem Verse oder Reim in Prose; oder:
Dem Knabbermuffeln einer Zunderbüchse gleich; oder:
Gleich dem Gesunden mit Franzosen-Seuch'; oder:
Gleich einem Hufnagel, in Einzelpence schraffiert; oder:
Gleich wie man Präsens-Praeter-Perfect konjugirt:
  So ist der Mensch; der starb, und dann vor Lachen sich vergaß,
  da er als seine Grabschrift so sonderbare Zeilen las.

Mark, how the lanterns cloud mine eyes!
See, where a moon-drake 'gins to rise!
Saturn crawls much like an *Iron Cat*
To see the naked moon in a slipshod hat.
Thunder-thumping toadstools crock the pots
To see the mermaids tumble;
Leather cat-a-mountains shake their heels
To hear the gosh-hawk grumble.
The rustic thread
Begins to bleed
And cobwebs' elbows itches;
The putrid skies
Eat mulsack pies
Baked up in logic breaches.

Munday trenchers make good hay,
The lobster wears no dagger;
Meal-mouth'd she-peacocks pole the stars
And make the low-bell stagger.
Blue crocodiles foam in the toe,
Blind meal-bags do follow the doe;
A rib of apple-brain spice
Will follow the Lancashire dice.
Hark, how the chime of Pluto's pisspot cracks,
To see the rainbow's wheel ganne, made of flax.

RICHARD CORBETT (1582 - 1635)
A Non Sequitur

Merk auf: Laternen wölken meine Augen!
Sieh, wie ein Entenmondmann dort aufgeht!
Grad wie'ne Bügeleisenkatze schleicht Saturn,
Daß er den Mond seh nackend in ner Schlampenmütz.
Donnerfausthämmernde Blätterpilze zerdeppern die Töppe,
Um die Seejungfrauen sich tummeln zu sehn;
Ihre Fersen schütteln Lederbergkatzen
Um den Hühnerhabicht grummeln zu hörn.
Das ländliche Garn
Fängt zu bluten an
Und Spinnwebenellenbogen juckts;
Die verfaulten Himmel
Essen Maulsackpasteten
Aufgebacken in logischen Hosen.

Montagsschneidbretter machen gut Heu,
Keinen Dolch trägt der Hummer;
Zimperliche Pfauenzimmer stängeln die Sterne,
Bringen Niederglocken zum Pummern.
Blaue Krokodile schäumen im Zeh,
Blinde Mehlsäcke folgen dem Reh;
Eine Rippe von Apfelhirnwürze
Wird folgen dem Lancashirewürfel.
Horch, wie das Glockenspiel von Plutos Pißpott knackst,
Das Fuchsradregenbogenbelln zu sehn, aus Flachs.

Dear Lord, receive my son, whose winning love
To me was like a friendship, far above
The course of nature or his tender age;
Whose looks could all my bitter griefs assuage:
Let his pure soul, ordain'd seven years to be
In that frail body which was part of me,
Remain my pledge in Heaven, as sent to show
How to this port at every step I go.

SIR JOHN BEAUMONT (1583 - 1627)
Dear Lord, receive my son

O HErr, nimm meinen Sohn/ des liebende Gewalt/
Mir wie ein Freundschaft war/ vil höher noch gestellt/
Denn der Natur Verlauf/ und seine zarten Jahr';/
Des Blick mein bitter Leid/ konnt lindern ganz vnd gar:/
Laß seine reine Seel/ die sieben Jahre lang/
In dem fragilen Leib/ Teil meines schwachen eigen/
Mein Himmels-Lotse sein/ vorausgeschickt, zu zeigen/
Wie ich mit jedem Schritt/ in gleichen Port gelang'./

91   Thou black, wherein all colours are composed,
And unto which they all at last return,
Thou colour of the sun where it doth burn,
And shadow, where it cools, in thee is closed
Whatever nature can or hath disposed
In any other hue: from thee do rise
Those tempers and complexions, which, disclosed
As parts of thee, do work as mysteries
Of that thy bidden power: when thou dost reign,
The characters of fate shine in the skies,
And tell us what the heavens do ordain,
But when earth's common light shines to our eyes,
Thou so retirest thyself, that thy disdain
All revelation unto man denies.

EDWARD, LORD HERBERT OF CHERBURY (1583 - 1648)
Black itself

Du *Schwarz*: darein ein jede Farb geschossen,
zu dem sie all am Ende kehren ein,
Du Sonnenfarbe, wo ihr Kohlen-Schein
und Schatten, wo er kühlt, in Dir beschlossen,
was die Natur vermag und angelegt
in jeder andern Farb': aus Dir her sprossen
die Complexion, der Safft, das Temprament (: erschlossen
als deine Elemente) sich als Secretum regt
Deiner verborgenen Macht: wenn *Schwarz* das Szepter trägt,
am Firmamente dann des Schicksals Zeichen glimmen
die sagen, was die Himmel uns bestimmen;
doch wenn das erd-gemeine Licht aufs Aug uns scheint:
dann wendest Du Dich ab, daß Dein Ergrimmen
alls, was den Menschen offenbart ist, jäh verneint.

Black beauty, which above that common light,
Whose Power can no colours here renew
But those which darkness can again subdue,
Dost still remain unvary'd to the sight,
And like an object equal to the view,
Art neither chang'd with day, nor hid with night;
When all these colours which the world call bright,
And which old Poetry doth so pursue,
Are with the night so perished and gone,
That of their being there remains no mark,
Thou still abidest so intirely one,
That we may know that blackness is a spark
Of light inaccessible, and alone
Our darkness which can make us think it dark.

EDWARD, LORD HERBERT OF CHERBURY (1583 - 1648)
Black beauty, which above that common light

Du Schönheit *Schwarz*: hoch über dem gemeinen Licht,
des Macht läßt einzig Farben hier erfunkeln,
die neu zu Schwärze macht das Dunkel,
bleibst still du, unveränderlich der Sicht,
und wie dem Anblick ein Objekt stets gleicht,
bei Tage unverwechselt und nicht versteckt bei Nacht;
wenn alle Farben, die der Welt als Pracht
erscheinen, der Alten Poesie Verlangen,
so mit der Nacht verschwunden sind, vergangen,
daß keine Spur von ihrem Sein dem Nichts sich kann entreißen,
bleibst *Du* identisch in dir selbst befangen,
daß wir erkennen können: das Schwarze ist ein Gleißen
von unerreichbar fernem Licht, ein Funken,
den einzig unsrer Dumpfheit Dünkel uns ‹dunkel› denken heißen.

93 The last and greatest herald of Heaven's King,
   Girt with rough skins, hies to the deserts wild,
   Among that savage brood the woods forth bring,
   Which he than man more harmless found and mild.
   His food was blossoms, and what young did spring,
   With honey that from virgin hives distilled;
   Parched body, hollow eyes, some uncouth thing
   Made him appear, long since from earth exiled.
   There burst he forth: All ye whose hopes rely
   On God, with me amidst these deserts mourn,
   Repent, repent, and from old errors turn!—
   Who listened to his voice, obeyed his cry?
   Only the echoes, which he made relent,
   Rung from their marble caves, Repent! Repent!

WILLIAM DRUMMOND OF HAWTHORNDEN (1585-1649)
Saint John Baptist

Der letzte, größte Herold unsers Heilands,
in rauhe Häut' gehüllt, eilt in die Wüsten wild
zur grausen Brut, den Thieren dieses Lands
die er harmloser fand denn Menschen, und mehr mild.
Zikaden warn sein Speiß, der jungen Sprossen kleine
mit Honig aus einsamen Bienenstöcken.
Gedörrt der Leib – die Augen hohl – erschrecken
ließ sein der Welt schon lang abhandendes Erscheinen.
Da bricht's aus ihm: «Ihr, deren Hoffen ruht
auf GOtt, klagt mit mir in dem Wüstengrab!
Bereut! Bereut! Vom alten Adam lasset ab!»
Wer hörte seine Stimme? Gehorchte seiner Wut?
Einzig sein Echo, das der Wind zerstreuet,
erstarb aus MarmelHöhlen: «Bereuet! Ach bereuet!»

I know that all beneath the moon decays,
And what by mortals in this world is brought,
In Time's great periods shall return to nought;
That fairest states have fatal nights and days;
I know how all the Muse's heavenly lays,
With toil of spright which are so dearly bought,
As idle sounds of few or none are sought,
And that nought lighter is than airy praise.
I know frail beauty like the purple flower,
To which one morn oft birth and death affords;
That love a jarring is of minds' accords,
Where sense and will invassal reason's power:
Know what I list, this all can not me move,
But that, O me! I both must write and love.

WILLIAM DRUMMOND OF HAWTHORNDEN (1585 - 1649)
I know that all beneath the moon decays

Ich weiß, daß alles unterm Mond verfällt
und daß, was Todgeweihte in diese Welt gebracht,
muß in den mächtgen Intervalln der Zeit zurück in nichtge Nacht;
daß von fatalen Tagen, Nächten, auch noch das Edelste vergällt;
und weiß, daß sich für aller Musen Leyer
mit ihrer Schwierigkeit-des-Leichten, teuer acquirirt,
als ‹müßiges Getön› fast niemand intressiert,
und daß nichts leichter sei als in die Luft gesprochnes Lob-Geseier.
Ich weiß, daß wie der Purpurblume schön Zerbrechlichkeit
für die ein einzger Morgen Geburt und Tod gleich bringt,
die Liebe in des Geistes Harmonien als Mißton klingt
wo Wille sich und Sinne versklaven die Vernünftigkeit...
Wißt: was die Liste aufgereiht, das alls kann mich nicht trüben –
Nur daß ich gleicherweis muß schreiben, ach! und lieben.

95   Sleep, Silence' child, sweet father of soft rest,
     Prince whose approach peace to all mortals brings,
     Indifferent host to shepherds and to kings,
     Sole comforter of minds with grief opprest;

     Lo, by thy charming-rod all breathing things
     Lie slumbering, with forgetfulness possest,
     And yet o'er me to spread thy drowsy wings
     Thou spares, alas! who cannot be thy guest.

     Since I am thine, O come, but with that face
     To inward light which thou art wont to show;
     With feigned solace, each a true-felt woe;
     Or if, deaf god, thou do deny that grace,
     Come as thou wilt, and what thou wilt bequeath,—
     I long to kiss the image of my death.

WILLIAM DRUMMOND OF HAWTHORNDEN (1585 - 1649)
Sleep, silence' child, sweet father of soft rest

Schlaf: Schweigens Kind, süß Vater sanfter Rast!
Prinz, dessen Nahn all Sterblichen bringt Frieden!
Wirt, vor dem jeder gleich: ob Könige, ob Hirten!
Du einzger Tröster nur von gramgepreßtem Geist!

Schau, alls was atmet, legst mit Zauberstäben
In Schlummer, in Vergessen;
Doch über mir die Dämmerflügel weben,
Der ich dein Gast nicht sein darf, willst du lassen?

Ich bin doch dein! Ach komm! Allein nur mit dem Schein
Des innern Lichts, was du gewohnt zu zeigen
Mit tröstlicher Erfindung ein jeder wahrempfundnen Pein;
Doch, tauber Gott, willst du die Gnade weigern?:
Komm wie du willt, was du auch lassen willt auf meinen Kissen,
Still mein Verlangen, die Imago meines Tods zu küssen!

Of this fair volume which we World do name
If we the sheets and leaves could turn with care,
Of him who it corrects and did it frame,
We clear might read the art and wisdom rare:
Find out his power which wildest powers doth tame,
His providence existing everywhere,
His justice which proud rebels doth not spare,
In every page, no, period of the same.

But silly we, like foolish children, rest
Well pleased with coloured vellum, leaves of gold,
Fair dangling ribands, leaving what is best,
On the great writer's sense ne'er taking hold;

Or if by chance our minds do muse on ought,
It is some picture on the margin wrought.

WILLIAM DRUMMOND OF HAWTHORNDEN (1585 - 1649)
The Book of the World

Wenn wir von diesem Prachtband namens *Welt*
Die Bögen, Seiten könnten sorgsam wenden,
Könnten von IHm wir, der's verfaßt, gebunden,
Die Kunst, ein einig Wissen, lesen unverstellt,
SEin Macht, die noch die wildsten Mächte zähmt, entdecken,
Wie SEine Vorsehung, die über allem thront,
SEin Richtschwert, das auch den Rebell nicht schont,
Ob jede Seit sich, jeden Punkt selbda erstrecken.

Doch albern – läppisch – kindisch gleich dem Narrn
Erbaun wir uns am Buntpapier, am Goldrandschnitt,
Am hübschen Lesebändel. Das Beste bleibt uns fern :
Vom Sinn des großen Dichters bekommen wir nichts mit.

Falls unser Geist doch einmal, rein zufällig, gebannt –
Dann von 'ner Abbildung als Fußnote am Rand.

97	Mortality, behold and fear!
What a change of flesh is here!
Think how many royal bones
Sleep within this heap of stones:
Here they lie had realms and lands,
Who now want strength to stir their hands:
Where from their pulpits seal'd with dust
They preach, «In greatness is no trust.»
Here's an acre sown indeed
With, the richest, royall'st seed
That the earth did e'er suck in
Since the first man died for sin:
Here the bones or birth have cried—
«Though gods they were, as men they died.»
Here are sands, ignoble things,
Dropt from the ruin'd sides of kings;
Here's a world of pomp and state,
Buried in dust, once dead by fate.

FRANCIS BEAUMONT (1586-1616)
On the Tombs of Westminster Abbey

Halt inne/ *Sterblichkeit/* und fürchte!:
Sieh hier das Fleisch sich in Verwesung wandeln!
Denck/ Wie viel königlich Gebein
Inmitten dieser Hauffen Stein
Hier ruht. Einst Land & Reich regierend
Erflehn sie Krafft/ die Händ zu rühren,
Von iren Canzeln/ unterm Stawb gebannt/
Nun predigend daß Größe kein Garant.
Wahrlich/ gesät ist hier ein Acker
Aus reichster königlichster Saat/
So je die Erde eingeschluckt
Seit Adams erster Sündenthat.
Hier ward den adelichten Knochen
Deß Weinens Beben außgetruckt:
Die Götter zwar im Leben/ als Menschen starben sie.
Sand rieselt itzt/ und eyn unreines Rinnen
Seitab von angeschlagnen Köningen tropft hie;
So ist des Pomps & Staates Welt
In Staub vergilbt/ einst hingefällt/ zerbrochen
Vom Fatum selbst.

98   Underneath this sable Herse
Lies the Subject of all Verse:
Sydney's Sister, Pembroke's Mother—
Death! ere thou Kill'st such another
Fair, and good, and learnd as SHEE,
Time will throw his Dart at thee.

WILLIAM BROWNE (1588-1643)
Epitaph on Mary Herbert, Countess of Pembroke

Hier unter diesem Leichenstein
ruht aller Verse Grund allein:
Pembrokes Mutter/ Sidneys Schwesterlein.
Tod, eh du wieder mordest ein'
wie sie so gut/ gelehrt/ vnd fein,
ziel' *Zeit* Dir ihre Pfeile ins Gebein!

99   May! Be thou never graced with birds that sing,
     Nor Flora's pride!
     In thee all flowers and roses spring,
     Mine only died.

WILLIAM BROWNE (1588-1643)
Epitaph in Obitum M. S. X° Maij, 1614

Mai! Sei nimmermehr geziert mit Vogelsange,
Mit Floras stolzer Blütengarb'!
In Dir jeds Blümlin, alle Rosen prangen –
Nur meine starb.

I dare not ask a kiss,
I dare not beg a smile,
Lest having that, or this,
I might grow proud the while.

No, no, the utmost share
Of my desire shall be
Only to kiss that air
that lately kissèd thee.

Robert Herrick (1591 - 1674)
To Electra

Ich wags nicht, einen Kuß,
ein Lächeln zu erflehn –
Denn hätt ich's, gäbs Verdruß:
Würd mich vor Stolz nur blähn.

Mein höchst Begehr vielmehr,
das sey, daß ihrs nur wißt:
Dem Äther hiermit ei-
nen Kuß! da er Dich küßt'.

Here, she lies, a pretty bud,
Lately made of flesh and blood:
Who as soon fell fast asleep
As her little eyes did peep.
Give her strewings, but not stir
The earth that lightly covers her.

ROBERT HERRICK (1591 - 1674)
Epitaph upon a Child that died

Ein Knospen zart hier ruht
War kaum aus Fleisch und Blut
Ist rasch in Schlummer eingenickt
Eh noch die Äuglein aufgeweckt
Streut Blumen ihr doch gebt fein acht
Rührt nicht die Erd die sie ganz sacht
Zum Schlafen hier nur zugedeckt

Man is a *tennis-court*: His flesh, the *wall*;
The gamesters *God* and *Satan*; th'heart's the *ball*.
The higher and the lower *hazards* are
Too bold *presumption* and too base *despair*.
The *rackets* which our restless *balls* make fly,
Adversity and sweet *prosperity*.
The angels keep the *court*, and mark the place
Where the *ball* falls, and chalk out ev'ry *chase*.
The *line*'s a civil life we often cross
Or which, the *ball* not flying, makes a *losse*.
Detractors are like *standers-by*, and bet
With charitable men: our life's the *set*.
Lord, in this *conflict*, in these fierce *assaults*,
Laborious *Satan* makes a world of *faults*;
Forgive them, Lord, although he ne'er implore
For favour: They'll be set upon our *score*.
O take the *ball* before it come to th'ground,
For this base *court* has many a *false rebound*.
Strike, and strike hard, but strike above the *line*:
Strike where thou please, so as the *set* be thine.

FRANCIS QUARLES (1592 - 1644)
Man is a tennis-court

MENSCH kömmt mir vor als eine *Tennis-bahn.*/ Sein Fleisch: der *Wall*/
Die Spieler: *Gott & Satan*/ Sein Herze ist der *Ball.*/
Die *Risiken* ‹zu hoch› gleichwie ‹zu flach›/
sind: kühnste *Präsumption*/ zu tiefes *Ungemach.*/
Die *Schläger*/ so den Ball luftschmettern stet/
sind *Unglück*/ gleichwie süß *Prosperität.*/
Punct-richter sind die Engel/ die markiern den *Place*/
des Balles Aufschlag/ und außkreiden jede *Chace.*/
Die *Lein*: rechtschaffen Leben/ so man oft überspringt/
was/ wenn der *Ball* nicht fliegt/ Verlust uns bringt./
Verläumder sind gleich *Zuschauern*/ die *Wetten* geben/
mit gutgesinnten Menschen:/ der *Einsatz*: unser Leben./
HErr! In dem Wett-streit/ in dem wüsten Quälen/
macht *Satan*/ umtriebig/ ein ganze Welt von *Fehlen.*/
Vergib sie, HErr/ ob er gleich nimmer win-/
sele um Gnad/ uns sey der *Punct-gewinn*!/
O nimm den *Ball*/ eh er zu Boden fällt/
Denn von *der* niedern Bahn viel *Fehlerschlag ab prällt.*/
Schlag'/ und schlag hart!/ Doch schlag über die *Lein'*:/
Schlag wo Du willt/ daß die *Partie* sey Dein!/

Perhaps 'twas but conceit. Erroneous sense,
Thou art thine owne distemper and offence.
Imagine then that thick, unwholesome steam
Was thy corruption, breath'd into a dream.

Nor is it strange, when we in charnels dwell,
That all our thoughts of earth and frailty smell.

Man is a candle whose unhappy light
Burns in the day, and smothers in the night.
And as you see the dying taper waste,
By such degrees does he to darkness haste.

Here is the diff'rence: when our body's lamps,
Blinded by age, or chok'd with mortal damps,
Now faint and dim and sickly, 'gin to wink
And in their hollow sockets lowly sink;
When all our vital fires, ceasing to burn,
Leave nought but snuff and ashes in our urn:

God will restore those fallen lights again,
And kindle them to an eternal flame.

HENRY KING (1592 - 1669)
Being Waked out of my Sleep by a Snuff of Candle which Offended me,
I thus thought

Vielleicht wars nur ein Bild. Du irrer Sinn
Bist deine eigne Seuche und dein Abschaum.
So mag dir dünken/ der dicke ungesunde Schmauch
Wär deiner eigenen Verwesung Hauch im Traum.

Es ist so seltsam kaum/ da unser Heim die Leichenhalle/
Wenn unser Denken alle nach Erd & Faulschleim stincken.

Der Mensch ist eine Kertz/ deß unglückselges Licht
Am Tage brennt/ erstikkt des Nachts/
Uns sieh! gleichwie die Flamē allmehlich lischt zunicht:
So raast er stufenweis ins Schwartz.

Das ist der Unterscheid: Wenn unsers Leibes Leuchten
Von Alter blind/ gewürgt von Todesfeuchten/
Nun kräncklich/ matt/ und trübe plötzlich blinken/
In ire hohlen Sockel langsam sinken/
Wenn unsers Lebens Fewer kalt erblassen/
Nur Kohlen Stawb/ und Aschen/ in unsrer Urne lassen:

Wird GOtt solch ausgezüngelt Glühen neu begründen
Und es zu einer ewig hellen Flammen-Lohe zünden.

The Lady Mary Villiers lies
Under this stone; with weeping eyes
The parents that first gave her birth,
And their sad friends, laid her in earth.
If any of them, Reader, were
Known unto thee, shed a tear;
Or if thyself possess a gem
As dear to thee, as this to them,
Though a stranger to this place,
Bewail in theirs thine own hard case:
   For thou, perhaps at thy return
   May'st find thy Darling in an urn.

THOMAS CAREW (1595 (?) -1639 (?))
Epitaph/ On the Lady Mary Villiers

Hier unterm Stein die Lady darfst du schaugen:
MARIA VILLIERS mit verweinten Augen
vom Älternpaar, das sie ins Leben bracht,
vnd manchem Trawer-Freund gesenket in den Schacht.
Sey dir vielleicht der eine, andere bekannt –
dann gönn', Betrachter, diesem eine Thräne.
Oder, besitzest selber du ein' Schatz
gleich lieb dir, so wie diesen Jene –
dann kenn, wiewohl ein Fremder diesem Platz,
in *ihrem* deinen *eignen* schweren Stand:
    Denn leicht, tust du die Schritte heimwärts wenden,
    könntst du dein Liebstes schon in einer Urne finden.

The glories of our blood and state
Are shadows, not substantial things;
There is no armour against Fate;
Death lays his icy hand on kings:
  Sceptre and Crown
  Must tumble down,
And in the dust be equal made
With the poor crookèd scythe and spade.

Some men with swords may reap the field,
And plant fresh laurels where they kill:
But their strong nerves at last must yield;
They tame but one another still:
  Early or late
  They stoop to fate,
And must give up their murmuring breath
When they, pale captives, creep to death.

The girlands wither on your brow;
Then boast no more your mighty deeds!
Upon Death's purple altar now
See where the victor-victim bleeds.
  Your heads must come
  To the cold tomb:
Only the actions of the just
Smell sweet and blossom in their dust.

JAMES SHIRLEY (1596 - 1666)
Death the leveller

Die Glorie unsers Bluts & Stands/
ist Schemen/ vnd nicht wesenhaft/
Gen Fatum bist du nicht bewafft;/
Den König holt der Todtentanz:/
  Szepter & Kron/
  das muß ja davon,/
Und muß im Stawbe gleich ze gleich geraten/
mit schlimmer HakenSense/ vnd dem Spaten.

Man mag das Feld mit Schwerten mähn/
vnd/ wo man tödt/ new Lorbeer säen/
Der Nerven Stärcke muss zuletzt doch lähmen,/
Sie können ja einander nur bezähmen:/
  Früh oder spät/
  sind *sie* gemäht/
Und müssen enden ihres Otems Fauchen/
wenn sie/ gefangen bleich/ zum Tode krauchen.

Der Lorber welkt schon auf der Brau'/
So prahl nicht mehr der mächtgen Taten!/
Auf Todes PurpurAltar,/ schau!/
wie itzt die Sieger-Opfer bluten:/
  Eur Kopf muß ab/
  ins kalte Grab!/
Denn nur das Handeln des Gerechten-Guten/
riecht süß/ vnd treibt auß TodtenErde Blüten.

I saw my Lady weep,
And Sorrow proud to be advancèd so
In those fair eyes there all perfections keep.
Her face was full of woe;
But such a woe (believe me) as wins more hearts
Then Mirth can do with her enticing parts.

Sorrow was there made fair,
And Passion wise; Tears a delightful thing;
Silence beyond all speech, a wisdom rare:
She made her sighs to sing,
And all things with so sweet a sadness move
As made my heart at once both grieve and love.

O fairer than aught else
The world can show, leave off in time to grieve!
Enough, enough: your joyful look excels:
Tears kill the heart, believe.
O strive not to be excellent in woe,
Which only breeds your beauty's overthrow.

ANONYM, from John Dowland's Second Booke of Songes (1600)
I saw my Lady weep

Ich sah MyLady weinen
und Kummer stolz, daß man sich ihm so näh'r
in jenen schönen Augen, wo ruhet die Vollkommenheit.
Ihr Antlitz war voll Leid;
doch, glaubt mir, solch ein Leid, das Herzen mehr
gewinnt denn aller Frohsinn mit Verlockens Schein.

So ward der Kummer schön
Und Leiden weis'; Thrän ward ein köstlich Ding
und rar die Weisheit: keine Wort' verlieren:
Sie hieß die Seufzer *singen*
und alle Dinge mit so holder Trauer rühren:
das ließ mein Herz im Nu gleich lieben wie zerspringen.

O Schöneres kaum mehr
die Welt erzeigt; laß Leid zu rechter Zeit!
Genug, genug! Dein Freudenblick ist höh'r:
glaub mir, Thrän tödt das Herz.
O streb nicht nach Vollkommenheit im Schmerz
was deiner Schönheit Unterwerfung ja nur dräut.

Weep you no more, sad fountains;
What need you flow so fast?
Look how the snowy mountains
Heaven's sun doth gently waste!
But my Sun's heavenly eyes
View not your weeping,
That now lies sleeping
Softly, now softly lies
Sleeping.

Sleep is a reconciling,
A rest that peace begets;
Doth not the sun rise smiling
When fair at even he sets?
Rest you then, rest, sad eyes!
Melt not in weeping,
While she lies sleeping
Softly, now softly lies
Sleeping.

ANONYM, from John Dowland's
Third & Last Booke of Songs & Airs (1603)
Weep you no more, sad fountains

Weint nicht mehr, traurige Brunnen, Fontänen;
Was müßt ihr so schnelle denn rinnen?
Seht auf den Bergen die SchneeMoränen
Unter der Sonnen Helle sacht tauen!
Doch meiner Sonne himmlische Augen
Schauen nicht euren Thränenkummer,
Da Jene im Schlummer
Ruht, sanft, ganz sanft nun
Im Schlummer.

Schlaf ist ein holdes Versöhnen:
Labende Ruhe, die Frieden gezeugt.
Lächelt die Sonne nicht, wenn sie dem Abend
Golden zu nieder sich beugt?
Ruht denn, bekümmerte Augen!
Taut nicht in Thränen, in Kummer,
Da Jene im Schlummer
Liegt, sacht, ganz sacht nun
Im Schlummer.

I saw fair Chloris walk alone
Where feather'd rain came softly down,
And Jove descended from his tower
To court her in a silver shower;
The wanton snow flew to her breast
Like little birds into their nest,
And overcome with whiteness there
For grief it thaw'd into a tear,
Thence falling on her garment's hem,
For grief it freez'd into a gem.

WILLIAM STRODE (1602 - ca 1644/45)
On a Gentlewoman walking in the snow

Schön-Cloris sah ich einsam sich bewegen
durch sacht hernieder rieselnden gefiedert Regen,
und Jupitern von seinem Turme steigen
um ihr in einem Silberschauer seine Gunst zu zeigen.
So schalkhaft flog der Schnee ihr an die Brust
wie kleine Vögel in ihr Nest,
und dort, von all der Weiße überkommen,
ist er vor Weh in eine Thräne gleich zerschwommen,
die tropft' auf ihrs Gewandes Spitzenflor,
wo sie vor Gram zu einem Edelstein gefror.

109   Music, thou queen of souls, get up and string
        Thy pow'rful lute, and some sad requiem sing,
        Till rocks requite thy echo with a groan,
        And the dull clifts repeat the duller tone.
        Then on a sudden with a nimble hand
        Run gently o'er the chords, and so command
        The pine to dance, the oak his roots forego,
        The holm and aged elm to foot it too;
        Myrtles shall caper, lofty cedars run,
        And call the courtly palm to make up one;
        Then, in the midst of all their jolly train,
        Strike a sad note, and fix'em trees again.

THOMAS RANDOLPH (1605 - 1635)
Music, thou Queen of Souls

Auf denn, Musik! Du Seelenkönigin, nun schlage
mit Macht die Laute, sing die Totenklage:
: des Echo im Gestein mit Stöhnen gegenschallt,
und von betrübten Felsen in trübern Tönen widerhallt.
In einem Hui dann gleite mit der weichen,
gewandten Hand über die Saiten: gib das Zeichen:
: Die Föhre tanze! Es entwurzle sich die Eiche!
Stechpalme & bejahrte Ulme: reiht euch ein!
Lauft, hohe Zedern! Myrten, springet drein!
Ruf auch die höf'sche Palme, daß sie gavottieren kann!
Mittzwischen in des Lustgewühls Rumoren dann
schlag einen TrauerKlang: – ! – : stehn wieder baum. Im Bann.

The seas are quiet when the winds give o'er;
So calm are we when passions are no more.
For then we know how vain it was to boast
Of fleeting things, so certain to be lost.
Clouds of affection from our younger eyes
Conceal that emptiness which age descries.

The soul's dark cottage, batter'd and decay'd,
Lets in new light through chinks that Time hath made:
Stronger by weakness, wiser men become
As they draw near to their eternal home.
Leaving the old, both worlds at once they view
That stand upon the threshold of the new.

Edmund Waller (1606 - 1687)
Old Age

Still wird die See, da schwach die Winde wehn.
So sind auch wir, wenn uns das Sehnen schwindet;
Da lernen wir, wie leer es war, zu tönen
Ob flüchtger Dinge, zu vergehn bestimmt.
Durch Fühlens Dunst verschwimmt uns jungen Augen
Die Leere, so dem Alter klar zu sehn.

Der Seele dunkles Cottage, verfallen und zerschlissen,
Durch Spalten, die die Zeit gerissen,
Läßt Neulicht ein.
Die werden weiser und durch Schwäche stärker sein,
Die sich dem ewgen Port entgegen freuen,
Und, fern der alten schon, zwei Welten schauen,
Die auf der Schwelle stehn der andern, neuen.

When I consider how my light is spent,
Ere half my days in this dark world and wide,
And that one talent which is death to hide
Lodged with me useless, though my soul more bent
To serve therewith my Maker, and present
My true account, lest he, returning, chide,
«Doth God exact day-labour, light denied?»
I fondly ask. But Patience, to prevent
That murmur, soon replies, «God doth not need
Either man's work or his own gifts. Who best
Bear his mild yoke, they serve him best. His State
Is kingly. Thousands at his bidding speed,
And post o'er land and ocean without rest;
They also serve who only stand and wait.»

JOHN MILTON (1608 - 1674)
On his Blindness

Wenn ich erwäge, wie mein Licht in Fernen
noch vor der Hälfte meiner Tage schwand, in dieser dunkelweiten Welt,
und daß mir ein Talent (: Tod wär's, wenn es nichts gält)
nutzlos gegeben ist, ob meine Seel gleich gerne
dem Schöpfer mit ihm diente, und zög die subalterne-
aufrichtige Bilanz, damit SEin Schelten mir nicht in die Ohren gellt:
Verlangt GOtt Tages Arbeit, wenn kein Lichtstrahl hellt?
Narr, der ich frag. Geduld nämlich, die här'ne,
erwidert bald, dem Murr'n zu wehrn, «Gott brauchet nicht
des Menschen Arbeit oder Gaben. Wer da trägt
SEin mildes Joch, dient IHm am besten. SEin Gericht
ist königlich: ein einzger Wink viel tausende bewegt
zu Land, und ozeanisch ruhelosen Fahrten.
Die aber dienen auch, die einzig stehn und warten.»

Well-shadow'd landscape, fare ye well:
How I have lov'd you, none can tell
　At least so well
As he that now hates more
Than e'er he lov'd before.

But, my dear nothings, take your leave,
No longer must you me deceive,
　Since I perceive
All the deceit, and know
Whence the mistake did grow.

As he, whose quicker eye doth trace
A false star shot to a mark'd place,
　Does run apace,
And thinking it to catch,
A jelly up doth snatch,

So our dull souls tasting delight
Far off, by sense and appetite,
　Think that is right
And real good; when yet
'Tis but the counterfeit.

SIR JOHN SUCKLING (1609 - 1642)
A Farewell to love

Leb wohl denn, Landschaft aus den Schattentagen:
Wie ich dich liebte: kaum einer kanns sagen
   so gut, so sehr
wie der, so itzt hat grimmern Mut
denn all sein Lieb zuvor.

Doch, liebe Nichtigkeiten: nehmt euren Abschied schön!
Ihr sollt mich nimmer hintergehn,
   da ich erlug's,
all des Betrugs versteh,
woher mein Täuschung mir erwuchs.

Wie der, des Auge flink erspäht, es fällt
ein falscher Stern auf einer Markung Feld,
   vom Wege schnellt,
und banget ihn zu fangen –
und Feldschlamm nur erlanget:

So glauben unsre Seelen dumpf im Schmecken
entlegner Lust, durch Sinne & durch TriebErwecken,
   es wäre recht
und gut und echt – doch keine Spur! Sie blicken
nicht andres als ein Trugbild nur.

113 In darkness let me dwell,
the ground shall Sorrow be;
the roof Despair to bar
all cheerful light from me,
the walls of marble black
that moisten'd still shall weep;
my music hellish jarring sounds
to banish friendly sleep.
Thus wedded to my woes
and bedded to my tomb,
O let me living die,
till death do come.

ANONYM, from John Dowland jun.'s A Musicall Banquet (1610)
In darkness let me dwell

Im Dunckel laß mich hausen,
Trauer der Boden sein;
das Dach Verzweifelung schleuß aus
des Lichtes heitren Schein;
die Wänd aus schwartzem Marmelsteyn,
daran gedämpfte Stille tropf' in Thränen,
indeß meine Musick mit hellisch Missetönen
den holden Schlaff vertreibet vnd verbannt.
Also vermählt mit meinen Nöten,
gebettet in mein Grabgemach,
laß mich lebendig sterben, ach
bis daß der Tod mich kömmt zu tödten.

Still do the stars impart their light
To those that travel in the night;
Still time runs on, nor doth the hand
Or shadow on the dial stand;
The streams still glide and constant are:
Only thy mind
Untrue I find,
Which carelessly
Neglects to be
Like stream or shadow, hand or star.

Fool that I am! I do recall
My words, and swear thou'rt like them all,
Thou seem'st like stars to nourish fire,
But O how cold is thy desire!
And like the hand upon the brass
Thou poin'st at me
In mockery;
If I come nigh
Shade-like thou'lt fly,
And as the stream with murmur pass.

WILLIAM CARTWRIGHT (1611 - 1643)
Falsehood (Still do the stars impart their light)

Die Sterne teiln doch noch ihr Licht
Mit allen Reisenden zur Nachtesstund/
Noch rennt die Zeit davon/ auch will der Zeiger nicht
Und nicht der Schatten stillstehn auf dem Ziffernrund/
Die Ström' in ihrem Gleiten doch stets beständig sind/
Nur deinen Sinn
Find untreu ich/
Leichtsinniglich
Weigerst du dich
Dem Zeiger/ Schatten/ Strom/ und Stern zu gleichen.

Narr, der ich bin! Ich widerruf
Mein Wort/ und schwör, du gleichest diesen allen/
Gleich Sternen machst du daß wir Feuer fangen/
Doch ach/ wie kalt ist dein Verlangen/
Und wie der Zeiger auf dem Uhrmetalle
Zeigst du auf mich
Mit Spöttelstich/
Doch komm ich nah/
Wie schattenähnlich fliehst du da/
Und wie der Strom fließt du vorbei mit bangem Murmelschalle.

To these whom death again did wed
This grave's the second marriage-bed.
For though the hand of Fate could force
'Twixt soul and body a divorce,
It could not sever man and wife,
Because they both lived but one life.
Peace, good reader, do not weep;
Peace, the lovers are asleep.
They, sweet turtles, folded lie
In the last knot that love could tie.
Let them sleep, let them sleep on,
Till the stormy night be gone,
And the eternal morrow dawn;
Then the curtains will be drawn,
And they wake into a light
Whose day shall never die in night.

RICHARD CRASHAW (1612 - 1649)
An Epitaph upon Husband and Wife

Für die der Tod erneut vermåhlt
Ist diese Gruft ein zweites Ehe-bett
Obzwar des Fatums Hand erstritt
Die Scheidung zwischen Seel vnd Leib
Konnt sie nicht trennen Mann vnd VVeib
Da sie eyn einig Leben beid gewåhlt
Husch! Guter Leser, weine nicht
Still! Die Verliebten schlummern nun
Zween Turteltåubchen liegen eingebogen
Im lezten Knoten den die Liebe flicht
Lass sie schlafen lass sie ruhn
Bis die Sturmnacht sich verzogen
Vnd der ewge Morgen bricht
Dann werdn die Vorhånge beiseit gezogen
Vnd sie erwachen in ein Licht
Des Tag soll nie in Nacht verglühn

Dear relics of a dislodg'd soul, whose lack
Makes many a mourning paper put on black!
O stay awhile, ere thou draw in thy head,
And wind thyself up close in thy cold bed.
Stay but a little while, until I call
A summons worthy of thy funeral.
Come then, Youth, Beauty, and Blood, all ye soft powers,
Whose silken flatteries swell a few fond hours
Into a false eternity. Come man;
Hyperbolised nothing! know thy span!
Take thine own measure here, down, down, and bow
Before thyself in thine idea; thou
Huge emptiness! contract thy bulk; and shrink
All thy wild circle to a point. O sink
Lower and lower yet; till thy small size
Call Heaven to look on thee with narrow eyes.
Lesser and lesser yet; till thou begin
To show a face, fit to confess thy kin,
Thy neighbourhood to Nothing!
Proud looks and lofty eyelids, here put on
Yourselves in your unfeign'd reflection;
Here, gallant ladies! this unpartial glass
(Through all your painting) shows you your true face.
These death-seal'd lips are they dare give the lie
To the loud boasts of poor Mortality;
These curtain'd windows, this retired eye
Out-stares the lids of large-look'd Tyranny:
This posture is the brave one; this that lies
Thus low, stands up (methinks) thus, and defies
The World! All-daring dust and ashes! only you
Of all interpreters read Nature true.

RICHARD CRASHAW (1612 - 1649)
Death's Lecture and the Funerall of a Young Gentleman

Theure Reliquie einer fremdbehausten Seele, deren Fehlen
manch trauerndes Papier sich schwärzen macht,
o! bleib noch kurz, eh du den Kopf einziehest
und dich in deinem kalten Bett vergräbst!
Bleib nur ein Weilchen, bis zu einem Urtel
ich lade, würdig deiner Beisetzung.
So kömmt denn: Jugend – Schönheit – Blut! ihr sanften Mächte all,
die ihr mit SeidenSchmeichelei die wen'gen schwachen Stunden
zu falscher Ewigkeit aufbläht! Komm, Mensch,
du hyperbolisch Nichts! Kenn' deiner Täge Maß!
Nimm hier das Maaß an dir: hinab! hinab! bück dich
vor dir in deiner Konception, du
ohngeheure Leere: den Umfang contrahier'! Schrumpf ein
den ganzen wüsten Circel bis zum Punct. O sinke
noch tiefer, immer tiefer, bis deine Winzigkeit
vom Himmel heischt, dich *nur aus Augenschlizen* zu betrachten.
Geringer! Noch geringer! Bis ein Gesicht
zu zeigen du beginnst, das deine Herkunft offenbarte:
die Nachbarschaft zum Nichts!
Hochmütge Lider, stolze Augen, hier:
in eurer unverfälschten Reflektion seid confrontirt!
Galante Ladies: hier!: dies unpartei'sche Glas, es zeigt
durch alle Tünche euer wahres Antlitz.
Die Lippen mit des Tods Sigill, sie wagen es, der Lüge
das laute Brüsten armer Sterblichkeit zu zeihen.
Das zugehängte Fenster: dies retirirte Aug, es stiert
entsetzlicher als die weitaufgerissnen Lider der Tyrannis.
Die Haltung ist ja tapfer nur, die da so niedrig
erst liegt – sich dann (wie mich bedünkt) erhebt – und so der Welt
beut Trutz! Staub-Aschen, alles-wagend: einzig ihr
von allen Interpreten legt die Natur wahr aus.

117 Sure, it was so. Man in those early days
         Was not all stone and earth,
     He shin'd a little, and by those weak rays
         Had some glimpse of his birth.
     He saw heaven o'r his head, and knew from whence
         He came (condemned) hither,
     And, as first love draws strongest, so from hence
         His mind sure progress'd thither.
     Things here were strange unto him: Sweat and till;
         All was a thorn, or weed;
     Nor did those last, but (like himself) died still
         As soon as they did *seed*,
     They seem'd to quarrel with him; for that act
         That fell him, foil'd them all;
     He drew the curse upon the world, and cracked
         The whole frame with his fall.
     This made him long for *home*, as loathe to stay
         With murmurers and foes;
     He sigh'd for Eden, and would often say
         «Ah! What bright days were those?»
     Nor was Heav'n cold unto him; for each day
         The valley, or the mountain
     Afforded visits, and still *Paradise* lay
         In some green shade, or fountain.
     Angels lay *ledger* here; each bush and cell,
         Each oak and highway knew them,
     Walk but the fields, or sit down at some well,
         And he was sure to view them.
     Almighty *Love!* Where art thou now? Mad man
         Sits down and freezeth on;
     He raves and swears to stir nor fire, nor fan,
         But bids the thread be spun.

Jaja, so wars: der Mensch in jenen fruhen Tagen
 war nicht ganz Stein & Erd.
Er *scheinete* ein wenig. Und hatte von dem zarten Strahlen
 ein kleines Wissen seiner Abkunft.
Er sah den Himmel über seinem Haupt: und wußte
 woher er kam: *hierher verdammt*;
Und so wie Erste Liebe stärker bindet, schwang sich
 sein Geist gewiß dorthin zurück.
Hier war ihm alles feindlich: Schweiß & Müh;
 jed Ding ward Dorn & Nessel,
Die auch nicht blieben, sondern starben ab (gleich ihm)
 sobald zur Saat sie reif.
Es schien, als haderten sie ihm: für jene Tat die *ihn*
 gestürzt, sie *alle* warn zuschanden.
Er zog der Welt den Fluch herbei, zertrümmerte
 mit seinem Fall das Weltgebäu.
Das macht' ihn *heimwehkrank*, so müd zu leben
 bei Flüsterern & Feinden.
Um Eden seufzt' er, und sprach häufig also:
 «Ach! was für lichte Tage waren das!»
Auch war der Himmel ihm nicht kalt: tagtäglich
 gewährten ihm Besuch
Tal oder Berg. Und noch lag da das Paradeis
 in manchem grünen Schatten oder Born.
Dort formten Engel einen Baldachin: jed Busch & Höhl,
 jed Weg & Eichbaum kannte sie:
Geh übers Feld – setz dich an eine Quelle –
 : und er war sicher, sie zu sehn.
Allmächtge Lieb! Wo bist du hin? Mensch, außer sich,
 setzt sich, ihn fröstelt.
Er raast und schwört dem Feuer wie dem Wedel ab –
 und läßt das Garn doch spinnen.

I see, thy curtains are close-drawn; thy bow
    Looks dim too in the cloud,
Sin triumphs still, and man is sunk below
    The center and his shroud;
All's in deep sleep and night; thick darkness lies
    And hatcheth o'r thy people;
But hark! What trumpets that? What angel cries
    «Arise! Thrust in thy sickle.»

HENRY VAUGHAN (ca 1621/22 - 1695)
Corruption

Ich sehe: dicht verhängt sind deine Fenster. Und dein Bogen
   schaut trübe im Gewölk.
Noch triumphiert die Sünd; der Mensch ist tief gesunken
   unter die Mitte, in sein Leichentuch.
Alls liegt in Nacht und tiefem Schlaf. Dick Dunkel herrscht
   und heckt ob Deinem Volk.
Doch – was trompetet dort? : – horch! was der Engel schreit:
   «*Auf! Auf! Mit deiner Sichel itzo schneid'!*»

I think not on the State, nor am concerned
Which way soever the great helm is turned:
But as that son, whose father's danger nigh
Did force his native dumbness, and untie
The fettered organs—so this is a cause
That will excuse the breach of Nature's laws.
Silence were now a sin; nay, passion now
Wise men themselves for merit would allow!
What noble eye could see, and careless, pass,
The dying lion kicked by every ass?
Has Charles so broke God's laws he must not have
A quiet crown, nor yet a quiet grave?
Tombs have been sanctuaries, thieves lie there
Secure from all their penalty and fear.
Great Charles his double misery was this:
Unfaithful friends, ignoble enemies.
Had any heathen been this Prince's foe,
He would have wept to see him injured so.
His title was his crime; they'd reason good
To quarrel at the right they had withstood.
«He broke God's Laws, and therefor he must die?»
And what shall then become of thee and I?
Slander must follow treason; but yet, stay!
Take not our reason with our King away.
Though you have seized upon all our defence,
Yet do not sequester our common sense.
«Chist will be King?» but I ne'er understood
His subjects built His Kingdom up with blood,
Except their own; or that He would dispense
With His commands, though for His own defence.
O to what height of horror are they come
Who dare pull down a crown, tear up a tomb!

KATHERINE PHILIPS (1631 -1664)
Vpon the Double Murther of K. Charles I.: in Answer to a Libellous Copy of Rhymes by Vavasor Powell

Mir gehts nicht um den Staat; mich kümmert nicht,
in welche Richtung man das Große Ruder reißt.
Denn so, wie seines Vaters drohende Gefahr dem Sohn,
dem Stummheit angeboren, seiner Zunge Fesseln
gelöst, so ist auch dies ein Fall,
der der Naturgesetze Bruch entschulden muß.
Schweigen? – : wär Sünde jetzt! Ja, Leidenschaft
würd *als Verdienst* sogar sich anrechnen der Weise.
Welch edles Aug säh ungerührt passiren, wie jedweder Eselshuf
den Leu im Tode noch zu treten sich erfrecht?
Brach Charles die Satzung Gottes so, daß weder ruh'ge Krone
noch stilles Grab ihm bleiben darf?
Als unantastbar galten Gräber stets: sogar der Dieb
durft da vor Furcht und Strafe sicher ruhn.
Oh großer Charles! Dein zwiefach Elend heißt:
Untreue Freunde – Feinde sonder Ehre!
Wär je ein Heide diesem Prinz unhold gewesen,
er würde weinen itzt, ihn so verletzt zu sehn.
Ja, sein Verbrechen war sein Titel: nur vernünftig,
dem Recht zu hadern, dem sie widerstanden.
«*Gottes Gesetze brach er: deshalb muß er sterben*»?
Und was soll werden dann aus Euch und mir?
Auf Treubruch folgt Schimpf: doch, haltet ein,
tragt nicht mit unserm König die Vernunft von hinnen!
Unsre Verteidigungen habt Ihr sämmtlich confiscirt –
doch unsern *common sense* sollt Ihr nicht mit Beschlag belegen.
«*Christus soll König sein*» – ich hab das nie begriffen:
daß SEine Untertanen *mit Blut* SEin Königreich erbauen –
nur nie mit ihrem eigenen; daß ER ein solch Gesetz,
und wärs zu SEinem Schutz, je ausgegeben.
Ach! Welche Horror-Höhe haben die erklommen,
die ihm die Kron abreißen und seine Gruft aufstemmen!

119 O the sad day!
When freinds shall shake their heads, and say
Of miserable me—
«Hark, how he groans!
 Look, how he pants for breath!
  See how he struggles with the pangs of death!»
When they shall say of these dear eyes—
«How hollow, O how dim they be!
 Mark how his breast doth rise and swell
  Against his potent enemy!»
When some old friend shall step to my bedside,
Touch my chill face, and thence shall gently slide.
But—when his next companions say
«How does he do? What hopes?»—shall turn away,
Answering only, with a lift-up hand—
«Who can his fate withstand?»

Then shall a gasp or two do more
Than e'er my rhetoric could before:
Persuade the world to trouble me no more!

THOMAS FLATMAN (1637 - 1688)
The sad day

O der betrübten Tage!
Wenn Freunde, köpfewiegend, sagen
von mir, der ich so elend bin:
«Horcht, wie er stöhnt!
　Schaut, wie sein Odem pfeift!
　　Seht, wie die Todesklaue nach ihm greift!»
Wenn man von diesen theuren Augen ruft:
«Wie hohl, o wie so trüb sie sind!
　Merkt, wie die Brust ihm schwillt, sich dehnt
　　im Streit mit seinem mächtgen Feind!»
Wenn an mein Bette tritt manch alter Freund,
die Hand legt auf die kalte Stirn, sich sacht entfernt,
und wenn, der bei ihm steht, dann meint
«Wie geht es ihm? Ist Hoffnung noch?» nur ab sich wendt
und *resigniret*, mit erhobner Hand:
«Wer wagte seinem Schicksal Widerstand?»

Dann überred' mein Keuchen, was bisher
mein' Redekünste nicht vermocht, dies Tal so jammerschwer,
Daß es mich ennuyiere nimmermehr!

Let not Death boast his conquering power,
She'll rise a star that fell a flower.

ANONYM (about 1650)
On Eleanor Freeman/ who died 1650, aged 21

Tod!: brüst' dich nicht der Tyrannei ob's Leben –
Sie, die als Blume fiel – wird sich als Stern erheben.

121 See, how the human animal is fed,
How nourishment is wrought, and how conveyed:
 The mouth, with proper faculties endued,
First entertains, and then divides, the food;
Two adverse rows of teeth the meat prepare,
On which the glands fermenting juice confer;
Nature has various tender muscles placed,
By which the artful gullet is embraced;
Some the long funnel's curious mouth extend,
Through which ingested meats with ease descend;
Other confederate pairs for Nature's use
Contract the fibres, and the twitch produce,
Which gently pushes on the grateful food
To the wide stomach, by its hollow road;
 That this long road may unobstructed go,
As it descends, it bores the midriff through;
The large receiver for concoction made
Behold amidst the warmest bowels laid;
The spleen to this, and to the adverse side
The glowing liver's comfort is applied;
Beneath, the pancreas has its proper seat,
To cheer its neighbour, and augment its heat;
More to assist it for its destined use,
This ample bag is stored with active juice,
Which can with ease subdue, with ease unbind,
Admitted meats of every different kind;

So frisset nun das Menschentier. Sieh, wie die Atzung
verarbeitet und weiter transportirt wird:
   Der Mund, mit tauglicher Gerätschaft ausgekleidet,
er nimmt die Nahrung gastlich auf, zerteilet sie;
zwei adversale Reihen Zähne bereiten
den Speißbrei dem die Drüsen Gärungssaft beymischen;
Natur hat da etliche zarte Müsceln hingepflanzt,
von ihnen wird der Schlund sinnreich umcränzt: die einen
dehnen des großen Trichters curieuse Mündung
durch die der ingestive Brei leichtweg hinuntergleitet;
antagonistisch andre (denn *in Zwecken* denkt
Natur): sie contrahirn die Fibern, producirn den Schub
der die dankbare Nahrung sachte würgt
durch cavernöse Straße dem weiten Magen zu.
   Damit ganz ungehemmet sei der lange Weg hinab,
schraubt er sich durch das *Zwerchfell*;
der große Recipient, geschaffen zur Verdauung,
er liegt im wärmsten Eingeweide: sieh mal an!
Ihm sind der *Spleen* (die Milz) und gegenüber
der glühnden *Leber* Labsal beygesellt;
darunter hat der *Pankreas* den rechten Sitz, daß er
des Nachbarn Wärme mehre, ihn erheitere.
Mehr noch: um seinem Sinn & Zweck zu assistirn,
ist dieser weite Sack mit tätgem Safft gefüllt,
der leichtweg binden – leichthin lösen kann
den zugeführten Speisebrei etwelcher Art.

This powerful ferment, mingling with the parts,
The leavened mass to milky chyle converts;
The stomach's fibres this concocted food,
By their contraction's gentle force, exclude,
Which by the mouth on the right side descends
Through the wide pass, which from that mouth depends;
In its progression soon the laboured chyle
Receives the confluent rills of bitter bile,
Which by the liver severed from the blood,
And striving through the gall-pipe, here unload
Their yellow streams, more to refine the flood;
The complicated glands, in various ranks
Disposed along the neighbouring channel's banks,
By constant weeping mix their watery store
With the chyle's current, and dilute it more;
Th'intestine roads, inflected and inclined,
In various convolutions turn and wind,
That these meanders may the progress stay,
And the descending chyle, by this delay,
May through the milky vessels find its way,
Whose little mouths in the large channel's side
Suck in the flood, and drink the cheering tide.
    These numerous veins (such is the curious frame!)
Receive the pure insinuating stream;
But no corrupt or dreggy parts admit,
To form the blood, or feed the limbs unfit;
Th'intestine spiral fibres these protrude,
And from the winding tubes at length exclude.

SIR RICHARD BLACKMORE (1652 - 1729)
from «Creation: The Digestive System»

Dies mächtige Ferment, sich mit den Teilchen mischend,
es convertiret die gegorne Masse zu *Milch-Speisesaft*;
mit sanft Gewalt, vermittels Contractionen, wird die Speiß,
die angedaute, von den Magenfibern ausgeschieden,
glitscht durch die Mündung rechterhand hinab
durch eine weite Furt (: von jener dependirend);
auf seiner Bahn empfängt der durchgewalkte *Chylus*
alsbald die confluenten Rinnsale von bittrer *Galle*,
die, von der Leber abgespalten aus dem Blut,
sich, durch den Gallengang genötigt, dann des gelben
Liquors entledigt, um das Flüssige noch mehr
zu läutern. Die complicirten Drüsen, in mannigfachen Reihen
entlang benachbarter Kanäle Ufer disponirt,
mischen mit stätem Weinen ihren wässerichten Stoff
mit jenes Chylus' Fluß, verdünnen ihn noch mehr;
die intestinen Wege, gebogen & gekrümmt,
drehn sich und winden sich in vielen Convulsionen
auf daß für Weiterkommen sorge das Mäandern
und, mittels der Verzögerung, der Chylus sich im Abstieg
durch milchige Gefäße bahne seinen Weg,
des kleine Mündungen inseiten der Kanäle
den Brei einsaugen, trinken von der leckern Flut.
   Von unzählbaren Äderchen (: so die curieuse Wandung)
wird der einschleichend reine Brei nun aufgezehrt –
Doch nicht gestattet ists, daß trübe-faule Teilchen
den Gliedern Gifft zuführen, dem Blute bey sich mischen;
des Eingeweids Spiralfibern, sie drücken's weg:
und ausgeschieden wirds der Länge nach aus den gewundnen Tuben.

Thy soul within such silent pomp did keep,
As if humanity were lull'd asleep;
So gentle was thy pilgrimage beneath,
Time's unheard feet scarce make less noise,
Or the soft journey which a planet goes:
Life seem'd all calm as its last breath.
A still tranquillity so hush'd thy breast,
As if some Halcyon were its guest,
And there had built her nest;
It hardly now enjoys a greater rest.

JOHN OLDHAM (1653 - 1683)
A Quiet Soul

Dein Seel bewahrte sich ein derart leises Prunken
Als wäre Menschtum-selbst in Schlaf gesunken
So sacht war deine Pilgerfahrt hienieden
Kaum weicher könn' der Zeit unhörbar Füsze gahn
Kaum sanfter kreisen der Planeten Bahn
Dem letzten Atemzug war Ruhe nur beschieden
Tranquillitas huscht' leicht ob deine Brust
Als wär bey ihr zu Gast ein Halkyon
Und hätt gebauet dort sein Nest
Kaum größern Friedens wird sie sich anjetzt erfreun

123   Far from the parlour have your kitchen placed,
Dainties may in their working be disgraced.
In private draw your poultry, clean your tripe,
And from your eels their slimy substance wipe.
Let cruel offices be done by night,
For they who like the thing abhor the sight.
   Next, let discretion moderate your cost,
And, when you treat, three courses be the most.
Let never fresh machines your pastry try,
Unless grandees or magistrates are by:
Then you may put a dwarf into a pie.
Or, if you'd fright an alderman and mayor,
Within a pasty lodge a living hare;
Then midst their gravest furs shall mirth arise,
And all the Guild pursue with joyful cries.
   'Tis the dessert that graces all the feast,
For an ill end disparages the rest:
A thousand things well done, and one forgot,
Defaces obligation by that blot.
Make your transparent sweet-meats truly nice,
With Indian sugar and Arabian spice:
And let your various creams encircled be
With swelling fruit just ravished from the tree.
Let plates and dishes be from China brought,
With lively paint and earth transparent wrought.

Salon und Küche seien weit geschieden. Man möchte sonst
der Leckerei, wo man sie zubereit', die Gunst entziehn.
Diskret nur wasch die Kutteln und rupfe das Geflügel,
und von den Aalen schab' die schleimige Substanz *privatim* nur.
Grausame Zurichtungen praeferier' *bei Nacht*,
Denn wer die Sache *mag*, der schätzt nicht auch den *Blick*.
  Dann: laß Bescheiden deinen Aufwand mäßigen, und wenn
du einlädst, sei'n drei Gänge 's äußerste.
Laß dein Gebäck nie neue Künstelein erproben,
es sey denn, Edle oder Ratsherrn wärn dabei:
Dann darfst du einen Zwerg in der Pastet' verstecken
oder, willst einen Bürgermeister oder Stadtrat schrecken,
setz in den Auflauf den lebendgen Hasen: dann wird
auch aus dem schwersinnigsten Pelz der Frohsinn steigen,
die ganze Gilde einstimmen mit groß Hallo.
  Es ist der Nachtisch, der das Dinner krönt. Ein schlechtes Ende
kompromittiert den ganzen Rest.
Tausenderlei geraten wohl – und *eins* vergessen: schon
wird die Verbindlichkeit mit einem Schlag zuschanden.
Mach die opaquen Süßigkeiten wirklich hübsch,
mit indianisch Zucker, Gewürzen aus Arabien;
und deine mannigfachen Crèmes, sie sei'n umründet
von schwellndem Obst, frisch von dem Baum geklaubt.
Dein Tafelporzellan, es komm von China,
lebhaft bemalt, durchscheinend zart getöpfert.

The feast now done, discourses are renewed,
And witty arguments with mirth pursued.
The cheerful master, midst his jovial friends,
His glass «to their best wishes» recommends.
The grace-cup follows to his sovereign's health,
And to his country, «plenty, peace, and wealth».
Performing then the piety of grace,
Each man that pleases re-assumes his place;
While at his gate, from such abundant store,
He showers his god-like blessings on the poor.

WILLIAM KING (1663 - 1712)
from «The Art of Cookery»

Man hebt die Tafel auf. Diskurse werden wieder aufgegriffen,
geistreiche Streitgespräche, mit Fröhlichkeit durchmischt.
Der heitre Gastgeber, in mitten der jovialen Freunde,
empfiehlt sein Glas «Auf euer Wohl». Es folgt
der Große Toast «Auf die Gesundheit unsers Königs
und unsers Landes: Wohlstand! Frieden! Heil!»
Nachdem das Dankgebet man dann gesprochen,
nimmt jeder, dem's gefällt, dem Platz nun wieder ein,
dieweil am Torgatter, aus Überflusses Vorrat,
gottähnlich Segen auf die Armen regnet.

Now hardly here and there a hackney-coach
Appearing, showed the ruddy morn's approach.
Now Betty from her master's bed had flown,
And softly stole to discompose her own.
The slipshod prentice from his master's door,
Had pared the dirt, and sprinkled round the floor.
Now Moll had whirled her mop with dexterous airs,
Prepared to scrub the entry and the stairs.
The youth with broomy stumps began to trace
The kennel-edge, where wheels had worn the place.
The smallcoal-man was heard with cadence deep,
'Till drowned in shriller notes of chimney-sweep.
Duns at his lordship's gate began to meet,
And Brickdust Moll had screamed through half a street.
The turnkey now his flock returning sees,
Duly let out a-nights to steal for fees.
The watchful bailiffs take their silent stands,
And school-boys lag with satchels in their hands.

JONATHAN SWIFT (1667 - 1745)
Description of a Morning

Nun, wo schon hie und da ein Droschkenwagen rüttelt,
Kriecht auch der rote Morgen frisch heran.
Aus ihres Meisters Bett ist Betty jetzt entwischt,
Schlüpft sacht davon, in Wirrnis sich zu schütteln.
Der schlampge Lehrling hat von seines Meisters Tür
Den Koth gekratzt & naßgesprengt den Flur.
Nach virtuoser Mode wringt jetzt die Moll den Mop,
Um, hop!, die Diele abzuschrubben & die Trepp.
Mit Besenstumpen fährt der Bursch die Spur entlang,
Die an der Rinnsteinkant' die Räder aufgerührt.
Des Bruchkohlmannes tiefen Ruf hört man; solang
Bis der ertränkt im schrillern Klang des Rauchfangkehrers.
An Seiner Lordschaft Pforte stehn Gläubger zum Empfang,
Und durch die halbe Straß entlang die Brickdust-Molly kreischt.
Nun sieht der Schließer heimkehrn seine Schäflein, die zur Nacht
Ordnungsgemäß sich für ein Scherflein fortzustehln erheischt.
Achtsame Wachtbeamte postiern sich auf den Schanzen,
Saumselig trödeln in die Schul die Rangen mit dem Ranzen.

A BEAUTIFUL YOUNG NYMPH GOING TO BED

Written for the Honour of the fair Sex from Dr Jonathan Swift

Corinna, pride of Drury Lane,
For whom no shepherd sighs in vain;
Never did Covent Garden boast
So bright a battered, strolling toast;
No drunken rake to pick her up,
No cellar where on tick to sup;
Returning at the midnight hour;
Four stories climbing' to her bower;
Then, seated on a three-legged chair,
Takes off her artificial hair:
Now, picking out a crystal eye,
She wipes it clean, and lays it by.
Her eye-brows from a mouse's hide,
Stuck on with art on either side,
Pulls off with care, and first displays 'em,
Then in a play-book smoothly lays 'em.
Now dextrously her plumpers draws,
That serve to fill her hollow jaws.
Untwists a wire; and from her gums
A set of teeth completely comes.
Pulls out the rags contrived to prop
Her flabby dugs and down they drop.
Proceeding on, the lovely goddess
Unlaces next her steel-ribbed bodice;
Which by the operator's skill,
Press down the lumps the hollows fill.

EINE LIEBLICHE JUNGE NYMPHE
BEGIEBT SICH ZU BETTE

Zu Ehren des schönen Geschlechts
verfaßt von Dr Jonathan Swift

CORINNA, *Drury Lane's* Gewinst,
für die kein Schäfer seufzt umsonst
(nie rühmte *Covent Garden* sich
'ner schönren Fetze auf dem Strich),
da kein Saufaus, sie aufzugabeln,
kein Schenkenloch, nen Schluck zu schnabeln,
zur mitternächtgen Stund kehrt heim
vier Stiegen hoch ins Kämmerlein;
bockt sich auf einen Dreibein-Stuhlen,
ihr künstlich Haupthaar abzupulen;
pflückt auß ein Aug, so von Crystallen,
wischt's rein, und läßts aufs Schränkchen fallen;
die Brauen, die von Mäusefellen
kunstreich ob jedem Auge angeklebt,
tut für ein Schauspielbüchel ab sie pellen,
wo sie mittzwischen glatten Seiten abgelegt;
entfernt sich flink die Wattepfropfen,
die ihre hohlen Wangen stopfen;
knüpft auf nen Draht: und ihrem Gaum' entgähnt
ein künstlich Set, komplett bezähnt;
zieht aus den Fetzen, so statt eines Mieder
die schlaffe Zitze stützt. Die hängt nun nieder.
Sodann sieht man das göttlich-holde Wesen
den stahlgerippten Schnürleib lösen,
der nach dem Heilsplan seines Schöpfers soll
das Dicke flacher machen und das Hohle voll.

Up goes her hand, and off she slips
The bolsters that supply her hips.
With gentlest touch, she next explores
Her shankers, issues, running sores,
Effects of many a sad disaster;
And then to each applies a plaster.

But must, before she goes to bed,
Rub off the daubs of white and red;
And smooth the furrows in her front,
With greasy paper stuck upon't.
She takes a bolus ere she sleeps;
And then between two blankets creeps.
With pains of love tormented lies;
Or if she chance to close her eyes,
Of Bridewell and the Compter dreams,
And feels the lash, and faintly screams;
Or, by a faithless bully drawn,
At some hedge-tavern lies in pawn;
Or to Jamaica seems transported,
Alone, and by no planter courted;

Or, near Fleet Ditch's oozy brinks,
Surrounded with a hundred stinks,
Belated, seems on watch to lie,
And snap some cully passing by;
Or, struck with fear, her fancy runs
On watchmen, constables and duns,
From whom she meets with frequent rubs;
But, never from religious clubs;
Whose favour she is sure to find,
Because she pays them all in kind.

Hoch fährt die Hand: die soll entspreiten
die Bolster so die Hüften breiten;
beginnt dann zärtlich zu erkunden
die Pickel, Mitesser & nassen Wunden:
gar manchen traurigen Desasters Würkung.
Auf jedes wird ein Pflästerchen gepappt zur Stärkung.

Doch eh' sie sich ins Bette retirirt,
wird noch der rot & weiße Schminkputz abgeschmiert,
die Furchen in der Stirn geglättet
mit Schmierpapier, das eingefettet;
muß noch ne Doctors-Pille schlucken
und kreucht dann zwischen zween Decken.
Liegt dort in Liebes-Marter-Pein;
doch – schläft sie endlich einmal ein –
spricht TRAUM: *Bridewell, Compter, erschein!*
Sie fühlt die Peitsch', hört leis sich schrein,
sieht sich, verführt von eines losen Luden Lügen,
in ner Provinz-Kaschemm' als Pfandgut liegen,
oder, allein, nach Trinidad verfracht' –
Da ist kein Pflanzer, der den Hof ihr macht!

Sie scheint in *Fleet Ditchs* Schlammgefild,
von hundertley Gestancke eingehüllt,
nachts, abzupassen irgend einen Deppen,
ihn, wer's auch sey, wer just vorbeikömmt, abzuschleppen;
ihr schreckhaft Traumgesichte scheint zu rinnen
zum Konstabler – zum Gläubiger – zur Grünen Minnen
mit denen sie schon manch Rencontre heckte –
doch freilich nie mit einer frommen Sekte
um deren Gunst sie nimmer sich genirt,
da sie sie alle artig financiert.

Corinna wakes. A dreadful sight!
Behold the ruins of the night!
A wicked rat her plaster stole,
Half ate, and dragged it to his hole.
The crystal eye, alas, was missed;
And puss had on her plumpers pissed.
A pigeon picked her issue-peas;
And Shock her tresses filled with fleas.

The nymph, though in this mangled plight,
Must every morn her limbs unite.
But how shall I describe her arts
To recollect the scattered parts?
Or show the anguish, toil, and pain,
Of gathering up herself again?
The bashful muse will never bear
In such a scene to interfere.
Corinna in the morning dizened,
Who sees, will spew; who smells, be poisoned.

JONATHAN SWIFT (1667-1745)
A Beautiful Young Nymph Going to Bed
WRITTEN FOR THE HONOUR OF THE FAIR SEX

Corinn' erwacht: welch gräßlich Blick ihr lacht!
Seht die Ruinen einer Nacht:
Das Pflästerchen, von einer miesen Ratz gemopst,
halb angeknabbert, ins Versteck gestopst;
das Glasaug, wehe! wird vermißt;
Puss hat die Plumper-Pfropfen vollgepißt;
'ne Taube hat die Pickelerbsen aufgepickt
und Shock mit Flöhen ihre Lockenfüll' gefickt.

Die Nymphe muß, also in Fetzen,
sich jedes Glied am Morgen neu zusammensetzen.
Doch wie beschreib ich ihr Geschick,
sich einzusammeln jedes Stück?
Wie zeig die Mühe ich – die Qual – die Wut,
mit der sie selber sich zusammenbaut?
Musa, die bloede, wird nie überwinden
sich einer solchen Scene einzublenden.
Corinna: ausstaffiert, am Morgen:
Wer's riecht, riecht Gift – wer's sieht, muß würgen.

*Epigram on a Lady who shed her water
at seeing the tragedy of Cato;
occasioned by an Epigram on a Lady
who wept at it*

Whilst maudlin Whigs deplore their Cato's fate,
Still with dry eyes the Tory Celia sate:
But though her pride forbade her eyes to flow,
The gushing waters found a vent below.
Though secret, yet with copious streams she mourns,
Like twenty river-gods with all their urns.
Let others screw an hypocritic face,
She shows her grief in a sincerer place!
Here Nature reigns, and passion void of art;
For this road leads directly to the heart.

NICHOLAS ROWE (1674-1718)
*Epigram on a Lady who shed her water at seeing the tragedy of Cato;
occasioned by an Epigram on a Lady who wept at it*

EPIGRAMM/ Auf eine Lady die ihr Wasser ließ,/ als sie der Tragödie CATO beiwohnte/ angelegentlich eines Epigramms auf eine Dame/ die dabey Zähren vergoß.

Dieweil *CATOs* Geschick gerührte Whigs bewimmern,
noch trocknen Auges da die Tory *Celia* saß; doch ob
ihr Stolz gleich wehrte dem Auge feuchtzuschwimmern,
fand weiter unten ein Ventil das rauschend Naß.
Zwar klagt sie heimlich, doch mit reichem Guß,
als wären's zwanzig Tritonen mit Krügen;
laß Andre heucheln ihre Mienen vor Verdruß –
Sie zeigt den Gram an einer Stell die kann nicht lügen:
Hier führt *NATUR* das Scepter, ungekünstelt Schmerz,
denn diese Straße führt *directe* in das Herz.

127 . . . . See! there she goes,
She reels along, and by her gait betrays
Her inward weakness. See, how black she looks!
The sweat, that clogs th'obstructed pores, scarce leaves
A languid scent. And now in open view
See, see, she flies! each eager hound exerts
His utmost speed, and stretches every nerve.
How quick she turns! their gaping jaws eludes,
And yet a moment lives; till, round enclosed
By all the greedy pack, with infant screams
She yields her breath, and there reluctant dies.

So when the furious Bacchanals assailed
Thracian Orpheus, poor ill-fated bard!
Loud was the cry; hills, woods, and Hebrus' banks,
Returned their clamorous rage; distressed he flies,
Shifting from place to place, but flies in vain;
For eager they pursue, till panting, faint,
By noisy multitudes o'erpowered, he sinks
To the relentless crowd a bleeding prey.

.... : Da!: Hier geht ihr Weg –
Sieh, dort taumelt sie lang, ihre Gangart verrät
Die innerliche Schwäche. Sieh, wie schwarz ihr Blick!
Der Schweiß, der die verklebten Poren stopft, läßt schwach
Zurück nur ihre Witterung. Und hier in freier Sicht:
Sieh, wie sie flieht! Ein Äußerstes an Eifer
Und jeden Nerv spannt itzt die geiferige Meute.
Wie quick sie Haken schlägt!, entkommt noch einen Augenblick
Den klaffenden Gebissen – lebt!, bis eingekesselt rings
Von all dem giergen Pack, mit Kinderkreischen
Haucht sie den Odem aus und stirbt im Widerstreben.

So griffen an die wütenden Mänaden
Den armen Bard': den thrazischen Orfeo!
Laut war ihr Schrei; Wald, Hügel, Hebrus' Ufer
Erzitterten vor ihrer Wut; er flieht in Not,
Springt hierhin, dorthin, doch er fleucht umsonst,
Denn heftger die Verfolgung nur; bis keuchend, matt
Von lautgewalter Masse überwältigt, sinkt er hin
Der gnadenlosen Meut zur blutbetreuften Beute.

The huntsman now, a deep incision made,
Shakes out with hands impure, and dashes down
Her reeking entrails and yet quivering heart.
These claim the pack, the bloody perquisite
For all their toils. Stretched on the ground she lies
A mangled corpse; in her dim glaring eyes
Cold Death exults, and stiffens every limb.
Awed by the threatening whip, the furious hounds
Around her bay; or at their master's foot,
Each happy favourite courts his kind applause,
With humble adulation cowering low.
All now is joy. . . . .

WILLIAM SOMERVILLE (1675-1742)
from «The Chase»

Itzt sticht der Waidmann einen tiefen Schnitt,
Schüttelt und wirft aus sudeligen Händen
Die dampfenden Gedärme, das noch pulsiernde Herz.
Das ist des Rudels Anspruch, der blutige Gewinst
Für ihre ganze Müh. Zu Boden hingestreckt liegt sie
Als Leiche ausgefleischt; in ihrem trüben Blicke stiert des
Kalten Tods frohlockend Triumphieren. Starr wird ein jedes Glied.
Rings um sie belln, der drohnden Peitsch' bewußt,
Der wilden Meute Hunde, und seinem Herrn bei Fuß
Scharwenzelt jeder Liebling geduckt um seine Gunst
Mit Speichellecken demütig & niedrig.
Der Rest ist Freude. . . . .

ELEGY
To an Old Beauty

In vain, poor nymph, to please our youthful sight
You sleep in cream and frontlets all the night,
Your face with patches soil, with paint repair,
Dress with gay gowns, and shade with foreign hair.
If truth, in spite of manners, must be told,
Why really fifty-five is something old.
   Once you were young; or one, whose life's so long
She might have borne my mother, tells me wrong.
And once, since Envy's dead before you die,
The women own, you played a sparkling eye,
Taught the light foot a modish little trip,
And pouted with the prettiest purple lip.
   To some new charmer are the roses fled,
Which blew, to damask all thy cheek with red;
Youth calls the Graces there to fix their reign,
And airs by thousands fill their easy train.
So parting summer bids her flowery prime
Attend the sun to dress some foreign clime,
While withering seasons in succession, here,
Strip the gay gardens, and deform the year.
   But thou, since Nature bids, the world resign,
'Tis now thy daughter's daughter's time to shine.
With more address, or such as pleases more,
She runs her female exercises o'er,
Unfurls or closes, raps or turns the fan,
And smiles, or blushes at the creature man.
With quicker life, as gilded coaches pass,
In sidling courtesy she drops the glass.
With better strength, on visit-days she bears

ELEGIE
auf eine verblichene Schönheit

Vergebens, arme Nymphe, schläfst, unsrer JugendSicht
zu schmeicheln, du alle Nacht mit Stirnband und in Crèm gepicht,
klebst das Gesicht mir Pflästerchen, willst es mit Tünche wahren,
trägst fröhlichbunte Röcke, deckst dich mit fremden Haaren.
Ich darf doch ehrlich sein? – auch wenn der Anstand mir iezt grollt –
und sagen: ey, funfundfunzig ist ein bißchen alt.
 Einst warst du jung – wenn eine, die so lang gelebt
daß sie mein Muttersmutterl sein könnt, mir keine Lügen webt –,
einst ließest du (die sterben ja: der Weiber Neidgefühlen,
noch eh *du* stirbst) ein blitzend Auge spielen,
lehrtest die leichten Füß den modisch TrippelLauf
und warfst zum Schmollmündchen die schönsten Purperlippen auf.
 Zu einer neuen Zaubrin Reiz die Ros nun flieht,
sie, die einst deine Wangen zu damaszieren blüht':
dort ruft die Grazien die Jugend an, die solln ihr Szepter schwingen,
und den beschwingten Reien rührt tausendfältig Singen.
So heißt der Sommer seine Blütenzier, im Scheiden
der Sonne aufzuwarten, in fremdem Clima sich zu spreiten;
dieweil nun *hier* es folgt, daß dürrende Gezeiten
das Jahr entstelln, den heitren Gartenschmuck entkleiden.
 Dir aber, da's *Natur* so will: laß dir die Welt verdunkeln –
s'ist nun der Tochterstochter Zeit, zu funkeln.
Mit besserer Manier – weil's mehr plaisiert –
hat sie die Frauenzimmerkunst studiert,
enfaltet sie den Fächer, klopftklapptundwendet ihn,
errötet oder lächelt dem Lebewesen ‹Mann›.
Mit mehr Behendigkeit näh'rt sie sich wenn der goldenen Phaeton
vorbey rollt, höfisch von der Seit, entsinkt ihr das Lorgnon.
Mit bessrer Kraft kann sie, an Visitirens Tagen,

To mount her fifty flights of ample stairs.
Her mien, her shape, her temper, eyes, and tongue,
Are sure to conquer—for the rogue is young:
And all that's madly wild, or oddly gay,
We call it only pretty Fanny's way.
   Let time, that makes you homely, make you sage,
The sphere of wisdom, is the sphere of age.
   'Tis true, when beauty dawns with early fire,
And hears the flattering tongues of soft desire,
If not from virtue, from its gravest ways
The soul with pleasing avocation strays.
But beauty gone, 'tis easier to be wise;
As harpers better by the loss of eyes.
Henceforth retire, reduce your roving airs,
Haunt less the plays, and more the public prayers,
Reject the Mechlin head, and gold brocade,
Go pray, in sober Norwich crepe arrayed.
Thy pendant diamonds let thy Fanny take
(Their trembling lustre shows how much you shake);
Or bid her wear thy necklace rowed with pearl,
You'll find your Fanny an obedient girl.
So for the rest, with less encumbrance hung,
You walk through life, unmingled with the young,
And view the shade and substance, as you pass,
With joint endeavour trifling at the glass,
Or Folly dressed, and rambling all her days,
To meet her counterpart, and grow by praise:
Yet still sedate yourself, and gravely plain,
You neither fret, nor envy at the vain.
   'Twas thus, if man with woman we compare,
The wise Athenian crossed a glittering fair,
Unmoved by tongue and sights, he walked the place,

die fünfzig Stufen ihrer Treppenfluchten steigen.
Ihr Antlitz, Form, Gemüth, die Augen und die Zung:
sie garantiern Succeß, denn diese Dirn ist *jung*;
und alles was schräg-aufgedreht, exzentrisch & agil,
das nenn'n wir nur den *Pretty Fanny Stil.*
 Zeit, die dich unschön macht: sie mach' dich weise –
der Weisheit Sphäre ist die Sphär' der Greise.
 Es stimmt: wenn Schönheits Feuer früh erglimmt,
von sanften Sehnsüchten die Schmeichelwort' vernimmt,
dann (zwar von Tugend nicht, so doch) von schwersten Wegen
weicht ab die Seele in ergötzlichem Zerstreun.
Doch ist die Schönheit hin – ist's leichter, weis zu sein,
wie der Verlust des Augenlichts dem Harpfner kömmt entgegen.
Zieh dich zurück denn, reducier die Schwärmlichkeit!
Such weniger die Oper heim – mehr öffentlichs Gebet!
Verschmäh die Brüssler Spitzen und den GoldBrokat!
Geh beten, in nüchtern' Norwich-Krepp gekleidt!
Laß deine Fanny dein Brillantgehäng ausführen
(sein Zitterglanz bespräch nur deinen Tatterich);
heiß sie, mit deiner Perlenkette sich zu zieren:
wirst deine Fanny ungehorsam finden nicht.
Was bliebe dann? – Mit Schwernis kaum behungen
gingst du durchs Leben, hieltst dich fern von Jungen,
betrachtet'st durchs Lorgnon, in dem Vorübergehn,
wie *Schatten & Substanz* sich um vereinte Läppischkeit bemühn,
wie *Narrheit*, aufgedonnert, ihren Tag durchtobt,
zu treffen ihr Pendant – zu schwelln noch, wenn gelobt.
Doch ruhig bey dir selbst, gesetzt & schlicht,
zernagtest nicht dein Herz, neidet'st die Eitlen nicht.
 'S war so (wenn Mann & Frau man in Vergleichung läßt):
Der Weise von Athen kam einst zu einem fashionablen Fest
und schritt hindurch, ließ nicht bewegen sich von Worten oder Blick,

Through tape, toys, tinsel, gimp, perfume, and lace;
Then bends from Mars's hill his awful eyes,
And—«What a world I never want?» he cries:
But cries unheard: for Folly will be free.
So parts the buzzing gawdy crowd and he:
As careless he for them, as they for him:
He wrapped in wisdom, and they whirled by whim.

THOMAS PARNELL (1679-1718)
An Elegy, To an Old Beauty

durch Borten Band & Tand, Brokat Parfum & Chic,
beugt sich vom Martis Hügel, die Augen schmerzgerollt,
und brüllt zurück «Was für ne Welt, die ich so nie gewollt!»
Der Schrei blieb ungehört. Frei will die Narrheit sein.
So kömmts, daß sich die wuselfrohe Schar und er entzwein:
Er scheert sich nicht um sie – sie nicht um ihn –
In Weisheit eingewickelt: er – sie: wirbelspinnt im Spleen.

129 Strange the formation of the eely race,
That know no sex, yet love the close embrace.
Their folded lengths they round each other twine,
Twist amorous knots, and slimy bodies join;
Till the close strife brings off a frothy juice,
The seed that must the wriggling kind produce.
Regardless they their future offspring leave,
But porous sands the spumy drops receive.
That genial bed impregnates all the heap,
And little eelets soon begin to creep.
Half-fish, half-slime they try their doubtful strength,
And slowly trail along their wormy length.

*

Justly might female tortoises complain,
To whom enjoyment is the greatest pain,
They dread the trial, and foreboding hate
The growing passion of the cruel mate.
He amorous pursues, they conscious fly
Joyless caresses, and resolved deny.
Since partial Heaven has thus restrained the bliss,
The males they welcome with a closer kiss,
Bite angry, and reluctant hate declare.
The tortoise-courtship is a state of war.
Eager they fight, but with unlike design,
Males to obtain, and females to decline.

Seltsam die Stellungen der Gattung ‹Aale›,
Die, des Geschlechts unkundig, doch eng Umarmung lieben,
Sich längsseits eingezwirbelt rund umeinander schmiegen,
Zu Amorsknoten schlingen, sich schleymig wohnen bey,
Bis dieses Schlachtgekringel herfürbringt schaumgen Brei:
Die Saat, die ihre Schlängelbrut soll zeugen. –
Der künftgen Sprößlinge mißachtend, ergreifen sie die Flucht,
Doch die geschäumten Tropfen empfängt poröser Sand:
Dies ingeniöse Bett befrucht' die ganze Menge,
Bis bald die kleinen Schlingel schon krepeln umeinand;
Halb Fisch – halb Schleim (noch zweifelhaft) erproben
Sie ihre Kraft, und schleichen lang in Wurmeslänge.

*

Zu Recht dürft sich das Schildkrötweib beklagen
Für die jedwede Lustbarkeit ein einzig Mißbehagen.
Sie fürchten die Belästigung und hassen ahnend schon
Des grausen Partners schwellende Passion.
Der wirbt verliebt – sie fliehn im Wissen
Vor lustlos Schnäbelein, und sagen «Nein!» entschlossen.
Da der parteische Himmel das Glück also verschlossen:
Die Männchen, welche sie mit Küssen «Willkomm!» heißen,
Beißen im Zorn sie und erklärn ihr ungeneigtes Hassen.
Die Schildkröthochzeit ist ein Kriegszustand.
Grimmer der Kampf, doch mit ungleichem Plan:
Das Männchen soll obsiegen – das Weibchen unterliegen.

The conflict lasts, till these by strength o'ercome
All sorrowing yield to the resistless doom.
Not like a bride, but pensive captive, led
To the loathed duties of an hated bed.
The seal, and tortoise copulate behind
Like earth-bred dogs, and are not soon disjoined;
But secret ties the passive couple bind.

*

WILLIAM DIAPER (1685-1717)
from «Oppian's Halieutics»

Der Streit hält an, bis überwältigt sie
Ins Unvermeidliche sich gramvoll schickt
Nicht gleich der Braut, nein, als Gefangene, gebückt
Ins Ekeljoch des Ehebetts.
Schildkröt wie Robben copulirn von hinten,
Gleich landgebornen Hunden, sind bald nicht auseinander:
Passives Paar, gebunden von insgeheimen Banden.

*

ON A LADY
PREACHED INTO A COLIC
by One of her Lovers

Bellona the fierce, who held man in disdain,
And despised her own sex, to whom love could give pain;
Went to church, in defiance, and met with her fate,
From a pulpited Cupid, who there lay in wait:
But her head was so armed, and so hard was her heart,
That his arrows rebounded, in scorn of his art,
Then, with voice of revenge, he exalted his pipes,
Shot in spleen at her belly, and gave her the gripes.
Thus I wound her, cried he, in a whimsical place,
'Cause she covers kind wishes, with haughty grimace.
Let her now twist and screw — 'twill but fasten the dart;
She has love in her bowels, though she hates in her heart.

AARON HILL (1685-1750)
On a Lady, Preached into a Colic, by One of her Lovers

AUF EINE LADY
DER MAN DIE KOLIK GEPREDIGT
von einem ihrer Anbeter

Die grimme Bellona, die auf Männer nur speit,
ihr Geschlecht geringschätzte: Liebe brächt ja «nur Leid»,
ging zum Trotz in die Kirche, und ihr Schicksal beschloß,
daß Cupido, lauernd, von der Canzel sie schoß.
Doch so hart war ihr Herz und ihr Sinn eisenbrav,
daß die Pfeile abprallten, und keiner sie traf.
Revanche im Mund, hob er's Blasrohr-Visier,
schoß im Grimm in den Bauch: 's machte Bauchgrimmen ihr.
Ha: getroffen! rief er, ja die Stelle macht Spass,
weil sie Wünsche verdränget mit stolzer Grimass'.
Um so fester der Pfeil, je mehr windt' sich das Weib:
Denn sie hasset im Herzen, doch sie liebet im Leib.

Newgate's Garland;
BEING
A NEW BALLAD, SHOWING
HOW MR JONATHAN WILD'S THROAT
WAS CUT FROM EAR TO EAR WITH A PENKNIFE,
BY MR BLAKE, ALIAS BLUESKIN, THE BOLD
HIGHWAYMAN,
AS HE
STOOD HIS TRIAL IN THE OLD-BAILEY, 1725

Ye gallants of Newgate, whose fingers are nice,
In diving in pockets, or cogging of dice;
Ye sharpers so rich, who can buy off the noose;
Ye honester poor rogues, who die in your shoes;
Attend and draw near,
Good news ye shall hear,
How Jonathan's throat was cut from ear to ear;
How Blueskin's sharp penknife hath set you at ease,
And every man round me may rob, if he please.

When to the Old Bailey this Blueskin was led,
He held up his hand, his indictment was read,
Loud rattled his chains, near him Jonathan stood,
For full forty pounds was the price of his blood.
Then, hopeless of life,
He drew his penknife,
And made a sad widow of Jonathan's wife.
But forty pounds paid her, her grief shall appease,
And every man round me may rob, if he please.

NEWGATE'S GARLAND
Das ist
Ein neue BALLAD, zeigend
wie Mr JONATHAN WILD's Kehl
von Ohr zu Ohr mit einem FEDERMESSER geschnitten ward
von Mr BLAKE/ alias BLUESKIN/ dem kühnen Highway-Mann
als er
A. D. 1725 im OLD-BAILEY vor Gericht stand
(nach der Melodie von THE CUT-Purse)

Ihr Cavaliere von Newgate, deren Finger so klug
Beim TaschenEintauchen, beim WürfelBetrug,
Ihr Ganoven so reich, daß den Henker ihr schmiert,
Ihr Edelhalunken, so in Schuhen crepirt,
Paßt auf & kommt nähr,
Ihr hört gute Mär,
Wie Jonathans Kehle ritsch-ratsch! von Ohr zu Ohr,
Daß Blueskins scharf Messer euch Leichterung sey,
Und jeder darf stehln hier, er sei nur so frei!

Als jener Blueskin zum Old Bailey geführt,
Da schwört seine Hand & die Anklag man hört,
Laut rasselt seine Kett', bei ihm Jonathan stund,
Denn der Preis auf sein Blut war gut vierzige £;
Müd an Leben & Leib
Zog er's Messers Geschneid,
Macht ne traurige Witwe aus Jonathans Weib,
Gab die vierzig £ ihr, ihren Gram zu versöhn'n –
Und jedermann um mich darf stehln, bit-te-schön!

Some say there are courtiers of highest renown,
Who steal the king's gold, and leave him but a crown;
Some say there are peers, and some parliament-men,
Who meet once a year, to rob courtiers again:
Let them all take their swing,
To pillage the king,
And get a blue ribbon instead of a string.
Now Blueskin's sharp penknife hath set you at ease,
And every man round me may rob, if he please.

Knaves of old, to hide guilt by their cunning inventions,
Called briberies grants, and plain robberies pensions;
Physicians and lawyers (who take their degrees
To be learnèd rogues) called their pilfering, fees:
Since this happy day,
Now every man may
Rob (as safe as in office) upon the highway.
For Blueskin's sharp penknife hath set you at ease,
And every man round me may rob, if he please.

Some cheat in the customs, some rob the excise,
But he who robs both is esteeméd most wise.
Churchwardens, too prudent to hazard the halter,
As yet only venture to steal from the altar:
But now to get gold,
They may be more bold,
And rob on the highway, since Jonathan's cold.
For Blueskin's sharp penknife hath set you at ease,
And every man round me may rob, if he please.

JOHN GAY (1685 - 1732)
Newgate's Garland

Man sagt, es gäb Hofleut von höchstem Ansehn,
Die des Königs Gold klaun, nur die Krone verschmähn,
Man sagt, es gäb Oberhaus-, Unterhausleut,
Treffen 1 mal im Jahr sich, bestehln die Hofleut erneut: –
Laßt doch allen den Swing,
Zu plündern den King,
N Ordensband kriegen anstelle ner Schling',
Blueskins Federmesser bringt euch Freiheit zutag,
Und jedermann um mich darf stehln, wenn er mag.

Einst nannten (zu verschleirn ihre Tricks, Inventionen)
Schurken *Zuschuß* ihr Schmiergeld und ihr Rauben *Pensionen*;
Doctoren & Richter (die die Robe nur kriegen
Um studiert zu betrügen) nannten Beute *Bezüge*;
Seit dem glücklichen Tag
Nun jedermann mag
Klaun – sicher, wie im Dienst – auf Straße & Weg,
Denn Blueskins Federmesser macht euch aufatmen schier –
Und jedermann um mich darf stehln, bit-te-sehr.

Manche mausen beim Zoll, mancher mopst die Akzis,
Doch wer beide bestiehlt, den schätzt man höchst weis.
Hochwürden, zu klug um den Strang zu riskiern,
Erlaubt vom Altar sich zu ex-pro-pri-iern;
Doch zu kommen ans Gold,
Könn' sie dreister sein bald,
Und klaun auf der Straß nun, da Jonathan kalt.
Denn Blueskins scharf Messer euch frei anheim stellt:
Jeder stehle & raube nur, was das Zeug hält!

Where the mob gathers, swiftly shoot along,
Nor idly mingle in the noisy throng:
Lured by the silver hilt, amid the swarm,
The subtle artist will thy side disarm.
Nor is the flaxen wig with safety worn;
High on the shoulder, in a basket borne,
Lurks the sly boy, whose hand, to rapine bred,
Plucks off the curling honours of thy head.
Here dives the skulking thief, with practised sleight,
And unfelt fingers make thy pocket light.
Where's now the watch, with all its trinkets, flown?
And thy late snuff-box is no more thy own.
But, lo! his bolder thefts some tradesman spies,
Swift from his prey the scudding lurcher flies;
Dexterous he 'scapes the coach with nimble bounds,
Whilst every honest tongue «stop thief!» resounds.
So speeds the wily fox, alarmed by fear,
Who lately filched the turkey's callow care;
Hounds following hounds grow louder as he flies,
And injured tenants join the hunter's cries.
Breathless, he stumbling falls. Ill-fated boy!
Why did not honest work thy youth employ?
Seized by rough hands, he's dragged amid the rout,
And stretched beneath the pump's incessant spout:
Or, plunged in miry ponds, he gasping lies,
Mud chokes his mouth, and plasters o'er his eyes.

*

Beschleunige die Schritte, wo sich zum Mob der Haufe ballt!
Misch dich nicht müßig in die rohe Menge!
Es lockt der Silberknauf: in dem Gedränge
wird vom subtilen Künstler dir der Degen abgeschnallt.
Auch sitzt die flachsene Perucke nie ganz fest:
Auf Schultern hoch, im Korbe lurend, duckt
der pfiffge Knirps, des raub-erzogne Hand
dir die gelockte Würd' vom Kopfe pflückt.
Hier tastet mit geübter Schläue der verschlagne Dieb,
und ungefühlte Finger erleichtern deine Tasche.
Wohin sind Uhr & Berlocken entschwunden?
Die neue Tabatière ist auch nicht mehr dein eigen!
Doch sieh: ein Händler merkt, wie man ihn dreist bestiehlt!
Flink läßt der Fiesler seine Beute fahren! – : und im Wetzen
weicht knapp der Kutsch' er aus, mit wieselschnellen Sätzen;
«Haltet den Dieb!» tönt jeder biedre Mund.
So schießt der Schlaufuchs hin, von Furcht entsetzt,
da er des Puters neugeschlüpfte Brut entwand,
und immer lauter hetzt ihn Hund auf Hund
und in den Jagdruf stimmen Pächter ein, vergrätzt.
Er, außer Atem, strauchelt – : fällt! Unsel'ger Bengel!
Was wähltest du, so jung, nicht bieder Tagewerk?
Die Rotte schleift ihn, der gepackt von Händen stark:
und zwangsgetäuft unter dem Pumpenschwengel
oder in Pfützenschlamm getunkt, liegt keuchend er;
Koth stopft den Mund ihm und verklebt die Augen.

*

Where Lincoln's Inn, wide space, is railed around,
Cross not with venturous step; there oft is found
The lurking thief, who, while the daylight shone,
Made the walls echo with his begging tone:
That crutch, which late compassion moved, shall wound
Thy bleeding head, and fell thee to the ground.
Though thou art tempted by the link-man's call,
Yet trust him not along the lonely wall;
In the mid-way he'll quench the flaming brand,
And share the booty with the pilfering band.
Still keep the public streets, where oily rays,
Shot from the crystal lamp, o'erspread the ways.

*

Who can the various city frauds recite,
With all the petty rapines of the night?
Who now the guinea-dropper's bait regards,
Tricked by the sharper's dice, or juggler's cards?
Why should I warn thee, ne'er to join the fray,
Where the sham quarrel interrupts the way?
Lives there in these our days so soft a clown,
Braved by the bully's oaths, or threatening frown?
I need not strict enjoin the pocket's care,
When from the crowded play thou lead'st the fair;
Who has not here or watch or snuff-box lost,
Or handkerchiefs that India's shuttle boast?

Kreuz' *Lincoln's Inn*, weitläuficht abgezäunt,
nicht mit riskantem Schritt! Man findt
da oft den LauerDieb, der wohl bei Tagesschein
läßt von den Mauern widerhalln des Bettlers Litanein –
Doch just die Krücke, die dein Mitleid rührte, prägt
ein Haupt voll Blut und Wunden: zu Boden sie dich schlägt!
Der Ruf des Fackelträgers möchte dich verleiten –
doch trau-schau-wem: entlang verlassner Wand,
auf halbem Weg, löscht er der Flamme Brand ...
und teilt den Raub sich mit den Co-Banditen.
Halt an die öffentlichen Straßen dich, wo Öl-Laternen
mit Strahlen, so crystall-zerstreut, den Weg besternen.

*

Wer zählt die vielen City-Trügereien auf
mit all den kleinen Räubereien im Verlauf
der Nacht? Wen falsche Würfel & gezinkte Karten narren,
paßt der noch auf des *Guinea-Droppers* Köder?
Was soll ich dich noch warnen: *nie* den Kopf
in Menschenauflauf stecken, wo Scheinkämpfe den Weg versperren?
Gibts denn heut noch nur *einen* schwachköpfichten Tropf,
der sich an Drohgebärd & Raufbolds Schwur ‹bewährt›?
Muß ich noch mahnen?: auf die Tasch' zu passen,
wenn deine Schöne du aus vollem Schauspielhaus geleitst:
Wen hat noch nicht die Uhr, die Tabatière verlassen
oder das Taschentuch, das Indiens Weberschiffchen ehrt?

O! may thy virtue guard thee through the roads
Of Drury's mazy courts, and dark abodes!
The harlots' guileful paths, who nightly stand
Where Catharine Street descends into the Strand!
Say, vagrant Muse, their wiles and subtle arts,
To lure the strangers' unsuspecting hearts:
So shall our youth on healthful sinews tread,
And city cheeks grow warm with rural red.
'Tis she who nightly strolls with sauntering pace,
No stubborn stays her yielding shape embrace;
Beneath the lamp her tawdry ribbons glare,
The new-scoured manteau, and the slattern air;
High-draggled petticoats her travels show,
And hollow cheeks with artful blushes glow;
With flattering sounds she soothes the credulous ear,
«My noble captain! charmer! love! my dear!»
In riding-hood near tavern-doors she plies,
Or muffled pinners hide her livid eyes.
With empty bandbox she delights to range,
And feigns a distant errand from the 'Change;
Nay, she will oft the quaker's hood profane,
And trudge demure the rounds of Drury Lane.
She darts from sarsenet ambush wily leers,
Twitches thy sleeve, or with familiar airs
Her fan will pat thy cheek; these snares disdain,
Nor gaze behind thee, when she turns again.

JOHN GAY (1685 - 1732)
from «Trivia»: Theves & Whores

O leite dich die Tugend durch die Gassen
der labyrinth'schen Höfe *Drury's*, seine finstren Löcher:
Der Hure Schleichpfade, die nächtlich ihren Stand
da hat, wo *Cathrin Street* hinabführt in den *Strand*.
O weltgewandte Muse: nenn die subtilen Tricks, den Amorsköcher,
die dort des Fremden arglos Herz verleiten:
daß auf gesunden Wegen unsre Jugend schreite,
mit rustikaler Wärme die City-Wang' sich röte.
'S ist die, die nachts mit Bummeln fürder schlendert;
kein Stützkorsett umfaßt den willfährigen Leib;
Im Lampenschein glitzt: Flitterputz, bebändert –
der frischgereinigte Manteau – das Air des Schlumpenweibs.
Verschmutzte Unterröck' zeig'n ihre weiten Wege
und hohle Wangen glühn in kunstrot Fieber
und dem geneigten Ohr kömmt Schmeichellaut entgegen:
«Mein nobler Captain! Na, wie wär's, du Lieber?»
Im Reit-Cape streunt sie bei der Schenkentür,
schaut blei-lidrig aus der umhüllten Haub' herfür;
gern zieht sie mit der leeren Putzschachtel entlang:
fingiert (vom '*Change*:) den weiten Botengang;
oft wird des Quäkers Hut sie profanieren
und ehrbar-sittsamlich um *Drury Lane* spaziren.
Aus Sarsenet-Versteck blinzt ihr verschmiztes Schmachten,
sie zupft am Ärmel dich, oder, ganz im Vertrauen,
patscht mit dem Fächer deine Wang'. Die Fallstricke verachte!
Wags nicht, wenn sie den Kopf herwider wendt, zurückzuschauen!

133   Words are like leaves; and where they most abound,
      Much fruit of sense beneath is rarely found.
      False eloquence, like the prismatic glass,
      Its gaudy colours spreads on every place;
      The face of Nature we no more survey,
      All glares alike, without distinction gay:
      But true expression, like th'unchanging sun,
      Clears, and improves whate'er it shines upon,
      It gilds all objects, but it alters none.
      Expression is the dress of thought, and still
      Appears more decent, as more suitable;
      A vile conceit in pompous words expressed,
      Is like a clown in regal purple dressed:
      For different styles with different subjects sort,
      As several garbs, with country, town, and court.

                            *

Wörter sind Blättern gleich. Wo diese abundant,
reift drunter kaum viel Sinn.
Falsche Beredsamkeit will gleich dem Prisma streuen
auf jede Stelle ein verlogen Bunt.
Das Antlitz der Natur ermessen wir nicht mehr:
Alls glänzet gleich – ohn Unterscheiden – leer.
Doch wahrer Ausdruck, wie die Sonn unwandelbar,
klärt und veredelt, was er auch bescheint,
vergüldet alle Gegenstände – ändert keinen.
Ausdruck ist des Gedankens Kleid. Und, traun,
scheint um so schlichter, desto passender zu sitzen.
Ein schlechtes Denken, das mit expressiver Hitzen
gesagt, ist wie der Königshermelin am täppschen Clown.
Ein jedes Thema seinen eignen Stil sich sucht
gleichwie mit je verschiedner Tracht Stadt, Hof & Land sich tucht.

*

But most by numbers judge a poet's song,
And smooth or rough, with them, is right or wrong;
In the bright Muse though thousand charms conspire,
Her voice is all these tuneful fools admire;
Who haunt Parnassus but to please their ear,
Not mend their minds; as some to church repair,
Not for the doctrine, but the music there.
These equal syllables alone require,
Though oft the ear the open vowels tire;
While expletives their feeble aid do join;
And ten low words oft creep in one dull line;
While they ring round the saine unvaried chimes,
With sure returns of still expected rhymes.
Where'er you find «the cooling western breeze»,
In the next line, it «whispers through the trees»:
If crystal streams «with pleasing murmurs creep»,
The reader's threatened (not in vain) with «sleep».
Then, at the last and only couplet fraught
With some unmeaning thing they call a thought,
A needless Alexandrine ends the song,
That, like a wounded snake, drags its slow length along.

ALEXANDER POPE (1688 - 1744)
from «An Essay on Criticism»

Anhand von *Zahlen* richt' die Zeilen im Gedicht!
‹Ungrade› oder ‹grade› heißt ‹schlecht› hier oder ‹recht›.
Auch wenn bei *Musa* tausend Zauber sich verschwören,
scheint ihre *Stimme* alles, was klangverliebte Narrn verehren.
Wer den Parnaß erklimmt, dem Ohr nur zu gefallen,
tut seinem Geiste keinen Dienst: gleich jenen, die zur Kirche wallen,
weil's da Musike gibt, nicht für die Lehr'.
Der Sylben Gleichmaaß nur begehr'!
Wiewohl das Ohr oft müd von offenen Vokalen,
dieweil zu schwacher Hülf Füllworte eilen:
zehn stumpfe Worte dümpeln oft in *einer* dumpfen Zeilen.
So versfüßelt's dahin: des Rhythmus leyerichter Seim
und wes man harrt, das kömmt denn auch: der ewiggleiche Reim:
Wo immer steht *the cooling western breeze*,
folgt garantiert *it whispers through the trees*.
Wenn die kristallnen Bäche *with pleasing murmurs creep*,
droht man dem Leser (nicht umsonst) mit *sleep*.
Dann, bei dem letzten, einzigen Reimpaar
mit Sinnlosem behäuft, das sie auch noch ‹Gedanke› nennen,
endet ein unnützer Alexandriner den Gesang,
der wie die kranke Schlang/ kreucht schleichend-matt entlang.

P. Ask you what provocation I have had?
The strong antipathy of good to bad.
When truth or virtue an affront endures,
Th'affront is mine, my friend, and should be yours.
Mine, as a foe professed to false pretence,
Who think a coxcomb's honour like his sense;
Mine, as a friend to every worthy mind;
And mine as man, who feels for all mankind.
   F. You're strangely proud.
   P. So proud, I am no slave:
So impudent, I own myself no knave:
So odd, my country's ruin makes me grave.
Yes, I am proud; I must be proud to see
Men not afraid of God, afraid of me:
Safe from the bar, the pulpit, and the throne,
Yet touched and shamed by ridicule alone.
O sacred weapon! left for Truth's defence,
Sole dread of folly, vice, and insolence!
To all but Heaven-directed hands denied,
The Muse may give thee, but the gods must guide:
Reverent I touch thee! but with honest zeal;
To rouse the watchmen of the public weal,
To virtue's work provoke the tardy Hall,
And goad the prelate slumbering in his stall.
Ye tinsel insects! whom a Court maintains,
That counts your beauties only by your stains,
Spin all your cobwebs o'er the eye of day!
The Muse's wing shall brush you all away:
All his Grace preaches, all his lordship sings,
All that makes saints of queens, and gods of kings,
All, all but truth, drops dead-born from the press,
Like the last Gazette, or the last address.

ALEXANDER POPE (1688 - 1744)
from »Epilogue to the Satires»

P.: Du fragst den Ansporn meiner Wut? – :
Die Feindschaft zwischen Schlecht und Gut!
Wenn Wahrheit/Tugend leiden Pein,
gilt der Affront auch mir, mein Freund, und sollte deiner sein.
Mir, dem erklärten Feind unechter Prätension
die ihrem Narrsinn setzt die rechte Geckenkron';
Mir, jeden edlen Geistes ächtem Freund;
und mir als Mensch, der um die ganze Menschheit weint.
F.: Bist seltsam stolz.
P.: So stolz, daß ich nicht Sklave bin;
so kühn, daß ich verzicht auf Schurkensinn;
und blöd genug, daß mich bewegt meins Vaterlands Ruin.
Ja, ich bin stolz! *Muß* stolz sein im Erleben
daß Menschen nicht vor Gott – vor mir nur beben
der ich vor Kanzel, Thron & Richterstuhl sicher bin –
verwundt-beschämt vom Ridiküln allein.
O letztes frommes Schwert, das noch die Wahrheit kämpfet frei:
des Dummen, Bösen, Unverschämten einzge Scheu!
Der Hand, die nicht der Himmel führt, wirds nicht geschenkt;
Die Muse leihts dir – doch von Göttern wirds gelenkt.
Ehrfürchtig schwing ich dich, mit aufrechtem Appell
: die Wächter öffentlicher Wohlfahrt wachzuschütteln
: zum Tugendwerk das träge Rathaus aufzurütteln
: zu pieken das Prälatschwein, das grunzt im Chorherrnstall.
Die funkelnden Insekten, die da bei Hofe flunkern
der ihre Schönheit zählt nach ihren bunten Klunkern:
wollt nur eur Spinngeweb auf Tages Lider legen – :
Der Musen Schwinge soll hinweg euch fegen!
Was SEine Gnaden predigt – wann SEine Lordschaft lacht –
was Götter macht aus Köni*gen*, aus *-ginnen* Heil'ge macht –
Alls, alles, nur nicht Wahrheit, fällt totgeboren aus der Presse
so wie die neuste Zeitung, die letzte Grußadresse.

.... The sickly taper
By glimmering through thy low-browed misty vaults,
(Furred round with mouldy damps, and ropy slime,)
Lets fall a supernumerary horror,
And only serves to make thy night more irksome.
Well do I know thee by thy trusty yew,
Cheerless, unsocial plant! that loves to dwell
'Midst skulls and coffins, epitaphs and worms:
Where light-heeled ghosts, and visionary shades,
Beneath the wan cold moon (as fame reports)
Embodied, thick, perform their mystic rounds.
No other merriment, dull tree! is thine.
And buried 'midst the wreck of things which were:
There lie interred the more illustrious dead.
The wind is up: hark! how it howls! Methinks
Till now, I never heard a sound so dreary:
Doors creak, and windows clap, and night's foul bird
Rooked in the spire screams loud: the gloomy aisles
Black-plastered, and hung round with shreds of 'scutcheons
And tattered coats of arms, send back the sound
Laden with heavier airs, from the low vaults
The mansions of the dead. Roused from their slumbers
In grim array the grizzly spectres rise,
Grin horrible, and obstinately sullen
Pass and repass, hushed as the foot of night.
Again! the screech-owl shrieks: ungracious sound!
I'll hear no more, it makes one's blood run chill.

ROBERT BLAIR (1699 - 1746)
from «The Grave»

.... Die müde Kerze
im Zwielicht deiner dämmernden Gewölbe
(Verhangen rings von Moderdampf & Flechtenschleim)
Wirft ab ein unnennbares Grau'n, und macht
Nur noch beschwerlicher und ärger deine Nacht.
Erkenn dich wohl an deinem treuen Judenbaum,
Freudloses, ungeselliges Gewächs! das seine Wohnstatt
Gern unter Schädeln, Särgen, Würmern, Grabinschriften hat,
Wo visionäre Schemen, leichtfüszige Geister
Unter dem bleichen kalten Mond (so geht die Red)
In leiblich Körpern ihre myst'schen Kreise ziehn.
Kein anderes Vergnügen, trüber Baum, ist dein!
Mitsamt Ruinen von gewesnen Dingen
Sinds die erlauchtren Toten, die hier beigesetzt.
Der Wind ist los! Horch, wie er heult! Mich deucht,
Noch nie hört ich so düster ein Geräusch:
Türknarren, Fensterklappen, eklen Nachtgefleuches Wimmern
Kreucht auf der Turmspitz und kreischt laut: in dämmernd Gängen
Hängt rings ums Pflasterschwarz der Wappenschilder Trümmer,
Verschlissne Waffenröck': von dort hallts wider,
Die Luft beschwert vom Dunst aus niedren Grüften
Der Totenhäuser. Gräulich stehn auf aus ihrem Schlummer
Geister, zu grimmem Angriff angefacht,
Und gräßlich grinsend, aufgestört ohn Unterlaß
Ziehn hin & wider sie, verschwiegen wie der Grund der Nacht.
Horch! Wieder tönt der Eul' ungnädges Schnarren!
Wills nicht mehr hören, 's macht das Blut erstarren.

I am resolved, this charming day,
In the open field to stray;
And have no roof above my head,
But that whereon the gods do tread.
Before the yellow barn I see
A beautiful variety
Of strutting cocks, advancing stout,
And flirting empty chaff about,
Hens, ducks, and geese, and all their brood,
And turkeys gobbling for their food;
While rustics thrash the wealthy floor,
And tempt them all to crowd the door.

JOHN DYER (1699 - 1758)
from «The Country Walk»

Resolviret bin ich, diesen reizenden Tag
Übers offene Feld, durch den freien Hag
Zu streifen, und ob dem Kopfe kein Dach
Ich hab – bis auf das wo die Götter spazieren.
Vor der gelben Scheune kann ich sehn
Eine Compagney, schön, mannigfach,
Von stolzierenden Hähnen, die kühn *avanciren*,
Und die Hülsen der Spreu verstreund, *coquetiren*
Gänse & Güsseln & Enten & Hennen
Und Truthähne kollern um Fuderschüsseln;
Das Landvolk indes drischt auf üppiger Tenne,
Lockt über die Schwelle des Fiederschwarms Menge.

137 See the fading many-coloured woods,
Shade deepening over shade, the country round
Imbrown; a crowded umbrage, dusk, and dun,
Of every hue, from wan declining green
To sooty dark. These now the lonesome muse,
Low-whispering, lead into their leaf-strown walks;
And give the season in its latest view.
Meantime, light shadowing all, a sober calm
Fleeces unbounded ether; whose least wave
Stands tremulous, uncertain where to turn
The gentle current: while, illumined wide,
The dewy-skirted clouds imbibe the sun,
And through their lucid veil his softened force
Shed o'er the peaceful world. Then is the time
For those whom wisdom and whom nature charm
To steal themselves from the degenerate crowd,
And soar above this little scene of things;
To tread low-thoughted vice beneath their feet,
To soothe the throbbing passions into peace,
And woo lone quiet in her silent walks.
Thus solitary, and in pensive guise,
Oft let me wander o'er the russet mead,
And through the saddened grove, where scarce is heard
One dying strain to cheer the woodman's toil.
Haply some widowed songster pours his plaint,
Far, in faint warblings, through the tawny copse;
While congregated trushes, linnets, larks,
And each wild throat, whose artless strains so late
Swelled all the music of the swarming shades,
Robbed of their tuneful souls, now shivering sit
On the dead tree, a dull despondent flock!
With not a brightness waving o'er their plumes,

Sieh hier der Wälder ausgezehrt-vielfarbige
Schattierungen tief eingeschattet, rings das Land
in Braun; ein dunkles Umbra, falb & matt
Aus jeder Farb: von fahl verschossnem Grün
Bis rußig-düster. Die alle leiten leise wispernd
Die Muse einsam auf den blattbestreuten Gang
Und präsentiern das Jahr in seinem späten Bilde.
Dieweil verdämmert alls, und milder Friede
Wattiert den Äther grenzenlos, des feinstes Wehen
Steht zitternd still, unschlüssig, wie zu drehen
Den sachten Windhauch, während, weit erleuchtet,
Taufeucht geschürzte Wolken sich die Sonn einsaugen,
Deren gedämpfte Kraft dann durch luzide Schleier
über die Welt ausgießen friedevoll. Dann ist es Zeit
Für die, so Weisheit & Natur in Bann geschlagen,
Sich aus der stumpfgewordnen Menge fortzustehlen,
Sich hoch zu schwingen über diese Schmierenbühne,
Niedrige Sinnung auszutreten unterm Fuß,
Der Leidenschaften Pochen zu kalmieren,
Schweigsamen Wegs zu trachten nach der Einsamkeit.
So ganz allein, gewandet in des Schwersinns Falten,
Laß oft mich wandern über Wiesen rostrotbraun
Und durch betrübten Hain, wo kaum zu hören
Ein einzger Sterbenston, des Waldmanns Müh zu freun.
Vielleicht, daß seine Witwerklag verströmt' ein Sänger
In schwachem Flöten fern durchs ockergelbe Holz;
Indessen Drosseln, Lerchen, Hänflinge in Scharen
Und jede wilde Kehl, die mit kunstloser Weis erst jüngst
Des schwärmerischen Dunkels Lied ließ schwellen,
Kaurt, der melodschen Seel beraubt, itzt schaudernd
Auf totem Baum in dumpf verzagter Heerde!
Kein Schimmer, der ihr matt Gepluster fiederte,

And nought save chattering discord in their note.
Oh, let not, aimed from some inhuman eye,
The gun the music of the coming year
Destroy; and harmless, unsuspecting harm,
Lay the weak tribes, a miserable prey,
In mingles murder, fluttering on the ground!

JAMES THOMSON (1700-1748)
Solitude (from «The Seasons»)

In ihrer Stimme nichts als schwatzhaft Mißakkord.
Ach daß (von eines Unmensch Aug gerichtet)
Doch nicht die Flintenbüchs des kommnden Jahres Lieder
Vernichte!, und nicht zu harmlos-unschuldigem Harm
Für armselige Beut die schwachen Glieder,
Im Totschlag hingestreckt, wirr flattern auf dem Grund!

As those we love decay, we die in part,
String after string is sever'd from the heart;
Till loosen'd life, at last but breathing clay,
Without one pang is glad to fall away.

Unhappy he who latest feels the blow!
Whose eyes have wept o'er every friend laid low,
Dragg'd ling'ring on from partial death to death,
Till, dying, all he can resign is—breath.

JAMES THOMSON (1700-1748)
On the Death of a particular Friend

Da, was wir lieben, *welket* – sterben wir stückchenweis:
Saite um Saite springt vom Herzen leis,
bis das gemorschte Leben (nur atmend' Staub am End)
ohn einen Schmerzenslaut sich nur zu gern abtrennt.

Unselig der so spät den Schlag empfindt!
Wes Aug ob jedem hingemähten Freund geweint,
mühsam geschleift von TeilTod zu TeilTode, bis, sterbend, er
von einem nur noch Abschied nimmt: dem Odem.

Around th' adjoining brook, that purls along
The vocal grove now fretting o'er a rock,
Now scarcely moving through a reedy pool,
Now starting to a sudden stream, and now
Gently diffused into a limpid plain
A various group the herds and flocks compose.
Rural confusion! on the grassy bank
Some ruininating lie; while others stand
Half in the flood, and often bending sip
The circling surface. In the middle droops
The strong laborious ox, of honest front,
Which incomposed he shakes; and from his sides
The troublous insects lashes with his tail,
Returning still. Amid his subjects safe,
Slumbers the monarch swain; his careless arm
Thrown round his head, on downy moss sustained;
Here laid his scrip, with wholesome viands filled;
There, listening every noise, his watchful dog.
Light fly his slumbers, if perchance a flight
Of angry gadflies fasten on the herd;
That startling scatters from the shallow brook,
In search of lavish stream. Tossing the foam,
They scorn the keeper's voice, and scour the plain,
Through all the bright severity of noon;
While, from their labouring breasts, a hollow moan
Proceeding, runs low-bellowing round the hills.

JAMES THOMSON (1700-1748)
Cattle in Summer (from «The Seasons»)

Um den Bach nahebei, der den tönenden Hain
Murmelt entlang, dort über Felsen sich fiedert,
Hier sich nur mählich schleicht durch den rohrichten Tümpel,
Jetzt zu plötzlicher Strömung ansetzt, dann wieder
Sacht sich verbreitet in eine durchscheinende Fläche,
Lagern sich Heerden & Schafe & Vieh in Vielfalt vereint.
Ländliche Confusion! Auf grasigem Uferstreif liegen
Wiederkäuend die einen, andere stehen
Halb in der Strömung, beugen den Nacken und schlürfen
Von des Wassers Kreise ziehender Fläche. Geduckt inmitten,
Schüttelt der kräftige Lastochs das ehrbare Haupt
Ohne Ruh, wedelt das lästige Ziefer
Von seinen Flanken sich ab mit dem Schweif,
Verharrt so still. – In seinem Volke geborgen
Schläft den Schlaf des Monarchen der Landmann, den Arm ohne Sorgen
Rund um den Kopf sich geschwungen, gestützt auf flaumiges Moos:
Hier liegt sein Ränzel, mit nahrhafter Speise gefüllt,
Dort, jedem Laute zuhorchend, sein wachsamer Hund.
Leicht flieht der Schlaf ihn, falls etwan ein Schwarm
Zorniger Zecken sich heft' an die Herde,
Die, voll Schrecken, bricht aus dem seichten Gewässer,
Tiefere Strömung begehrend. Schaumaufwühlend
Spotten des Wächters Stimm sie und vagabundieren
Durch der Ebene mittäglich herben Glanz, dieweil
Aus der mühsamen Tiefe der Brust ein dumpfhohles Stöhnen
Als brüllendes Echo von Hügel zu Hügel sich pflanzt.

140 .... The cherished fields
Put on their winter robe of purest white.
'Tis brightness all; save where the new snow melts
Along the mazy current. Low the woods
Bow their hoar head; and, ere the languid sun
Faint from the west emits his evening ray,
Earth's universal face, deep-hid and chill,
Is one wild dazzling waste, that buries wide
The works of man. Drooping, the labourer-ox
Stands covered o'er with snow, and then demands
The fruit of all his toil. The fowls of heaven,
Tamed by the cruel season, crowd around
The winnowing store, and claim the little boon
Which Providence assigns them. One alone,
The redbreast, sacred to the household gods,
Wisely regardful of the embroiling sky,
In joyless fields and thorny thickets leaves
His shivering mates, and pays to trusted man
His annual visit. Half-afraid, he first
Against the window beats; then, brisk, alights
On the warm hearth; then, hopping o'er the floor,
Eyes all the smiling family askance,
And pecks, and starts, and wonders where he is—
Till, more familiar grown, the table-crumbs
Attract his slender feet.

JAMES THOMSON (1700-1748)
Robin Redbreast (from «The Seasons»)

.... Das Feldgeheg
legt seine Winterrobe an von reinstem Weiß.
Hell ist nun alles – bis auf da, wo Neuschnee schmilzt
an Baches Windungen entlang. Tief beuget das Gehölz
die rauhbereiften Häupter; und eh die zage Sonne
aus Westen matt die Abendstrahlen sendet,
ist klirrend, tief vermummt, der Erde All-Gesicht
ein' einzige wild-wirre Wüstenei, die weithin deckt
des Menschen Werk. Sich härmend, steht
der Arbeits-Ochs, ganz schneebehäuft, und fodert
die Früchte seiner Müh'. Des Himmels Vögel,
gezähmt von grausamer Saison, sie hocken nun
ums Futterhaus und heischen die Brosamen,
so Vorsicht ihnen weist. Einer allein:
das Rotkehlchen, geweiht des Heerdes Göttern,
klug in Betracht des confusiven Himmels,
verläßt, aus Dornen-Dickicht & freudlos Gefilde,
die zitternden Gefährten; und zollt vertrauten Menschen
den jährlichen Besuch. Halb-furchtsam erst,
klopfts an das Fenster; hüpft dann flink
auf den gewärmten Ofen; dann, übern Boden hopsend,
beäugts, schief von der Seit', die lächelnde Familie,
und pickt; hüpft wieder; fragt sich, wo es sey –
bis, schon vertrauter nun, die Krumen von der Tafel
die Füße zierlich locken.

141   But soon th'endearments of a husband cloy,
Her soul, her frame incapable of joy:
She feels no transports in the bridal-bed,
Of which so oft sh'has heard, so much has read;
Then vexed, that she should be condemned alone
To seek in vain this philosophic stone,
To abler tutors she resolves t'apply,
A prostitute from curiosity:
Hence men of every sort and every size,
Impatient for Heaven's cordial drop, she tries;
The fribbling beau, the rough unwieldy clown,
The ruddy templar newly on the town,
The Hibernian captain of gigantic make,
The brimful parson, and th'exhausted rake.

SOAME JENYNS (1701-1787)
from «The Modern Fine Lady»

Bald sind ihr fad des Gatten Täppischkeiten
die weder Seelenfreud noch Leibeslust bereiten;
sie fühlt im Ehebett nicht dies Erotisch Wesen
von dem sie schon so oft gehört, so viel gelesen;
Vexirt dann ob des Fluchs, daß sie allein
vergebens suchen sollt' des Weisen Stein,
beschließt sie sich bei fäh'gern Lehrern umzusehn,
aus purer Neugier auf den Strich zu gehn.
Lechzend nach jenem Himmel-Herzens-Tropfen
läßt sie von Männern aller Art & Form sich stopfen:
vom müßgen Stutzer und vom rohen plumpen Laffen....
errötend frisch vom Lande, am *Temple*: vom stud. jur....
vom irländischen Hauptmann mit der Pfundsfigur....
vom ausgelaugten Wüstling.... vom schwerbesoffnen Pfaffen....

Just broke from school, pert, impudent, and raw,
Expert in Latin, more expert in taw,
His Honour posts o'er Italy and France,
Measures St Peter's dome and learns to dance.
Thence, having quick through various countries flown,
Gleaned all their follies, and exposed his own,
He back returns, a thing so strange all o'er,
As never ages past produced before:
A monster of such complicated worth,
As no one single clime could e'er bring forth;
Half atheist, papist, gamester, bubble, rook,
Half fiddler, coachman, dancer, groom, and cook.
Next, because business is now all the vogue,
And who'd be quite polite must be a rogue,
In parliament he purchases a seat,
To make the accomplished gentleman complete.
There safe in self-sufficient impudence,
Without experience, honesty, or sense,
Unknowing in her interest, trade, or laws,
He vainly undertakes his country's cause:
Forth from his lips, prepared at all to rail,
Torrents of nonsense burst, like bottled ale,
Though shallow, muddy; brisk, though mighty dull;
Fierce without strength; o'erflowing, though not full.

SOAME JENYNS (1701 - 1787)
from «The Modern Fine Gentleman»

Frech, schaamlos, naseweis, grad ledig seines Ranzen,
lateingeschult, geschulter noch im Murmelspiel,
kutscht Seine Gnaden mit Italien-Frankreich-Ziel,
mißt aus den Petersdom, erlernt das Tanzen.
Aus aller Herren Ländern, die er quick durchgeigt,
Tollheiten aufgeschnappt – die eignen *exponirt*,
kehrt er dann heim: ein Etwas, *manirirt*,
wie's noch kein Zeitalter iemalen hat erzeugt,
ein Monstrum von so *complicirtem* Wert
wie's noch kein einzig Clima je beschert:
Halb Fiddler, Spieler, Gauner, Schaumschläger, Papist –
Halb Kutscher, Tänzer, Groom & Koch, halb Atheist.
Dann, weil itzt Business *en vogue*, und der
ein Schuft sein muß, den man ‹geschliffen› nennt,
kauft er sich einen Sitz im Parlament,
um den *Vollend'ten Gentleman* zu completiren.
Geborgen da in selbstzufriedner Leckerheit,
ohne Erfahrung noch Vernunft noch Ehrbarkeit,
will eitel er des Staats Gewalten zieren,
des Handel & Intressen & Gesetze ihm ganz fremd:
Bereit, ob alles herzuziehen, schwemmt
ein Schwall von Nonsense über seine Lippen, gleichwie Bier
das schlammig abgestanden – mit Schaum, doch trübe sehr:
Pomp ohne Mark – ein Überfluß, der leer.

143 Here lies Sam Johnson:—Reader, have a care,
    Tread lightly, lest you wake a sleeping bear:
    Religious, moral, generous, and humane
    He was; but self-sufficient, proud, and vain,
    Fond of, and overbearing in dispute,
    A Christian, and a scholar—but a brute.

SOAME JENYNS (1701-1787)
Epitaph on Dr Samuel Johnson

Hier ruht SAM JOHNSON – bitt' dich Leser: brav,
tritt sacht! Weck nicht 'nen Bär aus seinem Schlaf!
Human & sittlich – religiös – aus edlem Holz
war er – doch dünkelhaft auch – eitel – stolz –
rechthaberisch – im Wortstreit nie frugal:
Ein Christ & ein Gelehrter – doch brutal.

144

Ye who amid this feverish world would wear
A body free of pain, of cares a mind;
Fly the rank city, shun its turbid air;
Breathe not the chaos of eternal smoke
And volatile corruption, from the dead,
The dying, sickening, and the living world
Exhaled, to sully Heaven's transparent dome
With dim mortality. It is not air
That from a thousand lungs reeks back to thine,
Sated with exhalations rank and fell,
The spoil of dunghills, and the putrid thaw
Of nature; when from shape and texture she
Relapses into fighting elements:
It is not air, but floats a nauseous mass,
Of all obscene, corrupt, offensive things.

*

Wollt ihr in dieser Fieberwelt euch wahren
von Schmerzen baar den Leib, den Geist sonder Beschwer:
dann flieht der Stadt Gestank! Der City Pest-Odeur
vermeidet, das Chaos ewgen Qualms zu atmen,
geflügelter Verderbnis, ausgedunstet
von toter, kranker und lebendger Welt,
den transparenten Dom des Himels zu beflecken
mit trüb Hinfälligkeit. Das ist nicht Luft,
was aus unzählgen Lungen raucht in eure,
gesättigt mit Abdämpfen, scheulich, widerbar,
dem Dung von Jauchegüllen und dem Schimmeltau
aller Natur, so sie aus Form, Gefüg, Gestalt
zurückefallt in ihrer Urmaterie Widerstreit:
Das ist nicht Luft – nein, eyn verderbt Gebräu
von Allem schlüpfrig, böse, und bespeit.

*

What dexterous thousands just within the goal
Of wild debauch direct their nightly course!
Perhaps no sickly qualms bedim their days,
No morning admonitions shock the head.
But, ah! what woes remain! life rolls apace
And that incurable disease, old age,
In youthful bodies more severely felt,
More sternly active, shakes their blasted prime;
Except kind Nature by some hasty blow
Prevent the lingering fates. For know, whate'er
Beyond its natural fervour hurries on
The sanguine tide; whether the frequent bowl,
High-seasoned fare, or exercise to toil
Protracted; spurs to its last stage tired life,
And sows the temples with untimely snow.

   When life is new the ductile fibres feel
The heart's increasing force; and, day by day,
The growth advances: 'till the larger tubes
Acquiring (from their elemental veins,
Condensed to solid cords) a firmer tone,
Sustain, and just sustain, th'impetuous blood.
Here stops the growth. With overbearing pulse
And pressure, still the great destroy the small;
Still with the ruins of the small grow strong.
Life glows meantime, amid the grinding force
Of viscous fluids and elastic tubes;
Its various functions vigorously are plied
By strong machinery; and in solid health
The man confirmed long triumphs o'er disease.

Was lenken Tausende geschäftig ihre Schritte
nächtlich ins Ziel von wüstem Debauchiren?
Vielleicht bedüstern keine üblen Dämpfe ihre Tage,
pocht an ihr Haupt kein morgendliches Warnsignal?
Doch ach – was bleibt an Leid! rasch rollt das Leben ab,
und jene unheilbare Krankheit *Alter*,
in Jugendkörpern strenger noch gefühlt, noch krasser würkend,
weht mit des Todes Anhauch über ihre Blüthe,
es sey denn, daß Natur mit einem hast'gen Schlag
gnädig verwehrt' das schleichende Geschick. Denn wisse:
Was immer fortstürmt über den natürlichen Elan hinaus
mit Blutes Hochflut – : sei's der häuf'ge Punsch;
die stark gewürzte Kost; Sport, überdehnt zur Mühsal –
treibt das erschöpfte Leben in sein letztes Stadium,
bestreut die Schläfen unzeitig mit Schnee.

    Wenns Leben jung noch, fühlen die geschmeidgen Fibern
wachsen des Herzens Kraft; und dieses Wachstum
nimmt täglich zu, bis dann die größern Tuben
von ihren Capillargefäßen, zu festen Strängen condensirt,
den kräftigeren Tonus kriegen,
umfassen (nur umfassen!) das ungestüme Blut.
Hier endet Wachstum. Und mit mächtgem Puls
und Druck zerstört das Große noch das Kleine,
erstarket an des Kleinen Resten noch.
Derweil glüht Leben in der mahlenden Gewalt
dickflüssiger Liquorum & der elast'schen Röhren;
heftig oblieget seinen mannigfachen Zwecken
der starke Mechanismus: und in solidem Wohlergehn
feiert der Mensch lange Triumphe übers Kranksein.

But the full ocean ebbs: there is a point,
By Nature fixed, when life must downward tend.
For still the beating tide consolidates
The stubborn vessels, more reluctant still
To the weak throbs of th'ill supported heart.
This languishing, these strengthening by degrees
To hard unyielding unelastic bone,
Through tedious channels the congealing flood
Crawls lazily, and hardly wanders on;
It loiters still; and now it stirs no more.
This is the period few attain; the death
Of Nature; thus (so Heaven ordained it) life
Destroys itself; and could these laws have changed
Nestor might now the fates of Troy relate;
And Homer live immortal as his song.

JOHN ARMSTRONG (1709 - 1779)
from «The Art of Preserving Health»: Air Pollution/ Causes of Old Age

Doch senket sich die Tide. Es gibt da einen Punct,
den hat Natur bestimmt, wo sich des Lebens Waage neiget.
Denn noch consolidiret die pulsiernde Flut
die hartwandigen Blutgefäße, die schon widerstreben
dem schwachen Klopfen des vernachlässigten Herzens.
Da schon erschlafft, verstärkt es nach & nach
(auf Knochen hart & unnachgiebig, unelastisch)
den eingedickten Fluß; der durch ermattete Kanäle
träg; schleicht; und kaum noch; kömmt voran.
Noch – sickert er – –. Nun rührt er sich nicht mehr.
Dies ist das Stadium, das Wenige erreichen: der Natur
End-Punct. Also zerstört (so hat's der HErr bestimmt)
das Leben selbst sich. Und könnt dies Gesetz man ändern,
könnt Nestor itzo Trojas Schicksal melden,
Homer unsterblich leben wie sein Sang.

145   Incessant now their hollow sides they pound,
Loud on each breast the bounding bangs resound;
Their flying fists around the temples glow,
And the jaws crackle with the massy blow.
The raging combat every eye appals,
Strokes following strokes, and falls succeeding falls.

Now drooped the youth, yet, urging all his might,
With feeble arm still vindicates the fight,
Till on the part where heaved the panting breath,
A fatal blow impressed the seal of death.
Down dropped the hero, weltering in his gore,
And his stretched limbs lay quivering on the floor.

So, when a falcon skims the airy way,
Stoops from the clouds, and pounces on his prey;
Dashed on the earth the feathered victim lies,
Expands its feeble wings, and, fluttering, dies.

His faithful friends their dying hero reared,
O'er his broad shoulders dangling hung his head;
Dragging its limbs, they bear the body forth,
Mashed teeth and clotted blood came issuing from his mouth.

PAUL WHITEHEAD (1719-1774)
from «The Gymnasiad»: The Boxers

Itzt, ohne Pause, dreschen sie sich ihre Weichen;
in beiderlei Brustkorb halln wider die batschenden Schwinger;
um die Schläfen glühet der fliegenden Fäuste Gefuchtel;
und bei jedem massigen Schlage knirschen die Kiefer.
Ein jegliches Auge entsetzet der raasende Wettstreit:
Hieb folgt auf Hieb, und ein Sturz folget dem andern.

Nun sank ermattet der Jüngling, die Kräfte doch sammlend
behauptet er schwächlichen Armes annoch den Kampf –
bis, auf die Stelle, wo keuchend der Odem sich hebet,
ein Hieb, ein fataler, das Sigel des Todes gedrückt.
Hin stürzt der Held, schwimmend im eigenen Blute,
und die Glieder ruhn, zuckend, zu Grunde gestreckt.

Gleichwie, die himmlischen Lüfte durchkeilend, der Falke
aus Wolken sich stürzt, auf die Beute herabstößt,
das gefiederte Opfer, zerschmettert, liegt auf der Erde,
die schwächlichen Flügel spreitet, und, flatternd noch, stirbt.

Auf huben die treulichen Freunde den sterbenden Helden;
über die Schultern, die breiten, hing pendelnd sein Haupt;
an den Gliedern ihn zerrend, schleppten den Leichnam sie fort
dem aus dem Munde Zahnbrei und klumpichtes Blut troff.

Rezitative
Of Constance holy legends tell,
The softest sister of the cell;
None sent to Heaven so sweet a cry,
Or rolled at mass so bright an eye.
No wanton taint her bosom knew,
Her hours in heavenly vision flew,
Her knees were worn with midnight prayers,
And thus she breathed divinest airs.

Air
In hallowed walks, and awful cells,
Secluded from the light and vain,
The chaste-eyed maid with virtue dwells,
And solitude, and silence reign.
The wanton's voice is heard not here,
To Heaven the sacred pile belongs;
Each wall returns the whispered prayer,
And echoes but to holy songs.

Recitative
Alas, that pampered monks should dare
Intrude where sainted vestals are!
Ah, Francis! Francis! well I weet
Those holy looks are all deceit.
With shame the Muse prolongs her tale,
The priest was young, the nun was frail,
Devotion faltered on her tongue,
Love tuned her voice, and thus she sung.

Rezitativ:
Manch fromme Legend von Konstanze erzählt,
Der sanftesten Nonn in des Klosterbaus Zellen,
Keine zum Himmel die Schrei so süß gellt,
So helle zur Messe die Augen tat rollen.
Keine Anfechtung je ihrem Busen ward kund,
In himmlisch Gesichten zerfloß ihr die Stund,
Die Kniee vom Mitternachtsbeten schon wund,
So hauchte sie die göttlichsten Airs:

Arie:
In hallenden Gängen und schrecklichen Zellen
Haust, abgeschieden vom eitlen Licht,
Die Magd mit Tugend & Keuschheit so helle,
Und Schweigen hier Cränze der Einsamkeit flicht.
Hier hört man nicht des Gelüstens Stimme,
Die Heilige Säule gehört nur dem Himmel;
Von jeder Wand echot des Betens Gewisper,
Hallt wider der frommen Gesänge Gelispel.

Rezitativ:
Ach, warum müssen kecke Mönche sich erdreisten,
Zu schleichen in der heiligen Vestalin Bau!
Ach Francis, Francis! Ich weiß genau,
All diese frommen Blicke sind bloß Hinterlisten!
Mit Scham verlängt die Muse der Erzählung Gang:
Schwach war die Nonne ... und der Priester jung ...
Da stockt Ergebenheit auf ihrer Zung,
Und Liebe stimmte an ihren Gesang, also:

Air
«Alas, how deluded was I,
To fancy delights as I did!
With maidens at midnight to sigh,
And love, the sweet passion, forbid!
O, father! my follies forgive,
And still to absolve me be nigh;
Your lessons have taught me to live,
Come teach me, O! teach me to die!»

To her arms in a rapture he sprung,
Her bosom, half-naked, met his;
Transported in silence she hung,
And melted away at each kiss.
«Ah, father!» expiring she cried,
«With rapture I yield up my breath!»
«Ah, daughter!» he fondly replied,
«The righteous find comfort in death.»

EDWARD MOORE (1712 - 1757)
THE NUN. A Cantata

Arie:
«Oh GOtt, wie ward ich irrgebracht
Ob meiner launschen Lüst' Gebieten!
Mit Mädchen zu seufzen um Mitternacht
Und Liebe, die süße Passion, zu verbieten!
Ach Vater!, sprecht los mich vom närrischen Streben,
Seid nah mir! Noch möcht ich Vergebung beerben!
Ihr ließet mich lernen die Lehre zu leben –
Kommt, lehrt mich, ach! Lehrt mich, zu sterben!»

In ihre Arme entzückt er da sprang,
Ihr Busen, halb-nackt, preßt den seinen,
In Schweigen hingerissen sie hang,
Und schmolz dahin in der Küsse Vereinen.
«Ah Vater!» schluchzt aushauchend sie da,
«Der Odem will vor Entzücken mir schwinden!»
«Ja, Tochter!» gab zärtlich er wider,
«Der Gerechte wird Tröstung im Tode finden!»

147   Next, in a low-browed cave, a little hell,
A pensive hag, moping in darkness, sits
Dolefully-sad: her eyes (so deadly-dull!)
Stare from their stonied sockets, widely wild;
For ever bent on rusty knives, and ropes;
On poignards, bows of poison, daggers red
With clotted gore. A raven by her side
Eternal croaks; her only mate Despair;
Who, scowling in a night of clouds, presents
A thousand burning hells, and damned souls,
And lakes of stormy fire, to mad the brain
Moon-strucken. Melancholy is her name;
Britannia's bitter bane. Thou gracious Power,
(Whose judgments and whose mercies who can tell!)
With bars of steel, with hills of adamant
Crush down the sooty fiend; nor let her blast
The sacred light of Heaven's all-cheering face,
Nor fright from Albion's isle, the angel Hope.

WILLIAM THOMPSON (1712 (?) -1766 (?))
from «Sickness»

In einer dumpfen Höhl, 'ner kleinen Hölle
Hockt eine Hex gedankenschwer, im Dunkel brütend
Trübselig-matt; die Augen (so tödlich-öd!)
Aus ihren steinern Höhlen stieren wild & weit
In Starr' gebannt auf Stricke, rostge Messer,
Auf Säuren, Giftkästchen & Dolche, rot
Von trocken Blut. An ihrer Seit ein Rabe
Krächzt immerdar: Ihr einziger Gesell *Verzweifelung*
Die, in 'ner Wolkennacht mit finstrem Dräun,
Beut tausend Flammenhöllen und verdammte Seelen
Und Seen von Feuerstürmen: 's macht das Hirn
Lunatisch. *MELANCHOLIA* ist ihr Name:
Britanniens bitterer Fluch. DU Gnadenmacht
(Wer könnt DEin' Richtsprüch, DEin Erbarmen zählen!),
Mit stählern Stangen, Bergen von Demant
Zerschlag die rußge Feindin; auch laß sie nicht
Das heilge Licht ausblasen von des Himmels heitrem Antlitz,
Den Engel *Hoffnung* schrecken vor Albions Insel.

148   'Twas on a lofty vase's side,
Where China's gayest art had dyed
The azure flowers, that blow;
Demurest of the tabby kind,
The pensive Selima reclined,
Gazed on the lake below.

Her conscious tail her joy declared;
The fair round face, the snowy beard,
The velvet of her paws,
Her coat, that with the tortoise vies,
Her ears of jet, and emerald eyes,
She saw; and purred applause.

Still had she gazed; but 'midst the tide
Two angel forms were seen to glide,
The genii of the stream:
Their scaly armour's Tyrian hue
Through richest purple to the view
Betrayed a golden gleam.

The hapless nymph with wonder saw:
A whisker first and then a claw,
With many an ardent wish,
She stretched in vain to reach the prize.
What female heart can gold despise?
What cat's averse to fish?

Da wo die Vase praesidirt,
die Chinas Pinselkunst geziert
mit blauen Blumen reich,
lehnt' artig ein klein Tabby-Lynx:
Selima, nachdenklich wie Sphynx,
schaut' nieder auf den Teich.

Ihr wissend Schweif die Freud' bespricht:
den Bart schneeweiß – lieb Rundgesicht –
die Pfoten sammetweich –
den Pelz gescheckt wie Schildpatt nett –
Smaragdpupillen – Ohren jett –
: sah sie; schnurrt Beyfall sich.

Sie spiegelt sich im Flutgehäus
zwei Engelsformen glitten leis:
Flußgenien im Flor:
ihrs Schuppenpanzers tyrisch Licht
mit reichstem Purpur täuscht der Sicht
ein goldnes Glänzen vor.

Mit Staunen sahs die Unglückskatz.
Den Schnurrbart erst, und dann 'ne Tatz
mit eifrigstem Bemühn
streckt' sie vergebens nach dem Lohn.
Welch Weiberherz kann Gold verschmähn,
Katz Fischen widerstehn?

Presumptuous maid! with looks intent
Again she stretched, again she bent,
Nor knew the gulf between.
(Malignant Fate sat by, and smiled)
The slippery verge her feet beguiled,
She tumbled headlong in.

Eight times emerging from the flood
She mewed to every watery god,
Some speedy aid to send.
No dolphin came, no nereid stirred:
Nor cruel Tom, nor Susan heard.
A favourite has no friend!

From hence, ye beauties, undeceived,
Know, one false step is ne'er retrieved,
And be with caution bold.
Not all that tempts your wandering eyes
And heedless hearts, is lawful prize;
Nor all, that glisters, gold.

THOMAS GRAY (1716-1771)
Ode/ On the Death of a Favourite Cat/
Drowned in a Tub of Gold Fishes

Miss Arrogance, mit Gierigkeit
streckt' sich erneut, bog sich erneut,
sah nicht den Abgrund dräun.
(Bös Fatum, grinsend, saß gebannt:)
Die Pfoten trog der glatte Rand:
kopfüber plumpst sie rein.

Achtmal noch taucht sie aus der Flut
und maunzt zu jedem Wassergott,
dass rasche Hülf er send!
Kein Triton kam, und kein Delphin,
Susann schien taub – Tom hört nicht hin –
Ein Liebling hat kein' Freund!

Ihr arglos Schönen, habet acht:
Ein Fehltritt ist nie gutgemacht!
Seid keck *mit Vorsicht* meist!
Nicht alls, was eure Herzen bang
und Blicke fängt, ist rechter Fang,
nicht alles Gold, was gleißt.

*On Seeing
a Tapestry Chair-Bottom Beautifully Worked
by His Daughter for Mrs Holroyd.*
WRITTEN IN THE YEAR 1793

While Holroyd may boast of her beautiful bottom,
I think of what numberless ills may bespot 'em;
'Tis true they're intended for clean petticoats;
But beware of th'intrusion of bold Sansculottes;
Who regardless of Charlotte's most elegant stitches,
May rudely sit down without linen or breeches:
Would you know from what quarter the mischief may come,
When the battery's unmasked then beware of the bomb.

RICHARD OWEN CAMBRIDGE (1717-1802)
On Seeing a Tapestry Chair-Bottom Beautifully Worked by His Daughter for Mrs Holroyd. WRITTEN IN THE YEAR 1793.

Beim Betrachten eines
von seiner Tochter für Mrs. Holroyd süperb gestickten
Gobelin-Stuhlsitzpolsters
GESCHRIEBEN IM JAHRE 1793

Ihres herrlichen Polsters mag die Holroyd nun jubeln –
Ich denk: 's können zahllose Übel sie sudeln:
Denn sie sind zwar gewiß für reine Unterröck gedacht –
Aber hüt dich vor dem Sitz der Sanskülotten ungeschlacht,
die Charlottens eleganter Stickerei ungeacht'
ohne Linnen oder Hosen darauf platznehmen rüd:
Wissest du, aus welchem Sitzquartier das Unheil dir blüht,
wenn die Batterie entblößt: vor der Bombe sey in acht!

Time was, a wealthy Englishman would join
A rich plum-pudding to a fat sirloin;
Or bake a pasty, whose enormous wall
Took up almost the area of his hall:
But now, as art improves, and life refines,
The demon Taste attends him when he dines;
Serves on his board an elegant regale,
Where three stewed mushrooms flank a larded quail;
Where infant turkeys, half a month resigned
To the soft breathings of a southern wind,
And smothered in a rich ragout of snails,
Outstink a lenten supper at Versailles.
Is there a saint that would not laugh to see
The good man piddling with his fricassee;
Forced by the luxury of taste to drain
A flask of poison, which he calls champagne!
While he, poor idiot! though he dare not speak,
Pines all the while for porter and ox-cheek.
Sure 'tis enough to starve for pomp and show,
To drink, and curse the clarets of Bordeaux:
Yet such our humour, such our skill to hit
Excess of folly through excess of wit,
We plant the garden, and we build the seat,
Just as absurdly as we drink and eat.

JAMES CAWTHORN (1719-1761)
from «Of Taste»

Nen satten Plumpudding würd einst ein wohlhäbiger Brite
nachrückend machen einer fetten Lendenschnitte,
Pasteten backen, deren imposanter Wall
würd fast an Wucht gleichkommen seiner Hall.
Doch nun, da Künste blühn, und's Leben raffinirt,
begleitet ihn *Dämon GESCHMACK*, wo er dinirt,
servirt ein elegant Menu ihm auf die rohen Planken,
wo 3 soufflirte Trüffelchen ziern einer Wachtel Flanken;
wo'n Truthähnchen, zwei Wochen grad entlassen
in sanften Südens säuselnden Zephyr geschickt,
würd, in 'nem reichen Schneckenragoutfin erstickt,
vor Neid ein Fastenessen zu Versailles erbleichen lassen.
Selbst Heilige könnt lachen machen dieser Blick:
Wie in dem Fricassé der gute Mann muß stochern,
gezwungen vom *GESCHMACK*, zu bechern
'nen Kolben Gift, das er Champagner nennt!,
indes, obwohl's nicht sagen wagt der Fant, der Idiot
allzeit nach Porter jankt und deftger Ochsenschnut.
Ja, 's ist genung!: zu hungern – just für Prunk & Show,
zu trinken – doch zu fluchen dem Rotwein von Bordeaux.
Doch das ist unser Spleen und unsre Kunst: wir mausen
ein Übermaß an Narrheit – durch ein Zuviel an Witz:
Den Garten leg'n wir an und baun den Herrensitz
grad so verstiegen wie wir trinken, schmausen.

If ought of oaten stop, or pastoral song,
May hope, chaste Eve, to soothe thy modest ear,
Like thy own solemn springs,
Thy springs, and dying gales,
O nymph reserved, while now the bright-haired sun
Sits in yon western tent, whose cloudy skirts,
With brede ethereal wove,
O'erhang his wavy bed:
Now air is hushed, save where the weak-eyed bat,
With short shrill shriek flits by on leathern wing,
Or where the beetle winds
His small but sullen horn,
As oft he rises 'midst the twilight path,
Against the pilgrim borne in heedless hum:
Now teach me, maid composed,
To breathe some softened strain,
Whose numbers stealing through thy darkening vale,
May not unseemly with its stillness suit,
As musing slow, I hail
Thy genial loved return!
For when thy folding star arising shows
His paly circlet, at his warning lamp
The fragrant hours, and elves
Who slept in flowers the day,
And many a nymph who wreaths her brows with sedge,
And sheds the freshening dew, and lovelier still,
The pensive pleasures sweet
Prepare thy shadowy care.
Then lead, calm votaress, where some sheety lake
Cheers the lone heath, or some time-hallowed pile,
Or upland fallows grey
Reflect its last cool gleam.

Wenn aus der Rohrblattflöte etwas, oder Hirtensang,
Dürft hoffen, keusche Abendin, dein sittsam Ohr zu schmeicheln,
Wie deine eignen andächtigen Böen
Bewegt sich heben und gerührt verwehen,
Schamhafte Nymphe, während nun in ihres Haares Glanz die Sonn
Jenseits im Westen sitzt, im Zelt, des Wolkenränder
Verwoben mit ätherischem Herkommen
Ob ihr's geschwungnem Bette hängen;
Und still die Luft nun, bis auf da wo die schwachsichtge Fledermaus
Vorbei mit schrillem Schrei auf Lederschwingen huscht,
Und wo der Käfer bläst
Sein kleines, mürrischs Horn,
Wie er's so oft inmitten des zwielichtgen Pfades hebt
Dem Wanderer entgegen, der in achtlos Summ'n versponnen;
So lehre mich, gelassne Maid,
Eine gedämpfte Melodie zu hauchen
Mit Strophen, die verstohlen durch dein Dämmerthal
Nicht unziemlich sich seiner Stille fügen mögen,
Dieweil im Schwersinn ich willkommen heiße
Dein vielgeliebtes freundliches Heimkommen!
Denn wenn dein Hütestern im Steigen zeigt
Den bleichen Reif, bei seiner mahnenden Laterne
Duftige Stunden, und die Elfen,
Die tags in Blumen schliefen,
Und manche Nymph, die ihre Brau'n mit Riedgras flicht,
Des Taus Erquickung sprenkelt, und Schönres noch
Bereiten diese nachdenklichen Freuden
Hold deiner schattigen Fürsorge;
Dann leite mich, stille Geweihte, wo ein flachausgespannter See
Aufheitert die einsame Haid, oder ein Pfahl, gehöhlt von Zeit,
Oder des Hochlands graue Brachen
Sein letztes kühles Glosen reflektiern.

But when chill blustering winds, or driving rain,
Forbid my willing feet, be mine the hut,
That from the mountain's side,
Views wilds, and swelling floods,
And hamlets brown, and dim-discovered spires,
And hears their simple bell, and marks o'er all
Thy dewy fingers draw
The gradual dusky veil.
While spring shall pour his showers, as oft he wont,
And bathe thy breathing tresses, meekest Eve!
While summer loves to sport
Beneath thy lingering light;
While sallow autumn fills thy lap with leaves;
Or winter yelling through the troublous air,
Affrights thy shrinking train,
And rudely rends thy robes;
So long, sure-found beneath the sylvan shed,
Shall fancy, friendship, science, rose-lipped health,
Thy gentlest influence own,
And hymn thy favourite name!

WILLIAM COLLINS (1721-1759)
Ode to Evening

Doch wenn kalttosend Winde oder Regengüsse
Den willgen Füßen Einhalt bieten, sei die Hütte mein,
Die von des Berges Flanke
Auf Wildnis, schwellnde Fluten schaut
Und Weiler, braun, mit deutlich-undeutlichen Türmen,
Und ihre schlichte Glocke hört, und allweil achtet,
Wie deine tautropfichten Finger zeichnen
Den stufenweis getrübten Schleier.
Dieweil nun Lenz oft, wie's ihm ziemt, muß seine Schauer gießen
Und baden dein athmendes Haar, sanfteste Abendin!;
Dieweil der Sommer Kurzweil liebt
In deinem Zögerlicht;
Indes blaßgelber Herbst mit Blättern deinen Rockschoß füllt,
Und Winter gellend durch der Luft Tumult
Dein schrumpfendes Gefolge schreckt
Und rüde deine Roben zaust –
So lang also, stets unterm Walddachschutz zu finden,
Solln Wissen – Freundschaft – Phantasie – Gesundheit rosenmundig
Dein zarter Einfluß eigen sein, und hymnisch
Verklären deinen Namen!

Science! thou fair effusive ray
From the great source of mental day,
Free, generous, and refined!
Descend with all thy treasures fraught,
Illumine each bewildered thought,
And bless my labouring mind.

But first with thy resistless light,
Disperse those phantoms from my sight,
Those mimic shades of thee;
The scholiast's learning, sophist's cant,
The visionary bigot's rant,
The monk's philosophy.

MARK AKENSIDE (1721-1770)
from «Hymn to Science»

SCIENTIA! – : Du hellverströmend Strahlen
aus der gewaltgen Quelle des mentalen Tags:
sublim! großmüthig! frei!
Steig nur herab mit deinen Schätzen all,
leucht jedem Denken (das verwildert meist)
und segne meinen arbeitsamen Geist!

Doch scheuch erst mit dem Licht, dem widersetzen
sich keiner kann, den Spuck von meinem Blick:
sie, deines Zerrbilds Fratzen:
Scholasten-Rabulistik! Sophisten-Heuchelei!
Wirr brodelnder Chiliasten mystelnd Schwatzen:
die Mönchs-Philosophei.

153   For I prophesy that they will understand the blessing and virtue of the rain.
For rain is exceedingly good for the human body.
For it is good therefore to have flat roofs to the houses, as of old.
For it is good to let the rain come upon the naked body unto purity and refreshment.
For I prophesy that they will respect decency in all points.
For they will do it in conceit, word, and motion.
For they will go forth afield.
For the Devil can work upon stagnating filth to a very great degree.
For I prophesy that we shall have our horns again.
For in the day of David Man as yet had a glorious horn upon his forehead.
For this horn was a bright substance in colour and consistence as the nail of the hand.
For it was broad, thick and strong so as to serve for defence as well as ornament.
For it brightened to the Glory of God, which came upon the human face at morning prayer.

Denn wahrlich ich sage euch begreifen werden sie den Segen und die Kraft des Regens.
Denn Regen ist über die Maaßen gut für des Menschen Leib.
Denn es ist also gut die Dächer flach zu haben auf den Häusern wie von altersher.
Denn es ist gut zu besorgen daß der Regen auf den nackten Leib komme zur Reinigung und Erquickung.
Denn wahrlich ich sage euch sie werden in allen Punkten achten was sich schickt.
Denn sie werden's tun in Gedanken Wort und Tat.
Denn sie werden weit hinausgehn übers Feld.
Denn wenn der Unflat starrt hat der Teufel allerleichtes Spiel.
Denn wahrlich ich sage euch wir werden unsere Hörner wieder haben.
Denn in den Tagen Davids schon hatte der Mensch ein herrliches Horn auf seiner Stirn.
Denn dieses Horn war von glänzendem Stoffe in Farbe & Festigkeit wie der Nagel der Hand.
Denn groß hart dick diente's zur Verteidigung gleichwie zur Zierde.
Denn das glänzte zum Ruhme GOttes welches kam auf des Menschen Antlitz bei der Morgenandacht.

For it was largest and brightest in the best men.
For it was taken away all at once from all of them.
For this was done in the divine contempt of a general pusillanimity.
For this happened in a season after their return from the Babylonish captivity.
For their spirits were broke and their manhood impaired by foreign vices for exaction.
For I prophesy that the English will recover their horns the first.
For I prophesy that all the nations in the world will do the like in turn.
For I prophesy that all Englishmen will wear their beards again.
For a beard is a good step to a horn.
For when men get their horns again, they will delight to go uncovered.
For it is not good to wear any thing upon the head.
For a man should put no obstacle between his head and the blessing of Almighty God.
For a hat was an abomination of the heathen. Lord have mercy upon the Quakers.

Denn auf den Besten der Menschen war's am größesten & strahlendsten.
Denn es ward alles auf einmal weggenommen von ihnen allen.
Denn dies tat GOtt also da er verachtete die gemeine Kleinmütigkeit.
Denn dies geschah in der Zeit nach ihrer Rückkehr aus der Babylonischen Gefangenschaft.
Denn ihr Geist war gebrochen und ihre Mannheit geschwächet in der Zinsfron unter der Fremden Joch.
Denn wahrlich ich sage euch die Engländer werden ihre Hörner als erste wiedererlangen.
Denn wahrlich ich sage euch alle Völker der Erde werden's ihnen gleichtun.
Denn wahrlich ich sage euch alle Engländer werden ihre Bärte wieder tragen.
Denn ein Bart ist der erste Schritt zu einem Horn.
Denn wenn die Menschen ihre Hörner wiederbekommen werden sie entzückt sein unbedeckt zu gehen.
Denn es ist nicht gut zu tragen etwas auf dem Kopfe.
Denn der Mensch soll kein Hindernis legen zwischen sein Haupt und des Allmächtigen G. O. T. T. E. S. Segen.
Denn ein Hut war ein Greuel der Heiden. (Herr erbarme dich der Quäker.)

For the ceiling of the house is an obstacle and therefore we pray
   on the house-top.
For the head will be liable to less disorders on the recovery of its horn.
For the horn on the forehead is a tower upon an arch.
For it is a strong munition against the adversary, who is sickness
   and Death.
For it is instrumental in subjecting the woman.
For the insolence of the woman has increased ever since Man has been
   crestfallen.
For they have turned the horn into scoff and derision without ceasing.
For we are amerced of God, who has his horn.
For we are amerced of the blessed angels, who have their horns.
For when they get their horns again they will put them upon the altar.
For they give great occasion for mirth and music.
For our Blessed Saviour had not his horn upon the face of the earth.
For this was in meekness and condescension to the infirmities of human
   nature at that time.
For at his second coming his horn will be exalted in glory.
For his horn is the horn of Salvation.

CHRISTOPHER SMART (1722-1771)
from «Jubilate Agno»

Denn die Decke des Hauses ist ein Hindernis und also beten wir auf dem Dache.
Denn kaum mehr zur Unordnung neigen wird sich das Haupt bei der Wiedererlangung des Hornes.
Denn das Horn auf der Stirn ist ein Pulverturm auf einem Wachtbogen.
Denn es ist eine starke Wehr wider den Feind des Name ist Krankheit & Tod.
Denn es ist ein Mittel sich untertan zu machen das Weib.
Denn des Weibes Unbotmäßigkeit ist gewachsen immerdar seit der Mensch in Sünde gefallen.
Denn sie haben das Horn in Hohn & Spott verkehrt ohn Ende.
Denn wir sind in der Strafe GOttes der sein Horn hat.
Denn wir sind in der Strafe der gesegneten Engel die ihre Hörner haben.
Denn wenn sie ihre Hörner wiedererlangen werden sie sie auf den Altar stellen.
Denn sie geben einen glänzenden Anlaß zu Frohsinn & Musik.
Denn unser gepriesener Erlöser trug nicht SEin Horn auf dem Antlitz der Erde.
Denn dieses ließ sich in Sanftmut herab zu den Schwächen der menschlichen Natur in jener Zeit.
Denn bei SEiner Wiederkunft wird sein Horn verzückt sein in Glorie.
Denn SEin Horn ist das Horn der Erlösung.

154   Near yonder thorn, that lifts its head on high,
      Where once the sign-post caught the passing eye,
      Low lies that house, where nut-brown draughts inspired,
      Where gray-beard mirth, and smiling toil retired,
      Where village statesmen talked with looks profound,
      And news much older than their ale went round.

      Imagination fondly stoops to trace
      The parlour splendours of that festive place;
      The white-washed wall, the nicely-sanded floor,
      The varnished clock that clicked behind the door;
      The chest contrived a double debt to pay,
      A bed by night, a chest of drawers by day;
      The pictures placed for ornament and use,
      The Twelve Goods Rules, the royal game of Goose;
      The hearth, except when winter chilled the day,
      With aspen boughs, and flowers and fennel gay;
      While broken tea-cups, wisely kept for show,
      Ranged o'er the chimney, glistened in a row.

Dicht unterm Dornbusch der die Krone bauscht, wo einst
Der Wegweiser den Blick heischt' im Vorüber,
Duckt sich das Haus wo haselbraune Tränke wärmten,
Graubärtger Frohsinn & verschmitzte Müh kehrt' ein,
Gewichtig Dorfpolitikaster disputierten,
Und Klatsch, viel älter als ihr Bier noch, ging reihum.

Einbildungskraft versenkt sich zärtlich, hier zu lesen
Die Spur von Pracht aus diesem Festlokal:
Wand weißgetüncht, der Boden sandbestreuet;
Lackierter Standuhr Ticken hintertürs;
Die Truhe, für zwiefach Rechnung ausgedacht:
Als Bett zur Nacht – Commode untertags;
Die Bilder, zu Nutz & Zierde angebracht;
Die ‹Zwölf Gebote› und ‹Das Gänsespiel›;
Die Feuerstell (es sei denn, Winter kühlt' den Tag)
Mit Espenzweigen, Blumen, Fenchel heiter; dieweil
Gesprungne Teetassen, wohlweislich aufbewahrt,
In blankem Schmuck gereiht auf dem Kaminsims.

Vain transitory splendours! could not all
Reprieve the tottering mansion from its fall?
Obscure it sinks, nor shall it more impart
An hour's importance to the poor man's heart;
Thither no more the peasent shall repair,
To sweet oblivion of his daily care;
No more the farmer's news, the barber's tale,
No more the woodman's ballad shall prevail;
No more the smith his dusky brow shall clear,
Relax his ponderous strenght, and lean to hear;
The host himself no longer shall be found
Careful to see the mantling bliss go round;
Nor the coy maid, half willing to be pressed,
Shall kiss the cup to pass it to the rest.

OLIVER GOLDSMITH (1728 - 1774)
from «The Deserted Village»

Vergänglich-leerer Glanz! Konnts denn dem morschen Bau
Vor seinem Sturz noch eine Gnadenfrist gewähren?
Es fällt ja insgeheim, und nimmer solls dem Herz
Des armen Manns den Rang der einen Stund erhöhen;
Auch soll nie mehr der Landmann dorthin gehen
Zum süß Vergessen seiner täglichen Beschwerden;
Des Bauern Klatsch, des Baaders Schwadronieren,
Des Waldmanns BalladSongs solln nimmermehr hier dröhnen;
Nie mehr soll sich der Schmied die finstren Züge weichen,
Entspannt von schwerer Kraft zurück sich, lauschend, lehnen;
Den Schankwirt selbst solln wir nie mehr erblicken
Bedacht auf des Behagens Rund; auch soll
Die spröde Magd (doch ungern nicht läßt sie sich drücken)
Nie mehr den Humpen küssen und dann weiterreichen.

155 The tapered choir, at the late hour of prayer,
Oft let me tread, while to th'according voice
The many-sounding organ peals on high,
The clear slow-dittied chant, or varied hymn,
Till all my soul is bathed in ecstasies,
And lapped in paradise. Or let me sit
Far in sequestered aisles of the deep dome,
There lonesome listen to the sacred sounds,
Which, as they lengthen through the Gothic vaults,
In hollow murmurs reach my ravished ear.
Nor when the lamps expiring yield to night,
And solitude returns, would I forsake
The solemn mansion, but attentive mark
The due clock swinging slow with sweepy sway,
Measuring time's flight with momentary sound.

THOMAS WARTON (1728-1790)
from «The Pleasures of Melancholy»

Laß mich noch oft den spitzgewölbten Kor betreten
Zu des Gebetes später Stund wenn, deine Stimm begleitend,
Die tausendzüng'ge Orgel in die Höhe
Dröhnt rein-getragenen Gesang, vielfältge Hymnen,
Bis in Ekstase meine Seele ganz gebadet ist,
Ins Paradies verschlagen. Laß mich auch sitzen
In tiefer Cathedrale abgelegnen Schiffen,
Dort den geweihten Tönen einsam lauschen
Die da gezogen lang durchs gottische Gewölb
In hohlem Raunen nur mein hochentzücktes Ohr erreichen.
Würd auch, wenn die Latern zur Nacht den Hauch
Auslöscht des Lichts und Einsamkeit einkehrt, nicht weichen
Dem feierlichen Bau, doch aufmerksam gewahrn
Der strengen Uhr gemessnen Pendels Bogenschwung
Die Flucht der Zeiten messend mit dem Schlag des *Jetzt*.

Prologue/ ON THE OLD WINCHESTER PLAYHOUSE/
OVER THE OLD BUTCHER'S SHAMBLES

Whoe'er our stage examines, must excuse
The wondrous shifts of the dramatic Muse;
Then kindly listen, while the prologue rambles
From wit to beef, from Shakespeare to the shambles!
Divided only by one flight of stairs,
The monarch swaggers, and the butcher swears!
Quick the transition when the curtain drops,
From meek Monimia's moans to mutton-chops!
While for Lothario's loss Lavinia cries,
Old women scold, and dealers d—n your eyes!
Here Juliet listens to the gentle lark,
There in harsh chorus hungry bulldogs bark.
Cleavers and scimitars give blow for blow,
And heroes bleed above, and sheep below!
While tragic thunders shake the pit and box,
Rebellows to the roar the staggering ox.
Cow-horns and trumpets mix their martial tones,
Kidneys and kings, mouthing and marrow-bones.
Suet and sighs, blank verse and blood abound,
And form a tragi-comedy around.
With weeping lovers, dying calves complain,
Confusion reigns—chaos is come again!
Hither your steelyards, butchers, bring, to weigh
The pound of flesh, Antonio's bond must pay!
Hither your knives, ye Christians, clad in blue,
Bring to be whetted by the ruthless Jew!

PROLOG AUF DAS OLD WINCHESTER THEATER
ÜBER DER ALTMETZGER-FLEISCHEREY

Der muß entschuldigen, wer unsre Bühne prüft,
Dramatis Musæ curieuse Wechselschichten:
So lauscht nur huldvoll dem Prologe, der da streift
von Witz zu Wurst, von Shakespeare bis zum Schlachten!
Nur unterteilt von einer Stiegenflucht
Stelzt der Monarch dieweil der Metzger flucht!
Schnell ist der Übergang beim Vorhangfallen
Von Hamlets Handlungshemmungen zu Hammelballen!
Dieweil Levinia um den Verlust Lotharios weint,
D–n Händler eure Augen, zankt Vettelvolk vereint!
Hier lauscht die Julia der Lerche Klangverheißen,
Dort blaffen harschen Chorgesang hungrige Bullenbeißer.
Krummdolch wie Metzgermesser mit Schlag um Schlag verwunden,
Und Helden bluten oben, und Hammel bluten unten!
Dieweil tragische Donner Parkett & Rang erschüttern,
Kommt der rebellsche Ochs bei dem Radau ins Schlittern.
Kuhhörner & Fanfaren ihr Kriegsgetön verflechten,
MarkKnochen: markig Reden – KidneyNieren: Königsnichten,
Rindertalg: SeufzerTalk – reinlich Blankvers: reichlich Blut
Sich nur zu gut zu einer Tragicomœdie configurirt.
Mit schlúchzenden Líebenden klágen hier stérbende Kálber:
Verwirrung selber herrscht! Kaos erneut regirt!
Bringt eure Waagen her, ihr Metzger, um zu wägen
Das Pfund von Fleisch das des Antonios Pfand!
Hierher die Messer, Christenvolk im blau Gewand,
Daß sie Herr Shylock ruchlos wetzen möge!

Hard is our lot, who, seldom doomed to eat,
Cast a sheep's-eye on this forbidden meat—
Gaze on sirloins, which, ah! we cannot carve,
And in the midst of legs of mutton—starve!
But would you to our house in crowds repair,
Ye generous captains, and ye blooming fair,
The fate of Tantalus we should not fear,
Nor pine for a repast that is so near.
Monarchs no more would supperless remain,
Nor pregnant queens for cutlets long in vain.

THOMAS WARTON (1728-1790)
*Prologue/ ON THE OLD WINCHESTER PLAYHOUSE/
OVER THE OLD BUTCHER'S SHAMBLES*

Hart unser Loos, die wir ein Mahl stets meiden müssen,
Schafsdumme Augen werfen auf dies verbotne Essen,
Auf Lendenstück – ah! – starrn, die wir nicht schneiden wissen,
Inmitten unter Hammelkeulen lungernd dennoch hungern!
Doch kämt in unser Haus zu Haufen ihr, in Massen,
Ihr generösen Captains, Ihr Schönheiten indessen,
Dann könnten wir vermissen des Tantalus Geschick,
Nicht müßte uns das Wasser dann im Mund zusammenlaufen
Nach einem guten Bissen.
Monarchen bräuchten nimmer hier ein Abendbrot entbehren,
Und schwangre Königinnen nicht zu lang nach einem Kotlett gieren.

I hate that drum's discordant sound,
Parading round, and round, and round:
To thoughtless youth it pleasure yields,
And lures from cities and from fields,
To sell their liberty for charms
Of tawdry lace, and glittering arms;
And when Ambition's voice commands,
To march, and fight, and fall, in foreign lands.

I hate that drum's discordant sound,
Parading round, and round, and round:
To me it talks of ravag'd plains,
And burning towns, and ruin'd swains,
And mangled limbs, and dying groans,
And widows' tears, and orphans' moans;
And all that Misery's hand bestows.
To fill the catalogue of human woes.

JOHN SCOTT OF AMWELL (1730 - 1783)
Retort on the Foregoing

Ich *hass'* der Trommel missetönend BUMM,
im Gleichschritt marsch! und marsch! und marsch herum:
denkfauler Jugend sie nur Spaass vor Augen hält,
lockt sie aus Städten & vom Feld,
daß sie verramschet ihre Freiheit für den Tand
von Wappenflitter, Tressen, Litzenband
und, wenn des Ehrgeiz Stimm befiehlt,
für Marsch & Schlacht & Fall in fremdem Land.

Ich hass' der Trumel diskordantes WUMM,
im Gleichschritt: marsch! und: marsch! und: kehrtschwenktum:
Mir spricht sie von der Ebenen Zerstören,
von Städtebrand & Landmannes Verheeren,
von Stümmelgliedern und des Sterbens Qualgezisch,
von Witwenjammer & von Waisenzähren:
all dem, was Elends Hände aufgetischt,
den Katalog menschlicher Leiden zu vermehren.

158 Forth goes the woodman, leaving unconcerned
The cheerful haunts of man, to wield the axe
And drive the wedge in yonder forest drear,
From morn to eve his solitary task.
Shaggy, and lean, and shrewd with pointed ears
And tail cropped short, half lurcher and half cur,
His dog attends him. Close behind his heel
Now creeps he slow; and now with many a frisk
Wide scampering, snatches up the drifted snow
With ivory teeth, or ploughs it with his snout;
Then shakes his powdered coat, and barks for joy.
Heedless of all his pranks, the sturdy churl
Moves right toward the mark; nor stops for aught,
But now and then with pressure of his thumb
To adjust the fragrant charge of a short tube
That fumes beneath his nose: the trailing cloud
Streams far behind him, scenting all the air.

*

Fort stapft der Waldmann; ihn bekümmert nicht
des Menschen heitre Wohnstatt, doch die Axt zu schwingen,
den Keil zu treiben, drüben, in dem öden Forst:
das ist sein einsam Werk vom Morgen bis zum Abend.
Struppig, verschlagen, dürr, die Ohren spitzelnd
und eingekniffnen Schweifs, halb Pointer & halb Köter,
begleitet ihn sein Hund. Hier, dicht bei Fuß,
schlurcht lahm er hin – dort, weit voraus im Laufe
schnappt tänzelnd er, mit elfenbeinern Zähnen
nach pudernd Schnee; pflügt ihn gar mit der Schnauze,
schüttelt den weißbestäubten Pelz, und bellt vor Glück.
Nicht achtend solcher Possen, marschiert der derbe Kerl
geraden Wegs fürbaß; nichts läßt ihn innehalten;
nur dann und wann, mit einer Pressung seines Daumens,
drückt er der kurzen Pfeife duftge Füllung fest,
die unter seiner Nase qualmt: der Wolke Spur
verbreitet hinter ihm sich weit. Aroma tränkt die Luft.

*

God made the country, and man made the town.
What wonder, then, that health and virtue—gifts
That can alone make sweet the bitter draught
That life holds out to all—should most abound,
And least be threatened, in the fields and groves?
Possess ye therefore, ye who, borne about
In chariots and sedans, know no fatigue
But that of idleness, and taste no scenes,
But such as art contrives, possess ye still
Your element; there only can ye shine;
There only minds like yours can do no harm.
Our groves were planted to console at noon
The pensive wanderer in their shades. At eve,
The moonbeam, sliding softly in between
The sleeping leaves, is all the light they wish;
Birds warbling, all the music. We can spare
The splendour of your lamps; they but eclipse
Our softer satellite. Your songs confound
Our more harmonious notes: the thrush departs
Scared, and the offended nightingale is mute.
There is a public mischief in your mirth;
It plagues your country. Folly such as yours,
Graced with a sword, and worthier of a fan,
Has made—what enemies could ne'er have done—
Our arch of empire, steadfast but for you,
A mutilated structure, soon to fall.

*

Gott schuf das Land – der Mensch erschuf die Stadt.
Wen wunderts dann, daß Tugend & Gesundheit – Gaben, die
den bittern Trunk, den Leben allen beut, allein
versüßen können – im Überflusse und am wenigsten
bedroht sind auf Feldern und in Hainen?
Ja, klammert euch, die ihr in Sänften und Kaleschen
euch schaukeln laßt und nur die Müdigkeit
des Müßigganges kennt, und nur das Bild goutirt,
so Kunst ersinnet, klammert euch
an euer Element: dort könnt ihr prätendiren, da allein
kann ohne Schaden wirken euer Sinn.
Den nachdenklichen Wanderer am Mittag zu erquicken
im Schatten, ward unser Hain gepflanzt. Des abends ist
der Mondenstrahl, sacht gleitend durch der Blätter Schlaf,
das Licht, mit dem sei sich bescheiden; zur Musik
g'nügt ihnen Vogelsang. Gern missen wir
den Prachtschein eurer Lampen: die verdunkeln nur
den sanfteren Trabanten unsers Himmels. Euer Singen
stört unsre Harmonien: auf fliegt die Drossel,
aufgeschreckt, und die gekränkte Nachtigall verstummt.
Ein öffentliches Ärgernis ist eure Afferey:
's ist eine Pest dem Lande! Denn Geckentum wie eures,
degen-gegürtet aber würd'ger eines Fächers,
es hat erreicht, was noch kein Feind zustandgebracht:
daß (unerschütterbar, nur nicht von euch) der Bogen unsers Empire
ein morsches Bauwerk ward, einsturzgefährdet.

*

England, with all thy faults, I love thee still—
My country! and, while yet a nook is left
Where English minds and manners may be found,
Shall be constrained to love thee. Though thy clime
Be fickle, and thy year most part deformed
With dripping rains, or withered by a frost,
I would not yet exchange thy sullen skies,
And fields without a flower, for warmer France
With all her vines; nor for Ausonia's groves
Of golden fruitage, and her myrtle bowers.
To shake thy senate, and from heights sublime
Of patriot eloquence to flash down fire
Upon thy foes, was never meant my task:
But I can feel thy fortunes, and partake
Thy joys and sorrows, with as true a heart
As any thunderer there. And I can feel
Thy follies, too; and with a just disdain
Frown at effeminates, whose very looks
Reflect dishonour on the land I love.
How, in the name of soldiership and sense,
Should England prosper, when such things, as smooth
And tender as a girl, all essenced o'er
With odours, and as profligate as sweet;
Who sell their laurel for a myrtle wreath,
And love when they should fight; when such as these
Presume to lay their hand upon the ark
Of her magnificent and awful cause?

*

England! Hab dich noch lieb, trotz deinen Fehlern all,
mein Heimatland, und werd, solang auch nur *ein* Eckchen,
wo englisch Geist & Sitten noch zu finden,
dich lieben müssen. Wie unbeständig auch
dein Clima sey (dein Jahr meist derangirt
von Tröpfelregen; oder frostverdorret) –
würd' deine Himmel doch, die mürrischen, niemals,
auch nicht die unbeblümten Felder tauschen für
warm Frankreich, seine Reben; nicht für Ausoniens
Goldfrüchtewälder, ihre Myrtenlauben.
Deinen Senat zu schütteln, von erhab'nen Höhen
der patriot'schen Eloquenz den Bannstrahl wettern
auf deine Feinde, war mir nie bestimmt –
doch kann ich heiß empfinden die Fortüne, und teilhaben
an deinen Leid & Freuden: nicht minder ächt im Herzen
als jeder Donnerer. Und deine Torheiten,
die fühl' ich auch. Rümpf' meine Nas zu Recht,
runzel die Stirn: ob jenen Schwuchteln, deren Äugeln schon
Unehre wirft auf mein geliebtes Land.
Wie denn – im Namen von Vernunft & Militär –
soll England prosperirn, wenn sowas, weichlich,
verpimpelt wie ein Mädel, ganz odorirt
und parfumirt, so liederlich wie süßlich,
das seinen Lorbeer für ein Myrtenzweig verscherbelt,
und *liebt* wo's *kämpfen* sollte, wenn sowas,
wie's scheint, die Hand legt an die Wiege
ihrer großartigen, sublimen Abkunft?

*

Now stir the fire, and close the shutters fast,
Let fall the curtains, wheel the sofa round,
And while the bubbling and loud-hissing urn
Throws up a steamy column, and the cups
That cheer but not inebriate, wait on each,
So let us welcome peaceful evening in.
Not such his evening, who with shining face
Sweats in the crowded theatre, and, squeezed
And bored with elbow-points through both his sides,
Out-scolds the ranting actor on ihe stage.
Nor his, who patient stands 'till his feet throb
And his head thumps, to feed upon the breath
Of patriots bursting with heroic rage,
Or placemen, all tranquillity and smiles.
This folio of four pages, happy work!
Which not ev'n critics criticise, that holds
Inquisitive attention while I read
Fast bound in chains of silence, which the fair,
Though eloquent themselves, yet fear to break,
What is it but a map of busy life,
Its fluctuations and its vast concerns?
Here runs the mountainous and craggy ridge
That tempts ambition. On the summit, see,
The seals of office glitter in his eyes;
He climbs, he pants, he grasps them. At his heels,
Close at his heels a demagogue ascends,
And with a dexterous jerk soon twists him down
And wins them, but to lose them in his turn.
Here rills of oily eloquence in soft
Meanders lubricate the course they take;

Nun schürt die Glut, und schließt die Fensterläden;
senkt die Portieren nieder; dreht die Couch herum;
und da aus blubberndem, laut zischendem Gefäß
des Dampfes Säule steigt, und eines jeden
die Schale harret, die erheitert – nicht berauscht,
laßt uns den friedevollen Abend willkomm' heißen.
Nicht dessen Abend, der mit schimmerndem Gesicht
im vollen Schauspielhause schwitzt und, eingedruckt,
mit Rippenstößen, links & rechts gerammet,
den schwülst'gen Mimen von der Bühne buht.
Nicht des, der lammfromm harrt (bis es im Fuße
ihm pocht und's ihm im Haupte schwurbelt) sich zu weiden
am Air des Patrioten (: heroisch platzend schier vor Rage) oder
des Parvenu-Politikers: ganz Biedersinn & Feixen!
Dies Folio: 4 Seiten: glücklichs Werk!:
nicht mal der Kritiker würd's kritisiern, es beut
Neugier und Spannung, wenn beim Lesen
ich fasciniret bin in SchweigeFesseln, die zu lösen
sich meine Lieben (die doch selbst beredt) nicht trauen:
Ist's nicht die Landkarte geschäftgen Lebens selber,
seiner verzweigten Unternehmungen, Fluctuationen?
Hier läuft ein Felsengrat: steil reizet er
den Ehrgeiz: schau, von droben schon
glitzt ihm des Amtes Siegelwürd' ins Auge!
Er klimmt – er keucht – : er hascht sie! – Ihm zu Füßen
dicht auf den Fersen steigt ein Demagoge nach,
bringt ihn zu Fall mit feingesponnener Intrigue –
gewinnet sie! – nur um sie wieder zu verspielen.
Dort schmiert der ölichten Beredsamkeiten Rinnsal
in sanft Mäandern den Verlauf ein, den es nimmt:

The modest speaker is ashamed and grieved
T'engross a moment's notice, and yet begs,
Begs a propitious ear for his poor thoughts,
However trivial all that he conceives.
Sweet bashfulness! it claims, at least, this praise,
The dearth of information and good sense
That it foretells us, always comes to pass.
Cataracts of declamation thunder here,
There forests of no-meaning spread the page
In which all comprehension wanders lost;
While fields of pleasantry amuse us there,
With merry descants of a nation's woes.
The rest appears a wilderness of strange
But gay confusion, roses for the cheeks
And lilies for the brows of faded age,
Teeth for the toothless, ringlets for the bald,
Heaven, earth, and ocean plundered of their sweets,
Nectareous essences, Olympian dews,
Sermons and city feasts and favourite airs,
Ethereal journeys, submarine exploits...

WILLIAM COWPER (1731-1800)
from «The Task»: The Woodman/ Town & Country Life/
Effeminate Englishmen/ Reading the Newspaper

Der Redner, so bescheiden!, er schämt sich, ja ihn grämet
nur *einen* Augenblicks Aufmerksamkeit zu heischen, und doch fleht er,
barmt seinem schlicht Gedankchen *ein* geneigtes Ohr,
wie trivial auch alles sey, was er verzapft.
Süß Blödigkeit!: zumindest fodert sie dies Lob:
Den Mangel an Gehalt, Information, den sie
uns prophezeit – er kömmt verläßlich!
Der Declamatio Katarakte donnern hier –
dort dehnen Wälder sich des Nicht-Bedeutens aufs Papier
in denen jed Begreifen irrewandert. Wohingegen
uns hier die Felder der Ergötzung amusirn
mit flotten Gassenhauern von den Schmerzen der Nazion.
Der Rest erscheint als Wildnis: eine sonderbare
doch lustge Confusion: den Wangen Rosen...
Für des gewelkten Alters Stirne: Lilien...
Zähne dem Zahnlosen & Löckchen für den Kahlen...
Erd Himmel Ozean beraubet seiner Schätze;
Nektar-Essenzen... des Olymps Ambrosia...
Predigten... City-Feste... LieblingsArien...
Luft-Reisen... submarine Beutezüge...

159   Quæ lenta accedit, quam velox præterit hora!
	Ut capias, patiens esto, sed esto vigil!

*

Slow comes the hour; its passing speed how great!
	Waiting to seize it—vigilantly wait!

WILLIAM COWPER (1731-1800)
Motto for a Clock/ sculptured by Bacon for George III
(now adorning Her Majesty's presence chamber in Windsor Castle)

Quæ lenta accedit, quam velox præterit hora!
　Ut capias, patiens esto, sed esto vigil!

　　　　　　　　　＊

Die langsam anschleichet, schnell ja verfliegt sie, die Stund.
　Willst du sie halten – geduldig sey, doch auf der Hut auch!

160   Could Homer come himself, distress'd and poor,
        And tune his harp at Rhedycina's door,
        The rich old vixen would exlaim, (I fear,)
        «Begone! no tramper gets a farthing here.»

WILLIAM COWPER (1731-1800)
On the Neglect of Homer

Könnte Homer höchstselbst – abgerissen und ärmlich –
Die Leyer anstimmen vor Alt-Rhedycinens Portal:
Ich fürcht', das wohlhäbige Oxford würd näseln,
«Verschwindet! Kein' Farthing bekömmet ein Landstreicher hier!»

161 To purify their wine, some people bleed
A lamb into the barrel, and succeed;
No nostrum, planters say, is half so good
To make fine sugar, as a negro's blood.
Now lambs and negroes both are harmless things,
And hence perhaps this wondrous virtue springs.
'Tis in the blood of innocence alone—
Good cause why planters never try their own.

WILLIAM COWPER (1731-1800)
Epigram

Um ihren Wein zu *raffiniren*, gießen manche 's Blut
von einem *Lamm* ins Faß: und siehe, es wird gut!
Kein heimlich Mittel, sagt der Pflanzer, ist nur halb so gut
für Zucker-Raffinade, als eines *Neger-Sclaven Blut.*
Gut, Neger-Lämmer harmlos' Dinge seyn:
daher vielleicht die wunderlichen Bräuche sprießen.
Es lieget wohl am *Unschulds*-Blut allein –
Kein Wunder dann, daß Pflanzer nie ihr eignes gießen.

Rebellion is my theme all day;
   I only wish 'twould come
(As who knows but perhaps it may?)
   A little nearer home.

Yon roaring boys, who rave and fight
   On t'other side the Atlantic,
I always held them in the right,
   But most so when most frantic.

When lawless mobs insult the court,
   That man shall be my toast,
If breaking windows be the sport,
   Who bravely breaks the most.

But oh! for him my fancy culls
   The choicest flowers she bears,
Who constitutionally pulls
   Your house about your ears.

Such civil broils are my delight,
   Though some folks can't endure them,
Who say the mob are mad outright,
   And that a rope must cure them.

A rope! I wish we patriots had
   Such strings for all who need 'em—
What? hang a man for going mad!
   Then farewell British freedom.

WILLIAM COWPER (1731-1800)
The Modern Patriot

Mein Elixier heißt *Rebellion*;
 Ich wünschte nur, sie wär
(vielleicht ja doch, wer weiß es schon?)
 mehr näher, käme her.

Den Schreihals, der die Messer wetzt
 jenseits Atlantiks Meer,
hab ich schon immer hochgeschätzt:
 je wüster, desto höh'r.

Nun Mob gesetzlos höhnt dem Recht,
 leer ich mein Glas auf den
(da Scheibenschmeißen Kurzweil heißt)
 der da die meisten Fenster schmeißt.

Doch, oh! dem sammlet mein Gemüth
 den rarsten Blütenflor,
der konstitutionell itzt zieht
 dein Haus dir übers Ohr.

So'n Bürgerkampf ist mein Plaisir,
 auch wenn's nicht alle teilen:
das hält dem Mob den «Irrsinn» für,
 ein «Strick» nur könnt ihn heilen.

Was Strick! Ach hätten doch wir Patrioten
 jedem Bedürft'gen einen zugedacht!
Wie? – hängen, nur weil's Idioten? – :
 Dann, Brit'sche Freiheit, Gute Nacht!

163 Sweet nymph, who art, it seems, accused
    Of stealing George's pen,
  Use it thyself, and having used,
    E'en give it him again;

  The plume of his that has one scrap
    Of thy good sense expressed,
  Will be a feather in his cap
    Worth more than all his *crest*.

WILLIAM COWPER (1731-1800)
Lines on a late Theft

Man hat Euch, Nymphchen, angeklagt
 des Raubs von GEORG's Feder:
So scribbelt nur, wie's Euch behagt,
 und gebt erst dann sie wieder.

Den Kiel, mit dem Ihr kratzen tut,
 gut & vernünftig schrappen,
wird ihm zur Feder-auf-dem-Hut:
 mehr wert, denn all sein Wappen.

Maria, could Horace have guess'd
   What honour awaited his ode
To his own little volume address'd,
   The honour which you have bestow'd,—
Who have traced it in characters here,
   So elegant, even, and neat,
He had laugh'd at the critical sneer
   Which he seems to have trembled to meet.

And, «Sneer if you please,» he had said,
   «A nymph shall hereafter arise,
Who shall give me, when you are all dead,
   The glory your malice denies;
Shall dignity give to my lay,
   Although but a mere begatelle;
And even a poet shall say,
   Nothing ever was written so well.»

WILLIAM COWPER (1731-1800)
To Mrs. Throckmorton/ On her beautiful Transcript
of Horace's Ode «Ad librum suum»

Maria: wenn Hóraz vernähme,
   welche Ehr seiner Ode erkiesen
(der Ode, gebettet in seinen klein Band)
   die Ehre, die *du* ihm erwiesen,
in Lettern sorgsam entblättert,
   in Buchstaben, fein, elegant – :
er lachte des Kritikers Häme,
   vor der er sonst furchtsam gezittert.

Und spräche: «Ey, höhnt nur so frei!
   Seht die Nymphe, die nach uns dort geht:
die gereicht mir – wenn wir alle tot –
   zum Ruhm, den die Neider mir wehren,
meinen Versen sogar Dignität,
   wiewohls nur'n Opusculum sey.
Ja, ein Dichter höchstselbst wird erklären:
   Nichts ward je geschrieben so gut.»

165   Yon ancient prude, whose withered features show
She might be young some forty years ago,
Her elbows pinioned close upon her hips,
Her head erect, her fan upon her lips,
Her eyebrows arched, her eyes both gone astray
To watch yon amorous couple in their play,
With bony and unkerchiefed neck defies
The rude inclemency of wintry skies,
And sails with lappet head and mincing airs
Duly at clink of bell to morning prayers.
To thrift and parsimony much inclined,
She yet allows herself that boy behind;
The shivering urchin, bending as he goes,
With slipshod heels, and dewdrop at his nose,
His predecessor's coat advanced to wear,
Which future pages yet are doomed to share,
Carries her Bible tucked beneath his arm,
And hides his hands to keep his fingers warm.
   She, half an angel in her own account,
Doubts not hereafter with the saints to mount,
Though not a grace appears on strictest search,
But that she fasts, and *item*, goes to church.
Conscious of age, she recollects her youth,
And tells, not always with an eye to truth,
Who spanned her waist, and who, where'er he came,
Scrawled upon glass Miss Bridget's lovely name,
Who stole her slipper, filled it with tokay,
And drank the little bumper every day.

Schau an: der prüde Besen: ihre Ausgedörrtheit zeigt,
sie möcht vor circa vierzig Jahren jung gewesen sein:
fest an die Hüften sind die Ellbogen geklemmt;
aufrecht der Kopf, der Fächer an den Lippen,
die Brauen hochgezogen, seitabwärts schieln die Blicke
ein amouröses Paar bei seinem Spiele zu verfolgen;
knochig & unbetucht der Hals, er trotzt
des Winterhimmels gnadenloser Tücke: und so segelt
mit Zipfelkopfputz & gezierter Haltung die Fregatte
punct Glockenschlag pflichteifrig in die Morgenmette.
Obschon auf Sparsamkeit, ja, Geiz geaicht,
erlaubt sie, daß ein Bub ihr schlurchet nach:
Der Bengel, bibbernd, beuget sich beim Gehen
in alten Latschen; Tau träuft ihm vom Nasendach;
der Mantel seines Vorgängers ist ihm vermacht
(und seinem Nachfolger wird gleiches Erbe dräuen),
schleppt ihr die Bibel untern Arm gepreßt,
gräbt ein die Hände, da sich seine Finger bläuen.
 Sie, eignem Maß zufolge fast ein Engel, hegt nicht Zweifel,
dereinst dort oben mit den Heiligen zu wandeln,
doch, wie genau man hinsäh auch, an Christentugend
zeigt sich nur, daß sie fastet, *item*, in die Kirche geht.
Des Alters eingedenk, besinnt sie sich der Jugend,
erzählt, doch freilich ohne's mit der Wahrheit zu genau zu nehmen,
wer ihr die Taille maß, und wer, um anzubandeln,
Miss Bridgets holden Namen in die Scheibe kratzte;
wer ihr die Schühchen raubte, sie mit Tokajer füllte
um jeden Tag den kleinen Kelch zu leeren.

    Of temper as envenomed as an asp,
Censorious, and her every word a wasp,
In faithful memory she records the crimes,
Or real, or fictitious, of the times;
Laughs at the reputations she has torn,
And holds them dangling at arm's length in scorn.
    Such are the fruits of sanctimonious pride,
Of malice fed while flesh is mortified:
Take, madam, the reward of all your prayers,
Where hermits and where Brahmins meet with theirs;
Your portion is with them; nay, never frown,
But, if you please, some fathoms lower down.

WILLIAM COWPER (1731 - 1800)
An Ancient Prude

So giftigen Gemüts wie eine Aspisviper,
vor Schmähsucht strotzend (jedes Wort ein Wespenstich),
hat ihr getreu Gedächtnis aufgespeichert jedes
reale oder eingebildete Verbrechen ihrer Zeit;
lacht jedem guten Ruf, den *sie* compromittirt,
und hält ihn rümpfend eine Armeslänge von sich weit.
  Dies sind die Früchte frommer Aufgeblasenheit,
von Bosheit wohlgenährt, dieweil das Fleisch kasteit:
Nehmt hin, mein Fräulein, der Gebete Lohn,
wo Eremiten & Brahminen sich mit diesen gatten:
Teilt euch den Lohn! – Nein, runzelt nicht die Brau'n –
please, ein paar Faden tiefer! – : wolln Madame verstatten? –

166   Other stones the era tell,
When some feeble mortal fell;
I stand here to date the birth
Of these hardy sons of Earth.
  Which shall longest brave the sky,
Storm and frost—these oaks or I?
Pass an age or two away,
I must moulder and decay;
But the years that crumble me
Shall invigorate the tree,
Spread its branch, dilate its size,
Lift its summit to the skies.
  Cherish honour, virtue, truth,
So shalt thou prolong thy youth.
Wanting these, however fast
Man be fix'd, and form'd to last,
He is lifeless even now,
Stone at heart, and cannot grow.

*

Reader! behold a monument
That asks no sigh or tear,
Though it perpetuate the event
Of a great burial here.

WILLIAM COWPER (1731-1800)
Two Inscriptions: For a Stone/ erected at the Sowing of a Grove of Oaks at Chillington, The Seat of T. Giffard, Esq., June 1790/ For a Stone erected on a similar Occasion at the same Place in the following Year.

Ein ander Stein die Zeit erzählt
von schwachen Sterblichen dahingefällt
Doch ich datier das Wiegenfest
von diesen Erdensöhnen stark & fest
  Wer trotzt am längsten denn dem Frost
dem Sturm & Himmel – diese Eichen oder ich?
Laß ein, zwei Menschenalter nur vorüberwallen
schon muß ich wittern und verfallen
jedoch die Jahr' die brökeln mich
solln dem Baume Kraft zusagen
die Äste spreiten den Umfang breiten
bis seine Wipfel in den Himmel ragen
  Hege Wahrheit Ehre Tugend
also verlängre deine Jugend:
Er strebet auch danach, der Mensch, wie schnell
er auch geformt zu dauern in der Still' –
leblos ist er sogar nun.
Ein Stein am Herz. Kann nicht gedeihn.

*

Bleib, Leser, sinnend du am Monumente stehn
das heischt nicht Seufzen oder Zähr'
wiewohl's verewigt das Geschehn
von einem Großbegräbnis hier

167 Though once a puppy, and though Fop by name,
Here moulders one whose bones some honour claim;
No sycophant, although of spaniel race,
And though no hound, a martyr to the chase.
Ye squirrels, rabbits, leverets, rejoice!
Your haunts no longer echo to his voice;
This record of his fate exulting view,
He died worn out with vain pursuit of you.
«Yes,»—the indignant shade of Fop replies—
«And worn with vain pursuit, man also dies.»

WILLIAM COWPER (1731 -1800)
Epitaph on FOP,/ A Dog belonging to Lady Throckmorton.
(August, 1792.)

Zwar Püppchen einst und ‹Fop› genannt, hier modert
ein Knochenhauf der iedoch Ehrfurcht fodert:
Kein Sykophant zwar, doch ein Spaniel, wie man sagt;
Kein Hetzhund zwar, und doch ein Märtyrer der Jagd.
Ihr Häselchen & Eichhörnchen, jauchzt auf!
Nicht länger echot sein Gekläffe eurem Lauf:
Frohlocket nun! Hier, sein Geschicke schaugt!
: Er starb an sinnloser Verfolgung, ausgelaugt.
«Zum Sterben,» gibt Fops Geist, beleidigt, wider,
«vom eitlen Streben ausgelaugt, legt *auch der Mensch* sich nieder!»

Amid this fearful trance, a thundering sound
He hears, and thrice the hollow decks rebound;
Upstarting from his couch on deck he sprung,
Thrice with shrill note the boatswain's whistle rung:
All hands unmoor! proclaims a boisterous cry,
All hands unmoor! the cavern'd rocks reply.
Roused from repose, aloft the sailors swarm,
And with their levers soon the windlass arm:
The order given, up springing with a bound,
They fix the bars, and heave the windlass round,
At every turn the clanging pauls resound:
Up-torn reluctant from its oozy cave
The ponderous anchor rises o'er the wave.
High on the slippery masts the yards ascend,
And far abroad the canvas wings extend.
Along the glassy plain the vessel glides,
While azure radiance trembles on her sides;
The lunar rays in long reflection gleam,
With silver deluging the fluid stream.
Levant and Thracian gales alternate play,
Then in th'Egyptian quarter die away.
A calm ensues; adjacent shores they dread,
The boats, with rowers manned, are sent ahead;
With cordage fastened to the lofty prow,
Aloof to sea the stately ship they tow;
The nervous crew their sweeping oars extend,
And pealing shouts the shore of Candia rend:
Success attends their skill! the danger's o'er!
The port is doubled, and beheld no more.

WILLIAM FALCONER (1732 - 1769)
from «The Shipwreck»

In dieser fürchterlichen Trance hört er Grollen
wie Donner – dreimal die Decks hohl widerrollen –
auf sprang er von der Decksliege! Mit Gellen
der Maat dreimal ließ seine Pfeife schrillen:
Anker lichten alle Mann! läßt der rauh Befehl erschallen:
Anker lichten alle Mann! tönt der Grotten Widerhallen.
Aus rückt, aus ihrer Ruh geschreckt, flugs der Matrosen Schwarm:
Mit Armen rasch die Ankerspills bestückt!
Auf das Commando hin, als wär's mit *einem* Will'
befestigt man die Arme, spiert rund das Ankerspill;
mit jeder Windung widerhallt das *Klong!* des Pall:
Aus seiner schlammgen Höhle zögernd hochgezogen
erhebt sich der profunde Anker aus den Wogen.
Am glatten Mast zieht man die Rahen hoch:
und breit entspreitet sich des Takelns Canvas-Tuch.
Nun gleitet das Gefährt auf glasigem Geflimmer
und ein azurner Zitterglast um seine Flanken fließt;
des Mondes Strahl im langen Widerschimmer
das Kielwasser mit Silber übergießt.
Im Widerspiel von thrazisch-levantinisch' Winden
will gen Ägyptens Land das Lüftchen schwinden ...
und eine Flaute folgt. Von nächster Küste drohet Graus:
man schickt mit Ruderern bemannte Boot' voraus;
am hohen Vordersteven gut vertäut
pulln sie gen Luv das stattliche Gefährt,
und die nervöse Mannschaft die Ruderspann' erhöht,
bis tosendes *Hurra!* Candias stille Küste sehrt:
Erfolg lohnt ihr Geschick! Vorbei ist die Gefahr!
Die Backbordwache, doppelt, späht' nichts im Okular.

169   On parent knees, a naked new-born child,
Weeping thou sat'st while all around thee smiled:
So live, that sinking to thy life's last sleep,
Calm thou may'st smile, whilst all around thee weep.

Sir William Jones (1746-1794)
Epigram

Als Kind, nackt, neugeborn, auf des Vaters Beinen
Saßest du weinend, dieweil die Deinen sich lächelnd ergetzten.
Lebe denn! – : daß du einst, sinkend in Schlaf, den letzten,
in Frieden magst lächeln, dieweil alle rings um dich weinen.

Says Tom to Jack, «'Tis very odd,
These representatives of God,
In colour, way of life and evil,
Should be so very like the Devil.»
Jack, understand, was one of those,
Who mould religion in the nose,
A red hot Methodist; his face
Was full of puritanic grace,
His loose lank hair, his low gradation,
Declared a late regeneration;
Among the daughters long renowned,
For standing upon holy ground;
Never in carnal battle beat,
Though sometimes forced to a retreat.
But C—t, hero as he is,
Knight of incomparable phiz,
When pliant doxy seems to yield,
Courageously forsakes the field.
Jack, or to write more gravely, John,
Through hills of Wesley's works had gone;
Could sing one hundred hymns by rote;
Hymns which will sanctify the throat:
But some indeed composed so oddly,
You'd swear 'twas bawdy songs made godly.

THOMAS CHATTERTON (1752 - 1770)
The Methodist

«Ist sonderbar,» sagt Tom zu Jack,
«daß dieses Gotts-Vertreter-Pack
nach Aussehn, *Way of Life*, und Üwel
gar nich viel anders als der Düwel.»
Jack, *nota ben*, war einer von den'n,
die'n Glauben aus der Nas sich drehn:
Ein glühnder Methodist. In sein Gesicht
sich puritan'sche Milde flicht;
Sein dünnes glattes Haar, der leisen Stimme Ton
besprach 'ne späte *Regeneration*
bei allen Töchtern lang bekannt,
da auf geweihtem Grund er stand
und nie in Fleisches Kampf gerungen –
zum Rückzug manchmal nur gezwungen.
Doch C–t, Held ohne Camouflage,
Ritter Der Beispiellosen Visage,
wenn, scheints, sich ne Schnalle geschmeidig ihm macht,
räumt couragirt das Feld der Schlacht.
Jack, besser: Johann (: würdger! grösser!),
durch-Berge-von-Wesleys-Werken-Fresser,
konnt aus dem Steigreif zwar einhundert Hymnen nölen,
die wohl mit heilger Salbung seine Kehle ölen –
doch manche componirt so kraus,
daß, müßt man's hören, möcht man schwören:
's wärn Frommsongs aus dem Freudenhaus.

171 Theirs is yon house that holds the parish poor,
Whose walls of mud scarce bear the broken door;
There, where the putrid vapours flagging, play,
And the dull wheel hums doleful through the day;—
There children dwell who know no parents' care;
Parents, who know no children's love, dwell there;
Heart-broken matrons on their joyless bed,
Forsaken wives and mothers never wed;
Dejected widows with unheeded tears,
And crippled age with more than childhood-fears;
The lame, the blind, and, far the happiest they!
The moping idiot and the madman gay.
  Here too the sick their final doom receive,
Here brought amid the scenes of grief, to grieve;
Where the loud groans from some sad chamber flow,
Mixed with the clamours of the crowd below;
Here sorrowing, they each kindred sorrow scan,
And the cold charities of man to man:
Whose laws indeed for ruined age provide,
And strong compulsion plucks the scrap from pride;
But still that scrap is bought with many a sigh,
And pride embitters what it can't deny.

Und hier das Haus, das die Gemeinde-Armen birgt,
des Lehmwand kaum die brüch'ge Türe stützt,
hier wo putride Dämpfe schon von fern anwehen,
tagein-tagaus das stumpfe Rad sich kläglich dreht:
da hausen Kinder, unkundig der elterlichen Obhut;
Eltern, die Kindesliebe nie gekannt;
Gebrochnen Herzens Frauen auf freudeloser Bettstatt;
Verlassne Eheweiber – Mütter, die nie im Ehestand;
Verhohlnen Schluchzens Witwen ohne Hoffnung;
Krüpplichtes Alter, mit mehr Angst denn Kinder haben;
Der Lahme – Blinde – und, bei weitem glücklichste:
Der possenreiche Narr – der stumpfe Idiot.
　Hier harrt der letzten Stunde auch der Kranke:
inmitten Leidensszenen bracht, auf daß er leide;
wo aus manch finstrer Kammer lautes Röcheln dringt,
sich mit dem Lärm vermengt der Menge unten;
Hier liegt der Sorgen eine mit der andern auf der Waage
und mit der kalten ‹Nächstenlieb' von-Mensch-zu-Mensch›,
des Nothgesetz zwar Fürsorg' heischt fürs Alter
und strikter Zwang entpflückt dem Stolz Almosen ja –
Doch wird solch Nothdurft nur mit vielem Murr'n entrissen
und Stolz vergällt, was er nicht weigern darf.

    Say ye, oppressed by some fantastic woes,
Some jarring nerve that baffles your repose;
Who press the downy couch, while slaves advance
With timid eye, to read the distant glance;
Who with sad prayers the weary doctor tease,
To name the nameless ever-new disease;
Who with mock patience dire complaints endure,
Which real pain and that alone can cure;
How would ye bear in real pain to lie,
Despised, neglected, left alone to die?
How would ye bear to draw your latest breath,
Where all that's wretched paves the way for death?
    Such is that room which one rude beam divides,
And naked rafters form the sloping sides;
Where the vile bands that bind the thatch are seen,
And lath and mud are all that lie between;
Save one dull pane, that, coarsely patched, gives way
To the rude tempest, yet excludes the day:
Here, on a matted flock, with dust o'erspread,
The drooping wretch reclines his languid head;
For him no hand the cordial cup applies,
Or wipes the tear that stagnates in his eyes;
No friends with soft discourse his pain beguile,
Or promise hope till sickness wears a smile.

Sprecht!: ihr, gezwakt von manchem eingebild't Wehwehchen,
von Nervenflattern, das die Mittagsruh euch stört, wenn unter euch
der Daunenpfühl sich biegt, dieweil mit scheuem Blick
sich, schon von fern die Stimmung deutend, Diener nähern;
die ihr mit Winselflehn den müden Doctor nervt, er soll
die immerneue, namenlose Krankheit beim Namen nennen;
die ihr mit Scheingeduld ertragt die gräßlichsten Beschwernisse,
die wahrer Schmerz, nur er allein, könnt heilen:
Wie trüget ihr's, den letzten Atemzug zu tun
wo Elend nur und Jammer dem Tod die Wege ebnen?
  Dies ist der Raum, nur unterteilt von einem rohen Stamm,
und nackte Balken bilden hier die Schrägen, wo man
die schnöden Schnüre sieht: des Reets Befestigung,
und Lehm & Sparren, mehr ist nicht dazwischen,
bloß eine schmuddelichte Scheibe, grob gefügt, die läßt
den rauhen Sturm hindurch, doch hält das Tag-Licht draußen;
Hier, auf ei'm wirren Haufen, staubbedeckt, entsinkt
das matte Haupt dem hoffnungsleeren Armen;
Ihm reichet keine Hand den Labetrunk,
tupft ihm die Thräne, so im Aug ihm stockt;
kein Freund verkürzt den Schmerz mit sanftem Plaudern, oder
verheißet Hoffnung, bis ein Lächel-Strahl
durch Krankheits-Wolken bricht.

But soon a loud and hasty summons calls,
Shakes the thin roof, and echoes round the walls;
Anon, a figure enters, quaintly neat,
All pride and business, bustle and conceit;
With looks unaltered by these scenes of woe,
With speed that, entering, speaks his haste to go;
He bids the gazing throng around him fly,
And carries Fate and Physic in his eye;
A potent quack, long versed in human ills,
Who first insults the victim whom he kills;
Whose murderous hand a drowsy Bench protect,
And whose most tender mercy is neglect.
  Paid by the parish for attendance here,
He wears contempt upon his sapient sneer;
In haste he seeks the bed where misery lies,
Impatience marked in his averted eyes;
And, some habitual queries hurried o'er,
Without reply, he rushes on the door;
His drooping patient, long inured to pain,
And long unheeded, knows remonstrance vain;
He ceases now the feeble help to crave
Of man; and silent sinks into the grave.

GEORGE CRABBE (1754 - 1832)
from «The Village»: The poor-house

   Doch nun ergeht ein hast'ger, lauter Aufruf
von Wand zu Wand als Echo: da bebt das dünne Dach;
und rasch tritt 'ne Gestalt herein: geziert & püppisch,
ganz Stolz & Business, ganz Profession & Dünkel,
mit Blicken in die Rund, die dies Szenarium des Leids nicht rührt,
mit einer Eile, die beim Eintreten vom Fortgehn bereits spricht;
und die ihn starr'nd umringen, scheucht wedelnd er hinweg;
Fatum & Heilkunst spricht aus seiner Miene:
Ein Quacksalber-mit-Einfluß, versiert in vielen Übeln,
der erst beleidigt noch sein Opfer, eh er's killt;
des Mörderhand wird protegirt von schnarchender Justiz
und dessen zartste Gnade noch – Mißachtung ist.
   Von der Gemeinde financirt zwecks ärztlicher Betreuung,
zeigt er Verachtung nur im sapienten Rümpfen;
hurtig sucht er das Lager auf, wo Elend liegt;
den abgewandten Blick kennzeichnet Ungeduld;
und, routinirte Fragen abgespult, der Antworten
nicht harrend, eilt der Thür er zu.
Sein mutloser Patient, der Pein so lang gewöhnt
und lang schon unbeachtet, weiß: Einwand ist umsonst.
Nicht mehr verlangt ihn nach dem schwachen Barmen
der ‹Mitmenschen›. Er schweigt – sinkt hin: ins Grab.

When my mother died I was very young,
And my Father sold me while yet my tongue
Could scarcely cry «'weep! 'weep! 'weep! 'weep!»
So your chimneys I sweep, & in soot I sleep.

There's little Tom Dacre, who cried when his head,
That curl'd like a lamb's back, was shav'd: so I said
«Hush, Tom! never mind it, for when your head's bare
You know that the soot cannot spoil your white hair.»

And so he was quiet, & that very night
As Tom was a-sleeping, he had such a sight!
That thousands of sweepers, Dick, Joe, Ned, & Jack,
Were all of them lock'd up in coffins of black.

And by came an Angel who had a bright key,
And he open'd the coffins & set them all free;
Then down a green plain leaping, laughing, they run,
And wash in a river, and shine in the Sun.

WILLIAM BLAKE (1757-1827)
The Chimney-Sweeper

Als mein Mutter starb, war ich noch ganz jung,
und mein Vater verkauft' mich, als noch kaum meine Zung
von dem *sweep!* *'weep!* *'weep!*, von dem *weep!* was wußt,
und so kehr ich euern Rauchfang und so schlaf ich in dem Ruß.

Da ist Little Tom Dacre, der heulte als sein Haar,
das gelocket wie ein Lammfell, ward geschoren ganz & gar;
Also sprach ich «Husch, Tom! Macht doch nichts, wenn ganz bar
ist dein Haupt – denn der Ruß? nicht verdirbet dein weiß Haar.»

Und da weinte er nicht mehr. Und in just derselben Nacht,
da im Schlaf Little Tom, ihm ein Traumgesichte lacht:
Daß Tausende von Kehrern, Dick und Joe und Jack und Bert
wären allesamt in Särge ganz in Schwarz eingesperrt;

Und ein Engel mit ei'm funkelschönen Schlüssel käm herbei
und der öffnete die Särge und der ließ sie alle frei:
da sprängen sie ins Grün hinunt, und lachten voller Wonn'
und sie badeten im Strome & sie glänzten in der Sonn.

Little Mary Bell had a fairy in a nut,
Long John Brown had the devil in his gut;
Long John Brown loved little Mary Bell,
And the fairy drew the devil into the nutshell.

Her fairy skipped out and her fairy skipped in;
He laughed at the devil, saying ‹Love is a sin.›
The devil he raged, and the devil he was wroth,
And the devil entered into the young man's broth.

He was soon in the gut of the loving young swain,
For John ate and drank to drive away love's pain;
But all he could do he grew thinner and thinner,
Though he ate and drank as much as ten men for his dinner.

Some said he had a wolf in his stomach day and night,
Some said he had the devil, and they guessed right;
The fairy skipped about in his glory, joy and pride,
And he laughed at the devil till poor John Brown died.

Then the fairy skipped out of the old nutshell,
And woe and alack for pretty Mary Bell!
For the devil crept in when the fairy skipped out,
And there goes Miss Bell with her fusty old nut.

WILLIAM BLAKE (1757 - 1827)
Long John Brown and Little Mary Bell

Little Mary Bell hatt nen Kobold in der Nuß,
Long John Brown hatt den Teufel im Gekrös;
Long John Brown liebte Mary Bell klein,
Und der Kobold jagt' den Teufel in die Nuß-Schal hinein.

Ihr Kobold hüpfte raus, hüpfte rein, hüpfte rund;
Er höhnete den Teufel und sprach ‹Lieben ist Sünd'›.
Den Teufel packte Rage, und er ward wutgemein,
Und der Teufel sprang dem Jungen in die Suppe hinein.

Er war bald im Gedärm des verliebten jungen Geck,
Denn John aß; und John trank; doch das Liebweh ging nicht weg;
Und es half alles nichts: er ward dünner und dünner,
Ob er gleich aß und trank, wie zehn Männer bei dem Dinner.

Manche sagten, 's sei der Wolf ihm im Magen Tag und Nacht,
Manche sagten, 's sei der Teufel – : und diese hatten recht;
Der Kobold wippte eitel, voller Stolz, voller Freud',
Und er höhnete den Teufel, bis zu Ende John Browns Leid.

Doch da schlüpfte der Kobold aus der Alt-Nuß-Schal',
Und nun Weh! Und nun Ach! für die hübsche Mary Bell,
Denn der Teufel kroch hinein, als der Kobold schlüpfte 'naus,
Und hier stakst nun Fräulein Bell mit ihrer ranzig tauben Nuß.

Is this a holy thing to see
In a rich and fruitful land,
Babes reduc'd to misery,
Fed with cold and usurous hand?

Is that trembling cry a song?
Can it be a song of joy?
And so many children poor?
It is a land of poverty!

And their sun does never shine,
And their fields are bleak & bare,
And their ways are fill'd with thorns:
It is eternal winter there.

For where-e'er the sun does shine,
And where-e'er the rain does fall,
Babe can never hunger there,
Nor poverty the mind appall.

WILLIAM BLAKE (1757-1827)
Holy Thursday

Ist dies denn heilig anzusehn
In einem reichen, fruchtbarn Land,
Wie Kinder klein ins Elend gehn
Genährt aus kalter Wucherhand?

Ist jener Zitterschrei ein Lied?
Kann das ein Lied der Freude sein?
Und so viele Kinder arm?
Es muß ein Land der Armut sein!

Und ihre Sonn hat nimmer Schein,
Ihr Feld ist immer kahl und bar;
Ihr Weg ist stets mit Dornen voll:
Es ist dort Winter immerdar.

Doch wo auf ewig Sonnenschein,
Wo Regen fließt, die Flur zu decken,
Kann nimmer hungern Kindlein klein,
Kann Armut nie den Geist erschrecken.

And did those feet in ancient time
Walk upon England's mountains green?
And was the holy Lamb of God
On England's pleasant pastures seen?

And did the Countenance Divine
Shine forth upon our clouded hills?
And was Jerusalem builded here
Among these dark Satanic Mills?

Bring me my Bow of burning gold:
Bring me my Arrows of desire:
Bring me my Spear: O clouds unfold!
Bring me my Chariot of fire.

I will not cease from Mental Fight,
Nor shall my Sword sleep in my hand
Till we have built Jerusalem
In England's green & pleasant Land.

WILLIAM BLAKE (1757-1827)
Milton. Preface

Sah man solch Füß in alter Zeit
Auf Englands grünen Bergen gehn?
Und ward das heilge Gotteslamm
Auf Englands schöner Weid gesehn?

Konnt göttlichen Gesichtes Schein
Auf unsre Wolkenhügel zielen?
Ward hier Jerusalem gebaut
Bei diesen dunklen Satansmühlen?

Bringt meinen Bogen mir aus Brennegold!
Bringt meine Pfeile von Verlangen!
Den Speer!: Ihr Wolken, seid entwolkt!
Bringt mir aus Feuer meinen Wagen!

Ich will vom Geistes Kampf nicht lassen,
Nicht ruhn solls Schwert in meiner Hand
Bis wir Jerusalem gebaut
In Englands grünem, schönem Land.

176 I wander thro' each charter'd street,
Near where the charter'd Thames does flow,
And mark in every face I meet
Marks of weakness, marks of woe.

In every cry of every Man,
In every Infant's cry of fear,
In every voice, in every ban,
The mind-forg'd manacles I hear.

How the Chimney-sweeper's cry
Every black'ning Church appalls;
And the hapless Soldier's sigh
Runs in blood down Palace walls.

But most thro' midnight streets I hear
How the youthful Harlot's curse
Blasts the new born Infant's tear,
And blights with plagues the Marriage hearse.

WILLIAM BLAKE (1757 - 1827)
London

Dicht wo die gültge Themse kocht
Durch jede gültge Straß' ich geh
Und spür in jedem Antlitz doch
Die Spur von Schwachheit, Spur von Weh.

In jedem Schrei von Jedermann,
In jedem Kinderschrei der Pein,
In jeder Stimme, jedem Bann
Hör ich die Fesseln geistgeschmied't.

Und wie des Rauchfangkehrers Leid
Jed rußig Kirche bangen macht
Und wie der Unglückssöldner ‹Ach!›
Im Blut von Pallastwänden nässen.

Doch meist hör ich durch Mittnachtstraßen
Wie jugendlicher Dirne Fluch
Des Neugebornen Thräne sehrt,
Mit Plagen schlägt der Ehe Leichentuch.

If from the public way you turn your steps
Up the tumultuous brook of Green-head Ghyll,
You will suppose that with an upright path
Your feet must struggle; in such bold ascent
The pastoral mountains front you, face to face.
But, courage! for around that boisterous brook
The mountains have all opened out themselves,
And made a hidden valley of their own.
No habitation can be seen; but they
Who journey thither find themselves alone
With a few sheep, with rocks and stones, and kites
That overhead are sailing in the sky.
It is in truth an utter solitude;
Nor should I have made mention of this Dell
But for one object which you might pass by,
Might see and notice not. Beside the brook
Appears a straggling heap of unhewn stones!
And to that simple object appertains
A story—unenriched with strange events,
Yet not unfit, I deem, for the fireside,
Or for the summer shade. It was the first
Of those domestic tales that spake to me
Of Shepherds, dwellers in the valleys, men
Whom I already loved;—not verily
For their own sakes, but for the fields and hills
Where was their occupation and abode.

Wenn deinen Schritt vom öffentlichen Wege ab
du zweigst, den wilden Bach von *Green-head Gill* hinauf,
wird's dir so vorkommen, als stünde deinen Füßen
ein Kampf mit steilstem Pfad bevor: so schroff erheben
sich Aug in Aug vor dir die Hirten-Berge.
Allein, nur Mut! Denn neben jenes Baches Schäumen
treten die Berge jäh zurück, und öffnen sich
zu einem stillverborgnen Thale mitteninne.
Keine Besiedlung ist zu sehn – nur daß,
wer sich hierher verirrt, allein sich findet
mit ein paar Schafen, Steinen & Gefels, und dem Milan
der ihm zu Häupten in den Lüften kreist.
'S ist in der Tat ein Äußerstes an Einsamkeit;
und diese Schlucht hätt ich auch nicht erwähnt,
wär's nicht um eines Etwas wegen, das du im Passieren
zwar sehen aber nicht bemerken könntest: Bei dem Bach
liegt ein zerstreuter Haufe unbehau'ner Steine,
und dieser Stelle ist eine Geschichte eingesenkt,
die, wiewohl schmucklos, ohne groß Ereignen,
ich doch für Sommerschatten oder das Kaminfeuer
nicht unpassend eracht'. Es war die erste,
die frühst' jener Erzählungen, die mir
von *Schäfern* sprachen: Siedlern jener Thäler, Männern
die ich schon immer liebte – nicht so sehr
um ihrer selbst, als um der Felsen, Hügel wegen,
dort wo ihr Tagwerk & Behausung sind.

And hence this Tale, while I was yet a Boy
Careless of books, yet having felt the power
Of Nature, by the gentle agency
Of natural objects, led me on to feel
For passions that were not my own, and think
(At random and imperfectly indeed)
On man, the heart of man, and human life.
Therefore, although it be a history
Homely and rude, I will relate the same
For the delight of a few natural hearts;
And, with yet fonder feeling, for the sake
Of youthful Poets, who among these hills
Will be my second self when I am gone.

*

Upon the forest-side in Grasmere Vale
There dwelt a Shepherd, Michael was his name;
An old man, stout of heart, and strong of limb.
His bodily frame had been from youth to age
Of an unusual strength: his mind was keen,
Intense, and frugal, apt for all affairs,
And in his shepherd's calling he was prompt
And watchful more than ordinary men.
Hence had he learned the meaning of all winds,
Of blasts of every tone; and oftentimes,
When others heeded not, He heard the South
Make subterraneous Music, like the noise
Of bagpipers on distant Highland hills.
The Shepherd, at such warning, of his flock
Bethought him, and he to himself would say,
«The winds are now devising work for me!»

Und daher ließ mich die Geschichte, als ich noch
ein Knabe, der noch nicht die Bücher werthielt, doch dafür
die Mächte der Natur gefühlt, vermöge sachter Leitung
des, was Natur mir offenbarte, mitempfinden
die Leidenschaften, die nicht meine eig'nen, und im Übermaß
und unvollkommen in der Tat bedenken, was
der Mensch, was MenschenHerz, was MenschenLeben sei.
Und so (obschon's nur eine heimatlich-naive
Geschichte ist) will ich sie weitergeben
zur Freude ein'ger weniger einfältger Herzen
und mit noch zarterer Empfindsamkeit
zu gunsten jener jungen Dichter, die in diesen Hügeln
mein Zweites Ich sein werden, wenn ich nicht mehr bin.

*

In *Grasmere Vale*, an Waldes Seite, hauste
dereinst ein Schäfer, *Michael* genannt:
ein alter Mann, am Herzen stark, an Gliedern kräftig;
und ungewöhnlich' Zähigkeit, von Jugend bis ins Alter,
prägt' seines Körpers Bau. Sein Geist war scharf,
so intensiv wie anspruchslos; gewachsen jeder Lage.
Im Schäferamt war er verläßlich, rasch,
wachsamer auch, als sonst die meisten Menschen.
Und so hatt er gelernt, der Winde Sprach' zu deuten,
der Böen Töne aller Art; und oftmals,
wenn andre unachtsam, hört' er
des Südwinds subterrane Töne wie Musik
von Sackpfeifern auf fernen Hochland-Hügeln.
Dann, ob der Warnung, achtete der Schäfer seiner Herde,
und sprach wohl zu sich selbst:
«Die Winde schaffen Arbeit für mich nun.»

And, truly, at all times, the storm, that drives
The traveller to a shelter, summoned him
Up to the mountains: he had been alone
Amid the heart of many thousand mists,
That came to him, and left him, on the heights.
So lived he till his eightieth year was past. . . . . .

*

. . . . . Their cottage on a plot of rising ground
Stood single, with large prospect, north and south,
High into Easedale, up to Dunmal-Raise,
And westward to the village near the lake;
And from this constant light, so regular
And so far seen, the house itself, by all
Who dwelt within the limits of the vale
Both old and young, was named the *Evening Star*. . . . . .

*

. . . . . Three years, or little more, did Isabel
Survive her Husband: at her death the estate
Was sold, and went into a stranger's hand.
The Cottage which was named the *Evening Star*
Is gone—the ploughshare has been through the ground
On which it stood; great changes have been wrought
In all the neighbourhood:—yet the oak is left
That grew beside their door; and the remains
Of the unfinished Sheep-fold may be seen
Beside the boisterous brook of Green-head Ghyll.

WILLIAM WORDSWORTH (1770 - 1850)
from «Michael. A Pastoral Poem»

Und wirklich zwang ihn jedesmal der Sturm,
der einem Unterschlupf entgegen treibt den Wanderer,
hoch ins Gebürg: Er war allein gewesen
im Herzen vieler tausend Nebel, welche ihm
zustießen – von ihm wichen, auf den Höh'n.
So lebt' er, bis sein achtzigst Jahr vergangen. . . . . .

*

. . . . . Ihr Cottage, auf einem Stück erhabnen Grunds,
stund ganz allein, mit fernem Blick nach Nord und Süd,
bis *Easedale* weit, dort hoch nach *Dunmal-Raise*,
hier westwärts bis zum Dorfe an dem Loch;
Und weil sein Licht so stetig und klaren Maßes brannte,
fernhin zu sehen, ward das Haus
von alt und jung, all' die das Thal in Grenzen bannte,
gern nur *Der Abendstern* genannt. . . . . .

*

. . . . . Drei Jahr nur überlebte, oder wenig mehr,
den Gatten Isabel. Bei ihrem Tode ward der Grundbesitz
verkauft, und ging an einen Fremden.
Das Cottage, das *Der Abendstern* genannt:
es steht nicht mehr. Wo es gestanden, wühlte sich
die Pflugschar durch den Grund; und große Umwälzungen
sind auf die ganze Nachbarschaft gekommen. Nur die Eiche,
die an der Thüre wuchs, steht noch. Und jene Reste
des nicht vollendeten SchafPferches kannst du sehn
zuseit' des einsam-wilden Bachs von *Green-head Gill*.

Earth has not anything to show more fair:
Dull would he be of soul who could pass by
A sight so touching in its majesty:
This City now doth like a garment wear
The beauty of the moment; silent, bare,
Ships, towers, domes, theatres, and temples lie
Open unto the fields, and to the sky;
All bright and glittering in the smokeless air.
Never did sun more beautifully steep
In his first splendour valley, rock, or hill;
Ne'er saw I, never felt, a calm so deep!
The river glideth at his own sweet will:
Dear God! the very houses seem asleep;
And all that mighty heart is lying still!

WILLIAM WORDSWORTH (1770 - 1850)
Composed upon Westminster Bridge

Schwerlich erzeigt die Erde lieblichere Dinge.
Dumpf wär die Seele dessen, der vorüberginge
an einem Anblick, dessen Größe so bewegt:
Die schöne Morgenfrühe jetzo trägt
die City wie ein Kleid; ganz rein im Äther
ruhn Kuppeln, Schiffe, Tempel, Türme und Theater
lautlos vor Himmel und Gefilden ausgespannt
hell gleißend unterm rauchlos Firmament.
Nie übergoldete die Sonne mit dem ersten Strahl
so schön den Fels, den Hügel und das Thal –
nie hab so schönen Frieden ich besessen!
Der Fluß treibt milde hin, so wie er eben will –
ach, HErr, die Häuser selber scheinen schlafvergessen!
Und dieses tiefe Herz, es schlägt ganz still.

179   Outstreching flame-ward his upbraiding hand
        (O God of mercy may no earthly Seat
        Of judgment such presumptuous doom repeat!)
        Amid the shuddering throng doth Cranmer stand;
        Firm as the stake to which with iron band
        His Frame is tied; firm from the naked feet
        To the bare head, the victory complete;
        The shrouded Body, to the Soul's command,
        Answering with more than Indian fortitude,
        Through all her nerves with finer sense endued;
        Now wrapt in flames—and now in smoke embowered—
        'Till self-reproach and panting aspirations
        Are, with the heart that held them, all devoured;
        The Spirit set free, and crown'd with joyful acclamations!

WILLIAM WORDSWORTH (1770 - 1850)
Cranmer

Mit flammenwärts gereckter, vorwurfsvoller Hand
(Ach daß ein solch vermessen Richtspruch, Gnade Gott!,
nie mehr gefället werd von irdscher Richterstatt!)
inmitt der schaudervollen Zuschauer ist CRANMERS Stand,
fest wie der Scheiterpfahl, an den mit EisenBand
die irdsche Hüll' gezurrt; standhaft mit Macht
vom baren Haupte bis zum Fuß; der Sieg vollbracht.
Der Leib im Büßerkleid, auf seiner Seel Kommand',
gehorcht mit mehr denn indianisch Zähigkeit,
durch jeden Nerv mit feinerem Sensorium bekleidt;
– in Flammen jetzt gehüllt – jetzt hinter Qualm verborgen –
bis Selbstvorwurf und keuchend-quälend Sorgen
sind, mit dem Busen der sie hegte, ganz vorbei.
Der Geist ist frei: gekrönt von Jubel-Schrei.

With ships the sea was sprinkled far and nigh,
Like stars in heaven, and joyously it showed;
Some lying fast at anchor in the road,
Some veering up and down, one knew not why.
A goodly vessel did I then espy
Come like a giant from a haven broad;
And lustily along the bay she strode,
Her tackling rich, and of apparel high.
This ship was nought to me, nor I to her,
Yet I pursued her with a Lover's look;
This ship to all the rest did I prefer:
When will she turn, and whither? She will brook
No tarrying; where She comes the winds must stir:
On went She,—and due north her journey took.

WILLIAM WORDSWORTH (1770-1850)
With ships the sea was sprinkled far and nigh

Mit Schiffen war die See gesprenkelt nah und fern
Wie Stern' am Himmel: freudevoll sah's aus;
Die einen fest vor Anker in der Meeresstraß',
Die andern drehten ab & bei – warum, das wüßt man gern.
Da späht' ich eine stattliche Fregatte
Gigantengleich aus einem Hafen kommen,
Die Bucht entlang mit rüstger Kraft geschwommen,
Mit reichem Gaffelwerk & mächtigen Speigatten.
Für mich war dieser Schoner nicht, ich nicht für ihn bestimmt,
Und doch verfolgt ich ihn mit ein's Verliebten Blicken;
Es wollt dies Schiff vor allen andern mich bestricken:
Wann wird es wenden, und wohin? Gewiß, es leidet
Kein Säumen nicht; wo's kommt, muß sich die Brise regen:
Schon wars vorbei. Und nahm gen Norden seine Wege.

181 Hail, Twilight, sovereign of one peaceful hour!
Not dull art thou as undiscerning Night!
But studious only to remove from sight
Day's mutable distinctions. Ancient power!
Thus did the waters gleam, the mountains lower
To the rude Briton, when in wolf-skin vest
Here roving wild, he laid him down to rest
On the bare rock, or through a leafy bower
Looked ere his eyes were closed. By him was seen
The self-same vision which we now behold,
At thy meek bidding, shadowy power, brought forth;
These mighty barriers, and the gulf between;
The floods—the stars; a spectacle as old
As the beginning of the heavens and earth!

WILLIAM WORDSWORTH (1770-1850)
Twilight

Heil Zwielicht!: Souverän der einen Stunde friedensreich!
Nicht dumpf bist du gleichwie die Nacht, ohn Unterscheid –
Nein, nur bereit, dem Anblick zu verhüllen
Tag's scharf geschiedne Wechselfülle. – Uralte Macht!
So glomm das Wasser, dräut' das zackichte Gebürge
Dem rohen Brit', als er im Wolfsfell wild
Hier streift' umher, zur müden Ruh sich streckte
Auf nackten Fels, vielleicht durch Laub verborgen
Späht', eh das Aug er schloß. Da schaute er
Die selbige Vision, die wir itzund gewahren
Auf deinen sanften Ruf beschworen, schattenhaft' Gewalt:
Die Bucht, begrenzt von mächtigen Barrieren,
Die Ströme, Stern' . . . . ein Schauspiel, just so alt
Wie aller Anfang Himmels und der Erden!

It is not be thought of that the flood
Of British freedom, which, to the open sea
Of the world's praise, from dark antiquity
Hath flow'd, «with pomp of waters, unwithstood,»—
Roused though it be full often to a mood
Which spurns the check of salutary bands,—
That this most famous stream in bogs and sands
Should perish; and to evil and to good
Be lost for ever. In our halls is hung
Armoury of the invincible Knights of old:
We must be free or die, who speak the tongue
That Shakespeare spake; the faith and morals hold
Which Milton held.—In everything we are sprung
Of Earth's first blood, have titles manifold.

WILLIAM WORDSWORTH (1770-1850)
from «London 1802»

Das steht nicht zu befürchten: daß die Flut
der Brit'schen Freiheit, die zum offnen Meer
des Ruhms der Welt seit dunklem altersher
geströmt, *mit Pomp von Wassern & mit Heldenmuth,*
auch wenn sie sich oft türmt bis zu der Wut
die an den Hemnis-Zügeln reißt gesunder Bande –
: daß diese höchstberühmte Flut in Sumpf & Sande
versickern soll und wie zum Schlechten so zum Gut
verloren sei auf ewig. Es hängt in unserm Saal
geharnischt Mal von alter Kämpen Lanzenschwunge:
Wir müssen frei sein oder sterben, die in Shakespeares Zunge
wir reden – und: die wir Miltons Moral
und Glauben teilen. Denn wir sind allzumal vom Ursprunge
des Ersten Bluts der Erde, mit Titeln ohne Zahl.

«*MISERRIMUS!*» and neither name or date,
Prayer, text, or symbol, graven upon the stone;
Nought but that word assigned to the unknown,
That solitary word—to separate
From all, and cast a cloud around the fate
Of him who lies beneath. Most wretched one,
Who chose his Epitaph? Himself alone
Could thus have dared the grave to agitate,
And claim, among the dead, this awful crown;
Nor doubt that He marked also for his own,
Close to these cloistral steps a burial-place,
That every foot might fall with heavier tread,
Trampling upon his vileness. Stranger, pass
Softly!—To save the contrite, Jesus bled.

WILLIAM WORDSWORTH (1770 - 1850)
A Grave-stone upon the floor in the Cloisters of Worcester Cathedral

«*MISERRIMUS!*» und weder Nam', noch Zeit,
noch Text/Symbol/Gebet sind in den Stein graviert;
Nichts – nur dies Wort, dem Unbekannten designiert,
dies solitäre Wort: auf daß es scheid'
von Allem, und eine Wolke hülle um das Leid
des, der hier ruht. Dem unser ganzes Mitleiden gebührt:
Wer wählte diesen Epitaph? Er selbst wohl agitiert',
nur er allein, mit seiner Inschrift zur Unbötigkeit,
heischt' seine schrecklich' Krone bei den Todten.
Kein Zweifel auch, daß er sich selbst erstritt
gleich neben diese Klosterstufen die Begräbnisstatt:
Daß jeder Fuß mit schwererem Gefälle treten,
auf seine Schlechtheit trampeln solle. Fremder, tritt
nur sacht! – : Um des Zerknirschten Heils wollt Jesus bluten.

184   It is a beauteous Evening, calm and free;
       The holy time is quiet as a Nun
       Breathless with adoration; the broad sun
       Is sinking down in its tranquillity;
       The gentleness of heaven is on the Sea:
       Listen! the mighty Being is awake
       And doth with his eternal motion make
       A sound like thunder—everlastingly.
       Dear Child! dear Girl! that walkest with me here,
       If thou appear'st untouch'd by solemn thought,
       Thy nature is not therefore less divine:
       Thou liest in Abraham's bosom all the year;
       And worshipp'st at the Temple's inner shrine,
       God being with thee when we know it not.

WILLIAM WORDSWORTH (1770-1850)
from «At Sunset»

Es ist ein schöner Abend: frei und unbewegt.
Die fromme Stunde schweigt, wie eine Nonne
vor Anbetung den Atem anhält. Eine RiesenSonne
zur stillen Ruh sich niederlegt.
Des Himmels Sachtheit auf den Wassern schwebt:
horch nur, das mächtge Wesen ist erwacht!
Mit seiner unablässigen Bewegung macht
es ein Geräusch wie Donner, das da ewig webt.
Lieb Kind! Lieb Mädchen, das mit mir spaziert:
Wenn du von dem solennen Denken (scheinbar) unberührt,
ist doch nicht weniger sublim deine Natur:
An Abrams Busen liegest du das ganze Jahr –
dir öffnet sich zum Allerheiligsten die Tempeltür –
wir wissen's nicht – und doch: GOtt ist mit dir.

185 If thou indeed derive thy light from Heaven,
Then, to the measure of that heaven-born light,
Shine, Poet! in thy place, and be content:—
The stars pre-eminent in magnitude,
And they that from the zenith dart their beams,
(Visible though they be to half the earth,
Though half a sphere be conscious of their brightness)
Are yet of no diviner origin,
No purer essence, than the one that burns,
Like an untended watch-fire, on the ridge
Of some dark mountain; or than those which seem
Humbly to hang, like twinkling winter lamps,
Among the branches of the leafless trees;
All are the undying offspring of one Sire:
Then, to the measure of the light vouchsafed,
Shine, Poet! in thy place, and be content.

WILLIAM WORDSWORTH (1770 - 1850)
If thou indeed derive thy light from Heaven

Wenn du denn doch dein Licht vom Himmel selbst empfängst,
Dann – nach dem Maß des Lichts, geboren diesem Himmel: –
Leuchte, Poet! an deinem Platz, und sei's zufrieden.
Die Sterne, in ihrer Vielheit Überzahlen,
Und die, so vom Zenith die Strahlen pfeilen
(Ob gleich dem halben Globus hell; auch wenn
Um ihren Glanz die andre Hälfte weiß),
Sind ja nicht göttlicherer Herkunft,
Und keine klarere Essenz, als jener Einzge, brennend
Gleich einem Leuchtfeuer hoch auf dem Kamm
Von einem dunkeln Berg; gleich denen, welche flimmernd
Wie Winters niedrig schaukelnde Latern
Zwischen den Zweigen der entlaubten Bäume hängen;
Die alle sind die unsterbliche Abkunft *eines* HErrn;
Daher, nach Maßgabe des Lichts, das dir beschieden:
Leuchte, Poet! an deinem Platz, und sei's zufrieden.

186   One summer evening (led by her) I found
A little boat tied to a willow tree
Within a rocky cave, its usual home.
Straight I unloosed her chain, and stepping in
Pushed from the shore. It was an act of stealth
And troubled pleasure, nor without the voice
Of mountain-echoes did my boat move on;
Leaving behind her still, on either side,
Small circles glittering idly in the moon,
Until they melted all into one track
Of sparkling light. But now, like one who rows,
Proud of his skill, to reach a chosen point
With an unswerving line, I fixed my view
Upon the summit of a craggy ridge,
The horizon's utmost boundary; far above
Was nothing but the stars and the grey sky.
She was an elfin pinnace; lustily
I dipped my oars into the silent lake,
And, as I rose upon the stroke, my boat
Went heaving through the water like a swan;
When, from behind that craggy steep till then
The horizon's bound, a huge peak, black and huge,
As if with voluntary power instinct
Upreared its head. I struck and struck again,
And growing still in stature the grim shape
Towered up between me and the stars, and still,
For so it seemed, with purpose of its own
And measured motion like a living thing,
Strode after me. With trembling oars I turned,
And through the silent water stole my way
Back to the covert of the willow tree;

An einem Sommerabend (von ihr geleitet) fand ich
Ein kleines Boot, an einem Weidenbaum vertäut,
In einer Felsengrotte, seinem angestammten Platz.
Stracks löst ich seine Kette, sprang hinein,
Und stieß vom Ufer ab. Verstohlen wars,
Kein ungetrübt Vergnügen, und mein Boot
Glitt unbegleitet nicht vom Ruf der Bergechos dahin;
Und ließ zu jeder Seit' still hinter sich
Ein träges Glitzern kleiner Kreise unterm Mond,
Bis sie in einer einzgen Spur von Funkelschein
Zerschmolzen. Doch nun gleich einem, welcher stolz
Auf seines Ruderns Fertigkeit, fixiert ich meinen Blick
Um einen festgewählten Punct gradlinig anzusteuern,
Hoch auf den Gipfel eines Felsengrats:
Des Horizontes äußerste Begrenzung; weiter höh'r
Warn nur die Sterne noch, das graue Firmament.
Es war verhext, das Boot: mit Schwung
Taucht ich die Ruder in den stillen See,
Und wenn ich mich beim Schlagen streckte, schob der Nachen
Sich schwankend übers Wasser wie ein Schwan;
Als hinter jenem schroffen Grat (bis jetzt
Des Horizonts Begrenzung) schwarz-ungeheuerlich, ein Riesengipfel,
Gleichwie von Willenskraft bewogen insgeheim,
Sein Haupt erhob. Ich schlug & schlug das Ruder,
Und, wachsend an Statur noch, türmte
Das Ungetüm sich zwischen mich und alle Sterne,
Und, ja, so schien's, aus eigenem Entschluß,
Mit abgemesser Bewegung wie ein lebend Ding
Verfolgte's mich. Mit Grauen rudernd macht ich kehrt,
Stahl mich hinweg durch dieses schweigende Gewässer,
Bis ich geborgen wieder unterm Weidenbaum;

There in her mooring-place I left my bark,—
And through the meadows homeward went, in grave
And serious mood; but after I had seen
That spectacle, for many days, my brain
Worked with a dim and undetermined sense
Of unknown modes of being; o'er my thoughts
There hung a darkness, call it solitude
Or blank desertion. No familiar shapes
Remained, no pleasant images of trees,
Of sea or sky, no colours of green fields;
But huge and mighty forms, that do not live
Like living men, moved slowly through the mind
By day, and were a trouble to my dreams.

WILLIAM WORDSWORTH (1770 - 1850)
from « The Prelude, or, Growth of a Poet's Mind »

Dort ließ ich meine Barke an ihrem Ankerplatz, –
Ging durch die Wiesen heim, in Schwermut und
In nachdenklichem Sinnen; allein nachdem ich dieses Bild
Gesehn, war viele Tage in Bewegung noch
Mein Hirn mit trüber, unklarer Empfindung
Ob dieses Seins noch nichtgewußten Formen, mein Gemüth
War überschattet – nennt's Alleinesein,
Nennt's schiere Einsamkeit. Und kein vertrauter Umriß
Blieb da zurück, kein freundlich Bild von Bäumen,
Von Himmel oder See, und keine Farben grüner Felder;
Nur mächtge, ungetüme Formen, *lebend zwar,*
Doch nicht wie Menschen leben, bewegten träge sich bei Tage
Mir durch den Sinn, durch meine Träume mir zur Plage.

187 Fair Star of Evening, Splendor of the West,
Star of my Country! on the horizon's brink
Thou hangest, stooping, as might seem, to sink
On England's bosom; yet well pleas'd to rest,
Meanwhile, and be to her a glorious crest
Conspicuous to the Nations. Thou, I think,
Should'st be my Country's emblem; and should'st wink,
Bright Star! with laughter on her banners, drest
In thy fresh beauty. There! that dusky spot
Beneath thee, it is England; there it lies.
Blessing be on you both! one hope, one lot,
One life, one glory! I, with many a fear
For my dear Country, many heartfelt sighs,
Among Men who do not love her linger here.

WILLIAM WORDSWORTH (1770-1850)
Composed by the Sea-side, near Calais. August, 1802

Oh Glanz des Westens, schöner Abendstern:
Stern meines Lands! Auf Horizontes Rand, im Wiegen
hängst du als wollest du dich neigen
an Englands Busen – doch du ruhest gern
derweil, hast dich als RuhmesWappen ihm geweiht:
unübersehbar jeder anderen Nation. Bedünken
will mich, du solltst meins Landes Sinnbild sein und winken
mit Lächeln, holder Stern, von seiner Fahn herab, gekleidet
in juvenile Schönheit. Da!: das dunstge Stück
knapp unter dir: lieb-England lieget dort!
Euch beiden Segen! Und *ein* Hoffen, *ein* Geschick,
ein Leben – *eine* Glorie! – Ich, im Tort,
mich will mein Vaterland mit Seufzen bang betrüben,
da ich bei Menschen harren muß, die es nicht lieben.

Once again, but how chang'd since my wand'rings began
I have heard the deep voice of the lagan and bann,
and the pines of Clanbrassil resound to the roar
that wearies the echoes of fair Tullamore.
Alas! my poor bosom, and why shouldst thou burn!
With the scenes of my youth can its raptures return?
Can I live, the dear life of delusion again,
that flow'd when these echoes first mix'd with my strain?

It was then, that around me, though poor and unknown,
high spells of mysterious enchantment were thrown;
the streams were of silver, of diamond the dew,
the land was an Eden for fancy was new.
I had heard of our bards, and my soul was on fire
at the rush of their verse, and the sweep of their lyre:
to me 'twas not legend, nor tale to the ear,
but a vision of noontide, distinguish'd and clear.

Ultonia's old heroes awoke at the call:
and renew'd the wild pomp of the chace and the hall;
and the standard of Fion flash'd fierce from on high,
like a burst of the sun when the tempest is nigh.
It seem'd that the harp of green Erin once more
could renew all the glories she boasted of yore.
Yet why at remembrance, fond heart, shouldst thou burn?
They were days of delusion, and cannot return.

SIR WALTER SCOTT (1771-1832)
The Return to Ulster

Und aufs neu, doch wie anders, seit mein Wandern begann,
Horcht ich der tiefen Stille, dem versunkenen Bann
Und Clanbrassils Fichten rauschten wider vom Rumor,
Das die Echos schwächer dämpft aus dem schönen Tullamore.
Weh mein armes Herz, warum mußt du dich verzehren!
Sollt mit meiner Jugend Bildern dein Verzücken wiederkehren?
Darf ich das geliebte Leben voll Phantastik wieder leben,
Seit mit den gespannten Sinnen sich dies Echo einst verwoben?

Da wars, als ob um mich, leise erst und unbewußt,
Magie hätt einen mysteriösen Zauberkreis beschworen:
Die Ströme warn aus Silber, aus Diamant der Tau,
Ein Eden war das Land denn neu & jung war Phantasie.
Früh lausch ich unsern Barden, meine Seele brannt im Feuer
Bei dem Rausch ihrer Verse & dem Schlag ihrer Leyer:
Für mich wars keine Mär, nicht Legende noch Geschichte –
Nein, mittäglich Gesichte, so deutlich und so klar.

Ultonias alte Recken erweckte das Signal
Aufs neu zu wilder Festesfreud, zur Meutjagd & im Saal;
Und das Banner des Fionn zuckte glühend von den Höhn
Gleich dem Durchbruch der Sonne, wenn die Sturmwolken nahn.
Und es schien als könnt die Harfe von Erin so grün
All die alten kühnen Ruhmestaten einmal noch erneun.
Doch warum, stolzes Herz, sollst im Erinnern dich verzehren?
Das warn Tage schöner Träume, können ja nicht wiederkehren.

189   On the wide level of a mountain's head
(I knew not where, but 'twas some faery place),
Their pinions, ostrich-like, for sails outspread,
Two lovely children run an endless race,
A sister and a brother!
This far outstripp'd the other;
Yet ever runs she with reverted face,
And looks and listens for the boy behind:
For he, alas! is blind!
O'er rough and smooth with even step he pass'd
And knows not whether he be first or last.

SAMUEL TAYLOR COLERIDGE (1772 - 1834)
Time: real and imaginary. An Allegory

Auf eines Berggipfels weitem Plateau
(Wo, wußt ich nicht, doch verhext war der Platz)
Mit Schwingen wie ein Strauß, als Segel ausgespannt,
Kommen zwei liebliche Kinder ein endloses Rennen gerannt,
Bruder und Schwester!
Sie ist ihm weit schon voran,
Rennt aber immer mit rückwärts gewandtem Gesicht
Und späht nach dem Knaben und horcht hinter sich:
Denn der, ach mein Gott! ist blind.
Und ist über geraden wie rauhen Boden gerannt,
Ob Erster – ob Letzter? – er weiß es nicht.

My days among the Dead are past;
Around me I behold,
Where'er these casual eyes are cast,
The mighty minds of old:
My never-failing friends are they,
With whom I converse day by day.

With them I take delight in weal
And seek relief in woe;
And while I understand and feel
How much to them I owe,
My cheeks have often been bedew'd
With tears of thoughtful gratitude.

My thoughts are with the Dead; with them
I live in long-past years,
Their virtues love, their faults condemn,
Partake their hopes and fears;
And from their lessons seek and find
Instruction with an humble mind.

My hopes are with the Dead; anon
My place with them will be,
And I with them shall travel on
Through all Futurity;
Yet leaving here a name, I trust,
That will not perish in the dust.

ROBERT SOUTHEY (1774 - 1843)
His Books

Die Tage bei den Toten sind gezählt.
Ich blick mich um, betracht',
worauf mein schweifend Auge immer fällt,
verstorbner Geister Macht:
nie-unverläßliche Gefährten sind sie mir,
mit denen ich alltäglich disputier'.

Mein Wohl erfreut sich ihrer Huld
und Trost find ich im Wehe;
Wenn ich empfinde und verstehe
wie viel ich ihnen schuld',
sind meine Wangen oft betäut
von Thränen nachdenklicher Dankbarkeit.

Mein Denken um die Toten kreist; bei jenen
wohn ich seit meiner Jugend,
verdamm' ihr Fehlen, liebe ihre Tugend,
hab teil an ihren Sorgen, ihrem Wähnen;
In ihrem Unterrichten sucht ich stets und fand
Belehrung von demütigem Verstand.

Mein Hoffen bei den Toten weilt: alsdann
wird auch mein Platz bei ihnen sein;
Bald werde ich mit ihnen ziehn
vitam venturi saeculi hinan;
Doch laß ich einen Namen hier (mein fester Glaube!)
der nicht vergehen wird im Staube.

191 A wrinkled, crabbed man they picture thee,
    Old Winter, with a rugged beard as grey
    As the long moss upon the apple-tree;
    Blue-lipt, an ice-drop at thy sharp blue nose,
    Close muffled up, and on thy dreary way
    Plodding alone through sleet and drifting snows.

    They should have drawn thee by the high-heapt hearth,
    Old Winter! seated in thy great armed chair,
    Watching the children at their Christmas mirth;
    Or circled by them as thy lips declare
    Some merry jest, or tale of murder dire,
    Or troubled spirit that disturbs the night,
    Pausing at times to rouse the mouldering fire,
    Or taste the old October brown and bright.

ROBERT SOUTHEY (1774 - 1843)
Winter

Sie malen dich als Rumpelstilz mit Runzeln,
Du alter Winter! mit rauhem Bart, so gräulich
Wie an dem Apfelbaum die Moosrapunzeln,
Blaulippig, mit nem Tropfen Eis an deinem Nasenzapfen:
So sollst du einvermummt auf deinem Pfade scheulich
Durch Schneeverwehn & Schloßen einsam stapfen.

Sie hätten besser dich gemalt am aufgeschichten Feuer,
Du alter Winter! Im großen Lehnstuhl hingesetzt,
Wie du der Kinder achtest bei ihrer Weihnachtsfeier,
Oder, von ihnen eingeringt, wie deinen Lippen mancher Scherz
Entfleucht, wohl auch manch grause Mordgeschicht,
Oder manch unruhvoller Geist der poltert durch die Nacht
Setzt aus zuweilen bis aufs neu die müde Glut er facht,
Wohl auch wie sie probiern vom Alt-Oktober braun & licht.

.... A little way
He turned aside, by natural impulses
Moved, to behold Cadwallon's lonely hut,
That lonely dwelling stood among the hills,
By a gray mountain's stream; just elevate
Above the winter torrents did it stand,
Upon a craggy bank; an orchard slope
Arose behind, and joyous was the scene,
In early summer, when those antic trees
Shone with their blushing blossoms, and the flax
Twinkled beneath the breeze its liveliest green.
But, save the flax-field and that orchard slope,
All else was desolate, and now all wore
One sober hue; the narrow vale, which wound
Among the hills, was gray with rocks, that peered
Above its shallow soil; the mountain side
Was with loose stones bestrewn, which oftentimes
Sliding beneath the foot of straggling goat,
Clattered adown the steep; or huger crags,
Which, when the coming frost should loosen them,
Would thunder down . . . . .
.... Adown the vale,
Broken by stones, and o'er a stony bed,
Roared the loud mountain stream.

ROBERT SOUTHEY (1774-1843)
A Mountain Landscape

.... Auf einen Pfad
Abseits vom Wege schlug er sich; ein instinktiver
Ansporn trieb ihn, Cadwallons Hütt' zu schaun, allein
Duckt jene Ansiedlung sich zwischen Hügeln
An einem grauen Wildbach, wenig höher nur
Als Winters ungezähmte Strömung stand sie
Auf einem Ufer felsicht; eines Früchtegartens
Abhang stieg da hintan, und heiter war
Das Bild im Frühsommer, wenn jene Baumgrotesken
In ihrer Blüte Schaam erröcheten, und Flachs
Sein lebhafts Grün ließ funkeln in der Brise.
Doch abgesehn vom Flachsfeld & vom Gartenabhang
War alles trostlos sonst, und trug nur einen
Einzigen Farbton nüchtern, und das Thal
Wand zwischen Hügeln sich, grau von Gefels, das lugte
Aus karger Krume vor; des Berges Flanke
Besät mit lockerem Gestein, das oft
jäh gleitend unterm Stolperhuf der Geißen
Steil abwärts poltert, oder mächtge Brocken,
Die, sollt der komm'nde Frost sie lockern,
Mit Donnern in die Tiefe würden rollen . . . . .
. . . . Im Tale flach,
Im Bett aus Stein, von Steinen aufgebrochen,
Brüllte des Berges lauter wilder Bach.

193   I have had playmates, I have had companions,
In my days of childhood, in my joyful school-days—
All, all are gone, the old familiar faces.

I have been laughing, I have been carousing,
Drinking late, sitting late, with my bosom cronies—
All, all are gone, the old familiar faces.

I loved a Love once; fairest among women:
Closed are her doors on me, I must not see her—
All, all are gone, the old familiar faces.

I have a friend, a kinder friend has no man:
Like an ingrate, I left my friend abruptly;
Left him, to muse on the old familiar faces.

Ghost-like I paced round the haunts of my childhood,
Earth seem'd a desert I was bound to traverse,
Seeking to find the old familiar faces.

Friend of my bosom, thou more than a brother,
Why wert not thou born in my father's dwelling?
So might we talk of the old familiar faces—

How some they have died, and some they have left me,
And some are taken from me; all are departed—
All, all are gone, the old familiar faces.

CHARLES LAMB (1775 - 1834)
The Old Familiar Faces

Ich hatte Gespielen – ich hatte Gefährten –
In meinen Kindheitstagen, in meinen frohen Schultagen –
Sind alle, alle dahin: die alt vertrauten Gesichter.

Ich habe gelacht – ich habe gezecht –
Trank spät, saß spät, mit meinen Busenfreunden –
Sind alle, alle dahin: die alt vertrauten Gesichter.

Ich liebte einst ein Liebes, die schönste aller Frauen:
Ihre Türen sind mir verschlossen, ich darf sie nicht schauen –
Sind alle, alle dahin: die alt vertrauten Gesichter.

Ich hab einen Freund, einen gütigern hat keiner:
Meinen Freund verließ ich abrupt, wie ein Undankbarer,
Verließ ihn, um den alt vertrauten Gesichtern nachzusinnen.

Heimsucht' ich wie ein Geist die Stätten meiner Kindheit;
Eine Wüste schien die Erde, die ich zu queren hätte
Auf der Suche nach den alt vertrauten Gesichtern.

Freund meines Herzens: Ihr, mehr denn ein Bruder!
Was wart nicht Ihr in meinem Vaterhaus geboren?
So könnten wir von den alt vertrauten Gesichtern erzählen:

Wie die einen verstarben – die andern mich verließen –
Und wieder andere von mir gerissen; alle fortgegangen –
Sind alle, alle dahin: die alt vertrauten Gesichter.

194   If from my lips some angry accents fell,
Peevish complaint, or harsh reproof unkind,
'Twas but the error of a sickly mind
And troubled thoughts, clouding the purer well,
And waters clear, of Reason; and for me
Let this my verse the poor atonement be—
My verse, which thou to praise wert ever inclined
Too highly, and with a partial eye to see
No blemish. Thou to me didst ever shew
Kindest affection; and would oft-times lend
An ear to the desponding love-sick lay,
Weeping my sorrows with me, who repay
But ill the mighty debt of love I owe,
Mary, to thee, my sister and my friend.

CHARLES LAMB (1775-1834)
Composed in Hoxton Lunatic Asylum

Falls je ein ärgerlicher Tonfall meinem Mund entquoll,
Gereizter Jammerschwall und harschen Tadels Murren,
War's einzig nur der Irrtum eines irren,
Verstörten Denkens, was getrübt den reinen Quell:
Das Lauterwasser der Vernunft. Mir armem Sünder
Sei'n diese Verse hier der Buße Schuld,
Die du mit Huld geneigt stets warst zu finden
Doch allzu wert des Lobs, und mit partei'schen Augenbinden
Kein Fehl zu sehn, und drücktest immer dein Empfinden
Mir wohlgesonnen aus; wolltst öfter leihn
Dein Ohr geneigt der zagen liebeskranken Leyer
Und meinen Kummer weinen mit mir, der vergilt
Dir nur zu krank mein' mächtge Liebesschuld,
Maria, Schwester, Freundin mein!

195   I strove with none, for none was worth my strife.
Nature I loved and, next to Nature, Art:
I warm'd both hands before the fire of life;
It sinks, and I am ready to depart.

WALTER SAVAGE LANDOR (1775 - 1864)
Finis

Mit keinem hatt ich Händel. Den Streit war niemand wert.
Ich hatt Natur so lieb und, ihr zur Seit, die Kunst.
An dem Kamin des Lebens rieb warm ich mir die Hände.
Das Feuer geht zu Ende. Zur Abfahrt bin bereit.

At night, when all is still around,
How sweet to hear the distant sound
  Of footstep, coming soft and light!
What pleasure in the anxious beat
With which the bosom flies to meet
  That foot that comes so soft at night!

And then, at night, how sweet to say,
«'Tis late, my love!» and chide delay,
  Though still the western clouds are bright;
Oh! happy, too, the silent press,
The eloquence of mute caress,
  With those we love exchanged at night!

THOMAS MOORE (1779 - 1852)
At Night

Wenn ringsum Stille in der Nacht,
Der ferne Klang so selig macht
 von Schritten leichtfüszig & sacht!
Welch Jubel in dem Schlag, der jagt,
Mit dem die Brust entgegenfliegt
 Dem Fuß gelinden Tritts bei Nacht!

Und dann bei Nacht das Wort so hold
«'S ist spät, mein Lieb!» Verspätung schilt,
 ob noch im West hell Wolkenschein entfacht;
O selig auch der stumme Halt,
Beredsamkeit von Zartheit still,
 Der Liebe Zwiegespräch bei Nacht!

197 How sweet the answer Echo makes
    To Music at night
  When, roused by lute or horn, she wakes,
  And far away o'er lawns and lakes
    Goes answering light!

  Yet Love hath echoes truer far
    And far more sweet
  Than e'er, beneath the moonlight's star,
  Of horn or lute or soft guitar
    The songs repeat.

  'Tis when the sigh,—in youth sincere,
    And only then,
  The sigh that's breathed for one to hear—
  Is by that one, that only dear,
    Breathed back again.

THOMAS MOORE (1779 - 1852)
Echoes

Wie süß des Echos Antwort macht
   Musik zur Nacht!
Wenn *sie* von Laut' und Horn erwacht,
und weithin über Rasen, Seen
   Lichtechos gehn.

Auch Lieb hat Echo: echter noch,
   das süßer singt,
als jemals unter Mondlichts Stern
von Laut', Gitarre oder Horn
   ein Lied nachklingt.

'S ist, wenn der Hauch in Jugend echt
   und einzig dann
der Seufzer, in der Einen Ohr gehaucht,
wird von der *einen*, einzig Lieben
   zurückgegeben.

The Man

You strange, astonished-looking, angle-faced,
   Dreary-mouthed, gaping wretches of the sea,
   Gulping salt-water everlastingly,
Cold-blooded, though with red your blood be graced,
And mute, though dwellers, in the roaring waste;
   And you, all shapes beside, that fishy be,—
   Some round, some flat, some long, all devilry,
Legless, unloving, infamously chaste:—

O scaly, slippery, wet, swift, staring wights,
   What is't ye do? What life lead? eh, dull goggles?
How do ye vary your vile days and nights?
   How pass your Sundays? Are ye still but joggles
In ceaseless wash? Still nought but gapes, and bites,
   And drinks, and stares, diversified with boggles?

The Fish

Amazing monster! that, for augh I know,
   With the first sight of thee didst make our race
   For ever stare! O flat and shocking face,
Grimly divided from the breast below!
Thou that on dry land horribly dost go
   With a split body and most ridiculous pace,
   Prong after prong, disgracer of all grace,
Long-useless-finned, haired, upright, unwet, slow!

Der Mensch:

Ihr merkwürdigen *(Angel-)*Keilgesichter, ungescheut –
   mundmäulige Maulsperrentröpfe in der See, ja die
   ihr immerdar Salzwasser durch die Kiemen seiht
mit kaltem Blut (dem Rot doch Würde leiht)
und stumm, wiewohl ihr haust in brüllender Wüstenei;
   Ihr all, die fischig seid (und alle Formen mal beiseit:
   hier rund, da platt, dort lang), ganz Teufelei,
beinlos, notorisch keusch, gen Liebe scheu:

O schuppig schlüpficht feuchtflink SchieleAugen,
   was macht ihr? Und wie lebt ihr, eh? Ihr Glotzer dumm,
wie variiert ihr eure schnöden Nächte, Tage?
   Wie bringt ihr euren Sonntag zu? Laßt euch nur wriggeln um,
undulatorisch-endlos? Könnt ihr nur gaffen, *Blubb* nur sagen?
   zu Schlückeln, Starren, Koboldfurcht nur taugen?

Der Fisch:

Bemerkenswertes Ungetüm! das, wenn ich richtig unterricht't,
   unser Geschlecht, als wir erstmalig deinen Anblick litten,
   auf ewig glotzen macht': o flach schockierendes Gesicht,
vom Brustkorb unten grauslig abgeschnitten!
Du, der auf trocknem Lande fürchterlich spaziert
   mit eingekeiltem Rumpf und ridikülsten Tritten:
   Stichstelz-auf-Stechschritt, du Entwürd'ger jeder Würd,
haarig & sinnlos lang befloßt, kopfhoch, unnaß & retardiert!

O breather of unbreathable, sword-sharp air,
  How canst exist? How bear thyself, thou dry
And dreary sloth? What particle canst share
  Of the only blessed life, the watery?
I sometimes see of ye an actual *pair*
  Go by! linked fin by fin! most odiously.

The Spirit

Indulge thy smiling scorn, if smiling still,
  O man! and loathe, but with a sort of love;
  For difference must its use by difference prove,
And, in sweet clang, the spheres with music fill,
One of the spirits am I, that all his will
  Live in whate'er has life—fish, eagle, dove—
  No hate, no pride, beneath nought, nor above,
A visitor of the rounds of God's sweet skill.

Man's life is warm, glad, sad, 'twixt loves and graves,
  Boundless in hope, honoured with pangs austere,
Heaven gazing; and his angel-wings he craves : —
  The fish is swift, small-needing, vague yet clear,
A cold, sweet, silver life, wrapped in round waves,
  Quickened with touches of transporting fear.

Leigh Hunt (1784 - 1859)
The Fish, The Man, and the Spirit

O Atmer nicht zu atmender, schwertscharfer Air,
    wie kannst du sein? Wie dich ertragen, dieses Flair
der trocknen, trüben Tasse? Kann denn kein Teilchen um dich schweben
    von dem allein glückseeligen: dem wässerichten Leben?
Bisweilen seh ich gar von euch ein veritables Paar
    vorbeigehn: Floss'-in-Flosse! Kann es sowas geben?

Der Geist:

Frön deinem LächelSpott, doch nur mit Lächeln mild,
    o Mensch! Weich nur zurück, doch nie ganz ohne Lieben,
    denn Unterschied muß seine Prob' am Unterscheiden üben,
daß Vielklangs Harmonie die Sphären tönend füllt.
Ich bin der Geister einer, der auf SEin Gebieten wallt
    und lebt in allem was da Odem hat – Fisch, Adler, oder Tauben –
    nicht Haß, nicht Stolz, nichts drunten und nichts droben,
ein Gast nur der Gefilde von GOttes Handwerk alt.

Menschtum ist: traurig-froh, warm, zwischen Grab & Lieben, und
    im Hoffen grenzenlos, geadelt von herb Pein;
zum Himmel blickt, nach Engelschwingen sehnt sein Herz sich wund.
    Der Fisch: flink, schwankend, anspruchslos und rein,
ein kaltsüß Silberleben, getaucht in Wogenrund,
    dem vage Angstempfindungen die Wendigkeit verleihn.

Seamen three! What men be ye?
Gotham's three wise men we be.
Whither in your bowl so free?
To rake the moon from out the sea.
The bowl goes trim. The moon doth shine.
And our ballast is old wine.—
And your ballast is old wine.

Who are thou, so fast adrift?
I am he they call Old Care.
Here on board we will thee lift.
No: I may not enter there.
Wherefor so? 'Tis Jove's decree,
In a bowl Care may not be.—
In a bowl Care may not be.

Fear ye not the waves that roll?
No: in charmèd bowl we swim.
What the charm that floats the bowl?
Water may not pass the brim.
The bowl goes trim. The moon doth shine.
And our ballast is old wine.—
And your ballast is old wine.

THOMAS LOVE PEACOCK (1785-1866)
Three Men of Gotham

Matrosen ho! Wer mögt ihr sein?
Wir sind der Gotham-Weisen drei!
Wohin in eurer Schale frei?
Dem Meer die Mondin abzufrei'n!
Der Nachen jagt. Im Mondenschein.
Und unsre Ladung: Alter Wein. –
Und eure Ladung: Alter Wein.

Und wer seid Ihr, so schnell herbei?
Die Alte Sorge nennt man mich.
An Bord gleich eleviern wir dich!
Nein, das darf ja nimmer sein.
Warum nicht? Es ist Iovis Schluß:
Die Sorg' die Schale meiden muß. –
Die Sorg' die Schale meiden muß.

Graut euch nicht vor Wogenbraus?
Nein: gefeit ist unser Kahn!
Wie schaut solch Schalen-Zauber aus?
Wasser darf dem Rand nicht nah'n!
Der Nachen jagt. Im Mondenschein.
Und unsre Ladung: Alter Wein. –
Und eure Ladung: Alter Wein.

How sweet and solemn, all alone,
With reverend steps, from stone to stone,
In a small village churchyard lying,
O'er intervening flowers to move!
And as we read the names unknown
Of young and old to judgment gone,
And hear in the calm air above
Time onwards softly flying,
To meditate, in Christian love,
Upon the dead and dying!

Across the silence seem to go
With dream-like motion, wavering, slow,
And shrouded in their folds of snow,
The friends we loved, long, long ago!
Gliding across the sad retreat,
How beautiful their phantom feet!
What tenderness is in their eyes,
Turned where the poor survivor lies
'Mid monitory sanctities!
What years of vanished joy are fanned
From one uplifting of that hand,
In its white stillness! when the shade
Doth glimmeringly in sunshine fade
From our embrace, how dim appears
This world's life through a mist of tears!
Vain hopes! blind sorrows! needless fears!

Wie mild und andächtig, so ganz allein
Ehrfürchtgen Schritts, von Stein zu Stein
In eines kleinen Dorfes Gottesacker
Zu streifen durch die Blumen mitteninnen!
So lesen wir die unbekannten Namen
Von Jung und Alt, dahingegangen
Zum Urteilsspruch. Hoch uns in stiller Luft
Hörn wir die Zeit sänftlich vorüberrinnen
In Christi Lieb zum Eingedenken
Der Toten und der Sterbenden!

Da scheints, als ob von jenseits wallten
Durchs Schweigen, traumgleich mählich, schwankend,
Gehüllt in ihres Leichtuchs schneeicht' Falten
Die Freunde, die vor langer Zeit wir liebten!
Hin über ihre Trauerzuflucht gleitend
Auf geisterhaften Füszen wunderbar!
Wie zart die Augen ihnen sind, dahin gericht'
Wo der bedauernswert Lebendige gebannt
Nun unter mahnend heilge Pflicht!
Wie sind verflossner Freuden Jahr beschworen
Nur auf ein Zeichen der gehobnen Hand
In ihrem weißen Schweigen! Doch wenn der Schemen
Im Sonnenlicht, ein Schimmer nur, verflüchtigt
Sich der Umarmung uns, wie trüb erscheint
Dies Erdenleben durch der Thränen Schleier!
Grundlose Ängste! Blinde Sorg! Leer Hoffen!

Such is the scene a round me now:
A little churchyard on the brow
Of a green pastoral hill;
Its sylvan village sleeps below,
And faintly there is heard the flow
Of Woodburn's summer rill;
A place where all things mournful meet,
And yet the sweetest of the sweet,
The stillest of the still!
With what a pensive beauty fall
Across the mossy mouldering wall
That rose-tree's clustered arches! see
The robin-redbreast warily,
Bright, through the blossoms, leaves his nest;
Sweet ingrate! through the winter blest
At the firesides of men—but shy—
Through all the sunny summer hours,
He hides himself among the flowers,
In his own wild festivity.

What lulling sound, and shadow cool,
Hangs half the darkened churchyard o'er,
From thy green depths so beautiful,
Thou gorgeous sycamore!
Oft hath the holy wine and bread
Been blest beneath thy murmuring tent,
Where many a bright and hoary head
Bowed at that awful sacrament.
Now all beneath the turf are laid,
On which they sat, and sang, and prayed.

Dies nun ist um mich rings das Bild:
Ein kleiner Kirchhof auf der Kuppe
Von einem Weidehügel grün; darunter
Träumt einen Waldtraum tief das Dorf;
Nur schwach ist dort das Lallen zu vernehmen
Von Woodburns kleinem Sommerbach;
Ein Ort, wo sich zur Klage jedes trifft,
Und doch der lieblichste von allen,
Der stillste aller stillen!
Mit welcher nachdenklichen Schönheit fallen
Über bemooste steinzerbrochne Wälle
Des Rosenstrauchs geschwungne Büsche! Sieh hier
Das Rotkehlchen voll Umsicht späh'nd
Durch Blüten flink sein Nest verlassen,
Hold-undankbar's! Den Winter lang gefunden wirds
Am Heerd des Menschen (wenn auch scheu) –
Durch alle Sommersonnenstunden
Verborgen zwischen wilden Blumen
In seiner eignen scheuen Fröhlichkeit.

Welch einschläfrichter Ton und kühler Schatten
Hängt überm Kirchhof, halb im Dunkel schon
Von deiner Tiefe schönem Grün,
Du riesenhafte Sykomore!
Wie oft ward Christi Brodt und Wein
Gesegnet unterm Raunen deines Zelts,
Wo manches Haupt, ergraut schon oder hell,
Dem Sacrament sich neigt' in Demuth.
Die sind nun all hinunter in die Erd gegangen
Auf der sie saßen einst und beteten und sangen.

Above that consecrated tree,
Ascends the tapering spire, that seems
To lift the soul up silently
To heaven, with all its dreams;
While in the belfry, deep and low,
From his heaved bosom's purple gleams
The dove's continuous murmurs flow,
A dirge-like song, half bliss, half woe,
The voice so lonely seems!

JOHN WILSON (1785-1854 (?))
A Churchyard Scene

Hoch über den geweihten Baum
Ragt spitz der Kirchturm, der die Seel
Scheint schweigend in die Höh zu schwingen
Mit allen Träumen in den Himmelsraum;
Im Glockenstuhl gurrt leis und fein
Aus des beschwerten Busens Purpurschimmer
Der Taube Wimmern immerdar
Dem Todtenliede gleich, halb Seeligkeit halb Weinen,
So einsam tönt die Stimm', so ganz allein!

I

And, like a dying lady lean and pale,
Who totters forth, wrapp'd in a gauzy veil,
Out of her chamber, led by the insane
And feeble wanderings of her fading brain,
The moon arose up in the murky east
A white and shapeless mass.

II

Art thou pale for weariness
Of climbing heaven and gazing on the earth,
Wandering companionless
Among the stars that have a different birth,
And ever changing, like a joyless eye
That finds no object worth its constancy?

Percy Bysshe Shelley (1792 - 1822)
The Moon

I
Und, wie im Sterben eine Lady dünn und bleich
Torkelt dahin; in Gazeflor gehüllt;
Aus ihrer Kammer, vom wahnsinnigen
Und müden Wandern ihres welken Hirns verführt,
So hob der Mond sich hoch in trüben Ost
Als weiß-formlose Masse.

II
Bist du so blaß aus Müdigkeit
Den Himmel zu erklimmen; zu starren auf die Erd;
Im Wandern stets gefährtenlos
Unter den Sternen, deren Abkunft anders;
Und unstet, wie ein Auge freudelos
Kein Ding findt würdig seiner Stetigkeit?

I met a traveller from an antique land
Who said: Two vast and trunkless legs of stone
Stand in the desert. Near them, on the sand,
Half sunk, a shattered visage lies, whose frown,
And wrinkled lip, and sneer of cold command,
Tell that its sculptor well those passions read
Which yet survive, stamped on these lifeless things,
The hand that mocked them and the heart that fed;
And on the pedestal these words appear:
«My name is Ozymandias, king of kings:
Look on my works, ye Mighty, and despair!»
Nothing beside remains. Round the decay
Of that colossal wreck, boundless and bare
The lone and level sands stretch far away.

PERCY BYSSHE SHELLEY (1792-1822)
Ozymandias

Traf einen Globetrotter aus antiquem Land,
der sprach: Zwei mächtige rumpflose Beine, steinbehaun,
stehn in der Wüste ... und daneben, in den Sand
gesunken halb, liegt ein zerfalln Gesicht, an dessen Düsterbrau'n
Hohnschnauben und verkniffner Lippe, ich seine Eisgewalt erkannt
und daß sein Skulptor diese Leidenschaft wohl las,
die gar noch überlebt (gemeißelt in solch lebelose Dinge)
die Mimesis der Hand, das Herz (das gleichwohl an ihr hinge).
Und auf dem Piedestale stand in Lettern groß:
Ozymandias bin ich: König aller Könige!
Ihr Mächtigen: blickt auf meyn Werk – seid aller Hoffung bloß!
Sonst hat nichts überdauert. Rings um die Welkigkeit
des kolossalen Wracks, nackt bar und grenzenlos
dehnt sich gleichförmig-einsam der Sand in Fernen weit.

203 Music, when soft voices die,
    Vibrates in the memory;
    Odours, when sweet violets sicken,
    Live within the sense they quicken.

    Rose leaves, when the rose is dead,
    Are heap'd for the belovèd's bed;
    And so thy thoughts, when thou art gone,
    Love itself shall slumber on.

Percy Bysshe Shelley (1792-1822)
Music, when soft Voices die

Musik wenn leis die Stimm verklingt
im Gedächtnis widerschwingt
Veilchendüfte süß verblüht
leben im belebt' Gemüth

Rosenblüth vom Reise todt
wird auf der Liebsten Bett gestreut
so Liebe-selbst wenn Du auf ewig abgereist
wird schlummernd ruhn in deinem Geist

An old, mad, blind, despised, and dying king,—
Princes, the dregs of their dull race, who flow
Through public scorn,—mud from a muddy spring,—
Rulers who neither see, nor feel, nor know,
But leech-like to their fainting country cling,
Till they drop, blind in blood, without a blow,—
A people starved and stabbed in the untilled field,—
An army, which liberticide and prey
Makes as a two-edged sword to all who wield,—
Golden and sanguine laws which tempt and slay;
Religion Christless, Godless—a book sealed;
A Senate,—Time's worst statute unrepealed,—
Are graves, from which a glorious Phantom may
Burst, to illumine our tempestuous day.

PERCY BYSSHE SHELLEY (1792-1822)
Sonnet: England in 1819

Der König? – : alt, verhöhnt, blind, sterbend, halb verrückt –
Prinzen? – : der Auswurf ihrer dumpfen Rasse, ein Geschmeiß
für den publiquen Spott, Dreck aus der Quell' verdreckt –
Herrschaft: die weder siehet noch empfindet; von nichts weiß;
wie ein Vampyr an ihrem ohnmächtigen Lande nückt
bis ab sie fällt, hieblos, am Blut sich blindgeleckt –
Ein Volk: auf unbestelltem Feld verhungernd wie erschlagen –
Ein Heer: das Freiheitsmorden wie Beutgierigkeit
dem, der es leit', zu zweischneidigem Schwerte machten –
Gesetze: golden-blutig, die locken so wie schlachten –
Unchristlich-gottlos Religion: ein Buch mit 7 Siegeln –
Senat: der's Mißstatut bestätigt, das schlimmste unsrer Zeit –
: Die sind *ein* Grab. Doch ein Phantom wird ihm entragen
im Strahlenglanz den Sturmwind unsers Aufbruchs zu beflügeln.

205 The grey-eyed Morn was saddened with a shower
A silent shower, that trickled down so still
Scarce drooped beneath its weight the tenderest flower,
Scarce could you trace it on the twinkling rill,
Or moss-stone bathed in dew. It was an hour
Most meet for prayer beside thy lowly grave,
Most for thanksgiving meet, that Heaven such power
To thy serene and humble spirit gave.
«Who sow good seed with tears shall reap in joy.»
So thought I as I watched the gracious rain,
And deemed it like that silent sad employ
Whence sprung thy glory's harvest, to remain
For ever. God hath sworn to lift on high
Who sinks himself by true humility.

JOHN KEBLE (1792 - 1866)
At Hooker's Tomb

Mit grauen Augen schauernd der Morgen war betrauert,
mit einem Schweigeschauer, der tröpfelt' stillverloren;
kaum träufelnd unter seiner Last die zart'ste Blume kauert',
kaum konnt die Spur man auf des Rinnsals Blinken spüren,
noch auf dem Moos-Stein taugebadet. 'S waren Stunden,
zum Beten grade recht an deinem schlichten Grabe,
so recht zum Erntedank, daß solche Kraft gefunden
der Himmel deinem heitren, demütigen Geist zur Gabe.
Mit Freuden erndten wird/ wer sät die Saat mit Thränen:
Also bedachte ich des Schauers Gnad im Schauen:
daß dies sich-trauerschweigend-Regen, wollt ich wähnen,
ein Ausfluß DEines Ruhmes Ernte sei, zu dauern
für immer. GOtts ist der Schwur: hinaufzuwinken
die, so in wahrer Demut vor IHm zu Staube sinken.

Red o'er the forest peers the setting sun;
The line of yellow light dies fast away
That crown'd the eastern copse; and chill and dun
Falls on the moor the brief November day.

Now the tired hunter winds a parting note,
And Echo bids good-night from every glade;
Yet wait awhile and see the calm leaves float
Each to his rest beneath their parent shade.

How like decaying life they seem to glide
And yet no second spring have they in store;
And where they fall, forgotten to abide
Is all their portion, and they ask no more.

Soon o'er their heads blithe April airs shall sing,
A thousand wild-flowers round them shall unfold,
The green buds glisten in the dews of Spring,
And all be vernal rapture as of old.

Unconscious they in waste oblivion lie,
In all the world of busy life around
No thought of them—in all the bounteous sky
No drop, for them, of kindly influence found.

Man's portion is to die and rise again:
Yet he complains, while these unmurmuring part
With their sweet lives, as pure from sin and stain
As his when Eden held his virgin heart.

JOHN KEBLE (1792 - 1866)
November

Rot blizt im Untergehn die Sonne übern Wald;
Fast tot ist schon der Strich: des gelben Lichtes Flor
Der das Gehölz im Osten krönte; falb und kalt
Fällt des Novembers kurzer Tag aufs Moor.

Da pfeift der müde Jäger einen Scheideton,
Und Echo beut Gutnacht aus Wiesenrain und Matten;
Wart, schau, wie lautlos Blatt für Blatt
Zur stillen Ruh nun schweben in ihrer Ahnen Schatten.

Gleichwie verfallndes Leben dünkt ihr Gleiten,
Doch will kein zweiter Frühling sich für sie bereiten,
Und wo sie bleiben haben sie im Fallen schon vergessen:
Das ist ihr Teil, ihrem Bescheiden zugemessen.

Einst werden des Aprils glükliche Winde über ihnen singen,
Sich tausend wilde Blüthen um sie entfalten her,
Und grüne Knospen glitzernd im Thau des Lenzes schwingen,
Alls in vernalischem Entzücken wie von altersher.

Bewußtlos liegen sie in trostlos-wüst Vergessen;
In all der weiten Welt geschäftigem Gewimmel
Gilt ihnen kein Gedenken. Es will kein freigebiger Himmel schenken
Ein Tropfen Freundlichkeit, der ihnen niederflösse.

Des Menschen Theil ist: Sterben – Auferstehn,
Doch er beklagt sich, während jene klaglos scheiden
Von ihrem süßen Leben, gleich ihm an Sünde rein
Wie noch im Stand der Unschuld sein Herz bewahrt in Eden.

Within a thick and spreading hawthorn bush,
That overhung a molehill large and round,
I heard from morn to morn a merry thrush
Sing hymns to sunrise, and I drank the sound
With joy, and, often an intruding guest,
I watched her secret toils from day to day—
How true she warped the moss, to form a nest,
And modelled it within with wood and clay;
And by and by, like heath-bells gilt with dew,
There lay her shining eggs, as bright as flowers
Ink-spotted-over shells of greeny blue:
And there I witnessed in the sunny hours
A brood of nature's minstrels chirp and fly,
Glad as that sunshine and the laughing sky.

JOHN CLARE (1793-1861)
The Thrush's Nest

In einem dichvernestelt Weißdornbusch geborgen,
der eines kugelichten Maulwurfshügels Überhang,
hört ich die stillvergnügte Drossel jeden Morgen
den Sonnenhymnus singen, und den Klang
trank ich mit Lust. Und, oft als zudringlicher Gast,
späht' täglich ich nach ihrer insgeheimen Müh':
Wie sie das Moos fein wölbte für ein Nest
und es mit Lehm und Hölzchen modelliert',
und nach & nach, wie sich mit Thau die Haide ziert,
gleich Blumen schmuck, schimmernde Eier lagen hie:
die Schalen tintenklex-gesprenkelt, bläulich-grün.
Und dort, in sonn'gen Stunden, ward ich Zeuge,
wie der Natur *Trouvères*, ausfliegend, weiterziehn
der Sonne freudig zwitschernd, bis an des Himmels Neige.

I am! yet what I am who cares, or knows?
My friends forsake me like a memory lost.
I am the self-consumer of my woes;
They rise and vanish, an oblivious host,
Shadows of life, whose very soul is lost.
And yet I am—I live—though I am toss'd

Into the nothingness of scorn and noise,
Into the living sea of waking dream,
Where there is neither sense of life, nor joys,
But the huge shipwreck of my own esteem
And all that's dear. Even those I loved the best
Are strange—nay, they are stranger than the rest.

I long for scenes where man has never trod—
For scenes where woman never smiled or wept—
There to abide with my Creator, God,
And sleep as I in childhood sweetly slept,
Full of high thoughts, unborn. So let me lie,—
The grass below; above, the vaulted sky.

JOHN CLARE (1793-1861)
Written in Northampton County Asylum

Ich bin! – doch *wer* bin ich?: wer weiß es und wen schert's?
Verlorener Erinnrung gleich von jedem Freund verlassen
Bin ich der Selbstverzehrer nur von meinem Schmerz:
Der steigt empor . . . . und geht dann weg . . . . . zerstreuter Gast,
Ein's Lebens Geist, des wahre Seel vergessen.
Und doch – Ich bin!, ich leb! – wenn auch geschmissen

In diese Nichtigkeit von Lärm und bösem Lachen;
In die lebendge See von TraumesWachen,
Wo kein Empfinden mehr fürs Leben, kein Ergetzen –
Nur noch dies Scheiterschiff der Selbstachtung, dies Wrack
All dessen, was mir teuer. Die ich am liebsten schätzte,
Sind fremd – neinnein, gar fremder als die andern.

Wie sehn' ich mich nach Szenen, die nie ein Mensch erwandert,
Wo nie ein Weib gelächelt oder weint' in Kummer –
In meinem Schöpfergott geborgen mich zu wiegen,
Zu ruhn wie in der Kindheit süßem Schlummer,
Hoher Gedanken kund & niegeborn. Laßt mich da liegen
Im Grase tief – hoch über mir des Himmels Rund.

209 Old noted oak! I saw thee in a mood
Of vague indifference; and yet with me
Thy memory, like thy fate, hath lingering stood
For years, thou hermit, in the lonely sea
Of grass that waves around thee!—Solitude
Paints not a lonelier picture to the view,
Burthorp! than thy one melancholy tree,
Age-rent, and shattered to a stump. Yet new
Leaves come upon each rift and broken limb
With every spring; and Poesy's visions swim
Around it, of old days and chivalry;
And desolate fancies bid the eyes grow dim
With feelings, that earth's grandeur should decay,
And all its olden memories pass away.

JOHN CLARE (1793-1861)
Burthorp Oak

Alt-ächte Eiche: sah dich im Empfinden
von schwankem Gleichmut; doch hat immer mir
dein Denkbild wie Geschick zähwurzelnd fest gestanden
seit alters, Eremit! im menschenfernen Meer
aus Gras, das um dich wogt. – Verlassenheit kann kaum
ein' abgeschiedenere Landschaft vor die Augen malen,
Burthorp!, als deinen einsam-melanchol'schen Baum
hinfällig bis zum Stumpf. Doch stets aufs neu, aus dumpfem Holz
wiegt jedes Frühjahr sich der Blätterflor im Stolz:
Gesichte schweben drum, poetisch' Idealen
von guter, alter, ritterlicher Zeit;
und desolate Zukunft füllt das Herz mit Trübigkeit
bei dem Gedanken, daß der Erd' Grandeur zergehe,
daß Eingedenken an das Alte selbst verwehe.

If by dull rhymes our English must be chain'd,
And, like Andromeda, the Sonnet sweet
Fetter'd, in spite of pained loveliness;
Let us find out, if we must be constrain'd,
Sandals more interwoven and complete
To fit the naked foot of poesy;
Let us inspect the lyre, and weigh the stress
Of every chord, and see what may be gain'd
By ear industrious, and attention meet;
Misers of sound and syllable, no less
Than Midas of his coinage, let us be
Jealous of dead leaves in the bay wreath crown;
So, if we may not let the Muse be free,
She will be bound with garlands of her own.

JOHN KEATS (1795-1821)
If by dull rhymes our English must be chain'd

Wenn stumpfe Reime unser Englisch müssen binden
Und gleich Andromeda das liebliche Sonett
Trotz Schmerzensherrlichkeit in feste Fesseln fassen;
Dann laßt – da wir einmal im Zwang – uns finden
Eh'r feingeflochtene Sandalen und komplett
Dem baaren Fuß der Poesie zu passen;
Laßt uns die Leyer prüfen & die Spannung messen
Von jeder Sait, und sehn was wir erreichen
Mit fleißgem Ohr, Aufmerksamkeit nicht weichen!
Arm an Syllaben, arm an Klang sind wir nicht minder
Als Midas seiner Wortkraft, also lasset
Uns Leerlaub aus der Lorbeerkrone winden.
Ob wir gleich MUSA nicht entledgen ihrer Bande,
Wird sie doch fesseln sich mit eignen Ruhmgirlanden.

When I have fears that I may cease to be
Before my pen has gleaned my teeming brain,
Before high-piled books, in charact'ry
Hold like rich garners the full-ripened grain;
When I behold, upon the night's starred face,
Huge cloudy symbols of a high romance,
And think that I may never live to trace
Their shadows, with the magic hand of chance;
And when I feel, fair creature of an hour!
That I shall never look upon thee more,
Never have relish in the faery power
Of unreflecting love!—then on the shore
Of the wide world I stand alone, and think
Till Love and Fame to nothingness do sink.

JOHN KEATS (1795 - 1821)
When I have fears that I may cease to be

Wenn mich die Furcht ergreift, mein Leben könnt zerschmettern
Eh noch der Federkiel aus meines Hirns Gewimmel,
Eh noch ein Bücherberg in Druck und Lettern
Die reiche Ernte liest und in den Himmel
Türmt; wenn auf der Nacht besternten Mien'
Ich als Romantisches Symbol seh eine Wolkenwand
Und fühl, daß ich's nie kann: die Spuren nachzuziehn
Von ihren Schatten, mit der Verwandlung Zufallshand;
Wenn ich empfind, Du Wesen einer Stunde hold,
Daß nie mein Blick soll ruhn mehr unverwandt
Auf Dir, nie mehr gebannt von reizender Gewalt
Der leichtbedachten Liebe . . . . Am fernen Strand
Der Welt steh ich allein dann im Gedenken,
Bis Ruhm & Lieb in Nichtigkeit versinken.

When we were idlers with the loitering rills,
The need of human love we little noted:
Our love was nature; and the peace that floated
On the white mist, and dwelt upon the hills,
To sweet accord subdued our wayward wills:
One soul was ours, one mind, one heart devoted,
That, wisely doating, asked not why it doated,
And ours the unknown joy, which knowing kills.
But now I find how dear thou wert to me;
That man is more than half of nature's treasure,
Of that fair beauty which no eye can see,
Of that sweet music which no ear can measure;
And now the streams may sing for others' pleasure,
The hills sleep on in their eternity.

HARTLEY COLERIDGE (1796-1849)
Friendship

Als wir am saumseligen Bach noch müßiggingen,
spürten wir kaum den Wunsch nach MenschenLieb';
Natur war unsre Liebe: der Friede, der da trieb
auf weißen Nebeln und auf Hügelhängen,
zähmt' unsern Eigensinn zu süß-harmonisch Klingen:
ein Geist war unser, *eine* Seel, *ein* Herze lieb
das weise gab – nicht frug, warum es gab,
unser das unbewußte Glück (das mit dem Wissen ja zerginge).
Doch weiß ich nun, wie lieb du mir gewesen
und daß der Mensch der größte Reichtum: der Natur –
der Schönheit, die dem Auge zu erlesen –
jener Musik zu süß, unhörbar jedem Ohr.
Mög' unser Bach zu Andrer Seligkeit nun rauschen
und seiner Ewigkeit der Hügel stille lauschen!

213   There is a silence where hath been no sound,
There is a silence where no sound may be,
In the cold grave—under the deep deep sea,
Or in wide desert where no life is found,
Which hath been mute, and still must sleep profound;
No voice is hush'd—no life treads silently,
But clouds and cloudy shadows wander free,
That never spoke, over the idle ground:
But in green ruins, in the desolate walls
Of antique palaces, where Man hath been,
Though the dun fox, or wild hyaena, calls,
And owls, that flit continually between,
Shriek to the echo, and the low winds moan,
There the true Silence is, self-conscious and alone.

THOMAS HOOD (1798-1815)
Silence

Es gibt ein Schweigen, wo kein Laut war je.
Es gibt die Stille, wo vielleicht nie Laut:
Im kalten Grab – und in der tiefen, tiefen See –
in weiter Wüste: die nie Leben schaut,
die immer stumm, muß tief im Schlummer bleiben ...
nicht eine Stimme huscht ... nicht Lebens schweigsame Gebärde ...
nur Wolken, Wolkenschatten freihin treiben
nichtssagend über die verlorne Erde.
Doch in versunkener Paläste grün Verwesen,
in überwachsnen Mauern, wo einst *der Mensch* gewesen,
zwar wohl Schakale und Hyänen schrein
und Eulen hin und wieder krächzen
dem Echo im Gestein, und matte Winde ächzen –
Doch dort ist wahre Stille: *sich selbst bewußt*, allein.

They do but grope in learning's pedant round,
Who on the fantasies of sense bestow
An idol substance, bidding us bow low
Before those shades of being which are found
Stirring or still on man's brief trial ground;
As if such shapes and moods, which come and go,
Had aught of Truth or Life in their poor show,
To sway or judge, and skill to sain or wound.
Son of immortal Seed, high destined Man!
Know thy dread gift,—a creature, yet a cause;
Each mind is its own centre, and it draws
Home to itself, and moulds in its thought's span
All outward things, the vassals of its will,
Aided by Heaven, by earth unthwarted still.

JOHN HENRY NEWMAN (1801-1890)
Substance and Shadow

Die tasten nur borniert sich durch Erkenntnisrunden,
die den Fantasterein der Sinne einverleiben
ein idolatrisch Wesen, und uns zur Achtung treiben
vor Wesensschemen (: die sei's untätig befunden,
sei's wirkend), aus menschlich-kurzsichtigen Urteilsgründen.
Als hätten solche Launen, Larven, die da wabern-weben,
an ihrem armseligen Schein etwas von Wahrheit oder Leben:
zu richten – zu regieren, zu lindern – zu verwunden!
Sohn unsterblicher Saat, zu hohem Menschentum bestimmt,
Causa wie *Creatur*!: lern', was dir hehr gegeben:
Sein eigen Centrum ist ein jeder Geist, er nimmt
heim in sich selbst und prägt mit seines Denkens Streben
die ganze Außenwelt, der so sein Inneres gebeut.
Die Erde neidets nicht – der Himmel stehet ihm zur Seit!

215   Above yon sombres swell of land
      Thou see'st the dawn's grave orange hue,
      With one pale streak like yellow sand,
      And over that a vein of blue.

      The air is cold above the woods;
      All silent is the earth and sky,
      Except with his own lonely moods
      The blackbird holds a colloquy.

      Over the broad hill creeps a beam,
      Like hope that gilds a good man's brow;
      And now ascends the nostril-stream
      Of stalwart horses come to plough.

      Ye rigid Ploughmen, bear in mind
      Your labour is for future hours:
      Advance—spare not—nor look behind—
      Plough deep and straight with all your powers!

RICHARD HENRY HORNE (1803-1884)
The Plough. A Landscape in Berkshire

Fern überm dunkelwogend Land
Siehst du der Dämmrung tief orangne Feuerspur
Mit einem falben Streif wie gelber Sand,
Darüber ein Geäder von Azur.

Über die Wälder weht es kühl.
Ganz still sind Erd und Himmelszelt.
Versponnen in ihr einsames Gefühl
Ein Zwiegespräch die Amsel hält.

Ein Strich den weiten Hügel näher kraucht
Gleich Hoffnung, die des Braven Stirne ziert;
Schon wölkt, was aus den Nüstern raucht
Von stämmig Pferden, vor den Pflug geschirrt.

Ihr rauhen Pflüger, gebet acht:
Die Arbeit ist für zukünftiges Glück:
Voran – und nicht gesäumt – schaut nicht zurück –
Pflügt tief & grad' mit aller eurer Macht!

As yonder lamp in my vacated room
With arduous flame disputes the darksome night,
And can, with its involuntary light,
But lifeless things, that near it stand, illume;
Yet all the while it doth itself consume,
And, ere the sun begins its heavenly height
With courier beams that meet the shepherd's sight,
There, whence its life arose, shall be its tomb—

So wastes my light away. Perforce confined
To common things, a limit to its sphere,
It shines on worthless trifles undesign'd
With fainter ray each hour imprison'd here.
Alas! to know that the consuming mind
Shall leave its lamp cold, ere the sun appear.

CHARLES WHITEHEAD (1804-1862)
The Lamp

Wie meine Lampe in der Kammer Einsamkeit
in stetem Brand den Streit mit Finsternis ausficht
und, in der Näh, mit unfreiwillgem Licht
zwar toten Dingen Lebensschein verleiht,
doch alleweil sich dabei selbst verzehrt
und, eh die Sonne den Zenith erklimmt
mit Strahlen-Botschaft die des Schäfers Aug vernimmt,
was ihr den Ursprung schenkte, zugleich den Untergang beschert:

So schwindet auch mein Licht dahin. Zwanghaft geschlossen
an die Banalität, um die sein Bannstrahl kreist,
scheint's auf wertlosen Tand, und unfreiwillgermaßen,
mit jeder Stunde schwächer, die es gefangen schließt.
Zu wissen, ach! daß der verzehrnde Geist
soll seine Lampe, eh das Licht aufgeht, verlassen!

217   I tell you, hopeless grief is passionless;
That only men incredulous of despair,
Half-taught in anguish, through the midnight air
Beat upward to God's throne in loud access
Of shrieking and reproach. Full desertness
In souls, as countries, lieth silent-bare
Under the blanching, vertical eye-glare
Of the absolute Heavens. Deep-hearted man, express
Grief for thy Dead in silence like to death:—
Most like a monumental statue set
In everlasting watch and moveless woe,
Till itself crumble to the dust beneath.
Touch it: the marble eyelids are not wet;
If it could weep, it could arise and go.

ELIZABETH BARRET BROWNING (1806-1861)
Grief

Ich sag Euch, hoffnungslose Pein ist ohne Fühlen,
Daß nur die Menschen unglaubwürdig ihrer Qualen,
In Schmerzen halbgebildet, die Mitternacht durch schrein,
Hämmern an Gottes Thron, mit Kreischen, Wühlen,
Vorwürfen gar und Droh'n. Ein vollständiges *Aus*
In Seelen wie in Ländern liegt rein stille
Unter der starren vertikalen Augenhelle
Des Absoluten Himmels. Tiefherzger Mensch, drück aus
Den Schmerz um deine Todten so schweigend wie der Tod,
Ganz wie des Standbilds Mahnmal stehe
In immerwährnder Not, bewegungsloser Wacht im Leide,
Bis es zerbröckelnd gleich dem Staub verwehe.
Faß an nur: – sind nicht naß, die Marmoraugenlider!
Könnts weinen, könnts ja sich erheben, gehen.

Oft have I seen at some cathedral door
A laborer, pausing in the dust and heat,
Lay down his burden, and with reverent feet
Enter, and cross himself, and on the floor
Kneel to repeat his paternoster o'er;
Far off the noises of the world retreat;
The loud vociferations of the street
Become an undistinguishable roar.
So, as I enter here from day to day,
And leave my burden at this minster gate,
Kneeling in prayer, and not ashamed to pray,
The tumult of the time disconsolate
To inarticulate murmurs dies away,
While the eternal ages watch and wait.

HENRY WADSWORTH LONGFELLOW (1807 -1882)
On Translating the Divina Commedia

Oft sah an mancher Kathedralenpforte Schlund
Ich einen Arbeiter in Staub und heißem Ruß
Sein Bündel setzen ab, und mit ehrwürdgem Fuß
Eintreten, sich bekreuzen, auf den Grund
Herniederknien, mehrmals sein Vaterunser sprechen
Abhanden fern dem Lärm der Welt;
Der Straße tosender Tumult
Ward nur mehr undurchdringlich dröhnendes Gekoche.
Gleich so, da ich tagtäglich hier eintrete
(Mein Bündel bei des Münsters Tor gestellt)
Zum Beten knie', nicht schämend der Gebete,
Stirbt der Tumult der trostlosen Epoche
Dahin in dumpf undeutlich Murmellachen –
Dieweil die Ewigkeiten warten, wachen.

219

In Mather's Magnalia Christi,
Of the old colonial time,
May be found in prose the legend
That is here set down in rhyme.

A ship sailed from New Haven,
And the keen and frosty airs,
That filled her sails at parting,
Were heavy with good men's prayers.

«Oh Lord! if it be thy pleasure,»
Thus prayed the old divine,
«To bury our friends in the ocean,
Take them, for they are thine!»

But Master Lamberton muttered,
And under his breath said he—
«This ship is so crank and wolty,
I fear our grave she will be!»

And the ships that came from England,
When the winter months were gone,
Brought no tidings of this vessel
Nor of Master Lamberton.

This put the people to praying
That the Lord would let them hear
What, in his greater wisdom,
He had done with friends so dear.

And at last their prayers were answered:—
It was in the month of June,

In *Mather's Magnalia Christi*,
aus alt Kolonieen-Zeit,
steht eine Legende in Prosa,
die ich in Verse gekleidet:

Ein Schiff stach von New Haven;
schwer hallte der Eiswind, der weht'
und beim Abschied die Segel geblähet,
von guter Menschen Gebet.

«Oh HErr, ist's denn dein Wille,»
so betet der Geistliche fein,
«ins Meer unsre Freunde zu senken:
nimm hin – sie sind ja dein.»

Nur Master Lamberton murrte;
knurrt' halblaut in sich 'nein:
«Dies Schiff ist ein Seelenverkäufer,
's wird unsre Gruft wohl sein.»

Und die Segler, die von England her,
– das Frühjahr nahte schon –
sie brachten keine Zeitung
vom Schiff oder Lamberton.

Da flehten sie zum HErren,
daß Er ihnen Nachricht geb,
was Er in Seinem Ratschluß
getan mit den Freunden so lieb.

Ihr Beten ward endlich erhöret:
Im Monat Juni es war,

An hour before the sunset
Of a windy afternoon;

When steadily steering landward
A ship was seen below,
And they knew it was Lamberton, Master,
Who sailed so long ago.

On she came, with a cloud of canvas,
Right against the wind that blew,
Until the eye could distinguish
The faces of the crew.

Then fell her straining top-mast,
Hanging tangled in the shrouds,
And her sails were loosened and lifted,
And blown away like clouds.

And the masts, with all their rigging,
Fell slowly one by one,
And the hulk dilated and vanished,
As a sea-mist in the sun!

And the people who saw this marvel,
Each said unto his friend,
That this was the mould of their vessel,
And thus her tragic end.

And the pastor of the village
Gave thanks to God in prayer,
That to quiet their troubled spirits
He had sent this Ship of Air.

HENRY WADSWORTH LONGFELLOW (1807 - 1882)
The Phantom Ship

ein Stund vor Sonnenuntergang
eines windigen Nachmittags klar;

Als, stetig landwärts haltend,
eine Brigg man sah in der Weit';
und man wußte: 's war Lamberton Master,
verschollen seit langer Zeit.

Da kam sie: mit Wolken von Segeln
grad gegen den sausenden Wind,
bis das Aug die Gesichter der Mannschaft
klar unterscheiden konnt.

Da riß aus den Wanten der Topmast;
im Takelwerk pendelnd er hing;
Und die Segel lösten sich – schwebten –
und wehten wie Wolken dahin.

Und die Masten mit allem Getakel
fieln mählich nach einand;
Und der Schiffsleib, wie Nebel im Sonnschein,
verweste – und verschwand!

Und die solches Wunder gesehen,
ein jeder wisperts dem Freund:
«Das war unsers Schiffes Todtenmaske,
und so sein tragisches End.»

Und jenes Dorfes Pastor
zu Gott sein Dankgebet ruft,
daß Er um ihren Seelenfried'
gesandt dies Schiff-aus-Luft.

An old man in a lodge within a park;
The chamber walls depicted all around
With portraitures of huntsman, hawk, and hound,
And the hurt deer. He listeneth to the lark,
Whose song comes with the sunshine through the dark
Of painted glass in leaden lattice bound;
He listeneth and he laugheth at the sound,
Then writeth in a book like any clerk.
He is the poet of the dawn, who wrote
The Canterbury Tales, and his old age
Made beauiful with song; and as I read
I hear the crowing cock, I hear the note
Of lark and linnet, and from every page
Rise odors of ploughed field or flowery mead.

Henry Wadsworth Longfellow (1807-1882)
Chaucer

Ein alter Mann in einer Hütt' inmitten eines Parks.
Die Kammerwänd gespickt mit Bildern in der Runde.
Porträts vom Jägersmann. Vom Habicht, Hunde und
Waidwundem Hirsch. Er lauscht der Lerche
Deren Gesang tönt mit der Sonne durch das Dunkel
Von buntem Glas, in Bleirand eingebunden.
Er lauscht & lächelt zu dem Klanggefunkel,
Schreibt dann in einem Buch wie irgendein Verwalter.
Das ist der Dämmerung Poet gewesen und der Dichter
Der *Canterbury Tales*, verherrlicht hat sein Alter
Der Preisgesang; und da ich lese,
Hör ich die Hähne krähn, hör ich die Weise
Von Hänfling, Lerche, und aus jeder Seite steigen
Die Düfte von gepflügtem Feld und blumenbunter Wiese.

221 The shades of night were falling fast,
As through an Alpine village passed
A youth, who bore, 'mid snow and ice,
A banner with the strange device,
 Excelsior!

His brow was sad; his eye beneath,
Flashed like a falchion from its sheath,
And like a silver clarion rung
Tlie accents of that unknown tongue,
 Excelsior!

In happy homes he saw the light
Of household fires gleam warm and bright;
Above, the spectral glaciers shone,
And from his lips escaped a groan,
 Excelsior!

«Try not the Pass!» the old man said;
«Dark lowers the tempest overhead,
The roaring torrent is deep and wide!»
And loud that clarion voice replied,
 Excelsior!

«Oh stay,» the maiden said, «and rest
Thy weary head upon this breast!»
A tear stood in his bright blue eye,
But still he answered, with a sigh,
 Excelsior!

Die Dämmerung brach schnell herein,
Als durch ein Alpendörfchen schritt
Ein Knabe, der durch Eis und Schnee
Ein Banner trug mit fremder Schrift:
   Excelsior!

Die Stirne trüb; allein das Aug
Blitzt gleich dem Schwerte aus der Scheid';
Gleich silbernen Clarinen tönt
Der unbekannten Zunge Laut:
   Excelsior!

In biedern Häusern sah er warm
und hell das Licht des Herdes scheinen –
Die Gletscher droben glommen fahl –
Dem Mund ein Stöhnen sich entrang:
   Excelsior!

«Wag nicht den Paß!» der Alte sprach,
«Der finstre Sturm dräut dir hernied'!
Tief ist und breit der brüllnde Fluß!»
Trompetenhell die Antwort scholl:
   Excelsior!

«Bleib,» sprach das Mädchen, «bett' dein Haupt,
Dein müdes Haupt an meiner Brust!»
Ins Auge lichtblau trat die Thrän',
Mit Seufzen er zur Antwort gab:
   Excelsior!

«Beware the pine-tree's withered branch!
Beware the awful avalanche!»
This was the peasant's last Good-night;
A voice replied, far up the height,
    Excelsior!

At break of day, as heavenward
The pious monks of St Bernard
Uttered the oft-repeated prayer,
A voice cried through the startled air,
    Excelsior!

A traveller, by the faithful hound,
Half-buried in the snow was found,
Still grasping in his hand of ice
That banner with the strange device,
    Excelsior!

There in the twilight cold and gray,
Lifeless, but beautiful, he lay,
And from the sky, serene and far,
A voice fell, like a falling star,
    Excelsior!

HENRY WADSWORTH LONGFELLOW (1807 - 1882)
Excelsior

«Merk auf der Fichte toten Ast:
Die schreckliche Lawine fürchte!»
Dies war des Sennen letzt' Gutnacht.
Fern von der Höhe kam die Stimm':
   Excelsior!

Im Morgengraun, da himmelauf
St. Bernhards fromme Mönche sich
Zum täglichen Gebete fanden,
Schrie eine Stimm' durch Schreckensluft:
   Excelsior!

Ein Reisender von treuem Hund
Ward, schneebegraben halb, erspürt:
Noch klammerte die eis'ge Hand
Das Banner mit der fremden Schrift:
   Excelsior!

Dort in dem Zwielicht kalt und grau
Leblos, doch wunderbar, er lag;
Und aus dem heitren Himmel, der so weit,
Fiel eine Stimme wie ein Meteor:
   Excelsior!

Evangeline brough the draught-board out of its corner.
Soon was the game begun. In friendly contention the old men
Laughed at each lucky hit or unsuccessful manœuvre,
Laughed when a man was crowned, or a breach was made in the
    king-row.
Meanwhile, apart, in the twilight gloom of a window's embrasure,
Sat the lovers, and whispered together, beholding the moon rise
Over the pallid sea and the silvery mist of the meadows.
Silently, one by one, in the infinite meadows of heaven,
Blossomed the lovely stars, the forget-me-nots of the angels.
Thus passed the evening away.

Henry Wadsworth Longfellow (1807 - 1882)
from «Evangeline»

Evangeline bracht aus der Ecke das Dame-Brett. Schon ward
begonnen das Spiel. In freundlichem Wettstreit die Alten
lachten ob jedem gelungenen Zuge, mißglückten Manöver;
lachten, wenn einer gekrönt – wenn in die Reihe des Königs
die Bresche geschlagen. Dieweil beiseit, im Zwielichtdämmer des
FensterAlkovens saßen die Liebenden wispernd beisamm',
 in den Aufgang
des Mondes versunken hoch über der blaßgrauen See,
 dem silbrigen Schimmer
der Matten. Schweigend, eins nach dem andern,
 auf Himmels unendlicher
Wiese erblühten die lieblichen Sterne, der Engel Vergißmeinnicht.
So ging der Abend dahin.

223   Thou comest, Autumn, heralded by the rain,
With banners, by great gales incessant fann'd,
Brighter than brightest silks of Samarcand,
And stately oxen harness'd to thy wain;
Thou standest, like imperial Charlemagne,
Upon thy bridge of gold; thy royal hand
Outstretched with benedictions o'er the land,
Blessing the farms through all thy vast domain.
Thy shield is the red harvest moon, suspended
So long beneath the heaven's o'erhanging eaves;
Thy steps are by the farmer's prayers attended;
Like flames upon an altar shine the sheaves;
And, following thee, in thy ovation splendid,
Thine almoner, the wind, scatters the golden leaves!

HENRY WADSWORTH LONGFELLOW (1807-1882)
Autumn

Du nahest, Herbst: dein Herold ist der Regen
mit FächerFahnen, die die Sturmwinde entspreiten
leuchtkräftiger denn Samarkands lichtfarbene Seiden,
ein stolzes Ochsenpaar gespannt vor deinen Wagen.
Du stehest, wie einst Karl der Große stand,
auf deiner goldnen Brücke; die royale Hand
reichst du mit Wohlgebärde übers Land, wie milde
die Höfe weitum segnend übers reich' Gefilde.
Dein Wappen ist der rote ErnteMond, der rollt
so lang unter des Himmels Träufendach;
des Landmanns Bittgesang will deinen Gang begleiten;
zur Altarlohe ist der Garben Farb' entfacht;
und im Gefolge, Ovationen dir bereitend,
streut aus der Wind, dein Almosenier, der Blätter Gold!

Somewhat back from the village street
Stands the old-fashioned country-seat.
Across its antique portico
Tall poplar-trees their shadows throw;
And from its station in the hall
An ancient time-piece says to all,—
  «For ever—never!
  Never—for ever!»

Halfway up the stairs it stands,
And points and beckons with its hands
From its case of massive oak,
Like a monk, who, under his cloak,
Crosses himself, and sighs, alas!
With sorrowful voice to all who pass,—
  «For ever—never!
  Never—for ever!»

By day its voice is low and light;
But in the silent dead of night,
Distinct as a passing footstep's fall,
It echoes along the vacant hall,
Along the ceiling, along the floor,
And seems to say, at each chamber-door,—
  «For ever—never!
  Never—for ever!»

Leicht abseits von des Dorfes Straß'
alt-modisch steht das Herrenhaus.
Auf den antiquen Portikus
fällt ranker Pappeln Schattenfluß.
Von seinem Standort in der Halle
ein uralt Uhrwerk spricht zu allen:
　«Für immer – nimmer!
　Nimmer – für immer!»

Es steht am Treppenabsatz dort
und weist mit seinen Zeigern fort
aus dem massiven Eich-Gehäus,
wie aus der Kutte sich das Kreuz
der Klosterbrüder schlägt, und seufzt
und Gram spricht jedem, der da läuft:
　«Für immer – nimmer!
　Nimmer – für immer!»

Bei Tage spricht es leicht und sacht –
Doch in der Todtenstill' der Nacht
deutlich wie eines Schrittes Fall
echot's entlang der leeren Hall,
die Deck' entlang – die Dielen lang –
vor jeder Kammertür so bang:
　«Für immer – nimmer!
　Nimmer – für immer!»

Through days of sorrow and of mirth,
Through days of death and days of birth,
Through every swift vicissitude
Of changeful time, unchanged it has stood,
And as if, like God, it all things saw,
It calmly repeats those words of awe,—
 «For ever—never!
 Never—for ever!»

In that mansion used to be
Free-hearted Hospitality;
His great fires up the chimney roared,
The stranger feasted at his board;
But, like the skeleton at the feast,
That warning time-piece never ceased,—
 «For ever—never!
 Never—for ever!»

There groups of merry children played,
There youths and maidens dreaming strayed;
O precious hours! O golden prime,
And affluence of love and time!
Even as a miser counts his gold,
Those hours the ancient time-piece told,—
 «For ever—never!
 Never—for ever!»

Durch Tage, froh und herb im Leid –
durch Todes- wie GeburtenZeit –
durch jede jähe Wechselstund
im Wandel unverwandt es stund;
Als ob, wie Gott, es Alles säh,
erneut es stet das Wort-der-Scheu:
　«Für immer – nimmer!
　Nimmer – für immer!»

In jenem Haus war stets bereit
die großherzigste Gastlichkeit;
Die Feuer den Kamin hoch brausten –
die Fremden an der Tafel schmausten –
Doch, wie der Sensenmann beim Fest,
die Standuhr immer mahnt' den Gast:
　«Für immer – nimmer!
　Nimmer – für immer!»

Dort herrschten lustger Kinder Spiel
und Jungfern-Jünglings-Träume viel:
O kostbar Stunden! Goldne Morgenröt'!
Und Überfluß an Lieb und Zeit!
Doch, wie ein Armer zählt sein Geld,
die alte Uhr die Stunden zählt':
　«Für immer – nimmer!
　Nimmer – für immer!»

From that chamber, clothed in white,
The bride came forth on her wedding night;
There, in that silent room below,
The dead lay in his shroud of snow;
And in the hush that followed the prayer,
Was heard the old clock on the stair,—
   «For ever—never!
   Never—for ever!»

All are scattered now and fled,
Some are married, some are dead;
And when I ask, with throbs of pain,
«Ah! when shall they all meet again?»
As in the days long since gone by,
The ancient time-piece makes reply,—
   «For ever—never!
   Never—for ever!»

Never here, for ever there,
Where all parting, pain, and care,
And death and time shall disappear,—
For ever there, but never here!
The horologe of Eternity
Sayeth this incessantly,—
   «For ever—never!
   Never—for ever!»

Henry Wadsworth Longfellow (1807 - 1882)
The Old Clock on the Stairs

Aus jener Kammer, weiß im Kleid
am Hochzeitsabend schritt die Braut;
Dort unten, in dem stillen Raum,
träumt' der Verstorbene den Todtentraum
und in des Betens Stille, von den Stufen
hört' man das alte Uhrwerk rufen:
 «Für immer – nimmer!
 Nimmer – für immer!»

Sind alle nun dahin, zerstreut:
im Eh'stand diese – jene tot –
Und wenn, aufschluchzend, ich dann frag:
«Wann seh ich wieder sie? – ach, sag!»,
wie in dem alt-vergangnen Leben
tut mir die Uhr zur Antwort geben:
 «Für immer – nimmer!
 Nimmer – für immer!»

Nimmer hier – für immer dort,
wo all Scheiden, Bangen, Tort
und Tod und Leid sind ewig fort:
Für immer dort – doch nie an diesem Ort!
Also macht mir das Herz bereit
dies Horologium der Ewigkeit.
 «Für immer – nimmer!
 Nimmer – für immer!»

In the long, sleepless watches of the night,
A gentle face—the face of one long dead—
Looks at me from the wall, where round its head
The night-lamp casts a halo of pale light.
Here in this room she died; and soul more white
Never through martyrdom of fire was led
To its repose; nor can in books be read
The legend of a life more benedight.
There is a mountain in the distant West
That, sun-defying, in its deep ravines
Displays a cross of snow upon its side.
Such is the cross I wear upon my breast
These eighteen years, through all the changing scenes
And seasons, changeless since the day she died.

HENRY WADSWORTH LONGFELLOW (1807 - 1882)
The Cross of Snow

In langen, schlaflosen Vigilien der Nacht
mich von der Wand herab ein zartes Haupt betracht':
das Antlitz einer, die längst tot. Und rund um dies Gesicht
flicht die Laterne einen Cranz aus bleichem Licht.
In diesem Raum starb sie. Und eine Seel, die *weißer* noch gewesen,
ward nie durch Fegefeuerpein geleit'
zu ihrer Ruh; in keinem Buche kann man lesen
von der Legende eines Lebens, das mehr benedeit.
Da steht ein Berg, im fernen West,
der, sonn-abweisend, in den Klüften tief,
an seinem Hang ein Kreuz aus Schnee enthüllt.
So ist das Kreuz auch, das ich auf der Brust
die achtzehn Jahr getragen durch alle wandelnde Gestalt
und Zeit, unwandelbar seit sie entschlief.

Blind Bartimeus at the gates
Of Jericho in darkness waits;
He hears the crowd;—he hears a breath
Say, «It is Christ of Nazareth!»
And calls in tones of agony,
Ιησου, ελεησον με!

The thronging multitudes increase;
Blind Bartimeus hold thy peace!
But still, above the noisy crowd,
The beggar's cry is shrill and loud;
Until they say, «He calleth thee;»
Θαρσει, εγειραι φωνει σε!

Then saith the Christ, as silent stands
The crowd, «What wilt thou at my hands?»
And he replies, «O give me light!
Rabbi, restore the blind man's sight!»
And Jesus answers, Υπαγε!
Η πιστις σου σεσωκε σε!

Ye that have eyes, and cannot see,
In darkness and in misery,
Recall those mighty Voices Three,
Ιησου, ελεησον με!
Θαρσει, εγειραι, υπαγε!
Η πιστις σου σεσωκε σε!

HENRY WADSWORTH LONGFELLOW (1807-1882)
Blind Bartimeus

In Dunkelheit vor Jericho
am Tor harrt Bartimeus. Oh,
er hört die Menge – hört Wispern stet
«Seht Christum dort von Nazareth»,
und ruft mit Schreien aus tiefstem Weh:
Ιησου, ελεησον με!

Die Menge schwillt sich drängend, müht:
Bartimeus, halte Fried'!
Doch weiter, über dem Tosen wild
des Bettlers gellendes Flehen schrillt;
bis man ihm sagt «ER ruft dich – geh'»
Θαρσει, εγειραι φωνει σε!

Da sprach Christus – die Menge stand –
«Was tastest du nach meiner Hand?»
Und er gab hin «Oh schenk mir Licht!
Rabbi, heile des Blinden Gesicht!»
Da sprach Herrjesus: Υπαγε!
Η πιστις σου σεσωκε σε!

Ihr, mit Augen die können nicht sehn,
in Dunkelheit, mit Elends Gestöhn,
gedenkt jener machtvollen Worte drei:
Ιησου, ελεησον με!
Θαρσει, εγειραι, υπαγε!
Η πιστις σου σεσωκε σε!

227   It was the schooner Hesperus,
         That sailed the wintry sea;
      And the skipper had taken his little daughter,
         To bear him company.

      Blue were her eyes as the lairy-flax,
         Her cheeks like the dawn of day,
      And her bosom white as the howthorn buds,
         That ope in the month of May.

      The skipper he stood beside the helm,
         His pipe was in his mouth,
      And he watched how the veering flaw did blow
         The smoke now west, now south.

      Then up and spake an old sailor,
         Had sailed the Spanish Main,
      «I pray thee, put into yonder port,
         For I fear a hurricane.

      «Last night the moon had a golden ring,
         And to-night no moon we see!»
      The skipper he blew a whiff from his pipe,
         And a scornful laugh laughed he.

      Colder and louder blew the wind,
         A gale from the north-east;
      The snow fell hissing in the brine,
         And the billows frothed like yeast.

War einst ein Schoner, *HESPERUS*,
  der kreuzt' die Winterseen;
Und der Schiffer hatt bracht sein Tochter klein
  die möcht ihm nahe sein:

Wie wilder Flachs die Augen blau,
  wie Morgenröt' die Wängelein,
der Busen weiß wie Hagedorn
  der blühet wohl im Mai'n.

Am Steuerhelm der Schiffer steht,
  im Mund die Pfeife fest,
späht, wie die Wechselbö zerweht
  den Rauch mal süd – mal west.

Da meldt ein alter Seemann Wort,
  kennt Spaniens Meere weit,
«Bitt', steuert an den nächsten Port:
  ein Hurrikan uns dräut!

Der Mond letzt nacht hatt ein' güldnen Reif,
  und heut ist gar kein Mon'!»
Der Schiffer schnaubte durch die Pfeif'
  und lachte nur im Hohn.

Kälter & lauter schon blus der Wind,
  die Bö schlug um nach Ost;
Schnee fauchte in die salzige See,
  die Dünung schäumt' wie Most.

Down came the storm, and smote amain
  The vessel in its strength;
She shuddered and paused, like a frighted steed,
  Then leaped a cable's length.

«Come hither! come hither! my little daughter,
  And do not tremble so;
For I can weather the roughest gale,
  That ever wind did blow.»

He wrapped her warm in his seaman's coat
  Against the stinging blast;
He cut a rope from a broken spar,
  And bound her to the mast.

«O father! I hear the church-bells ring,
  Oh, say, what may it be?»
«'Tis a fog-bell on a rock-bound coast!»
  And he steered for the open sea.

«O father! I hear the sound of guns,
  Oh, say, what may it be?»
«Some ship in distress that cannot live
  In such an angry sea!»

«O father, I see a gleaming light,
  Oh, say, what may it be?»
But the father answered never a word,
  A frozen corpse was he.

Auf kam der Sturm und drosch mit Macht
 den Schoner in die Breit',
der tänzelnd scheut', gleich dem bangen Roß,
 dann sprang – ein Kabel weit.

«Komm näher mir, mein Töchterlein,
 du mußt nicht zittern gar –
Ich kann ja trotzen dem rauhesten Sturm,
 den je die See gebar!»

Er hüllt sie warm in sein Seemannsfell –
 der Eiswind sticht und rast;
Von gesplitterter Spiere schnitt er das Seil,
 band fest sie an den Mast.

«O Vater, sagt: was mag das sein?
 Kirchglockenschall ich hör!»
«'S ist die Nebelglock an felsiger Küst'.»
 und hielt aufs offene Meer.

«O Vater, ich höre Kanonengedröhn:
 o sagt, was mag das sein?»
«'S ist ein Schiff in Not, das in tosender See
 ohn Hülfe und allein.»

«O Vater, ich sehe Lichterschein:
 o sagt, was mag das sein?»
Doch der Vater sprach nie mehr ein Wort:
 war froststarr-todt wie Stein:

Lashed to the helm, all stiff and stark,
   With his face turned to the skies,
The lantern gleamed through the gleaming snow
   On his fixed and glassy eyes.

Then the maiden clasped her hands and prayed
   That saved she might be;
And she thought of Christ, who stilled the wave
   On the Lake of Galilee.

And fast through the midnight dark and drear,
   Through the whistling sleet and snow,
Like a sheeted ghost, the vessel swept
   Towards the reef of Norman's Woe.

And ever the fitful gusts between
   A sound came from the land;
It was the sound of the trampling surf,
   On the rocks and the hard sea-sand.

The breakers were right beneath her bows,
   She drifted a dreary wreck,
And a whooping billow swept the crew
   Like icicles from her deck.

She struck where the white and fleecy waves
   Looked soft as carded wool,
But the cruel rocks, they gored her side,
   Like the horns of an angry bull.

Ans Steuer gezurrt, gen Himmel gewandt
  das Gesicht, ganz stier und steif;
die Lampe glomm durch den glimmernden Schnee
  auf die Augen, glasig im Reif.

Da faltet die Hände das Kind, und schickt
  um Rettung ein Gebet;
gedachte des Heilands, der die Wogen gestillt
  am See Genezareth.

Und pfeilschnell durch grause Mitternacht
  durch pfeifende Schloßen und Schnee
jagt das Schiff wie ein verhüllt Gespenst
  gegens Riff von *Norman's Woe*.

Und stetig durch unstete Bö'n
  kam ein Geräusch von Land:
Das war der stampfenden Brandung Gedröhn
  auf Sandbank, Fels und Strand.

Schon waren die Brecher unterm Bug
  – es driftet, verlorenes Wrack! –
da brüllten die Wogen: die Mannschaft fegt'
  wie Eiszapfen vom Deck.

Lief auf, wo die weißen flockigen Welln
  sahn weich wie Woll & Garn –
Doch das grausame Riff in die Flanken stieß
  wie des grimmen Bullen Gehorn.

Her rattling shrouds, all sheathed in ice,
   With the masts went by the board;
Like a vessel of glass, she stove and sank,
   Ho! ho! the breakers roared!

At daybreak, on the bleak sea-beach,
   A fisherman stood aghast,
To see the form of a maiden fair,
   Lashed close to a drifting mast.

The salt sea was frozen on her breast,
   The salt tears in her eyes;
And he saw her hair, like the brown sea-weed,
   On the billows fall and rise.

Such was the wreck of the Hesperus,
   In the midnight and the snow!
Christ save us all from a death like this,
   On the reef of Norman's Woe!

HENRY WADSWORTH LONGFELLOW (1807-1882)
The Wreck of the Hesperus

Die rasselnden Wanten, ummantelt in Eis,
  und die Masten ging'n über Bord –
Wie Glas zerschellte es und sank:
  Die Brecher brüllten Mord.

Bei Tagesgraun, am öden Strand,
  ein Fischer stand erstarrt:
Er sah an einen treibenden Mast
  ein liebliches Mädchen gezurrt:

Auf der Brust gefroren die salzige See –
  die Augen salzträngequollen;
Und ihr Haar sah er wie braunen Tang
  mit den Wellen fallen und wallen.

Das war das Wrack der *HESPERUS*
  in Mitternacht und Schnee.
HErr! Wahre uns vor solchem Tod
  am Riff von *Norman's Woe*!

O curfew of the setting sun! O Bells of Lynn!
O requiem of the dying day! O Bells of Lynn!

From the dark belfries of yon cloud-cathedral wafted,
Your sounds aërial seem to float, O Bells of Lynn!

Borne on the evening wind across the crimson twilight,
O'er land and sea they rise and fall, O Bells of Lynn!

The fisherman in his boat, far out beyond the headland,
Listens, and leisurely rows ashore, O Bells of Lynn!

Over the shining sands the wandering cattle homeward
Follow each other at your call, O Bells of Lynn!

The distant lighthouse hears, and with his flaming signal
Answers you, passing the watchword on, O Bells of Lynn!

And down the darkening coast run the tumultuous surges,
And clap their hands, and shout to you, O Bells of Lynn!

Till from the shuddering sea, with your wild incantations,
Ye summon up the spectral moon, O Bells of Lynn!

And startled at the sight, like the weird woman of Endor,
Ye cry aloud, and then are still, O Bells of Lynn!

HENRY WADSWORTH LONGFELLOW (1807 - 1882)
The Bells of Lynn,/ Heard at Nahant.

O löschendes Feuer der sinkenden Sonne! O Glocken von Lynn!
O Totenmesse des sterbenden Tages! O Glocken von Lynn!

Aus finsteren Türmen gewehet von Wolkenkathedralen
scheinet ihr wesenlos, luftig erhaben, zu treiben, o Glocken von Lynn!

Abendwind-her, quer über das Zwielicht aus Karmoisin,
über Land und See steigt ihr und fallet, o Glocken von Lynn!

In seinem Nachen der Fischer, weit draußen vom Lande entfernt,
lauschet, und rudert gemessen der Küste zu, Glocken von Lynn!

Über schimmernde Dünen – eins folget dem andern –
schreitet das Vieh stallwärts nach Hause, o Glocken von Lynn!

In der Ferne der Leuchtturm: er hört euch, gibt Antwort
mit Flammensignal das Losungswort weiter, o Glocken von Lynn!

Und die dunkelnde Küste hinunter rollet die Brandung,
klatscht in die Hände und ruft euch, o Glocken von Lynn!

Bis mit wilden Gesängen, empor aus der schaudernden See,
den Mond ihr gespenstisch befehlet, o Glocken von Lynn!

Und entsetzt bei dem Anblick, so wie die Hexe von Endor,
schreiet ihr laut – und verstummt, o Glocken von Lynn!

229 When Letty had scarce passed her third glad year,
    And her young artless words began to flow,
    One day we gave the child a coloured sphere
    Of the wide earth, that she might mark and know,
    By tint and outline, all its sea and land.
    She patted all the world; old empires peeped
    Between her baby fingers; her soft hand
    Was welcome at all frontiers. How she leaped,
    And laughed, and prattled, in her world-wide bliss;
    But when we turned her sweet unlearned eye
    On our own isle, she raised a joyous cry—
    «Oh! yes, I see it, Letty's home is there!»
    And while she hid all England with a kiss,
    Bright over Europe fell her golden hair.

CHARLES TENNYSON TURNER (1808 - 1879)
Letty's Globe

Als Letty grad ihr drittes Lebensjahr gewonnen,
Mit jungen Worten kunstlos zu sprudeln just begonnen,
Da schenkten wir ihr einmal einen Globus bunt-
Gemalt, daß sie benennen und erkennen könnt
An Farb & Form der weiten Erde Meer und Land.
Die Welt patscht sie reihum: da blinzten alte Reiche
Durch ihre Kinderfinger; ihre weiche Hand
An jedem Schlagbaum war willkommen; wie sie sich freut'
Und plapperte & lachte in ihrer WeltenreiseSeeligkeit!
Doch als wir ihre ungelehrten lieben Augen
Auf unsre Insel lenkten, brach sie in Jubel aus:
«Oh ja, ich sehs!: da ist der Letty Haus!»,
Vermocht mit einem Kuß ihr ganzes England zu bedecken:
Auf ganz Europa fiel der Glanz von eines Engels Locken.

One little noise of life remained—I heard
The train pause in the distance, then rush by,
Brawling and hushing, like some busy fly
That murmurs and then settles; nothing stirred
Beside. The shadow of our travelling earth
Hung on the silver moon, which mutely went
Through that grand process, without token sent,
Or any sign to call a gazer forth,
Had I not chanced to see; dumb was the vault
Of heaven, and dumb the fields—no zephyr swept
The forest walks, or through the coppice crept;
Nor other sound the stillness did assault,
Save that faint-brawling railways move and halt;
So perfect was the silence Nature kept.

CHARLES TENNYSON TURNER (1808 - 1879)
On the Eclipse of the Moon of October 1865

Ein schwaches Lebenszeichen blieb: ich hörte
den Zug in weiter Ferne halten, dann allhier
vorübergrollen, leis verhallen, wie ein Tier
das rumort – sich dann legt. Ansonsten rührte
sich nichts. Der Schatten unsrer Reise-Erd
lag auf dem Silbermond, der ungehört
den großartigen Fortschritt quert', ohn Zeichen
noch ausgesandt Signal: den Schau'nden zu erreichen –
hätt ichs nicht beiläufig gesehn. Stier war die Hülle
des Himmels. Stumm das Feld. Kein Zephyr huschte
auf Waldes Wegen, strichelt' durchs Gebuschte;
kein andrer Laut beschädigte die Stille
als nur des Zugs verwehtes Grollen, Stop & Spur:
Vollkommen war das Schweigen der Natur.

231

Now sleeps the crimson petal, now the white;
Nor waves the cypress in the palace walk;
Nor winks the gold fin in the porphyry font:
The firefly wakens: waken thou with me.

Now droops the milk-white peacock like a ghost,
And like a ghost she glimmers on to me.

Now lies the Earth all Danaë to the stars,
And all thy heart lies open unto me.

Now slides the silent meteor on, and leaves
A shining furrow, as thy thoughts in me.

Now folds the lily all her sweetness up,
And slips into the bosom of the lake:
So fold thyself, my dearest, thou, and slip
Into my bosom and be lost in me.

ALFRED TENNYSON, LORD TENNYSON (1809 - 1892)
Summer Night

Nun schläft das weiße Blütenblatt; nun das in Karmesin;
kein Hauch wogt am Palastweg durch Zypressen,
noch wankt die Goldflosse im Becken von Porphyr –
der Glühwurm wacht: so wache Du mit mir.

Nun senkt der Pfau, weiß wie ein Geist, sein Milchgefieder
– und wie ein Geist, so flimmert *sie* vor mir.

Nun liegt die Erd', ganz Danaë, bei Sternen
– und all Dein Herz, es öffnet sich vor mir.

Nun schießt der scheue Meteor dahin – zurück
bleibt nur die Funkenspur so, wie Dein Denken mir.

All ihre Süße faltet nun die Lilie ein
und gleitet in des Teiches Tiefe:
So falte dich, mein Liebstes, Du, und gleite
mir in die tiefe Brust, verliere Dich in mir.

Dear Lucy, you know what my wish is,—
I hate all your Frenchified fuss:
Your silly entrées and made dishes
Were never intended for us.
No footman in lace and in ruffles
Need dangle behind my arm-chair;
And never mind seeking for truffles,
Although they be ever so rare.

But a plain leg of mutton, my Lucy,
I pr'ythee get ready at three:
Have it smoking, and tender, and juicy,
And what better meat can there be?
And when it has feasted the master,
'Twill amply suffice for the maid;
Meanwhile I will smoke my canaster,
And tipple my ale in the shade.

WILLIAM MAKEPEACE THACKERAY (1811-1863)
Persicos Odi

Liebe Lucy, du kennst mein Begehren:
Ich hass' all den französischen Quark!
Deine faden *Entrées* und *Pâtieren*
Degoutieren wir fürderhin stark!
Kein Bedienter in Tressen und Rüffeln
Soll hinter dem Armstuhl uns schnüffeln;
Laß auch all dein Gesuche nach Trüffeln,
Und kämen sie zehntausend Mark!

Doch ne Keule vom Hammel, dear Lucy,
Bereite – ich bitt'dich – um 3^h:
Mach sie mürbe und kross und schön juicy,
Denn welch besseres Fleisch uns wohl sei?
Und wenn sie genähret den Master,
Sei der Knochen: der Magd ihr Plaisier;
Derweil paffe ich still meinen Knaster
Und süffel im Schatten mein Bier.

233 Riches I hold in light esteem,
And Love I laugh to scorn;
And lust of fame was but a dream
That vanish'd with the morn:
And if I pray, the only prayer
That moves my lips for me
Is, «Leave the heart that now I bear,
And give me liberty!»

Yea, as my swift days near their goal,
'Tis all that I implore:
In life and death a chainless soul,
With courage to endure.

EMILY BRONTË (1818-1848)
The Old Stoic

Der Reichen acht ich kaum,
Und Hohn lach ich der Liebe Tand;
Und Lust auf Ruhm war nur ein Traum
Der mit dem Morgen schwand:
Und – *falls* ich bet'! – das einzige Gebet
Das mir die Lippen regt,
Sei: «Laß das Herz, das mir nun schlägt,
Und gib mir Freiheit!»

Iä!! da vom Letzten Tag die Lebenstage scheiden,
Ist alls, um was ich bitte:
In Tod wie Leben eine Seele ohne Kette,
Und Mut zum Leiden.

My little Son, who look'd from thoughtful eyes
And moved and spoke in quiet grown-up wise,
Having my law the seventh time disobey'd,
I struck him, and dimiss'd
With hard words and unkiss'd,
—His Mother, who was patient, being dead.
Then, fearing lest his grief should hinder sleep,
I visited his bed,
But found him slumbering deep,
With darken'd eyelids, and their lashes yet
From his late sobbing wet.
And I, with moan,
Kissing away his tears, left others of my own;
For, on a table drawn beside his head,
He had put, within his reach,
A box of counters and a red-vein'd stone,
A piece of glass abraded by the beach.
And six or seven shells,
A bottle with bluebells,
And two French copper coins, ranged there with careful art,
To comfort his sad heart.
So when that night I pray'd
To God, I wept, and said:

Mein kleiner Sohn, der nachdenklichen Blicks
sich ganz erwachsen gab, auch schon so sprach,
Als er zum siebten Mal mein Reglement verletzt,
da schlug ich ihn; schickt' ihn zu Bett
mit harschen Worten; ohne Kuß (die Mutter freilich,
sie hatte mehr Geduld. Doch die war tot).
Dann, sorgend, daß sein Schmerz den Schlaf ihm wehrte,
sucht ich sein Bette auf;
Doch fand ich ihn in tiefem Schlummer:
die Lider abgeschattet, ihre Wimpern naß
vom letzten Schluchzer noch.
Und ich, aufstöhnend,
küßt' seine Tränen fort, netzt ihn mit eignen Tränen –
Denn, auf ein Tischchen, ihm zu Häupten,
hatt' er, in Reichweite, verteilt:
ein Kästchen Spielmarken; ein rotgeädert Mineral;
ein Stückl Glas, im Kiesstrand glattgeschliffen;
und so sechs, sieben Muschelschalen;
ein Fläschchen Glockenblumen;
und zwei französ' sche Kupfermünzen, mit Liebe arrangiert,
sein kummervolles Herz zu trösten.
Als ich, in jener Nacht, in Tränen,
und im Gebet mit Gott; da sprach ich:

Ah, when at last we lie with trancèd breath,
Not vexing Thee in death,
And Thou rememberest of what toys
We made our joys,
How weakly understood
Thy great commanded good,
Then, fatherly not less
Than I whom Thou hast moulded from the clay,
Thou'lt leave Thy wrath, and say,
«I will be sorry for their childishness.»

Coventry Patmore (1823 - 1896)
The Toys

Ach! Wenn uns einst der Lebensatem stockt,
wir Dich im Tod nicht ärgern mehr,
und Du der Freude eingedenk
die wir am Tändelkrame hatten,
und wie wir schwächlich nur begriffen
in Deinem grimmigen Befehl die Güte –
Dann, väterlich nicht minder
als ich, den Du aus Staube hast geformt,
soll Deine Wut verrauchen; sollst Du sagen:
«Dein' Kindlichkeit erbarmet mich».

235   A wind sways the pines,
And below
Not a breath of wild air;
Still as the mosses that glow
On the flooring and over the lines
Of the roots here and there.
The pine-tree drops its dead;
They are quiet, as under the sea.
Overhead, overhead
Rushes life in a race,
As the clouds the clouds chase;
And we go,
And we drop like the fruits of the tree,
Even we,
Even so.

GEORGE MEREDITH (1828 - 1909)
Dirge in the Woods

Ein Wind wiegt die Fichten,
Aber unten
Nicht ein Hauch stiller Luft;
Still wie die Moose glosen
Auf der Flur, dem Gefädel
Von den Wurzeln da und hier.
Aus den Fichten fällt es tot;
Sie sind still wie unterm Meer.
Über uns, über uns
Rauscht das Leben im Parforce
Wie die Wolken Wolken jagen;
Und wir gehn
Und wir fallen wie die Früchte von dem Baum,
Sogar wir,
Gerade so.

On a starr'd night Prince Lucifer uprose.
Tired of his dark dominion swung the fiend
Above the rolling ball in cloud part screen'd,
Where sinners hugg'd their spectre of repose.
Poor prey to his hot fit of pride were those.
And now upon his western wing he lean'd,
Now his huge bulk o'er Afric's sands careen'd,
Now the black planet shadow'd Arctic snows.
Soaring through wider zones that prick'd his scars
With memory of the old revolt from Awe,
He reach'd a middle height, and at the stars,
Which are the brain of heaven, he look'd, and sank.
Around the ancient track march'd, rank on rank,
The army of unalterable law.

GEORGE MEREDITH (1828 - 1909)
Lucifer in Starlight

Prinz Luzifer erhob sich aus besternter Nacht:
Der finstern Herrschaft müd, schwang sich der Feind
hoch ob den rollnden Ball der falb durch Wolken scheint
wo Sünder ihrer Scheinruh' nur bedacht:
seins aufwallenden Stolzes leichte Beute warn sie da.
Bald ließ er seine Schwing' im Westen spreiten –
bald wälzte sich die RiesenMasse über Afrika –
bald schattete der Schwarze Stern die nordpolaren Weiten.
Durch fern're Zonen streichend, wo die Wunde sticht:
des alten Aufstands wider Gottes Ehrfurcht eingedenk,
gewann er eine halbe Höhe, wo der Sterne Licht
(die's Himmels Hirn) er schaute – und versank.
Den alten Marschweg lang stampft' Reih um Reih das Dröhnen
unwandelbarer Satzung Divisionen.

237 Your hands lie open in the long fresh grass,—
The finger-points look through like rosy blooms:
Your eyes smile peace. The pasture gleams and glooms
'Neath billowing skies that scatter and amass.
All round our nest, far as the eye can pass,
Are golden kingcup-fields with silver edge
Where the cow-parsley skirts the hawthorn-hedge.
'Tis visible silence, still as the hour-glass.
Deep in the sun-searched growths the dragon-fly
Hangs like a blue thread loosened from the sky:—
So this wing'd hour dropt to us from above.
Oh! clasp we to our hearts, for deathless dower,
This close-companioned inarticulate hour
When twofold silence was the song of love.

DANTE GABRIEL ROSSETTI (1828 - 1882)
Silent Noon

Geöffnet liegen deine Händ' im hohen frischen Grün
durch das die Finger spitzeln wie rosig Blütenfunkeln;
Fried spricht dein Aug. Die Wiesen schimmern oder dunkeln:
hoch droben weit, zerzaust-geballt, die Wolken ziehn.
Um unser Nest, so weit das Auge schweift,
dehnt goldner *Kingcup* sich zu Silberborten
wo Schierling schürzt die Weißdornhecke dorten –
's ist sichtbar Schweigen: wie die Sanduhr läuft.
Tief im besonnten Sprießen die Libelle
hängt wie ein blaues Garn entrollt aus Himmels Helle:
so ließ von oben sich die FlügelStund zu uns hernied'.
Zu ew'ger Mitgift ja sei unsrer Herzen Quelle,
was die gemeinsame, selig-wortlose Stunde uns beschied
: Als doppelt Schweigen wob der Liebe Lied.

Here writ was the World's History by his hand
Whose steps knew all the earth; albeit his world
In these few piteous paces then was furled.
Here daily, hourly, have his proud feet spanned
This smaller speck than the receding land
Had ever shown his ships; what time he hurled
Abroad o'er new-found regions spiced and pearled
His country's high dominion and command.
Here dwelt two spheres. The vast terrestrial zone
His spirit traversed; and that spirit was
Itself the zone celestial, round whose birth
The planets played within the zodiac's girth;
Till hence, through unjust death unfeared, did pass
His spirit to the only land unknown.

Dante Gabriel Rossetti (1828 - 1882)
Raleigh's Cell in Tower

Hier ward geschrieben die *Historie der Welt*
von seiner Hand. Er schritt die ganze Erde aus. Inmitt'
der paar erbärmlichen QuadratYards ausgerollt
war seine Welt. Tagein-stundaus durchmaß der stolze Schritt
dies Eiland: winzger als sich in der Meeresweit'
die Küsten seinen Schiffen je gezeigt, da er zu seiner Zeit
fern über neuentdeckte Perlen- und Gewürz-Regionen
sein's Landes Oberherrschaft und Kommando warf.
Zwei Sphären kugeln hier: terrestrisch ausgedehnte Zonen
durchrast' sein Geist. Und dieser Geist so scharf
war selbst ein Himmels-Sphäroid, in dessen Rund
Planeten kreiselten in Zodiacus' Zirkelband
bis, furchtlos wider ungerechten Tod, sein HochVerstand
grenzüberschritt ins einzge nichtbekannte Land.

239   When I am dead, my dearest,
Sing no sad song for me;
Plant thou no roses at my head,
Nor shady cypress tree:
Be the green grass above me
With showers and dewdrops wet;
And if thou wilt, remember,
And if thou wilt, forget.

I shall not see the shadows,
I shall not feel the rain;
I shall not hear the nightingale
Sing on, as if in pain;
And dreaming through the twilight
That doth not rise nor set,
Haply I may remember,
And haply may forget.

Christina Georgina Rossetti (1830 - 1894)
Song

Wenn ich dahingegangen, Liebster,
sing mir keinen Trauersang;
pflanz mir zu Häupten keine Rosen
noch schattichten Zypressenstamm.
Sei nur ob mir das grüne Gras
von Regen und Tautropfen nass,
und wenn du willst, gedenke;
und wenn du willst – vergiß.

Ich soll ja die Schatten nicht sehen,
nie spüren die regnichte Zeit;
soll nimmer der Nachtigall hören
ihr Lied wie aus Herzeleid.
Und träumend durch das Dämmer,
das sich nicht senkt noch hebt,
werd ich, vielleicht, gedenken –
wer weiß? vergessen was lebt.

Remember me when I am gone away,
Gone far away into the silent land;
When you can no more hold me by the hand,
Nor I half turn to go yet turning stay.
Remember me when no more day by day
You tell me of our future that you planned:
Only remember me; you understand
It will be late to counsel then or pray.
Yet if you should forget me for a while
And afterwards remember, do not grieve:
For if the darkness and corruption leave
A vestige of the thoughts that once I had,
Better by far you should forget and smile
Than that you should remember and be sad.

CHRISTINA GEORGINA ROSSETTI (1830-1894)
Remember me

Gedenke mein, wenn ich dahingegangen,
weit fortgegangen in das SchweigeLand;
wenn du mich nicht mehr bei der Hand
nimmst – ich: zum Gehn mich wend', und doch befangen – .
Gedenke mein: wenn nicht mehr täglich-stet
von unsrer Zukunft du erzählst, die du geplant.
Gedenke nur. – Die Einsicht brütet der Verstand:
daß es zu spät nun sei für Ratschluß wie Gebet.
Doch solltest du einstweilen mich vergessen,
so gräm dich nicht, wenn du hernach gedenkest.
Denn wenn die Dunkelheit und die Verwesung lassen
ein Überbleibsel von dem Denken, das einst mein,
ists besser, wenn vergessend Lächeln du dir schenkest,
als zu erinnern und betrübt zu sein.

241   O Earth, lie heavily upon her eyes;
Seal her sweet eyes weary of watching, Earth;
Lie close around her; leave no room for mirth
With its harsh laughter, nor for sound of sighs.
She hath no questions, she hath no replies,
Hushed in and curtained with a blessèd dearth
Of all that irked her from the hour of birth;
With stillness that is almost Paradise.
Darkness more clear than noon-day holdeth her,
Silence more musical than any song;
Even her very heart has ceased to stir:
Until the morning of Eternity
Her rest shall not begin nor end, but be;
And when she wakes she will not think it long.

CHRISTINA GEORGINA ROSSETTI (1830-1894)
Rest

Leg dich getrost, ach Erd', auf ihre Augen schwer!
Ach siegle ihre schauensmüden Augen, Erde!
Schmieg dich um sie, laß keinen Raum für Frohgebärde,
Gelächter rauh. Mach, daß auch Seufzen sie nicht hör'!
Sie hat nicht Antworten, sie hat nicht Fragen,
gestillet und umhüllt vom Fehlen segensreich
all des, was sie gequält seit ihren frühen Tagen,
in einer Ruhe, die dem Paradiese gleich.
Ein Dunkel schirmt sie, reiner denn Mittage,
ein Schweigen, mehr Musik denn jeder Sang;
ihr Herze selbst hat aufgehört zu schlagen.
Bis zu der Ewigkeiten FrühAnfang
soll ihre Ruh nicht anfangen noch aufhörn, sondern *sein*:
Erwacht sie dann, wird ihr die Weile dünken klein.

She turned in the high pew, until her sight
Swept the west gallery, and caught its row
Of music-men with viol, book, and bow
Against the sinking sad tower-window light.

She turned again; and in her pride's despite
One strenuous viol's inspirer seemed to throw
A message from his string to her below,
Which said: «I claim thee as my own forthright!»

Thus their hearts' bond began, in due time signed.
And long years thence, when Age had scared Romance,
At some old attitude of his or glance

That gallery-scene would break upon her mind,
With him as minstrel, ardent, young, and trim,
Bowing ‹New Sabbath› or ‹Mount Ephraim.›

THOMAS HARDY (1840-1928)
A Church Romance

im chorgestühl wandt sie den kopf ihr blick gezogen
zur westempore schweifte – und haften blieb
an einer reihe musiker mit gamben noten bogen
vorm licht des turmfensters im schwinden trüb

aufs neu wandt sie den kopf in ihres stolzes trotz hinein
schien einer der mit schwung der gambe leben gab
von seinen saiten eine botschaft ihr herab
zu schwingen *ihr sollt noch heut meyn eigen sein*

so knüpft sich bald besiegelt ihrer herzen band
und jahre drauf als mit dem prosa-alter die romantik schwand
fiel ihr bei irgendeiner altvertrauten haltung plötzlich

bei einem blick von ihm das bild auf der empore wieder ein
mit ihm als minnespielmann jung und flamboyant
wie er ‹mount ephraim› ‹new sabbath› strich

Thirty-two years since, up against the sun,
Seven shapes, thin atomies to lower sight,
Labouringly leapt and gained thy gabled height,
And four lives paid for what the seven had won.

They were the first by whom the deed was done,
And when I look at thee, my mind takes flight
To that days tragic feat of manly might,
As though, till then, of history thou hadst none.

Yet ages ere men topped thee, late and soon
Thou didst behold the planets lift and lower;
Saw'st, maybe, Joshua's pausing sun and moon,

And the betokening sky when Caesar's power
Approached its bloody end; yea, even that Noon
When darkness filled the earth till the ninth hour.

THOMAS HARDY (1840-1928)
To the Matterhorn (June-July 1897)

's ist 32 jahre her nun daß im gegenlicht
der sonn den ferngläsern im tal ein 7-schemen-molekül
mühselig sprang den gipfelgrat erstieg
und mit vier leben zahlte für der sieben sieg

sie warn die ersten die das werk vollbracht
und wenn ich dich betracht mein sinn dann fliegt
hin zu dem tag da tragisch triumphierte menschenmacht
als hättst bis dahin du geschichte noch gar nicht

gehabt allein äonen eh die menschen dich erhöhten
sahst du den fall und aufstieg der planeten
sahst josua nachsinnen über sonn und mond

und himmels prophezeiung daß seinem blutgen ende
sich caesars herrschaft neige ja gar den gipfelsieg
da eine große finsternis bis zu der neunten stunde

Thy shadow, Earth, from Pole to Central Sea,
Now steals along upon the Moon's meek shine
In even monochrome and curving line
Of imperturbable serenity.

How shall I link such sun-cast symmetry
With the torn troubled form I know as thine,
That profile, placid as a brow divine,
With continents of toil and misery?

And can immense Mortality but throw
So small a shade, and Heaven's high human scheme
Be hemmed within the coasts yon arc implies?

Is such the stellar gauge of earthly show,
Nation at war with nation, brains that teem,
Heroes, and woman fairer than the skies?

THOMAS HARDY (1840-1928)
At a Lunar Eclipse

dein schatten erd vom pol bis zum äquatorstrich
stiehlt nun sich auf selenes mildem licht hinan
in monochromer meridianer zirkelbahn
einer serenität die unerschütterlich

wie soll ich diese sonnenprojizierte symmetrie
mit der gequält-zerrissnen form verbinden die dein bild
und dies profil wie eine götterbraue mild
mit kontinenten voller elend und voll schinderei

kann das denn sein daß nur so kleinen schattenraum
die ungeheure sterblichkeit dort wirft des himmels hoch-humaner bau
findt in den küstenlinien die der bogen einschließt seinen saum

ist dieses das stellare stichmaß unsrer erdenschau
nation im kriege mit nation des hirnes traum
helden und schöner als das firmament die frau

When you are old and gray and full of sleep
And nodding by the fire, take down this book,
And slowly read, and dream of the soft look
Your eyes had once, and of their shadows deep;

How many loved your moments of glad grace,
And loves your beauty with love false or true;
But one man loved the pilgrim soul in you,
And loved the sorrows of your changing face;

And bending down beside the glowing bars,
Murmur, a little sadly, how love fled
And paced upon the mountains overhead,
And hid his face amid a crowd of stars.

WILLIAM BUTLER YEATS (1865 - 1939)
When you are old and grey and full of sleep

Wenn du im Alter, grau und schlafensmatt,
Am Feuer nickst, nimm zu dir dieses Buch,
Lies langsam, träume von dem Blick so weich
Und jenen tiefen Schatten, die einst dein Auge hatt.

Wie viele liebten deine Zeiten frohen Witzes
Und deine Schönheit – seis mit falscher Lieb seis ohne Hehl,
Nur *ein* Mann liebt' in dir die Pilgerseel
Und liebt' den Kummer deines wechselnden Antlitzes.

Und im Herniedersinken, zuseit die Scheiter glimmen,
Murmle, ein wenig traurig, wie die Liebe floh
Und ins Gebürge schritt hoch über Gipfelhöh
Und ihr Gesicht barg in der Sterne Flimmern.

Cast a cold eye
On life, on death.
Horseman, pass by!

WILLIAM BUTLER YEATS (1865-1939)
Epitaph (Drumcliff, County Sligo)

Reiter, blick kalt
Auf Leben, auf Tod.
Weiter! Kein Halt!

247 Down the blue night the unending columns press
In noiseless tumult, break and wave and flow,
Now tread the far South, or lift rounds of snow
Up to the white moon's hidden loveliness.

Some pause in their grave wandering comradeless,
And turn with profound gesture vague and slow,
As who would pray good for the world, but know
Their benediction empty as they bless.

They say that the Dead die not, but remain
Near to the rich heirs of their grief and mirth.
I think they ride the calm mid-heaven, as these,
In wise majestic melancholy train,
And watch the moon, and the still-raging seas,
And men, coming and going on the earth.

RUPERT BROOKE (1887 - 1915)
Clouds

Endlose Säulenreih durch blaue Nacht hin dräut
In stimmlosem Tumult, zerspellt und wogt und fließt,
Den fernen Süden dort betritt – hier WirbelSchnee auf reißt
Hoch zu des weißen Monds verborgner Lieblichkeit.

Manch eine hält in wuchtgem Wandern unbegleit'
Und dreht sich vag und mählich mit profunder Geste
Wie der, der Gutes für die Welt bät', dennoch wüßte:
Ihr Wohlgeschenk aus ihrem Segen wäre Eitelkeit.

Man sagt, die Toten sterben nicht, sie bleiben
Den reichen Erben nah von ihrem Schmerz, von ihren Frohgebärden.
Ich denk: den stillen Zenith reiten sie, wie diese hier
In weiser Majestäten Trübsal treiben,
Und halten Wacht dem Mond, dem leis bewegten Meer,
Den Menschen, kommend-gehend auf der Erden.

248   If I should die, think only this of me:
        That there's some corner of a foreign field
        That is for ever England. There shall be
        In that rich earth a richer dust conceal'd;
        A dust whom England bore, shaped, made aware,
        Gave, once, her flowers to love, her ways to roam,
        A body of England's, breathing English air,
        Wash'd by the rivers, blest by suns of home.
        And think, this heart, all evil shed away,
        A pulse in the eternal mind, no less
        Gives somewhere back the thoughts by England given;
        Her sights and sounds; dreams happy as her day;
        And laughter, learnt of friends; and gentleness,
        In hearts at peace, under an English heaven.

RUPERT BROOKE (1887-1915)
The Soldier

Denkt einzig dies von mir, wenn sterben ich gesollt:
Daß hier ein Eckchen ist in einem fremden Feld
Das ein Stück England ewig sei. Hier ists geheckt,
Daß reiche Erd werd reicherm Staub zur Gruft:
Ein Staub, den Albion gezeugt, geformt, geweckt,
Ihm ihre Blumen gab zur Lieb, ihm Weg zum Wandern hielt,
Ein englisch Leib, atmend Anglias Luft,
Von Heimatsonn gesegnet, von ihren Flüssen abgespült.
Und denkt, dies Herz, das alles Übel abgespeit,
Schenkt, nur ein Puls im ewgen WeltengeistGewimmel,
Anglias Gabe wieder her: Gedanken, irgend wo;
Ihr Scheinen – Tönen – Träumen, gleich ihrem Tage froh;
Und Lachen beigebracht vom Freund; und Sachtigkeit
In friedvoll Herzen unter einem englisch Himmel.

Nachwort

Goethe sagt, Übersetzer seien als geschäftige Kuppler anzusehen, die uns eine halbverschleierte Schöne als höchst liebenswürdig anpreisen. Diese errege *eine unwiderstehliche Neigung nach dem Original*. Und Chaim Nachman Bialik meint, eine Übersetzung sei *wie ein Kuß durch ein Taschentuch*.

Now goth sonne under wod:/ Me reweth, Marye, thy faire rode./ Now goth sonne under tre./ Me reweth, Marye thy sone and thee. Das dunkle Tuch zu lüften, das über diesem anonymen Vierzeiler aus der Zeit der Magna Charta und Henrys III. liegt, wäre als Übersetzung ein Erkenntnisvorgang, der, wie Schillers Gedicht vom verschleierten Bildnis zu Saïs mahnt, das Aufheben des Schleiers, als das *Erkennen* nackter Wahrheit mit *Schuld* ineins setzte. Goethes kokett laszives Bild malt jenes Ineinander von Eros und Erkenntnis, auf dem dieser eigentümlich theologische Akzent lastet, während in Bialiks (psychoanalytisch aufschlußreichem) Aperçu das Motiv des *Tuchs*, Schleiers, Vorhangs oder Gewebes wieder auftaucht. Ungeachtet dessen, daß die *Schöne* dem Original voraus hat, daß sie immerhin *halb*, dieses aber ganz verschleiert sich zeigt; und sich nicht dem *Kuß* bietet, sondern prima vista selber *Tuch* nämlich Gewebe, also Textur ist. Weben/Flechten/Spinnen: wir sind im Reich Ariadnes & Arachnes. Cervantes läßt Don Quichotte sagen: *Mir scheint, daß es sich mit dem Übersetzen von einer Sprache in die andre so verhält, wie wenn einer flandrische Tapeten von der Rückseite betrachtet; man sieht zwar die Figuren, aber sie werden durch die Menge von Fäden ganz entstellt, und man sieht sie nicht in der Glätte und Farbenfrische der Vorderseite.*

Die Rückseite jener vierzeiligen englischen Tapete aus dem 13. Jahrhundert böte sich uns etwa wie folgt dar: Nun/jetzt geht/versinkt Sonne unter Holz:/ Mich barmt/reut/dauert, Maria, deine schöne Röte./ Nun/jetzt geht/versinkt Sonne unter Baum:/ Mich barmt/reut/dauert, Maria, deines Sohnes und deiner. Manch Übersetzer würde sich aus Demut vor der Integrität des Originals kaum weiter vorwagen wollen und allenfalls erklärend hintansetzen, mit *schöner Röte* sei das Inkarnat der Muttergottes als pars pro toto, also ihr Gesicht, mit *Holz* das Kreuzesholz und mit *Baum* der Kreuzesstamm gemeint. Hätte es damit sein Bewenden, bliebe der geliebte Gegenstand ungeküßt und dreiviertelverschleiert, so daß, was wie eine als Bescheidenheit sich tarnende Imaginationsschwäche aussähe, eher der Resignation des verzichtenden Liebenden gleichkäme. *Grammatische* Übersetzungen nennt Novalis in einem Blütenstaub-Fragment diese *Übersetzungen in gewöhnlichem Sinn. Sie erfordern sehr viel Gelehrsamkeit, aber nur diskursive Fähigkeiten.* Was über das Diskursive hinausginge, ein intentionaler Überschuß, wäre ein poetisches Prinzip, das Novalis *verändernd* nennt: *Der wahre Übersetzer dieser Art muß in der Tat der Künstler selbst sein und die Idee des Ganzen beliebig so oder so geben können.* Wer in Sprache kaum mehr als ein Kommunikationssystem zwischen Sender und Empfänger zu sehen pflegt, mag Hardenbergs hochfliegenden Anspruch, Übersetzen müsse eine spezifische Art von Meta-Dichtung sein (*with the magic hand of chance*: Keats) für anmaßend halten. Sein Recht hat der Anspruch aber an der Einsicht, daß durchaus nicht nur dichterische Sprache auch Mimesis ist. Dedecius: *Wir produzieren keine Produkte, sondern Prozesse.*

Die *gewisse Farbe der Fremdheit,* die nach Humboldt eine gute Übersetzung an sich trägt, weist darauf hin, daß Vertrautheit sich nach Fremdem sehnt; beide verzehren aneinander und gelangen zu etwas, auf das Sprache als *Spur einer Intention* (Eco) lediglich verweist. Diese Vorläufigkeit allen Übersetzens, sein Prozessuales als Spurenlese, als Magnetfeld zwischen Widerruf und Setzung,

Fragezeichen und Apodiktum ist inzwischen zum poetologischen Gemeinplatz gereift, und die Einsicht, jede Übersetzung sei eigentlich ein Stück konzeptueller, experimenteller Literatur, längst nicht mehr so verstiegen, wie es unterm Druck des Brotberufs hie und da noch scheinen mag. Daß in jeder Sprache, in jedem Wort ein Fremdes nistet, meint, daß ein konnotativer Hohlraum so einlädt, diese Leerstellen auszufärben, wie es die kindliche Lust am Ausfärben von Malbüchern früh erfährt. Meint auch: die poetische Durchlässigkeit der Sprachen zueinander, ihre *Kreolisierung*. Könnte es nicht sein, daß damit jene Horizontverschmelzung anvisiert wird, wie sie sich bei Leibniz in einem universalen Übersetzungsprogreß von der höchsten Monade bis in die vielfältigsten Verästelungen der Dingwelt darstellt? – : *Und obwohl die zwischen den Pflanzen des Gartens befindliche Erde und Luft, oder das zwischen den Fischen des Teichs befindliche Wasser weder Pflanze noch Fisch ist, so enthalten sie deren doch wieder, aber meistens in einer uns unerfaßbaren Subtilität*, heißt es in der Monadologie. Daraus mag folgen, daß poetisches, *veränderndes* Übersetzen zwar wohl ein Gelingen kennt, das sich nach seiner je eigenen Stimmigkeit oder Unstimmigkeit, also seiner Immanenz bzw. seinen ästhetischen Prämissen bemißt, nicht aber im normativen Sinn ein Richtig oder Falsch; jedenfalls dann nicht, wenn ein Übersetzer so mutig ist, *durch philologischen Verrat poetische Entsprechung herzustellen* (Ingold). Allerdings möchte die Kategorie *Entsprechung* selber fragwürdig sein.

Soll heißen: die Veränderung, *so oder so*, die *Zauberhand des Zufalls*, die *Fremdheit*, die *Kreolisierung*, der *Verrat* und Leibnizens Implikation, daß wir nicht eigentlich übersetzen sondern selber übersetzt werden, verweisen die Gefahr sogenannter sachlicher Fehler an einen Bereich, in dem unpoetische Richter über poetische Delinquenten zu Gericht säßen. Erfüllt eine im adäquanznormativen Sinne korrekte Übersetzung ihren Begriff – oder erschöpft sie sich nicht vielmehr in Tautologie? Ein Beispiel, hypothetisch: Gesetzt, ein übersetzender Dichter hätte die Zeile *Now goth sone under Tre*, prima vista irrtümlich, mit *Nun versinkt die Sonne unter Dreien* übertragen und sodann, verschreckt von wohlmeinenden Ratgebern, in einem nicht voraus- sondern nacheilenden Gehorsam *unterm Kreuzesstamm* geschrieben. Was läge hier vor? – : Verbesserung, Berichtigung, unverzichtbare Korrektur? Oder eine Selbstzensur, die das qua Analogie aufblitzend imaginierte Bild der Heiligen Trinität, oder des Gekreuzigten zwischen den zween Schächern, oder des Heilands mit Maria und Maria Magdalena selbdritt ängstlich sich versagt? Vielleicht paßt eine Kalendergeschichte von Hebel nicht schlecht hierher. Sie heißt MISSVERSTAND und geht so: *Im neunziger Krieg, als der Rhein auf jener Seite von französischen Schildwachen, auf dieser Seite von schwäbischen Kreissoldaten besetzt war, rief ein Franzos zum Zeitvertreib zu der deutschen Schildwache herüber: «Filou! Filou!» das heißt auf gut deutsch: Spitzbube. Allein der ehrliche Schwabe dachte an nichts so Arges, sondern meinte, der Franzose frage: Wieviel Uhr? und gab gutmütig zur Antwort: «Halber vieri.»*

Könnte es beim Übersetzen nicht eher darum gehen, sich vom Mißverstand leiten und Mißverständnisse schöpferisch werden zu lassen? Mißverständnisse gleichzeitig gezielt wie absichtslos so wirksam werden zu lassen wie die Rute des Wünschelrutengängers, um die Herrschaft des Auktorialen zu brechen? Zurück zu unserem Vierzeiler. Daß Stil und Konvention Ausdruck sui generis sind, erhellt: daher *holdes Antlitz* für *fair rode* dem Hohen Stil eher angemessen wäre. Womit zugleich die metrische Keimzelle des Ganzen gegeben ist: schlichter jambischer Wechsel von Hebung und Senkung, nach dem die Wahl des Verbs sich richtet: also *dauert*. Aus der Korrelation von Wort- und Versakzent entscheidet sich der Satzbau der Zeile; ein 11-Silber entsteht, mit einer ‹weiblichen› Endung, die der Anrufung der Muttergottes korrespondiert: *Dein holdes Antlitz dauert mich, Maria.* Da im Original diese 2. Zeile zur ersten in einer Paarreim-Bindung steht, für die sich eine Lösung schlechterdings nicht finden läßt, legen sich dem Übersetzer, der das Poetische nicht lediglich in der Semantik, sondern, bis in die Einzelphoneme hinein, in den Klangvaleurs sucht, Substitut-Verfahren nahe, Freudsche Verschiebungen auch; oder Ersatzmechanismen wie Binnenreime, Assonanzen, Lautversetzungen; oder Anagramme wie etwa dann, wenn aus Maria *Mar*, aus dauert *ert*, aus holdes *hol* und aus dem Antlitz das Schluß-*tz* abgespalten, umgestellt und sodann verschränkt werden zum Synonym für *wod*: nämlich: *Mar-ter-hol-tz*. Marterholtz mit archaisierendem Tz: heikel, no doubt about. Daß die verändernden Übertragungen, wie Novalis warnt, *leicht ins Travestieren fallen*, bestätigt dieses Prekäre. Indes gehts hier nicht um subjektives Stilempfinden. Wenn z.B. im martialischen Azincourt Carol von 1415 Sprache wie eine Rüstung in ihren Gelenken knirscht, dürfen Archaismen seine Zeilen auch dann mit der schweren Armatur ihres Harnischs wappnen, wenn ihr Bedeuten unterm schwarzen Visier sich verdunkelt. Das hätte mit Pasticcio nichts zu tun; wäre womöglich sogar eher geeignet, die historische Distanz freizusetzen, als es jene versierte Aktualisierung vermöchte, die sich des Alten im Raubgriff bemächtigte, um's im Triumph der Gegenwart als nivellierte Beute zuzuschlagen. Von der Gleichzeitigkeit des Historischen heute, seiner Parallelisierung kann auch ohne postmodernen Kontext gesprochen werden, von der Ironie, daß die kontemporäre allgegenwärtige Verfügbarkeit differenter Stilbildungen (*so oder so*: Novalis) von der Pflicht zur Observanz kontemporären Sprachgebrauchs, kontemporärer Orthographie gerade entbindet.

Dabei geht es um mehr noch als um Stil und Konvention. Wo die Sprache des Dichters, auch des übersetzenden, in der Erscheinung aufgeht, haben wir es zunächst mit *Schrift* zu tun, deren einzelne Zeichen nicht Spielmarken, sondern Träger von Ausdruck und Mimesis sind. Die Entscheidung, dem *Marterholtz* ein alterthümliches T-Z zu geben, folgt der Einsicht, daß Schrift *physiognomisch* ist; das TZ gibt dem Kreuzesstamm etliche Jahresringe mehr; zudem erscheint im T die Form & Gestalt des Kreuzes, monadisch, noch einmal. Und wiewohl *Tre* nicht *Drei* sondern *Baum*, und T entweder einen harten Dentallaut oder eine 3-endige Figur namens *Kreuz* bedeuten, so enthalten sie einander alle, aber in einer für uns unerfaßbaren Subtilität. Wer hier nicht folgen mag, lasse sich von Jean Selz, dem französischen Übersetzer Benjamins, die Anekdote erzählen, wie ihn eines Tages Benjamin mit der verblüffenden Behauptung überraschte, alle Wörter, gleich welcher Sprache, glichen in ihrem Schriftbild dem Ding, das sie bezeichneten. *Diese Idee begeisterte mich nicht besonders. Ich dachte daran, daß manche Wörter graphisch einem Wort aus einer anderen Sprache gleichen, welches das Gegenteil bedeutet. Das spanische Wort «mas» gleicht zum Beispiel eher dem französischen «moins» als dem französischen «plus» ..... «Wenn also das Wort ‹casserole› in einer Sprache Katze bedeuten würde, wären Sie wahrscheinlich der Ansicht, das Schriftbild des Wortes ‹casserole› sähe einer Katze ähnlich?» «Vielleicht», entgegnete nach einigem Nachdenken Benjamin, der nicht leicht zu schlagen war, «aber nur insofern, als eben eine Katze einem Kochtopf gleicht».»* Benjamin erteilt Lizenz, sich bis zum Einzelgraphem auf eine Analogie objektiver Gestaltqualitäten zu berufen dann, wenn sie poetische Signifikanz besitzt. Daß solche Signalements so verborgen bleiben können, daß sie nur dem Autor, nicht dem Leser einsichtig sind, spricht nicht gegen ihre Plausibilität im ästhetischen Kontext.

Daß *Marye* als *Maria* zu übersetzen ist, wäre keiner Erwähnung wert – verlangte nicht mitunter die *Idee des Ganzen*, Namen oder adverbielle/adjektivische Bestimmungen im Original zu belassen. In William Blakes (aus rhythmischen Gründen fast unübersetzbarem) *Long John Brown and Little Mary Bell* z.B. verlangt nicht nur der galante Hornpipe-Rhythmus, in dem die Sexualität des Gedichts sich aufschaukelt, den Versakzent unangetastet zu lassen und einzig den Buchstaben A im Wort «and» in ein U zu verwandeln. Denn nicht nur die Namen, einschließlich des hier nicht so sehr adjektivischen als heraldisch nominalen «Long», auch der besondere Klangreiz des Little ist unübersetzbar: nur so klingelt das Glöckchen, das Mary Bell in ihrer Nutshell hat. (Andererseits gibt es schwer übersetzbare Wörter wie «fancy» oder «spleen», die denn doch so fremd sind, daß sie nur mit Vorbehalten als *silberne Rippe* im deutschen Sprachleib sich halten ließen.) Vom Klang ist hier die Rede. Daraus erhellt, warum für das *Now* von Zeile 1 und 3 das schneidende *Jetzt* oder noch schärfere *Itzt* deplaciert wäre. Der Passionsszene angemessener wäre der tintige Indigo-Klang des *Nun* – allerdings nicht am Zeilenanfang, da sonst ein zu kräftiger Akzent auf ihn fiele. Aus den Forderungen des Metrums schält sich dann folgendes Fragment der ersten Zeile heraus: *Die Sonne geht nun unter.....Marterholtz*. Da «untergehen» intransitiv ist, bedarf das Kreuz einer Präposition, möglichst zweisilbig, um mit der Silbenzahl der 2. Zeile zu korrelieren. Das aber wird zur Crux der Übertragung. Denn die englische Konstruktion dieses lyrischen Tafelbilds entspricht vollkommen der unausgebildeten Perspektivtechnik in der Malerei um 1200. Die Entscheidung, trotzdem dem «unter» ein «hinter» beizufügen, reißt in eine zweidimensionale Bildfläche gleichsam stereoskopisch ein kleines Diorama des Golgatha. Aber solche Tiefenperspektive ist nicht zu umgehen. *Die Sonne versinkt nun unterm.....Nun taucht die Sonne hinab unter.... Die Sonne taucht nun hinunter....*: das hinkt und stolpert, wie man es auch dreht & wendet; inwieweit Zwang, Notwendigkeit und *verändernde* Freiheit sich bedingen: das wäre hier zu lernen.

Die dritte Zeile, der ersten wortgleich bis auf *tre* statt *wod*, verlangt lediglich nach einer Variante für *Marterholtz*. Gleichwohl ist es zwar anfechtbar, aber nicht illegitim, die gesamte Zeile zu variieren, denn: wenn ein und derselbe Text von verschiedenen Übersetzern verschieden übertragen werden kann, darf dann ein einzelner Übersetzer nicht die Wiederholung eines Textes verschieden übertragen? Wiederholung bedeutet ja nicht Identität dann, wenn der wechselnde Kontext einen Refrain ein ums anderemal neu färbt. Beispiel: In Charles of Orleans' Klage über den Verlust der geliebten Lady lautet die Refrainzeile dieses 5-versigen Gedichts aus der ersten Hälfte des 15. Jahrhunderts: *O! wretche, lesse ones thy speche.* Sollte die Übersetzung hier nicht die Lizenz haben, das Manische des Wiederholens umzuschmelzen in die Manie dessen, der mit Varianten um jene Sprache kreist, die ihr eigenes Verstummen sucht: *Laß einmal doch die Sprache schweigen..... Laß einmal doch dein Reden enden..... Laß einmal doch dein Wort verstummen....* usw. Die Zahl der *Intentionen* ist unbegrenzt, sofern sie nur stimmig miteinander korrespondieren.

Für die dritte Zeile ist zu fragen, ob die Reimbindung an die vierte diesmal gelänge. Dazu bedarfs zunächst der Klärung, wie der knifflige Satzbau der Endzeile einzulösen wäre. Da im Deutschen die infrage kommenden Verben an einen Genitivus objectivus gekoppelt sind, muß, um die Silbenzahl nicht auswuchern zu lassen und das Metrum nicht zu irritieren, irgendwo mit Elisionen gearbeitet werden. Das Dilemma ist bekannt. *Dienstag, den 30. Dezember 1823. Wir sprachen darauf von Übersetzungen, worauf Goethe mir sagte, daß es ihm sehr schwer werde, englische Gedichte in deutschen Versen wiederzugeben. «Wenn man die schlagenden einsilbigen Worte der Engländer», sagte er, «mit vielsilbigen oder zusamengesetzten deutschen ausdrücken will, so ist gleich alle Kraft und Wirkung verloren»,* berichtet Eckermann, versagt sich freilich beizufügen, daß es nun einmal ohne die Verhüllungstricks, zu denen Silbenkürzungen und Vokal-Elisionen zählen, auch nicht jene halbverschleierte englische Schöne gäbe, die, nicht ohne *Kraft und Wirkung*, in dem Weisen von Weimar eine unwiderstehliche Neigung nach dem nackten Original weckte. Am besten also, aus «deiner» ein «dein'» zu machen; statt «dauert» das kürzere «barmt» zu wählen; dieses statt des «und» zu wiederholen, sowie statt des zweisilbigen Possessivpronomens *deines* (Sohnes) den bestimmten Artikel *des* einzusetzen (da unmißverständlich ist, wer gemeint ist.). Bleibt nun jenes «dein'» in derselben Position wie das *thee*, kann es dort als Reim-Echo antworten dem *Holz der Pein*, vor dem sich nicht nur Maria, sondern die ganze Natur in Trauer neigt: *Nun neigt die Sonn sich unters Holz der Pein/ Mich barmt des Sohnes, barmt, Maria, dein'.*

Ein in Trauer erstarrtes Tafelbild also, gesehen von einem namenlosen lyrischen Subjekt, das nicht aus den Zeilen spricht, sondern in sie hinein, auf sie verweist, mit der Hand eines Evangelisten, in einem ausgesparten Gebilde, zart ausbalanciert zwischen Distanz und Misericordia. Christi Passion zwischen den Ulmen und Weiden von Devon oder Yorkshire oder Cumberland vor der großen Dunkelheit um die neunte Stunde, da die Efeugräber der englischen Churchyards sich auftaten. Und der Vorhang im Tempel zerriß: jener defloratorische Vorgang, der im Bild von der Erkenntnis, als die der Theologe den Sexus begreift, sein Emblem findet. Denn all die translatorischen Räsonnements, von denen hier die Rede war, können nicht verschleiern, daß die zahlreichen Entscheidungsprozesse des Übersetzers, die den Schleier zerreissen, Zugriffe, Übergriffe sind. Es bezeichnet die spezifische Verhaltensweise des translatorischen Geistes, daß jene zudringlich das Fremde ins Eigene ver- und umschlingen; und im Ausfüllen der konnotativen Hohlräume («Ich fühl mich so leer») wird etwas von dieser libidinösen Überwältigung deutlich. Auch das Penetrative des Vorgangs. Jene Räsonnements, all dies Abwägen,

Austarieren, Suchen und Tasten sind Strategien im Liebeskampf, Schachzüge im Liebeswerben, das dem kopulativen Prozeß der Wort- und Satzfindung teils vorausgeht, teils ihn begleitet. Dieser selbst ist ein eher ungalanter, nämlich gierig raptuöser, usurpatorischer Vorgang, und je stärker die libidinöse Besetzung des Fremdtextes (des Geliebten Gegenstands) durch den übersetzenden Dichter, desto beherzter um nicht zu sagen gewalttätiger sein Zugriff. Beispiele für diese Gewalt, die dem Leser als Ausdrucksgewalt sich mitteilt, gibt es zuhauf. Hölderlins Sophokles-Übertragungen, beseelt und getrieben von verzehrender Sehnsucht nach dem Fernen und Fremden, anverwandeln das Deutsche dem Griechischen in einer syntaktisch und lexisch bis zum Zerreissen angespannten Diktion; und wie der Schleier zu Saïs hier zerfetzt, ja das Standbild selbst in grandiosen Trümmern zurückgelassen wird, ist im deutschen Drama ohne Vergleich. Celans Mandelstam-Übersetzungen, nach Maßgabe von Übereinstimmung mit den Originalintentionen so fragwürdig, daß jeder Slawist den Finger darauf legen kann, sind nach Maßgabe deutscher Lyrik ebenso inkommensurable Gebilde wie Arno Schmidts Bulwer-Lytton-Übersetzungen nach Maßgabe deutscher Prosa. Von auktorialer Eitelkeit im Sinne von Verliebtheit in die eigenen sprachlichen Möglichkeiten läßt sich dabei nicht sprechen – eher von Begehren nach dem Anderen, Fremden, Neuen, Unbekannten. Kein privates Terrain wird hier eifersüchtig umzäunt. Denn auch wenn die Idiosynkrasien der Übersetzerdichter Individualhandschrift wären, Manier im Sinne von *maniera*, so doch nicht als Stilgebärde, als Attitüde, sondern als bloße Technik, auf die diese ein Monopol selten behaupten. Au contraire: Indem sie mit gewagtem Beispiel vorangehen, fordern sie, wenn auch unausgesprochen, zu mutiger Nachfolge auf.

Das ungarische Wort für «Übersetzer» meint auch: «Verschwender». Nietzsche: *Ich liebe den, dessen Seele sich verschwendet; denn er schenkt sich immer her und mag sich nicht bewahren.* Dies bezeichnet sehr schön den Überschuß in der Manier, das Luxurierende, das noch der kleinsten Sinnzelle verändernd sich schenkt. Das Begleitphänomen des Begehrens spricht gegen die Ideologie des *Dienens.* Übersetzende Dichter dienen dem geliebten Gegenstand mitnichten, sondern überwältigen ihn nach einer Phase buhlenden Umkreisens, und sind darin ebenso wenig *bescheiden* wie ein Liebender, der seine Ansprüche geltend macht – was ohne Regelverstoß, ohne Distanzüberschreitung ja nicht angehen kann. Die Sonne neigt sich unters Holz der Pein – wir verneigen uns vor dem Werk – aber dieser Demutsgestus bewährt sich de facto nur außerhalb der Werkgrenzen. Die *faire rode*, die schöne Röte des Schämens, wäre die Barriere, die im Akt des Übersetzens durchstoßen wird. Dieser meint nicht Symbiose, sondern Penetration: ein unmäßiger, vampyresker, jedenfalls identifikatorischer Vorgang. Getrost darf hier vor einer Fetischisierung sogenannter Professionalität gewarnt werden. Sie ist verlockend, weil die Insistenz auf Materialbeherrschung unmittelbar evident scheint. Aber Professionalität, die auf sich selbst pocht, gerät in Ideologieverdacht. Als sollten mit diesem Slogan, wie in vorindustriellen Zünften oder Gilden, die Reihen eng geschlossen werden zur Abwehr alles exzentrischen Außenseiterwesens. Die versammelten Reihen der *Professionellen* gleichen dem Auftritt der Meistersinger im 1. Akt, einschließlich jenes Merkers, der jeden Normverstoß des verliebten Stolzing gegen die Regeln der Tabulatur mit laut kreischenden Kreidestrichen annotiert. Es ist eine Sprachpolizei, die über die schiefe Alternative zwischen Dienen und Herrschen wacht. Wo das Dem-Werk-Dienen empfohlen oder gefordert wird, ist das Herrschen schon mitgedacht; konstituiert wird ein fataler Antagonismus; beide wären Chiffren von Unfreiheit. Diese hätte allenfalls im Triebleben der Sprache ihre Stätte: als Obsession. Einem Künstler *Bescheidenheit* anzuraten, hätte nicht nur etwas unangebracht Onkelhaftes, sondern auch etwas Kunstfremdes insofern, als ohne verwegenen Zugriff, ohne das Wagnis des Würfelwurfs, im Artifiziellen ebenso wenig etwas recht geraten kann wie im Eros. (Bescheidenheit als *Benehmen* ist löblich ja rühmlich, limitiert aber eo ipso den generativen Impuls. Dagegen Goethes *Nur die Lumpe sind bescheiden.*). Ärger wäre nur Übersetzen als *Völkerverständigung*, etwa analog zu Suhrkamps legendären «Verständigungstexten». Der Übersetzer als *kultureller Christophorus*. Das Pietistische, Nazarenische dieses Bildes; als ginge es um Dolmetschen. Korrektes Übersetzen im inkorrekten Leben kann es nicht geben.

Das vorliegende Buch ist im Kern ein Nachdruck der Anthologie *My Second Self/ When I am gone*, die 1991 in einer Auflage von 500 Exx. als Privatdruck, ausgestattet von Cornelia Feyll, gedruckt von P. R. Wilk und hergestellt von Friedrich Forssman, von der Hamburger Stiftung zur Förderung von Wissenschaft und Kultur in einer generösen mäzenatischen Geste finanziert und dem Verfasser zur privaten Verfügung überlassen wurde. (Die meisten Exemplare wurden verschenkt; einige wenige gelangten in den Handel.) Die Übersetzungen stammen aus den Jahren 1977-1989. Ergänzt werden sie hier um das Epithalamion von Edmund Spenser, das 1993 als Privatdruck in 50 Exx. erschien, sowie um sämtliche englischen Originale und das vorliegende Nachwort. Alle Übersetzungen wurden für den Neudruck durchgesehen, aber nur sehr zurückhaltend revidiert, um nicht der Imaginationslust des Erstdrucks durch Eingriffe zu viel von ihrer Frische zu nehmen, einer Frechheit, die ein Geschenk der Jugend war, das die Skrupel des Alters verschonen sollten. Die englischen Originale fanden sich in einem knappen Dutzend diverser Anthologien, deren editorische Kriterien sowohl zu heterogen als auch zu unbestimmt sind, als daß der Übersetzer für sie, im Einzelnen wie im Ganzen, Verantwortung übernehmen könnte. Seine Arbeit war eine literarische, keine anglistische; und nicht um eine sogenannte repräsentative Auswahl ist es ihm gegangen, sondern um eine private, intime Blütenlese, die mit seinen übrigen Werken in einem mehr oder weniger deutlichen Zusammenhang steht.

Wolfgang Schlüter
Wien/Irland 2002

Anfangszeilen-Register

All die ihr kreuzt die fromme Stätte hier   28
Als Kind, nackt, neugeborn   169
Als Letty grad ihr drittes Lebensjahr gewonnen   229
Als mein' Mutter starb, war ich noch ganz jung   172
Als wir am saumseligen Bach noch müßiggingen   212
Alt-ächte Eiche!: sah dich im Empfinden   209
An/ die ich auf der Welt am liebsten hab   22
An einem Heilquell, unterm Schlehendorn   32
An einem Sommerabend (von ihr geleitet) fand ich   186
An meinen treu-liebreizenden Galan   36
Ans Rotkehlgen/ den Zawnkönig/ dich wend   86
Auf denn, Musik! Du Seelenkönigin   109
Auf einen Pfad/ Abseits vom Wege   192
Auf eines Berggipfels weitem Plateau   189
Auffs Haubt geschlagen ist der schwarze Drachen   41

Bald sind ihr fad des Gatten Täppischkeiten   141
Beschleunige die Schritte, wo sich zum Mob   132
Bevor ein letztesmal ich Atem hol'   81
Bin I. N. R. I., kommen in die Schlacht   12
Bürger, Ihr habt so rotgepust't die Kohlen der Passion   46

CORINNA, *Drury Lane's* Gewinst   125

Da!: Hier geht ihr Weg   127
Das deucht mich ob der MinoritenBrüder wunders   14
Das Feldgeheg   140
Das steht nicht zu befürchten: daß die Flut   182
Da, was wir lieben, *welket*   138
Da wo die Vase praesidirt   148
dein schatten erd vom pol bis zum äquatorstrich   244
Dein Seel bewahrte sich ein derart leises Prunken   122
Denkt einzig dies von mir, wenn sterben ich gesollt   248

Denn wahrlich ich sage euch   153
DEO GRATIAS, ENGELLANT, REDDE PRO VICTORIA   23
Der Dinge drei sind's, die gedeihen schnell   57
Der Höllen Teufel TUTIVILL   26
Der König? – : alt, verhöhnt, blind   204
Der letzte, größte Herold unsers Heilands   93
Der muß entschuldigen, wer unsre Bühne prüft   156
Der Reichen acht ich kaum   233
Dicht unterm Dornbusch, der die Krone bauscht   154
Dicht wo die gültge Themse kocht   176
Die Dämmerung brach schnell herein   221
Die fliehn mich nun, die einst auf nackten Sohlen   49
Die Glorie unsers Bluts & Stands   105
Die grimme Bellona, die auf Männer nur speit   130
Die Kupel aus Azur   74
Die langsam anschleichet, schnell ja verfliegt sie   159
Die müde Kerze   135
Die Sonne geht nun unter   1
Die Sterne teiln doch noch ihr Licht   114
Die süsse Frühlingszeit   51
Die Tage bei den Toten sind gezählt   190
Die tasten nur borniert sich durch Erkenntnisrunden   214
Dieweil *CATO*s Geschick gerührte Whigs bewimmern   126
Die Zweige schlagen aus im Hag   7
Du Blindenstock! Du selbsterkorne Narrenschelle!   62
Du fragst den Ansporn meiner Wut?   134
Du nahest, Herbst: dein Herold ist der Regen   223
Du Schönheit *Schwarz*: hoch über dem gemeinen Licht   92
Du *Schwarz*: darein ein jede Farb geschossen   91

Ein alter Mann in einer Hütt'   220
Ein ander Stein die Zeit erzählt   166
Einen Mann, der fast blind   38

Ein Knospen zart hier ruht   101
Ein schwaches Lebenszeichen blieb   230
Ein Wind wiegt die Fichten   235
Endlose Säulenreih durch blaue Nacht   247
ER ging zuerst voran   75
Erwäge nur, wie dieser Staubesand   83
Es gibt ein Schweigen, wo kein Laut war je   213
Es ist ein schöner Abend   184
Es scheinet weiß – und ist doch rot   30
Euch, meiner Börse, keiner andern Maid   17
Evangeline bracht aus der Ecke das Dame-Brett   222
Ewigen Erinnerns Pein   37

Falls je ein ärgerlicher Tonfall   194
Fern überm dunkelwogend Land   215
Fort stapft der Waldmann   158
Frech, schaamlos, naseweis   142
Für die der Tod erneut vermählt   115

Gedenke mein, wenn ich dahingegangen   240
Geheimer Mord ward unlängst jüngst vollstreckt   53
Geöffnet liegen deine Händ' im hohen frischen Grün   237
Gleich einem armen Eremit, an düsterm Ort   56
Gleich ungesprochner Reden Donner-laut   88
Gleichwie im Sterben eine Lady dünn und bleich   201

Halt inne/ *Sterblichkeit*/ und fürchte!   97
Heil Zwielicht!: Souverän   181
Hier ruht/ in dieser Grub' verborgnen Bahre   59
Hier ruht SAM JOHNSON   143
Hier unter diesem Leichenstein   98
Hier unter diesem Marmorklotz   31
Hier unterm Stein die Lady darfst du schaugen   104

Hier ward geschrieben die *Historie der Welt*   238
Hüt' dich, Freisasse, Edelpage, Lanzenknecht   19

Ich bin aus Ireland   9
Ich bin das all's so leid   71
Ich bin! – doch *wer* bin ich?   208
Ich habe einen edlen Hahn   24
ich hab ein junge schwester   20
Ich *hass'* der Trommel missetönend BUMM   157
Ich hatte Gespielen – ich hatte Gefährten   193
Ich sag Euch, hoffnungslose Pein ist ohne Fühlen   217
Ich sah MyLady weinen   106
Ich schrieb ihren Namen in den Strand   52
Ich wag's nicht, einen Kuß   100
Ich weiß, daß alles unterm Mond verfällt   94
Ihr Cavaliere von Newgate   131
Ihr, die ihr eures Weges wallet   13
Ihres herrlichen Polsters mag die Holroyd   149
Ihr Heil'gen-Stürmer, sagt doch mal, warum   87
Ihr merkwürdigen *(Angel-)*Keilgesichter   198
im chorgestühl wandt sie den kopf   242
Im Dunckel laß mich hausen   113
In dieser fürchterlichen Trance hört er Grollen   168
In Dunkelheit vor Jericho   226
In einem dichtvernestelt Weißdornbusch geborgen   207
In einer dumpfen Höhl, 'ner kleinen Hölle   147
In langen, schlaflosen Vigilien der Nacht   225
In *Mather's Magnalia Christi*   219
Ist dies denn heilig anzusehn   174
«Ist sonderbar,» sagt Tom zu Jack   170
Itzt, ohne Pause, dreschen sie sich ihre Weichen   145

Ja! das ist *Zeit*: die nimmt getrost   58
Jaja, so war's: der Mensch in jenen fruhen Tagen   117

Könnte Homer höchstselbst   160
Komm, Schlaf/ o Schlaf! du fest vertäuter Frieden   63
Kyrie, ja, Kyrie   25

Laß mich noch oft den spitzgewölbten Kor   155
Leb wohl denn, Landschaft aus den Schattentagen   112
Leg dich getrost, ach Erd'   241
Leicht abseits von des Dorfes Straß'   224
Liebe Lucy, du kennst mein Begehren   232
Little Mary Bell hatt nen Kobold in der Nuß   173

Mai! Sei nimmermehr geziert mit Vogelsange   99
Manch fromme Legend von Konstanze bericht'   146
Man hat Euch, Nymphchen, angeklagt   163
Mann-im-Mond steht und stelzt fürbaß   8
Maria, wenn Hóraz vernähme   164
Matrosen ho! Wer mögt ihr sein?   199
Meine Galeere kreuzt   48
Mein Elixier heißt *Rebellion*   162
Mein geistlich Vater, mit Verlaub   39
Mein höchstedle Frawe   42
Mein kleiner Sohn, der nachdenklichen Blicks   234
Mein Lieb ist fahren in ein Land   43
Mein Leib, gefangen zwischen Wänden   55
Mein Lied!, das du, erdacht statt Goldgeschmeid   52B
MENSCH kömmt mir vor als eine *Tennis*-bahn   102
Merk auf: Laternen wölken meine Augen!   89
Mir gehts nicht um den Staat   118
«*MISERRIMUS!*» – und weder Nam'   183
Mit flammenwärts gestreckter, vorwurfsvoller Hand   179

Mit grauen Augen schauend   205
Mit keinem hatt ich Händel   195
Mit Lullay-Kinderschlafgesang   47
Mit Schiffen war die See gesprenkelt   180
Mit welch betrübten Schritten, Mond   61
Musik wenn leis die Stimm verklingt   203
Muß irren durch den Wald so wild   44

Nah fokussiert mein Aug auf deines   77
Nen satten Plumpudding würd einst ein rechter Brite   150
Nun schläft das weiße Blütenblatt   231
Nun sei willkommen, Lenz   16
Nun, wo schon hie und da ein Droschkenwagen   124

Oft sah an mancher Kathedralenpforte   218
Oh Glanz des Westens, schöner Abendstern   187
Oh Menschenheit   29
Oh wenn uns trennt' ein Hellespont von Crem   73
O der betrübten Tage   119
O HErr, nimm meinen Sohn   90
O löschendes Feuer der sinkenden Sonne   228
O Mörderin: bin ich erst tot   79

Prinz Luzifer erhob sich aus besternter Nacht   236

Reiter, blick kalt   246
Resolviret bin ich, diesen reizenden Tag   136
RICHERD! Zwâr bleistu stêt ein trichser   4
Rot blitzt im Untergehn die Sonne übern Wald   206
Rot wird die Ros bei meiner Dame Schreiten   66

Sah man solch Füß in alter Zeit   175
Salon und Küche seien weit geschieden   123

Schau an: der prüde Besen   165
Schlafe, schlafe, Kindlein: schlaf   10
Schlaf: Schweigen's Kind, süß Vater sanfter Rast   95
Schlag hurtig, Herz   27
Schön-Cloris sah ich einsam sich bewegen   108
Schwarzschlackiger Schmiede   34
Schwerlich erzeigt die Erde lieblichere Dinge   178
SCIENTIA! – : Du hellverströmend Strahlen   152
Seltsam die Stellungen der Gattung ‹Aale›   129
Sieh hier der Wälder ausgezehrt-vielfarbige   137
Sieh, wie die blasse Königin der stillen Nacht   70
Sie malen dich als Rumpelstilz   191
sing, kukuk nû   2
's ist 32 jahre her nun daß im gegenlicht   243
So frisset nun das Menschentier   121
SorgenBesänft'ger Schlaf!   68
Still wird die See, da schwach die Winde wehn   110

Theure Reliquie einer fremdbehausten Seele   116
Tod: brüst' dich nicht, auch wenn dich manche nennen   78
Tod!: brüst' dich nicht der Tyrannei   120
Traf einen Globetrotter aus antiquem Land   202
Traun, einer Lady darf ich mich erfreun   18

Um den Bach nahebei, der den tönenden Hain   139
Um ihren Wein zu *raffiniren*, gießen manche   161
Um toten Lebens wegen weiß ich um mein lebend Tod   40
Und aufs neu, doch wie anders, seit mein Wandern   188
Und hier das Haus, das die Gemeinde-Armen birgt   171

Vergebens, arme Nymphe, schläfst   128
Verhülle, *Absalon*, der goldnen Locken Zier   15
Verzeih, gepriesne Seel, der Zähren   67

Vielleicht wars nur ein Bild 103
vogellin im holze 6
Vom Seufzen verdorret, von Thränen versengt 76
von ein jungfraw will singen 21

wann mine ougen dämmern 5
War einst ein Schoner, *HESPERUS* 227
was barmet euch mein kinde nicht 11
Was liegst in seichtem Trott 82
Was unser Leben ist? – : Ein Schauerspiel 54
Was will denn dies? 50
Was wollten Dichter mit des Schmälens Zeilenlauf 65
Weint nicht mehr, traurige Brunnen, Fontänen 107
Wenn alle Farben nachts in *Schwarz* gefaßt 60
Wenn aus der Rohrblattflöte etwas 151
Wenn Brennesseln im Winter rote Rosen tragen 35
Wenn deinen Schritt vom öffentlichen Wege ab 177
Wenn denn Musik und Poesie sind überein 84
Wenn du denn doch dein Licht vom Himmel selbst empfängst 185
Wenn du im Alter, grau und schlafensmatt 245
Wenn erst der Roggen wieder reicht ans Kinn 64
Wenn ich dahingegangen, Liebster 239
Wenn ich erwäge, wie mein Licht in Fernen 111
Wenn Maßliebchen gescheckt mit Veilchen schmust 72
Wenn mein Grab neu aufgebrochen 80
Wenn mich die Furcht ergreift 211
Wenn ringsum Stille in der Nacht 196
Wenn stumpfe Reime unser Englisch müssen binden 210
Wenn vom Gesimse Eis in Zapfen starrt 72
Wenn wir von diesem Prachtband namens *Welt* 96
Werd sagen euch, was Liebe sonder Maßen sei 33
Westlich Wind, wann wirst du wehen 45
Wie meine Lampe in der Kammer Einsamkeit 216

Wie mild und andächtig, so ganz allein   200
Wie süß des Echos Antwort macht   197
Wie viele nichtswürdige, lachhaft angetünchte Viecher   69
Wollt ihr in dieser Fieberwelt euch wahren   144
Wörter sind Blättern gleich   133
wunniclich ists weil der summer weilt   3

Zeuch weg, eitles Genießen   85
Zwar Püppchen einst und ‹Fop› genannt   167

Autorenverzeichnis

AKENSIDE, Mark   152
AMWELL, John Scott of   157
ARMSTRONG, John   144

BARNFIELD, Richard   84
BARRETT BROWNING,
   Elizabeth   217
BEAUMONT, Francis   97
BEAUMONT, Sir John   90
BEST, Charles   70
BLACKMORE, Sir Richard   121
BLAIR, Robert   135
BLAKE, William   172-176
BRONTË, Emily   233
BROOKE, Rupert   247-248
BROWNE, William   98-99

CAMBRIDGE, Richard Owen   149
CAREW, Thomas   104
CARTWRIGHT, William   114
CAWTHORN, James   150
CHATTERTON, Thomas   170
CHAUCER, Geoffrey   15-17
CLARE, John   207-209
COLERIDGE, Samuel Taylor   189
COLERIDGE, Hartley   212
COLLINS, William   151
CONSTABLE, Henry   66-67
COWPER, William   158-167
CORBETT, Richard   87-89
CRABBE, George   171
CRASHAW, Richard   115-116

DANYEL, Samuel   68
DAVIES, of Hereford, John   73
DIAPER, William   129
DONNE, John   76-81
DRAYTON, Michael   69
DRUMMOND OF HAWTHORNDEN,
   William   93-96
DUNBAR, William   41
DYER, John   136

FALCONER, William   168
FLATMAN, Thomas   119
FLETCHER, John   85

GAY, John   131-132
GOLDSMITH, Oliver   154
GRAY, Thomas   148
GREENE, Robert   65
GREVILLE, Fulke,
   Lord Brooke   60

HARDY, Thomas   242-244
HERBERT OF CHERBURY,
   Edward Lord   91-92
HERRICK, Robert   100-101
HILL, Aaron   130
HOCCLEVE, Thomas   18
HOOD, Thomas   213
HORNE, Richard Henry   215
HOWARD, Henry,
   Earl of Surrey   51
HUNT, Leigh   198

James I. (King)   74
Jenyns, Soame   141-143
Jones, Sir William   169
Jonson, Ben   82-83

Keats, John   210-211
Keble, John   205-206
King, Henry   103
King, William   123

Lamb, Charles   193-194
Landor, Walter Savage   195
Longfellow,
  Henry Wadsworth   218-228

Meredith, George   235-236
Milton, John   111
Moore, Edward   146
Moore, Thomas   196-197

Newman, John Henry   214

Oldham, John   122
Orleans, Charles of   39-40

Parnell, Thomas   128
Patmore, Coventry   234
Peacock, Thomas Love   199
Peele, George   64
Philips, Katherine   118
Pope, Alexander   133-134

Quarles, Francis   102

Ralegh, Sir Walter   53-58
Randolph, Thomas   109
Rossetti,
  Christina Georgina   239-241
Rossetti,
  Dante Gabriel   237-238
Rowe, Nicholas   126

Scott, Sir Walter   188
Shakespeare, William   71-72
Shelley, Percy Bysshe   201-204
Shirley, James   105
Sidney, Sir Philip   61-63
Skelton, John   47
Smart, Christopher   153
Somerville, William   127
Southey, Robert   190-192
Spenser, Edmund   52-52B
Strode, William   108
Suckling, Sir John   112
Swift, Jonathan   124-125

Tennyson,
  Alfred, Lord Tennyson   231
Thackeray,
  William Makepeace   232
Thompson, William   147
Thomson, James   137-140
Turner,
  Charles Tennyson   229-230

VAUGHAN, Henry   117

WALLER, Edmund   110
WARTON, Thomas   155-156
WEBSTER, John   86
WHITEHEAD, Charles   216
WHITEHEAD, Paul   145
WILSON, John   200
WORDSWORTH, William   177-187
WOTTON, Sir Henry   75
WYATT, Sir Thomas   48-50

YEATS, William Butler   245-246

My Second Self When I Am Gone
Englische Gedichte, übersetzt von Wolfgang Schlüter

Gestaltung Marcel Schmid Basel
Gesetzt aus der New Baskerville
Druck Fuldaer Verlagsanstalt Fulda

ISBN 3-905591-52-9
© 2003 Urs Engeler Editor
D-79576 Weil am Rhein, Im Schwarzenbach 6
Telefon und Fax 0(049)7621 76238
CH-4057 Basel, Dorfstrasse 33
Telefon 0(041)61 631 46 81
A-1030 Wien, Rechte Bahngasse 28/19